HISTORY OF IMPERIAL CHINA

Timothy Brook, General Editor

CHINA'S LAST EMPIRE

THE GREAT QING

William T. Rowe

THE BELKNAP PRESS OF
HARVARD UNIVERSITY PRESS
Cambridge, Massachusetts
London, England
2009

To Muriel Bell

whose vision has immeasurably advanced
our understanding of Qing history

Library of Congress Cataloging-in-Publication Data
Rowe, William T.
China's last empire : the great Qing / William T. Rowe.
p.   cm.
Includes bibliographical references and index.
ISBN 978-0-674-03612-3 (alk. paper)
1. China—History—Qing dynasty, 1644–1912. I. Title.
DS754.R84 2009
951'.03—dc22   2009011232

CONTENTS

MAPS

FIGURES

CHINA'S LAST EMPIRE

The Great Qing

INTRODUCTION

THE GREAT Qing empire was by far the largest political entity ever to
center itself on the piece of earth known today as China.[1] It more than
doubled the geographic expanse of the Ming empire, which it displaced
in 1644, and more than tripled the Ming's population, reaching in its last
years a size of more than half a billion persons. Included within the Qing
empire were not only those people who saw themselves as "Chinese" but
also people who had never previously been incorporated into a Chinese
dynastic state, including Tibetans, Uighur Muslims, certain groups of
Mongols, Burmese and Tais along the southwestern frontier, indigenous
populations of Taiwan and other newly colonized areas both on the frontiers and in interior highlands, and also the people who occupied the
Qing throne itself and would come to be known as "Manchus." This
enormous territory, or at least the vast bulk of it, and this huge and con-
tinuously growing population, with all its attendant tensions, would be
bequeathed to its successor states, the Republic of China and the People's
Republic of China. For the Qing was many things, but one of those
things was the closing chapter of the two-thousand-year history of imperial China.

To govern this unprecedentedly expansive empire for nearly three hundred years, the Qing in its heyday worked out systems of administration
and communication more efficient and effective than any of its predecessors. And to feed this unprecedentedly large population, it achieved a
level of material productivity (indeed, prosperity) far beyond that of any
earlier Chinese dynasty, as well as institutions of economic management
probably more ambitious and effective than any seen previously any-

where in the world.[2] While scholars of Chinese art and literature may reasonably argue that the Qing's aesthetic output was not quite the equal of, say, Tang poetry, Song painting, or Ming porcelain, its vibrant cosmopolitan culture did make great contributions in all of these areas, and it also pioneered in new venues of artistic expression such as the novel and the theater, to say nothing of print journalism. And while it is a mistake to see China at any point in its imperial history as hermetically isolated from other parts of the world, there is no question that it was under the Qing empire that relations and mutual influences between the eastern and western ends of the great Eurasian landmass became qualitatively more intense, and also more conflictive, than they ever had been in the past. The implications of this are still being worked out today.

Historians understand the Great Qing empire much differently now than we did forty or fifty years ago. Indeed, it might be fair to say that in the 1950s and 1960s there really was no such thing as "Qing history" in most of the world. Of course, Chinese historians had long organized China's past in terms of successive ruling houses, which rose and fell according to the Confucian model of the "dynastic cycle," and the Qing could be seen as simply the last such ruling house. Accordingly, as had each new dynasty in the past, the fledgling government of the Chinese Republic after 1912 commissioned an official history of its predecessor, the *Draft History of the Qing (Qingshi gao)*, eventually published in 1927 under the editorship of the former imperial official Zhao Erxun.[3] Five years later, the intrepid private scholar Xiao Yishan published his own *General History of the Qing Dynasty (Qingdai tongshi)*, which came to serve in essence as the standard scholarly statement on the subject.[4]

By the second half of the twentieth century, however, Confucian historiography was no longer in favor, at least in the West. Instead, the effective father of modern Chinese history in the United States, John King Fairbank of Harvard University—who with incredible personal energy wrote textbooks, trained teachers for other universities, and oversaw a pioneering monograph publication series on modern East Asia—held firmly to a view that divided the history of China's past half millennium around 1842. All that fell before remained part of "traditional China," whereas "modern China" began with the Western "shock" of the Opium War and the Treaty of Nanjing.[5] The Qing was thus bifurcated, and different groups of scholars worked on the two separate parts. Fairbank never explicitly said (as others did) that late imperial history before the 1842 watershed was essentially "stagnant" and that genuine developmental change began only with China's response to the West, but this was implicit in his periodization.[6] The best textbooks of modern Chinese history produced under the influence of the Harvard school did, of course, allot brief coverage to the Qing's first two centuries, but the overwhelming focus of their attention was the era from 1842 to the present, the period of "true"—that is, Westernizing—modernity.[7]

For all the eurocentrism implicit in their periodization scheme, Fairbank and his followers were not challenged by historians in China itself. Under the Leninist assumption that Western imperialism was the single dominant force in recent Chinese history, the Chinese Academy of Social Sciences in Beijing organized its scholars into two separate research facilities, the Institute of History and the Institute of Modern History, with their jurisdictions divided by the Opium War. In Taiwan as well, the Nationalist authorities, under the heady influence of "modernization theory," similarly divided historians at the Academia Sinica into an Institute of History and Philology and an Institute of Modern History, studying respectively the periods before and after 1842. A comparable division of labor (though not quite so institutionally reinforced) underlay postwar Japanese scholarship on Qing history. Especially for scholars at the Marxist-influenced University of Tokyo, "modern" China began only with the Opium War.

There were minority voices in the 1970s, to be sure, voices that apprentice scholars such as myself found terribly exciting. But as far as I know there was only one scholarly initiative that radically proposed to study all of the dynasty's history as a piece, oblivious of the Opium War divide. It was a journal—a newsletter, really—boldly entitled *Ch'ing-shih wen-t'i* (*Problems in Qing History*) founded in 1965 at Yale University by Jonathan Spence, who was a graduate student at the time. In China itself, the estimable *Qingshi yanjiu* (*Studies in Qing History*), produced by the Qing History Institute of Chinese People's University, began publication only a quarter century later, in 1991.[8]

It seems in retrospect that the evolution of Qing historiography in the past half century, especially but not exclusively in the United States, has been marked by three important revisionist turns. The first of these—a social history turn—grew up slowly in the 1970s and 1980s and was influenced most importantly by studies of the European and American past sparked above all by the popular vogue of the French historical school and its flagship journal *Annales: économies, sociétés, civilisations*. The emphasis was not on political, military, or diplomatic events nor on great individual figures of the past but on social, economic, and cultural "structures" (as opposed to mere "conjunctures") that emerged and receded only very slowly over the "longue durée."[9] The somewhat belated impact of this school on the field of Chinese history was facilitated by American China scholars' gradual assimilation of the magnificent corpus of socioeconomic history that had been produced by Japanese China scholars since the Second World War, and then by the opening to outside researchers of the huge troves of Qing imperial archives (in Taiwan in the 1970s and in Beijing in the early 1980s), which enabled scholars to attempt the kind of bold, long-term history espoused by *Annales*.

The consequences of this social history turn were three. First, historians began to be newly critical of the instrumental view of China's recent past inherent in the "China's response to the West" model and to concentrate instead on changes in the country's own domestic history, seen now as anything but stagnant. This new trend was summarized, approvingly, by one of Fairbank's own chief disciples, Paul Cohen, with the phrase "discovering history in China."[10] The impact of the West on the Qing empire was increasingly marginalized in this revisionist narrative of Qing history—a necessary corrective, perhaps, but one that would invite subsequent correctives of its own. Eventually, historians would move to "bring the West back in" to the new Qing history, once we had come to understand it better on its own terms.[11]

A second consequence of the social history turn, abetted by the economic "miracles" of the East Asian Four Little Dragons (Hong Kong, Singapore, Taiwan, South Korea) and then of post-Mao China itself, was a gradual discarding of the failure narrative of Qing history. Research questions such as "Why was there no capitalism or industrialization in nineteenth-century China?" (often asked in unfavorable comparison to Meiji Japan) were now seen as based on misguided or even false assumptions. Comparative social scientists as well as American specialists in Chinese history began to argue that as late as the mid-eighteenth century the Qing empire may have had a more prosperous economy and a higher general standard of living than most of Western Europe.[12]

A third and most telling consequence came in the area of periodization. No sooner did the view of the Qing era as a coherent whole begin to trump the "traditional"/"modern" divide than dynastic markers themselves began to seem like mere surface ripples in the structural evolution of China's past. As Frederic Wakeman Jr. observed in 1975:

Gradually, social historians began to realize that the entire period from the 1550s to the 1930s constituted a coherent whole. Instead of seeing the [Qing] as a replication of the past, or 1644 and 1911 as critical terminals, scholars detected processes which stretched across the last four centuries of Chinese history into the Republican period. The urbanization of the of the lower [Yangzi] region, the commutation of labor services into money payments, the development of certain kinds of regional trade, the growth of mass literacy and increase in the size of the gentry, the commercialization of local managerial activities—all these phenomena of the late Ming set in motion administrative and political changes that continued to develop over the course of the [Qing] and in some ways culminated in the social history of the early twentieth century.[13]

But what to call this new era that transcended the Ming-Qing divide? The weaker, less encumbered term that gained great popularity was "late imperial." This phrase implied that not merely the Qing but also all or part of the preceding Ming was a single coherent historical era.[14] The stronger formulation, one which I endorsed, was the term "early modern."[15] But this category, too, had several obvious liabilities. For one thing, it seemed to imply some necessary transition to a full-fledged modernity, perhaps a modernity that looked a lot like Westernization, with its industrialization and representative government; and this was a notion that revisionist historians sought most deeply to challenge. More generally, "early modernity" was a concept deliberately appropriated from the historiography of Europe, and its use seemed to force onto China a set of Western-inspired expectations that risked obscuring the particular realities of the Chinese past itself.[16] The verdict on this issue is still out.

The second basic reconceptualization of Qing history is now often referred to as the Inner Asian turn.[17] This was an outgrowth of a cultural history revolution that followed on the heels of the social history revolution. With its emphasis on "representations" over inherent "facts," cultural history urged the de-essentialization of such categories as gender and race, seeing them as culturally negotiated and historically contingent rather than biologically given. Although new attention to changing gender roles has been one of the most fruitful and exciting developments in Chinese historiography during the past several decades, the related study of racial or ethnic identities has had more direct relevance to our reconceptualization of the Qing as a historical era.

Among the central arguments advanced by the revisionists was that "Manchu" identity was itself a historical construct, created largely subsequent to the conquest itself. The Qing takeover had been the work of a deliberately forged "conquest organization" within which racial or ethnic identity was important but fungible. This new Manchu-centered Qing differed fundamentally from most preceding imperial dynasties—and none so dramatically as the Ming—in that it was self-consciously conceived as a universal empire, a multinational polity within which China (the former Ming domain) was simply one component, though quite obviously the most central and economically productive one. The dissociation of the Great Qing empire from the long recurring pattern of imperial Chinese dynasties has led some scholars to insist on seeing 1636 (the year of the Qing's self-proclamation) rather than 1644 (the year of the Qing conquest of the Ming) as the empire's proper founding date.[18]

Far from wholeheartedly "sinicizing" their domain, Qing rulers merely played the Confucian role of Son of Heaven as one of many simultaneous roles they adopted to rule their myriad ethnic-national constituencies. The separate ethnic identities of these constituencies were not erased by sinicization but instead were deliberately cultivated by the Qing court (though often behind the backs of its Han Chinese ministers). Non-Chinese historical actors—those today usually subsumed under the political label "minority peoples"—were granted a new active subjectivity and autonomous agency. In this view, these minority groups and individuals worked in daily practice to negotiate their own identity, in concert with their Han and Manchu neighbors and rulers.[19]

This new Qing history gradually won the day, prompting a wave of investigations into the empire's adventurous expansion at its frontiers (an expansion often opposed by Han literati officials as a distraction from domestic needs in China proper). The emphasis shifted away from seeing China as a passive late nineteenth-century victim of Western or Japanese imperialism to seeing it as an active player in the imperialist project itself, most dramatically in the eighteenth century but also in the nineteenth and early twentieth as well. At the same time, however, just as the earlier movement to "discover history in China" had sought to overcome the biases of a eurocentric historiography, the new Qing historiography directly combated a sinocentric one. Influenced by the postcolonial critique of nationalism by historians of South Asia, it exposed flaws in the view that imperial history was but a long prologue to the emergence of a modern Han Chinese nation-state—and more generally in the underlying notion of the nation-state as the necessary end of history. Han-nationalist historiography was criticized as imposing a model of progress derived from the serendipitous experience of Western Europe on a quite different set of cultures, which—but for the actions of a core of self-interested twentieth-century nationalist elites—might have taken an altogether very different course.[20]

The third sea change in Qing historiography, which might be called the Eurasian turn, grew largely out of the second but also drew upon the longstanding subdisciplines of world history and ecological history, both of which in the past had only fitfully paid attention to developments on the Chinese subcontinent.[21] Where these fields first importantly intersected with the Qing was in studies by Chinese historians of the so-called general crisis of the seventeenth century and how this may have precipitated the Ming-Qing dynastic transition. In arguing for the impact of this crisis on late imperial China, a number of scholars stressed transnational economic factors, especially dramatic fluctuations in international bullion flows, but also the global climatic shift sometimes called the Little Ice Age.[22]

Ultimately, however, it was the comparative study of early modern empires that led to a new vision of Eurasian unity. The older binary history of European challenge and Asian response gave way to a new historical emphasis on different components of a holistic Eurasian landmass that followed local variant courses along a comparable developmental trajectory.[23] Rather than being an isolated exception, the Qing was now reconceived as effectively similar to the Ottoman, Moghul, Romanov, and perhaps even Napoleonic land-based empires in patterns of administrative centralization (aided by new communication technologies), deliberate multinational inclusion, and aggressive land settlement. Together, these new Eurasian powers worked from various directions to enclose and squeeze out older (often nomadic) cultures.[24]

This Eurasian revision carried significant implications for periodization as well. If the Inner Asian turn posed a problem for the hard-fought triumph of a China-centered Qing history, the Eurasian turn potentially challenged the revisionist conception of a "late imperial China" as including the Ming along with the Qing, and of an "early modern China" as starting sometime in the Ming's last century. In what might be seen as a manifesto for the Eurasian turn, Evelyn Rawski—revising in 2004 her

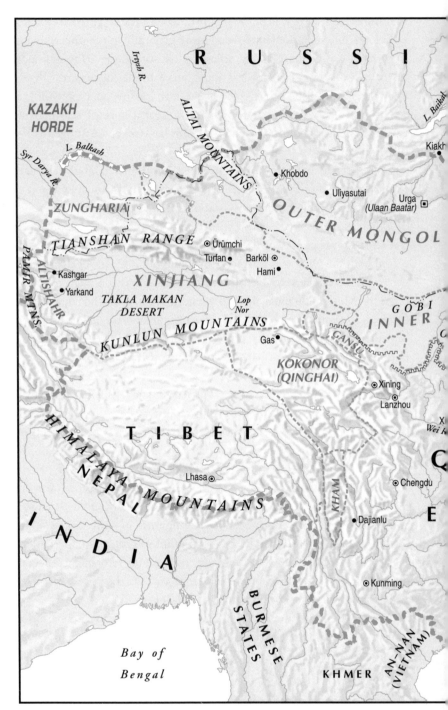

MAP 1

Nerchinsk •

Onon R.

•ulen R.

Orkhon R.

DESERT

MONGOLIA

Hohhot
⊙ (Guihua)

□ Beijing

Albazin •

GREATER KHINGAN MTNS.

Amur R.

Amur R.

MANCHURIA

Sungari R.

Ussuri R.

W. Liao R.

Shenyang (Mukden) □

Yalu R.

KOREA

Sea of
Japan

JAPAN

Bo Hai

Yellow R.

⊙ Jinan

Yellow
Sea

⊙ Kaifeng

N G

Nanjing ⊙

Han R.

Wuchang

Yangzi R.

Shanghai ⊙

East
China

Sea

I R E

Gan R.

Fuzhou ⊙

East
China
Sea

⊙ Guangzhou

TAIWAN

South
China
Sea

The Qing Empire
1800

□	Capital
⊙	Provincial capitals and major towns
•	Other towns
▰ ▰ ▰	Qing Empire 1800
- - - -	Qing internal regions
-·-·-	Present-day northern boundary of China
⊓⊓⊓⊓	Great Wall (after 1550)

0   500 km.

0   500 mi.

1996 position that the Qing was qualitatively different from previous Chinese dynasties—argued emphatically that such an unprecedentedly centralized empire was so deeply a specific function of Manchu rule that it was an impossibility under the ethnically Han rulers of the Ming. In other words, early modernity in China did indeed begin with the dynastic transition of 1644, and not before.[25] Perhaps the dynastic periodizers of the old Confucian tradition were not so far wrong after all.

The Great Qing empire discussed in this book, then, is a constantly moving target. What it was, and to what extent it constituted something incomparably distinctive in the longer run of Chinese history or in the vast expanse of Eurasian space, remain open questions. That is precisely why the study of this place and period, at our own moment in history, is so rewarding.

I

CONQUEST

IN 1688 Tong Guogang, an officer of the Chinese Plain Blue Banner, petitioned the Kangxi emperor to change his officially registered ethnicity from "Chinese-martial" (*Hanjun*) to "Manchu." His great-uncle Tong Bunian had been born in Liaodong around 1580 but moved to Wuchang in central China. As a Wuchang native, he passed the metropolitan examination in 1616, served the Ming as a county magistrate, and later headed up the dynasty's military defenses in the northeast. After a disastrous defeat, Tong Bunian was accused of treason and died in prison in 1625, fervently proclaiming his loyalty to the Ming. His son Guoqi grew up in Wuchang and there composed a genealogy defending his father's Chinese patriotism by demonstrating descent from no fewer than ten generations of heroic Ming soldiers. But when Guoqi was taken captive during the Qing conquest of the Yangzi region in 1645, he and his family were impressed into the Chinese Plain Blue Banner.

As it turned out, other Tong men of Liaodong ancestry—men whom Guoqi had candidly included in his genealogy—had been just as heroic in the cause of the conquering Qing armies as Tong Bunian had been in defense of the Ming. Indeed, one of these would become the maternal grandfather of the Kangxi emperor, making Tong Guogang himself Kangxi's uncle! The emperor thus granted Guogang's petition for reclassification as a Manchu, noting, however, that it would be administratively awkward to similarly reclassify too many of his distant kin. From that day forward, Tong Guogang and certain of his relatives became Manchus while others remained Chinese. In this time and place, ethnic identities were far from genetically predetermined but were flexible, ambiguous, and negotiable.[1]

Stories like this one have been central to a new kind of historical understanding of just who were the rulers of the dynasty that took over the throne of China in 1644. Not long ago, the accepted wisdom on the Manchus grew, on the one hand, out of an essentialist assumption that races were, after all, races—each, like the Manchus, biologically or genetically determined once and for all time. But this essentialist view was also based on a teleological Han nationalist historiography that saw a Han Chinese nation-state in the twentieth century as the inevitable outcome of China's two-thousand-year-old imperial history. According to this logic, all lasting imperial dynasties, including those of alien rule, were roughly analogous; alien "races" like the Mongols and Manchus might conquer the domain of the Han people, but if they were to hold onto that possession they would have to rule it as Chinese, and in effect become Chinese themselves.

According to this scenario of Qing rule, a Manchu race or people existed prior to the conquest of the Ming, though they were in all important ways "barbarians," culturally inferior to the Han. Once the conquest was accomplished, the Manchus, after some internal debate, opted to rule China as Confucian Chinese Sons of Heaven, a decision that inevitably led to the cultural "assimilation" and presumably also the biological eradication of the Manchu race. Some Manchu rulers such as the Qianlong emperor (r. 1736–1795) noted with alarm that their countrymen were losing their distinctiveness and fought a rearguard action to maintain "the Manchu way," but they were doomed to failure. When the Qing dynasty was itself replaced by the Chinese Republic in 1911, there were few real Manchus left, and these simply melted into the general Chinese population. One convenient implication of this narrative is that it supposedly exposed as fundamentally bogus the Japanese imperialist attempt in the late 1930s to establish the state of Manchukuo in northeast China as a nation-state of the Manchu people, since, in the Chinese view, a Manchu people no longer existed.

In the 1980s, however, historians of the Qing began to rewrite this narrative, almost to stand it completely on its head.[2] Through the influence of cultural studies, we came to distrust essentialized notions of biological categories such as race and to see racial classifications instead as the products of specific historical situations and sociopolitical processes of negotiation. Thus, according to this new view, in the seventeenth century there really was no such thing as Manchus. Instead, there were various groups of peoples along the northeast frontiers of the Ming empire, drawn from a wide variety of genealogical stocks and cultural traditions, with not a few of these people fully or partly of Han Chinese ancestry. The group that succeeded the Ming on the Dragon Throne was not a Manchu race but was instead an organization of persons deliberately created for the purpose of conquest. The leaders of this "Qing conquest organization" felt it useful to assign their members national identities such as Mongol, Chinese-martial, and even Manchu, but this assignment was based on political convenience rather than any preexisting biological fact. As seen in the case of the Tong family described above, this initial assignment might easily be rescinded or changed as situations demanded.

Whereas the older view saw an originally distinguishable Manchu people that was assimilated or otherwise effaced over time, the new Qing narrative saw the Manchus as actually having come into existence over the course of the dynasty. The strenuous activities of the Qianlong emperor and others were not so much defending a national culture threatened with extinction as working to create such a culture by providing it with an origin myth, a national language and literature, and a set of defined cultural traits. And in this project they were surprisingly successful. Ironically, if Manchus did not really exist before 1644, they certainly did in 1911, according to this scenario. In keeping with this view, the story of Manchukuo was pretty much as presented in Bertolucci's great film *The Last Emperor.* Puyi, in the movie, was roused out of his postimperial career as a Shanghai lounge lizard to answer what he sincerely felt to be the call of his Manchu people to head their national state in the northeast. What was hypocritical about Japan's Manchukuo project was not some pretense that a genuine Manchu people existed on which to base it (for such a group did exist at this time) but rather the pretense that these Manchus would have real self-determination.

This new narrative is itself subject to overstatement. A second generation of Manchu-centered scholarship argues for the reality of ethnic or racial difference, at least in the eyes of contemporaries, from the dynasty's very outset. A study of Manchu garrisons throughout Qing China, for example, has detected a significant degree of ethnic tension between their inhabitants and the surrounding Han populations.[3] Still, in one form or other most historians today prefer the new narrative to the older one, and that set of assumptions underlies our story here.

Organizing the Conquest

Whether the Qing conquerors were an ethnically distinct frontier people or a deliberately constructed multiethnic conquest organization, their achievement was truly remarkable.[4] How could such a motley assemblage possibly overcome the mighty Ming war machine, arguably the most formidable fighting force in the world at that time?

The rise of the Qing as a military and political force in the area that became known as Manchuria, and is today northeast China, was the work of three successive tribal chieftains of the clan known as Aisin Gioro. "Aisin" means "gold" and is written in Chinese with the character *Jin*— which was the dynastic name of the Jurchen-speaking people who ruled north China from 1115 to 1260 and from whom the Aisin Gioro claimed descent. The three chieftains were Nurhaci (d. 1626), Hong Taiji (d. 1643), and Dorgon (d. 1650). The efforts of these three men to deliberately prepare their subjects for the conquest of the Ming included confederation, centralization, and (to a debated degree) sinicization—the appropriation of Han Chinese organizational techniques and cultural traits.

For most of the Ming era, "Manchus" did not exist. Population groups in northeast China were widely diverse, and while several of them shared linguistic and no doubt genetic similarities, no overarching identity united the peoples of this large and ecologically variable region. Unlike the Jurchen of the past and the Mongols to their west, the Aisin Gioro and their immediate neighbors were not nomadic herdsmen. The economy of their Liao River valley home had over the late sixteenth and early seventeenth centuries developed into a mixture of agriculture and hunting, with a significant amount of intercultural trade, especially in furs and the highly prized medicinal root ginseng. Under Nurhaci, the Aisin Gioro gradually accumulated a monopoly on franchises to import ginseng to the Ming, where demand for the stimulant was growing rapidly just as indigenous sources became exhausted. Although, like all of the Ming's other trading partners, the Aisin Gioro took in exchange some silk and other fine Chinese manufactures, ginseng tipped the balance of trade greatly in Nurhaci's favor. In the early seventeenth century the Ming may have re-exported to the Aisin Gioro as much as 25 percent of the silver it took in from Europe and the New World. This profit from trade, applied to the acquisition of weaponry (including firearms) and the hiring of skilled military officers, very largely financed the conquest.[5]

Governance along the northeast borders was primarily in the hands of hereditary tribal chiefs. As had most imperial regimes before them, the Ming practiced a policy of divide and rule toward these mobile and frequently martial peoples, investing each tribal chief with a vassalage and sporadically attempting to stir up rivalries among them. Nurhaci was one such chieftain enjoying a vassal relationship with the court. Around the turn of the seventeenth century, urged on by the Ming, he declared a vendetta against a neighboring tribe, which he accused of murdering his father. In pursuit of this cause, he forged a series of alliances with other population groups through marital unions, coercion, and conquest. The result was the creation of a significant confederation.

Events such as these had happened several times previously under the Ming and were not in themselves alarming. If a confederation was to become a serious threat to the dynasty, it needed some sort of permanent institutionalization. This was precisely what Nurhaci attempted to provide. The first step was to create a written language for his growing population, which he accomplished by commissioning a team of local scholars in 1599 to adapt the Mongol script to the Jurchen speech: with that stroke, the language later known as Manchu was born. A more decisive step was his creation of the system of "banners" in the years before 1615. There were initially four, and subsequently eight, such banners—solid white, white bordered with yellow, solid blue, and so on. Each banner signified a fighting unit, but it also represented a unit of residence and economic production and included not merely fighting men but also their dependents. As the system was gradually worked out, each banner came to be identified with a discrete national grouping—Manchu, Mongol, Chinese-martial—though assignment of national identities and consignment to ethnic groups was a matter of expedience and ongoing readjustment. Like the Mamluk armies of the medieval Middle East, members of the eight banners were all legally slaves. Inasmuch as hierarchical relationships within and among the banners were governed by a military command structure that was simultaneously a system of administration and property ownership, this resembled a feudal system. It was not quite feudal, however, in that the system of proprietorship that underlay it was not land but rather slaves. In 1616 Nurhaci proclaimed his regime the Latter Jin.[6]

The banner soldier was a formidable fighting man (Fig. 1). Cavalry wore the uniform color of their banner and were protected by metal helmets with red tassels and cane shields. Each man was responsible for the maintenance of three horses. Soldiers carried distinctive swords and sometimes flails but were most accomplished in the use of the bow; their quiver housed thirty or more arrows. Manchu bows were short (four feet) but very powerful, requiring years of strength-training to master. The distinctive mode of firing arrows from horseback at full gallop—

Fig. 1 Manchu imperial bodyguard (Zhanyinbao). Courtesy
Metropolitan Museum of Art, New York.

holding the bow and the reins simultaneously in the left hand while drawing the bow with the right—was so original to banner warcraft that it had its own verb (*niyamniyambi*) in the Manchu language. Infantry included some archers as well, but they were more often musketeers or artillerymen. Use of muskets was something of a practiced specialty among Han Chinese bannermen. They had also learned from the Portuguese how to cast cannon, and they developed the strength to haul them into the field, earning the nickname *ujen cooha* (heavy troops).[7]

It fell to the second Latter Jin leader, Hong Taiji, to superimpose on this tribal or feudal arrangement a bureaucratic structure on the Ming model. Hong Taiji was no longer to be the first among equals within a caste of feudal princes. He was now also, and uniquely, the emperor (Son of Heaven) within a state structure, and the banner headmen were in part his state officials. This move was significant for at least two reasons: it provided a superior form of political organization suitable for the conquest of the vast lands to the south; and it also provided an unmistakable challenge to the Ming emperor, who now saw to his northeast not a collection of subservient vassals but instead a polity that claimed to be, for the moment at least, a separate but equal state.

Now, for sinicization. Our previous understanding was that the Manchus, like all other aspiring barbarian conquerors of China, adopted Chinese ways of governance and legitimation of their rule, becoming in effect civilized Chinese. We know now that nothing so complete ever happened. The Qing rulers wore many hats and governed their diverse constituencies (Jurchen, Mongol, Tibetan, Chinese) in differing ways simultaneously. If the Qing ruler was the Son of Heaven for his Chinese subjects, he was also the Khan of Khans for the Mongols, the Chakravartin (Wheel-Turning King) for the Tibetans, and so on. The Qing would be a diverse, multinational, and presumably universal empire, very different from the Chinese dynasties it succeeded.[8]

That said, the conquest organization in the northeast, starting with Nurhaci himself, proved very enthusiastic and adept at adopting Chinese ways in the project of exerting domination over their would-be Chinese subjects. They energetically recruited Chinese elites disaffected from the Ming or simply hungry for personal power to serve as civil bureaucrats and military leaders of their fledgling state. The military men brought with them European-style artillery and other novel techniques of warfare that the Ming had learned from the Jesuits. They assiduously studied the Chinese language and launched translation projects for the Chinese classics, importing in the process Confucian models of ethical conduct, public service, and statecraft. They gradually set up a shadow imperial government, with a Grand Secretariat, Six Boards, and so on, closely imitative of the Ming. And they began to cultivate diplomatic relations with the Ming's purportedly vassal states, most notably Korea.

In November 1629 Hong Taiji opted for the first time to turn his forces directly against the Ming domain. He breached the Great Wall to occupy four cities of the central plain: Luanzhou, Qian'an, Zunhua, and Yongping. Ignoring his explicit orders to treat the inhabitants graciously, however, his field commanders put the civilian populations of Qian'an and Yongping to the sword. It was a public relations disaster that cost Hong deeply in his efforts to win the hearts and minds of frontier peoples, and he accordingly subjected his guilty subordinates to public show trials.

Three years later, in 1631, Hong laid siege to the stoutly defended Ming garrison and trading city of Dalinghe, along the coast of today's Liaoning province (Map 3). Massively fortified and surrounded by a ring of castles, this was a formidable prize. Hong besieged it with more than 20,000 troops and pounded it with cannon recently acquired from the Portuguese. After weeks of fighting, negotiations, and dizzying shifts of allegiance by local commanders, Dalinghe fell to Hong's forces—a signal victory for the ascendant regime.[9] In 1636 Hong Taiji threw down the gauntlet in the most provocative way imaginable: he changed the name of his imperial regime from Latter Jin to Qing. According to the Chinese system of Five Elements, the Ming, whose dynastic name contained the element of fire, would surely triumph over (melt) the Jin, whose proper element was metal. But the Qing element of water would inevitably extinguish the Ming.

By the early 1640s the entire edifice was in place. Still, things did not go smoothly. Subjects of the Qing had also suffered from the era's bad harvests and had been forced to raid and forage for food. Banner armies made frustratingly little headway against the stalwart Ming general Wu Sangui, whose forces guarded the entrance to China proper, the Shanhaiguan Pass. In a regime accustomed to easy success, morale plummeted critically. Then in September of 1643 Hong Taiji himself died, succeeded by his young son Fulin, with Hong Taiji's brother Dorgon as regent. The very next year the long-awaited conquest opportunity presented itself. The Chinese rebel leader Li Zicheng captured Beijing, and his proclaimed Shun dynasty immediately demonstrated its talent for

plunder, brutality, and little else. The horrified Wu Sangui deserted his
post in the northeast and returned to the capital to dispatch Li, who fled
to Xi'an, then moved throughout central China until the summer of
1645, when he apparently was killed by militiamen of a village that his
few surviving followers had raided for food. The military and administrative establishment of the Qing followed Wu Sangui into Beijing, where
Fulin, at the age of six, was installed on the Dragon Throne on October
30, 1644, with the reign title Shunzhi, Vanquisher of the Shun.

Alien Rule

China had experienced a long history of periodic rule by peoples who
were not identified, by themselves or by the conquered, as Chinese. No
one really liked it, of course, but it could be justified ideologically in several ways. The Son of Heaven was, after all, the intermediary between the
active first principle of the universe, Heaven, and all human beings, not
simply the Chinese, and so logically Heaven might select any of its constituents to receive its mandate to rule. And the criterion for receiving that mandate was not bloodline but rather the personal virtue of the
candidate—with "virtue" defined fairly precisely in Confucian cultural
terms.

That said, China long had an indigenously-generated sense of essential,
perhaps even biological, difference among peoples, and the Qing conquest was one moment when such domestic racial thought came to the
fore. No one was more emphatic in this than the Hunanese philosopher
and erstwhile resistance leader Wang Fuzhi (1619–1692). After discussing how beasts with webbed feet and with cloven hooves necessarily separate themselves from each other, Wang wrote:

> The Chinese in their bone structure, sense organs, gregariousness
> and exclusiveness, are no different from the barbarians, and yet they
> must be distinguished absolutely from the barbarians. Why is this
> so? Because if man does not mark himself off from things, then the
> principle of Heaven is violated. If the Chinese do not mark them-
> selves off from the barbarians, then the principle of earth is violated.
> And since Heaven and earth regulate mankind by marking men off
> from each other, if men do not mark themselves off and preserve an
> absolute distinction between societies, then the principle of man is

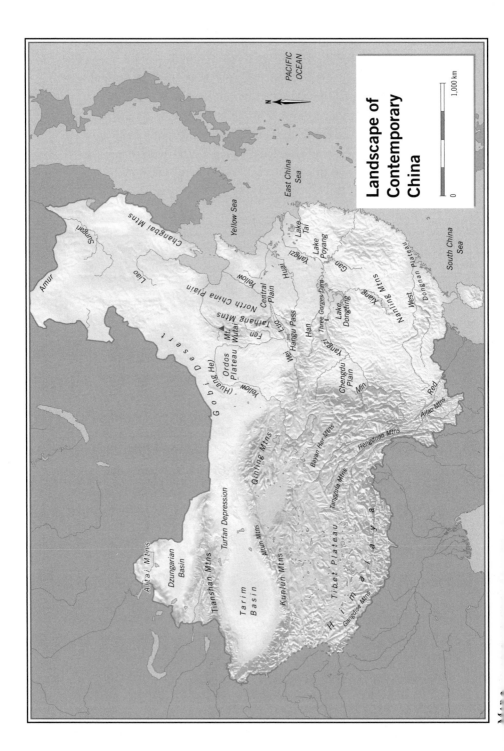

Landscape of Contemporary China

0   1,000 km

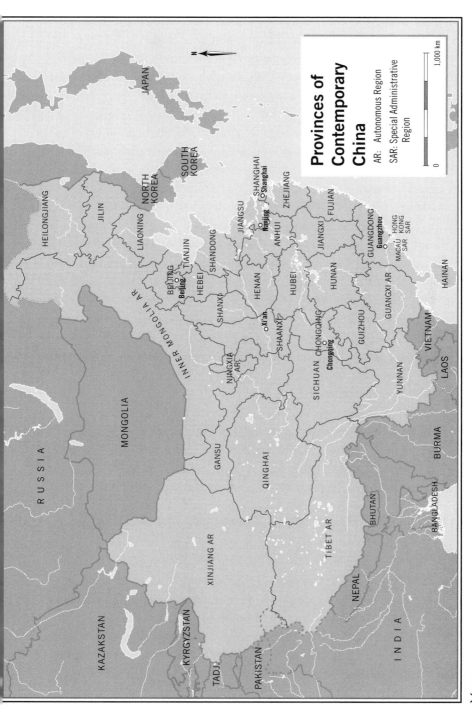

Provinces of Contemporary China

AR: Autonomous Region

SAR: Special Administrative Region

0   1,000 km

MAP 3

violated . . . Even the ants have leaders who rule their ant-hills, and if other insects come to attack their nests, the leader gathers the ants together and leads them against their enemies to destroy them and prevent further intrusion. Thus he who would lead the ants must know the way to protect his group. [10]

Unsurprisingly, Wang's writings were proscribed throughout much of the Qing era but reemerged to great popularity in the late nineteenth century, beginning with their republication in 1867 by the (presumably loyalist) anti-Taiping hero Zeng Guofan.[11]

In practice, the Qing takeover of much of north China was surprisingly easy and bloodless. In one county of Shandong, local elite-led militia, dismayed at the rapacious incompetence of the late Ming administration, eagerly handed their locality over to the arriving officials of Li Zicheng's Shun dynasty and then, just as readily, kicked out Li's officials and delivered it again to the Qing once the Shun proved even less able than the Ming.[12] But this early success may have been deceptive; it would take a full forty years after the conquest of Beijing for the Qing regime to establish itself with full security throughout the breadth of the former Ming domains, and for much of this period the new dynasty's eventual triumph was by no means determined.

Emboldened by their early success, and even before most of central China had been occupied, the new regime ordered all its male subjects to adopt the queue, a hairstyle traditional to the northeast in which the forehead was shaved and remaining hair was wound into a long braid. In early 1645 the Dorgon regency issued an imperial edict to the Board of Rites:

Within and without, we are one family. The Emperor is like the father, and the people are like his sons. The father and sons are of the same body; how can they be different from one another? If they are not as one then it will be as if they had two hearts and would they then not be like the people of different countries? . . . All residents of the capital and its vicinity will fulfill the order to shave their heads within ten days of this proclamation. For Zhili and other provinces compliance must take place within ten days of receipt of the order from the Board of Rites. Those who follow this order belong to our country; those who hesitate will be considered treasonous bandits and will be heavily penalized. Anyone who attempts to evade this or-

der or who uses cunning language to argue against it will not be
lightly dealt with.[13]

The court may have underestimated the degree of rage this queue-
wearing demand would generate among Han men, who not only saw
their traditional hairstyle as reflective of their cultural identity (a point
the Qing understood) but also viewed shaving their foreheads as a form
of self-mutilation and a breech of filial obligation owed to the parents
who had bequeathed them their bodies. Throughout the central China
highlands, local elites who had already accepted with deference the arrival of Qing county administrations responded to the demand with renewed revolt. They retreated to their mountain fortresses and held out,
often to the last man, for another five or six years.[14]

In the lower Yangzi region the outcome was bloodier still. Ming general Shi Kefa had ordered that the splendid city of Yangzhou be defended
to the death, and in May 1645 when it fell to Qing forces much of the
population was deliberately killed and survivors raped and murdered by
unruly Chinese soldiers in Qing employ. Despite this ominous example, and in direct response to the head-shaving decree, local elites in
the Yangzi delta opted to rebel against their newly established conquerors. In retaliation, furious Qing generals ordered the massacre of over
200,000 people in the county seat of Jiading and an even larger number
in Jiangyin.[15]

Cultural memories of these atrocities, especially the one at Yangzhou
for which an eyewitness account (Wang Xiuchu's *A Record of Ten Days
at Yangzhou*) circulated underground for centuries, would haunt the
Qing ever after. One sample from Wang's long catalogue of atrocities told
of a forced march of survivors, while the city lay in smoldering ruins:

Some women came up, and two among them called out to me . . .
They were partially naked, and they stood in mud so deep that it
reached their calves. One was embracing a girl, whom a soldier
lashed and threw into the mud before driving her away. One soldier
hoisted a sword and led the way, another leveled his spear and drove
us from behind, and a third moved back and forth in the middle to
make sure no one got away. Several dozen people were herded together like cattle or goats. Any who lagged behind were flogged or
killed outright. The women were bound together at their necks with

a heavy rope—strung one to another like pearls. Stumbling with each step, they were covered with mud. Babies lay everywhere on the ground. The organs of those trampled like turf under horses' hooves or people's feet were smeared in the dirt, and the crying of those still alive filled the whole outdoors. Every gutter or pond that we passed was stacked with corpses, pillowing each other's arms and legs. Their blood had flowed into the water, and the combination of green and red was producing a spectrum of colors. The canals, too, had been filled to level with dead bodies.[16]

Grafted on to "scientific" (that is, social Darwinist) notions of racial difference imported from the West in the late nineteenth and early twentieth centuries, and in company with the rediscovered writings of nativist writers such as Wang Fuzhi, such graphic accounts fed the mill of anti-Manchuism and Han nationalism that contributed mightily to the dynasty's overthrow in 1911.

For its part, the Qing regime remained undecided on just how much it was willing to play the game of Confucian rule. The old Jurchen Council of Princes—under the leadership of Dorgon, Jirgalang (who would succeed the regent following his death in 1650), and Ebai (who would serve as regent for the young Kangxi emperor from 1661 to 1669)—retained considerable authority. Literati opinion was largely disregarded, and the Chinese were treated effectively as a conquered people.[17] But with Kangxi's arrest of Ebai (who died in prison almost immediately) and assumption of personal rule, the tone of Qing policy moved in a dramatically different direction.

Dynastic Consolidation

It took the Qing conquerors nearly forty years from the time they captured Beijing and announced the founding of the dynasty to fully eliminate their competitors, and for much of this time it was by no means a certainty that the Qing would ultimately prevail. The first of these competitors was the rump regime of the defeated dynasty itself, called the Southern Ming. The Ming practice of enfeoffing imperial princes in various localities throughout the empire had left a variety of candidates for succession on the death of the Chongzhen emperor in 1644, but it also virtually ensured that conflict would ensue over just who should be the focus of loyalist efforts.

In June 1644 the Prince of Fu at Nanjing was reluctantly persuaded to declare himself the Hongguang emperor, but his reign lasted just one year before he was captured and killed by Qing forces. Thereafter one prince after another—usually several at once—claimed the mantle, running around the country seeking shelter and patronage from various paramilitary resistance forces or masters of mountain fortresses. The most lasting of these, the Prince of Yongming, was proclaimed the Yongli emperor in 1646 and then flitted around Guangdong, Guangxi, southern Hunan, and Yunnan for a dozen years before eventually fleeing to Burma. He was apprehended there by Wu Sangui and executed in May 1662, extinguishing the Ming once and for all.

A far more serious threat to the Qing was the rebellion of Wu Sangui himself. As the Ming general who had joined the Qing and led their forces into North China, he had been granted a fiefdom in Yunnan. Similar fiefs had been granted two other Ming turncoats—Shang Kexi in Guangdong and Geng Qimao in Fujian. By the early 1670s the Kangxi emperor had grown impatient with the autonomy of these "Three Feudatories" and put increasing pressure on the princes to resign and allow full integration of the south into the Qing bureaucratic administration. Wu Sangui responded on December 28, 1673, by declaring a rebellion, under the slogan "Overthrow the Qing and restore the Ming." He ordered his subjects to cut their queues and his troops to wear white garments and caps in mourning for the late dynasty.

At the same time, Wu also proclaimed his own new Zhou dynasty. He quickly advanced into western Hunan and then in early 1674 took the provincial capital, Changsha, the northern Hunan prefecture of Yuezhou, and Jingzhou in western Hubei. He was poised for an advance into the Yangzi valley, when the Kangxi emperor led his own troops south into Jiangxi to divide Wu from the other two feudatories and to find some route into Hunan to recapture Yuezhou, Wu's northernmost stronghold. The emperor achieved this in 1679, after five years of bitter fighting. But his victory turned the tide of what had seemed a life-and-death dynastic struggle, and within two years the rebellion had collapsed.[18]

The third challenger to the Qing was both the most persistent and by far the most interesting. It was a vast, integrated, armed, and eventually bureaucratized maritime empire built up and controlled by three successive generations of the Zheng family of traders from coastal Fujian.[19] Large armadas of Chinese armed smugglers had dominated the trade in

East Asian waters since the late fifteenth century, exchanging the prized silk, porcelain, and other manufactures of China for silver from Japan and the New World. The Ming ban on maritime trade only increased the power of these groups, while the Tokugawa expulsion of the Portuguese and its restriction of Dutch trade to the small island of Deshima in the 1630s dramatically reduced competition from these other maritime powers. In 1624 Zheng Zhilong assumed control of one such fleet of armed smugglers, and by 1630, at the age of twenty-six, he had unified them all under his single command.

Zheng engaged diplomatically with the Portuguese (who offered him the latest Western military technology in exchange for Chinese manufactures), the Dutch in Taiwan (for whom he had once worked as a translator and with whom he signed a treaty of mutual protection), the Japanese (who gave him the daughter of a high-ranking *daimyō* in marriage), and eventually the Ming (who, beleaguered by internal rebellion and Qing incursions in the northeast, in 1628 appointed Zheng an admiral of the fleet). His now very powerful empire was headquartered at Xiamen (Amoy) on the Fujian coast, where he made himself a popular hero by routinely seizing government granaries in years of dearth and distributing their contents to the coastal population. When the Qing captured Beijing in 1644, Ming loyalists saw Zheng as their champion, but in 1646 he withdrew his forces from Fujian and allowed the Qing to capture the local Ming pretender, the so-called Longwu emperor. His betrayal was met with another betrayal, however, when rather than honoring Zheng for his assistance the Qing instead took him prisoner and carted him off to Beijing. He was held there as hostage against his successors for some fifteen years, and in 1661 when he was no longer deemed useful he was executed.

Zheng Zhilong's son, Zheng Chenggong, assumed control of his father's Xiamen-based maritime empire in 1646 and immediately set out to bureaucratize its organization, dividing it into eastern and western fleets and five inland and five overseas companies, each divided into branches, and all overseen by several central ministries reporting to himself. Through agents at his inland base in Hangzhou, he purchased the best Jiangnan manufactures and became the undisputed master, both commercially and militarily, of the East China seas. But having in his youth been granted by the Longwu emperor the title Lord of the Imperial Surname, Chenggong took his Ming loyalism more seriously than his father had. In 1658 he launched a major attack on Jiangnan, announcing his attempt to reclaim it for the Yongli emperor (who was on the run in Yunnan). With a force of well over 100,000 men, he captured several coastal cities, then sailed up the Yangzi and took Zhenjiang.

On September 9, 1659, Zheng Chenggong attacked Nanjing but was turned back with heavy casualties. Throughout the following year the Qing, now fully determined to eliminate this nagging threat, besieged Zheng's Xiamen base. It withstood the siege, but Zheng nevertheless decided to withdraw from the mainland. For several decades his regime's relations with the Dutch had been souring, and so on April 30, 1661, he appeared with some 900 ships before Castle Zeelandia at Anping on the Taiwan coast. Landing without incident, he fought to dislodge the Dutch and on February 1, 1662, secured their negotiated withdrawal from Taiwan to Batavia. For this, he has been much honored as a Chinese nationalist hero.

Later that same year, however, Zheng Chenggong seemed to fall into a depression (prompted in part by reports of the execution of his father, with whom he had remained in communication during his long captivity) and committed suicide. After a succession struggle, his son Zheng Jing assumed command of the still prosperous maritime state. Familiar institutions of Chinese civil government—tax offices, Confucian academies, poorhouses, and widow homes—were set up in the regime's new Taiwan home. It survived for another two decades. Draconian moves by the Qing court to destroy its economic base by forcibly removing populations along the southeast coast proved more disastrous to the Qing than to the Zheng, who easily found other avenues of trade. Chinese naval attacks on Taiwan met with mixed success. Repeated Qing overtures for a negotiated surrender, in exchange for semiautonomous status for Taiwan, were met by procrastination. But finally, fatally weakened in 1674 by an ill-considered participation in Wu Sangui's Three Feudatories rebellion, beset by a worsening subsistence crisis, and damaged by another round of fratricidal fights over succession, the Zheng regime succumbed to a massive assault ordered by the Kangxi emperor in 1683. The Qing were now, at last, undisputed masters of all of China proper.

Forging an Accommodation

A key factor in the successful establishment of any dynasty in imperial China was the forging of an alliance between the local gentry and the central bureaucracy.[20] The literati class had historically remained fairly stable during dynastic transitions. Some individuals and families lost their lives in loyalist resistance, while others succeeded at promoting themselves under the new regime, but in aggregate they remained entrenched in support of their local interests. The gentry of the late imperial era were not in a position to assume the throne themselves—they were not an armed warrior caste like their Japanese counterparts, the samurai. Consequently, new dynasties were formed either by rebellious commoners such as the Ming founder or by alien conquerors such as the Qing. But no matter who took the reins of imperial rule, the gentry were absolutely necessary to the consolidation of a new dynasty in a number of ways.

Besides serving as a recruitment pool for imperial officials, they were the controllers of display in their localities—through teaching, delivering public lectures, performing sacrifices and other public rituals—and were therefore the critical voice in establishing the new regime's legitimacy. More practically, they stabilized local society through their philanthropic activities and other local leadership projects, and through a range of legal and quasi-legal channels they were critical to the regime's fiscal collection system. It was absolutely essential for an aspiring dynasty to secure an effective alliance with this group, and the Qing worked diligently at this over the course of its first several decades on the throne.

In the cultural sphere it immediately began to reestablish the examination system, providing upward mobility opportunities and securing tacit endorsement of its legitimacy on the part of all who consented to sit for the test. In 1679 it held a grand special examination offering civil service degrees well in excess of established quotas and intended specifically to capture the allegiance of scholars who may still have harbored loyalist sentiments toward the Ming. In 1658 it ceremoniously reestablished the postgraduate Hanlin Academy, that historically troublesome home of political criticism that the Ming in its last days had allowed to lapse. By the early 1680s it launched a massive compilation project, the *Mingshi*, for preserving the history of its predecessor, with the goal among other things of channeling the energies of literati who had special knowledge of, and nostalgia for, the now safely extinguished former dynasty.

The Qing was helped immeasurably in this project of cultural cooptation by its adept selection of officials. For example, in Yangzhou—the once-grand lower Yangzi city that had seen brutal devastation during the conquest—local literati in the late seventeenth century were seeking to rebuild their cultural hegemony by a busy process of poetry composition and publication, construction of pavilions, bridges, and other sites of real or invented historical significance, and collective meetings to drink, recite, admire the scenery, and generally vet one another's claims to cultural superiority. Much of this process was orchestrated by the young Shandong native Wang Shizhen (1643–1711), who was dispatched by the Qing to serve as a judge in the area and whose own literary gifts, personal charisma, and support for the project of elite reconstitution in no small way sold the idea of Qing rule in this pivotal locality. In the short term, at least, the massacre of 1645 was nearly effaced from local memory.[21]

The Qing moved to forge ties with the landed elite in more material ways, most strikingly by what it chose not to do. The Ming, which had come to power on a "land to the tiller" platform, had moved quickly to seize many large private landholdings and redistribute plots to household-scale cultivators. The Qing did no such thing. Although it carved out imperial, banner, and official estates in the environs of Beijing and elsewhere in north China, it did this primarily in areas that had been decimated by the Li Zicheng rebellion. Elsewhere, it announced its intent to respect existing ownership rights and help landowners displaced by the rebellions reclaim their property.

The Qing also helped elites regain control over their labor force. In Guangshan and Shangcheng counties of Henan's southern highlands, for example, bondservant labor in agriculture was the norm. The dynastic transition had been marked, here as elsewhere, by waves of rebellion among this unfree workforce. In 1658, on a rumor that the new Qing court had declared universal emancipation, the bondservants rose up one final time. But the recently arrived Qing prefect moved quickly to demonstrate that the rumor was untrue, throwing his military forces behind local militias to brutally suppress the challenge to landlord rule. This key event cemented the identity of interests between landlords and the state in a troublesome part of the empire where Ming loyalist and localist resistance movements died hard.

The most severe test of the throne-gentry alliance occurred, unsurprisingly, in the area of tax collection and especially, as one might expect, among the enormously wealthy anti-Qing families of the Yangzi delta. Though this was probably the most productive agrarian land in all of China, it was also disproportionately taxed. The Ming founder had instituted what amounted to confiscatory tax rates there in the fourteenth century in order to support his new imperial capital at Nanjing, and predictably these assessments had remained on the books even when his successor moved the principal capital to Beijing. The response of local landholders and officials over the centuries had been to work out what both parties agreed to be a reasonable tax yield, collect just this amount year after year, and declare the excess uncollectible due to natural calamities of one sort or another. As a result of this arrangement, by early Qing times there were enormous accumulated tax arrears on record for this region, arrears that no local authority had any intention of ever collecting.

Under the Ebai regency in 1661, however, the court suddenly announced its intention to clear these arrears. Deeply suspicious of the Jiangnan gentry's politics and hoping to break the back of their autonomous economic power, it announced a schedule of required repayment, posted officials to the area charged with prosecuting the tax clearance, and, when local landholders proved unable or unwilling to meet these demands, threw large numbers of influential gentry in local jails. Nationally, the irate response of the elite was overwhelming, and the court quickly recognized its mistake. It released the hostages, worked out financial agreements to save face on both sides, and scapegoated and cashiered (and in some cases even imprisoned) the very officials it had charged with clearing the taxes in arrears. The throne-gentry alliance in Jiangnan had, after a rocky start, ultimately survived the conquest.

2

GOVERNANCE

WHILE the Great Qing was an empire encompassing many disparate peoples, it was also a dynasty (*guo*) in the Chinese imperial tradition, and its ruling house confronted many of the same problems faced by its predecessors. The Chinese empire, the legacy of the First Emperor Qin Shihuang in the third century B.C., had demonstrated throughout its long history that it could be conquered but not permanently fragmented. Some self-righting mechanism seemed to dictate that periods of breakdown would be followed by longer eras of reintegration. The empire had been able to sustain its enormous size in the area known as "China proper" or "Inner China" for over two millennia. No other political unit of comparable scale—not the Roman or Holy Roman empires in the West, nor the Mamluk or Ottoman empires in the Islamic world, nor the Mongol empire in central Asia—had survived nearly so long. Why?

Usually an empire expands up to the point where the costs of maintaining military superiority over its neighbors along increasingly extensive borders, combined with the costs of internal administration and maintenance of stability, become unsustainably great.[1] The economy buckles under the mounting pressure as the imperial government tries to enlarge its share of the realm's economic product, and the society fractures as collection mechanisms for meeting the state's growing fiscal demands exacerbate inequality (as it is usually easier to collect proportionately more from the poor than from the rich). The resulting tension and animosity in turn make the costs of maintaining internal stability all the greater. In most cases, the empire breaks down under the strain into smaller, more governable polities or states, and at that point the imperial regime fades into history.

One way that the sprawling empire of the Son of Heaven was able to escape this fate was through two economic revolutions—in the Tang and Song, and again in the late Ming and early Qing—that greatly expanded the empire's productivity. By increasing the size of the pie, the imperial regime could take a larger slice without immiserating its subjects. This pattern continued until the unrelenting growth of the population in the mid-Qing made this strategy no longer feasible. Paired with growing economic productivity was a triumph of organizational logistics that allowed the budget of the Heavenly Empire to remain small relative to the society's total economic product. When it worked well, the Qing administration was governance on the cheap.

For example, in the matter of defense, military systems were so well developed that the empire could move men and supplies efficiently to any front that suddenly became critical. The Grand Canal, constructed under the Sui dynasty (589–618), shipped massive quantities of grain from the river valleys of central and southern China to provision troops in the less productive, more volatile north. In addition, the military colony (*tuntian*) system planted economically self-sufficient detachments of soldier-farmers and their families at key points along the defended frontier to support regular troops in the event of conflict. A third military innovation in the mid-Ming was an arrangement whereby enterprising private merchants were granted lucrative franchises within the imperial salt monopoly in proportion to the amount of grain they shipped and sold at low cost to military garrisons along the northern frontiers.[2] The net effect of these logistical maneuvers was that the empire was able to defend its enormous borders with an impressively small and inexpensive standing army. At its most expansive, the Qing standing army—including both the bannermen and the Chinese Green Standard Army—employed well under a million troops to pacify and defend a population of four to five hundred million.[3]

At least as significant as its efficiency in the military arena was the empire's ability to keep the civil administration small relative to the size of the overall society and economy it governed. One key factor was the state's use of Neo-Confucian political ideology as an instrument for maintaining order and stability. There were certainly limits to this: despite the heavy bias of Confucian rhetoric in favor of compliance and social harmony, late imperial Chinese society was probably at least as vi-

olent on a day-to-day basis as its contemporaries in the West and elsewhere. But overall, such instruments of indoctrination as the civil service
examination allowed unparalleled success in the use of normative and ritual means for social control. Another factor was the late empire's skillful
use of self-regulatory groups within the society itself—kinship organizations, agrarian villages, water conservancy communities, and merchant
and artisanal guilds—to achieve the state's goals of maintaining order,
providing welfare services, and so on.[4] And third, the state apparatus itself was organized into a rather tight and impressively efficient bureaucratic machine.

The smallness of the formal state under the Qing, in terms of personnel
and budget, was not just a practical advantage but a point of honor. "Benevolent governance" (renzheng)—governance by a few good men rather
than by proliferating, interventionist institutions—was a positive Confucian value self-consciously trumpeted by the regime itself. For much of
the Qing, it worked tolerably well and might even have been the best way
to rule China's expansive domain, given the available technology. But in
the Qing's last century, when faced internally with increasing population
pressure, social complexity, and geographic mobility, and externally with
a competitive international war of all against all, the need for a political
entity capable of mobilizing China's economic and human resources to a
much greater degree than ever before became wrenchingly apparent. But
the imperial government found it difficult to change. This problem of determining the optimum size of the state and then securing it against foreign invasion and domestic rebellion was a central theme of Qing history.

Political Institutions

Years before the actual conquest, the Qing had formed a set of governmental institutions modeled closely on those of the Ming, and it rather
seamlessly imposed these on the governance of China as a whole once it
entered the pass in 1644. Contemporaries divided this administrative apparatus conceptually into two parts: the "inner" administration located
at Beijing and the "outer" administration located in the provinces. The
inner or central administration included the Grand Secretariat, which
since the first Ming emperor's abolition of the post of chancellor had
been the closest thing to an executive institution within the formal bureaucracy. Before and just following the conquest, the Qing had filled the
functions of the Ming Grand Secretariat with an evolving collection of

smaller agencies, but in 1658 it reorganized these more precisely on the Ming model and gave it that same name.

The several positions known as "grand secretary" were, under the Qing, the highest to which Chinese or non-Chinese civil servants could aspire. Grand secretaries were very powerful men, not so much because they held this post but because they already wielded power that the post merely acknowledged explicitly. While the Grand Secretariat exercised little policymaking authority, it served as a channel of communications by collecting, ratifying, and forwarding "memorials" (*tiben*), reports sent to the emperor from other central and field officials. The system was clumsy, and in the early eighteenth century Qing emperors themselves became so frustrated that they devised ways to streamline communications and sidestep the Grand Secretariat.

A notch below the Grand Secretariat were the so-called Six Boards—Revenue, Civil Office (tasked with assigning personnel to specific bureaucratic posts), War, Criminal Justice, Public Works, and Rites. These were, again, more advisory than executive institutions, each with large clerical staffs headed by two presidents and several vice presidents, which were usually collateral posts held by important field administrators. Especially powerful was the Board of Rites. Because of the broad range of activities covered by the notion of "ritual" in Confucian China, this board was in charge not merely of imperial sacrifices, etiquette, and protocol at court but also of the civil service examination system, education more generally, moral conduct among the degree-holding gentry, and—as overseer of the so-called tribute system—many aspects of the empire's diplomatic relations with the outside world. Another important central government agency inherited from earlier dynasties was the Censorate, a group of more than fifty officials, usually young and ambitious, assigned to look over the shoulders of other metropolitan and field administrators and if necessary serve as whistle-blowers.[5]

A particularly sensitive institution was the recently reestablished Hanlin Academy, a venerable postgraduate school for the most successful products of the civil service examination system. Ostensibly charged with the compilation of historical archives and other documents, the Hanlin served in practice as a holding pool for talented scholars awaiting high office and, increasingly, as a locus of policy criticism by ambitious young hotshots who knew in their hearts they could do a better job than their seniors if only they were given these responsible posts. Political agitation from Hanlin scholars had prompted the late Ming court to allow the

Fig. 2   Temple of Heaven, Beijing.

academy to lapse, but the more ostentatiously self-confident Qing seized upon the opportunity to court literati favor by reopening the Hanlin in 1658.[6]

The "outer" or field bureaucracy had multiple levels with overlapping jurisdictions. The Qing posted governors to administer each of the empire's eighteen or so provinces and also governors-general to perform nearly the same functions for sets of contiguous provinces or for one especially large province (Map 4). Thus, while Hubei and Hunan provinces, or Guangdong and Guangxi, each had their own governor, the two-province units of Huguang (Hubei-Hunan) and Liangguang (Guangdong-Guangxi) each had a governor-general as well. The sprawling and populous Sichuan had both a governor and a governor-general of its own.

The posts of governor and governor-general were outgrowths of Ming precedents but were modified and made more substantial in the Qing dynasty's early years. Under the Ming, provincial governance had been most directly handled by several specialist commissioners: an administrative commissioner, a surveillance commissioner, and a military commissioner. Beginning in 1430, central government dignitaries were dis-

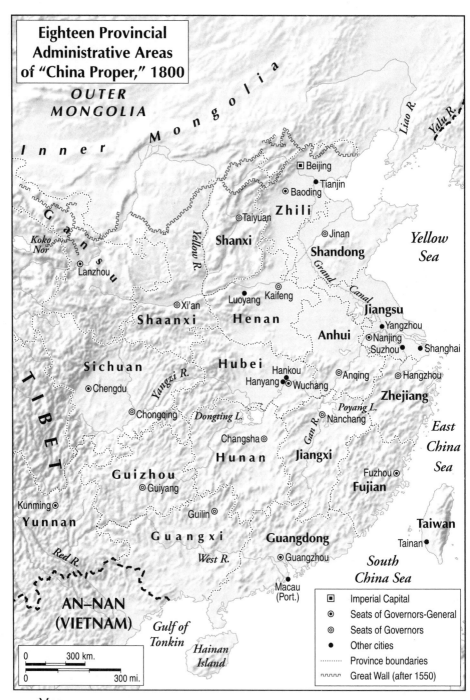

Eighteen Provincial Administrative Areas of "China Proper," 1800

OUTER MONGOLIA

I n n e r   M o n g o l i a

■ Beijing
• Tianjin
◎ Baoding

Zhili

◎Taiyuan

Shanxi

◎ Jinan

Shandong

Yellow Sea

Koko Nor

G a n s u

◎ Lanzhou

Yellow R.

◎Xi'an

Shaanxi

Luoyang Kaifeng◎

H e n a n

Grand Canal

Jiangsu
• Yangzhou
◎Nanjing • Shanghai
Suzhou•

Anhui

Sichuan

◎Chengdu

Yangzi R.

H u b e i
Hankou
Hanyang•◎Wuchang

◎ Anqing ◎ Hangzhou

Zhejiang

◎Chongqing *Dongting L.*

Poyang L.
◎ Nanchang

Gan R.

East China Sea

Changsha◎

H u n a n   Jiangxi

T I B E T

Guizhou
◎Guiyang

Fuzhou◎

Fujian

Kunming◎

Y u n n a n

Guilin◎

G u a n g x i

Guangdong

West R.

◎Guangzhou

Taiwan

Tainan•

South China Sea

Macau
(Port.)

Red R.

AN–NAN
(VIETNAM) *Gulf of Tonkin* Hainan Island

■	Imperial Capital
◉	Seats of Governors-General
◎	Seats of Governors
•	Other cities
....	Province boundaries
∼∼∼	Great Wall (after 1550)

0   300 km.

0   300 mi.

Liao R.   *Yalu R.*

MAP 4

patched, without staff or permanent residence in the provinces, to coordinate the activities of these several field commissioners. Gradually, these touring "grand coordinators" were regularized into provincial administrators, or "governors." In the same era, touring officials whose functions under the Ming had been strictly military and who in the early Qing were nearly always bannermen were regularized as "governors-general."[7]

Regional and provincial administrators had real decision-making power in the late imperial government. As often as not, policy initiatives came not from the throne but from them. The Son of Heaven exercised absolute power in theory, but in practice that power was limited by the need to observe ritual correctness and the precedents set by his forebears, the constraints of his personal energy and interest in his job (constraints that had severely curtailed the effectiveness of the late Ming rulers), and not least the limits of communication. The execution of imperial power has been compared to that of a switchboard operator: when the emperor heard of regional policy initiatives worked out on the scene by a field official, he would decide on their soundness and then forward the good ideas to other regional officials to implement as they deemed feasible in their own jurisdictions. Most provincial officials dutifully notified the throne of what they were up to and received guidance when they could. But the emperor could not rule upon matters that, for whatever reason, did not come to his attention.

Below the level of the province was the prefecture, administered by a prefect, and next was the county or district, under the authority of a county magistrate. With typically five or six counties per prefecture, roughly seven to thirteen prefectures per province, and eighteen or so provinces, the number of counties totaled nearly two thousand empire-wide. In most times and places the county was the lowest level of formal administration, the smallest unit to which a centrally-appointed, examination-certified bureaucrat was assigned. There might easily be a million people in a populous county, and the magistrate was responsible for knowing everything that went on within its borders and for all aspects of local defense and policing, maintenance of public works, popular livelihoods, education and local culture, and, most pressingly, civil litigation within his jurisdiction. It was an impossible task, and contemporaries understood this. In *The Death of Woman Wang*, Jonathan Spence has described cases of crime-solving and conflict resolution confronted by magistrates of a single remote Shandong county in the early Qing era. In each case, despite the diligent, judicious, passionately fair-minded, and often ingenious efforts of the magistrate to achieve social justice for the parties concerned, the wrong people almost always profited and the innocent parties suffered.[8] In the late empire's system of governance on the cheap, the frustrated magistrates simply did not have the resources to do the job their Confucian moral training impelled them to do.

In addition to this grid of Qing territorial administration, at both the provincial and the county levels there were also functional specialists such as provincial treasurers and provincial judges (successors of the Ming administrative and surveillance commissioners, respectively) and directors of education, all of whom reported to one of the Six Boards in Beijing rather than to the general territorial administrator in whose jurisdiction they served. There were also circuit intendants whose formal duties were to oversee units of jurisdiction (the circuit) midway between the province and the prefecture. But as these administrative units became increasingly vestigial over the course of the dynasty, circuit intendants either lapsed into sinecure holders or were assigned specialist duties such as hydraulic maintenance or, in areas of heavy contact with foreigners such as Shanghai, local management of diplomatic affairs. Paralleling this entire civil administration was a grid of military officials as well.

Thus, territorial administration under the Qing was an elaborate system of checks and balances designed to ensure effective central control over officials in the field. Governors and governors-general duplicated one another's efforts and monitored one another's obedience to central directives; functional specialists did the same for general administrators; military officials performed this oversight function for their civil counterparts; superiors submitted annual reports on the performance of their subordinates; and territorially specialized censors in the capital looked over everyone's shoulders all the while.

Especially critical to the goal of central control was the so-called law of avoidance, a package of practices regarding assignment of officials that the Qing inherited from its predecessors, expanded, and rigorously enforced. A cardinal principle of the law of avoidance was the separation of incumbent officials from their posts. Although officials were, almost of necessity, wealthy landholders and lineage leaders in their own right, their economic and social power centered on their distant native place, not on the jurisdiction where they served at the pleasure of their imperial master. A field official was never allowed to serve in his home district or even province, and in the system of checks and balances he was never paired with or adjacent to a relative or even a fellow provincial. An official of registered Chinese ethnicity would most often find himself serving with others of Manchu or Mongol registry, and vice versa. To avoid the possibility that an official would, over time, become entrenched in his assigned jurisdiction, officials were routinely rotated so that those at the provincial levels served tours of duty no longer than three years and those at the local level only half that time. It was an ingenious system, and for most of the dynasty it achieved its aims. But as everyone knew, the throne was trading off independent initiative on the part of its officials for the sake of central control. Rulers consistently railed against lethargic, careerist, time-serving local bureaucrats, but their dysfunctional behavior was built into the Qing system of governance, which tolerated and even encouraged it.

Administrative Innovation and Centralization

During its first century, the Qing regime made three significant innovations in its central administration, designed to enhance the regime's ability to function as an expansionist, multinational, early modern empire. Significantly, all three institutions operated outside the regular bureaucracy and were staffed by personal clients of the throne rather than by successful civil service examination candidates.

The first, known in Chinese as the Court of Colonial Affairs (*Lifan yuan*) but in Manchu as the Ministry for Ruling the Outer Provinces (*Tulergi golo be dasara jurgan*), was established on the eve of the conquest in 1638.[9] It was the first organ in China's imperial history created specifically to administer areas outside of China proper—Mongolia, Tibet, and so on—which the Qing now claimed as integral parts of its empire. The ministry had an office in the capital equivalent in status to the Six Boards as well as its own field bureaucracy of impressive size. Han literati were almost entirely excluded from this critical institution, and much of its operation was conducted in languages other than Chinese.

Among the ministry's most important functions was staging elaborate rituals designed to symbolically integrate Inner Asian populations into the Qing empire while demonstrating that the ruling house itself remained essentially one of them. These rituals included the Imperial Hunt, in which the court and its vassals jointly participated, and scheduled pilgrimages and tribute missions of borderland leaders to the throne. The Imperial Hunt originated among the Jurchen long before the conquest; pilgrimages and tribute missions derived from Ming practice but were reconceived under the Qing to reflect the special bonds between fellow peoples of pastoral origin. The Ministry for Ruling the Outer Provinces also managed the proliferating exchange markets that oversaw both state-sponsored and—increasingly over the eighteenth century—private trade across cultural frontiers.

The second Qing innovation, the Imperial Household Department, was dedicated to the emperor's personal service and to management of his various private financial interests throughout the realm. Though formally instituted by the regent Ebai upon the death of the Shunzhi emperor in 1661, it in fact had a much older prehistory, dating back to the Jurchen tribal leaders' personal monopoly on the ginseng trade and to private landed estates owned by the ruling house prior to the conquest. The Imperial Household Department was a means of circumventing the economic and political power of Chinese eunuchs, and Ebai's decision in the 1660s to formalize it was largely a response to perceptions of the reviving power of eunuchs in the last years of Shunzhi's reign. Instead of eunuchs (several of whom remained to provide the most intimate services for the emperor), the Imperial Household Department was staffed by bondservants, following a model of personal servitude that had deep roots in Jurchen culture. Its personnel were drawn from the upper three banners of the various Jurchen, Mongol, Chinese, and Korean ethnicities.

Apart from personal service to the throne, disbursing funds for the imperial family's daily expenses, and building and maintaining various imperial residences, the Imperial Household Department operated agrarian estates in the northeast and north China, managed the imperial silk manufactories in Nanjing and Suzhou, and held lucrative interests in the customs service, the salt administration, livestock husbandry, copper mining and trade, the ongoing ginseng trade, and gift exchanges associated with the tribute system. By the end of the eighteenth century it had become a large and growing bureaucracy comprising over 1,600 officials and an untold number of rank-and-file staff.[10]

Certainly the most dramatic of the Qing innovations in central administration, however, was the Grand Council. As implied by its Chinese name *Junjichu* (Office of Military Planning), the Grand Council began as an informal advisory commission for military affairs. On his various campaigns, the Kangxi emperor had brought along several of his most trusted military strategists, who also assisted him in running state business from his remote field headquarters. Over the last years of his reign, and especially under his energetically centralizing successor, Yongzheng, this informal body evolved into a permanent privy council in the palace itself, and its sphere of authority expanded to all arenas of imperial policy. However, it was never regularized into the formal bureaucratic structure of the empire, remaining something of a personal "star chamber" or "kitchen cabinet" granting private advice to the throne.

Typically some three to five members of the inner court would hold the rank of grand councilor at any one time. Though an especially trusted Chinese minister might be numbered among them occasionally, the composition of the council was overwhelmingly Manchu, its leading members often drawn from the emperor's closest circle of relatives and friends. In practice it proved to be a remarkably enabling instrument of personal rule for the more capable Qing emperors, and during the late Qing it accomplished what the Grand Secretariat during the Ming had not been able to do—it took up the slack in leadership when the throne lost its vigor.[11]

The unusual power of the Grand Council was in large part the result of an accompanying institutional innovation of the late Kangxi and Yongzheng reigns. The Qing paid great attention to the management of communications, which determined the throne's ability to exercise control over its vast domains. In the early decades of the dynasty, following Ming precedent, memorials from individual officials were channeled through the appropriate board—Rites, Works, Civil Office, and so on—and relayed to the throne and subsequently archived by the corresponding office of the Grand Secretariat. With the establishment of the Grand Council, however, a separate special category of communication was created known as secret or palace memorials (*zouzhe*). These were sent directly to the inner court for immediate reading by the emperor in consultation with the council, and only then were they recirculated downward to the Grand Secretariat and the appropriate board for comment or action.

These palace memorials did not supersede routine memorials and were theoretically used only for the most urgent items demanding immediate attention. Unsurprisingly, however, memorialists tended to think that whatever they had to say was necessarily urgent, and very quickly the privileged channel became the normal means of communication whenever policy decisions of even relatively marginal significance might be affected. Routine memorials, which still comprised the vast majority of communications, became confined to regular reports of weather, harvest yields, grain reserves, common criminal cases, maintenance of public works, and the like.[12]

The emergence of the palace memorial as the major forum for policy discussion had several other dramatic effects on Qing rule. In order to manage this new channel of direct access to the imperial ear, the Grand Council strictly limited the number of officials who were authorized to submit palace memorials. Altogether, fewer than a hundred individuals—presidents and vice presidents of the Six Boards, governors, governors-general, high ranking military officers, and selected others—were on the list at any given time. One implication of this constraint was to elevate the status of provincial officials over their prefectural and county subordinates. Another was that the cohort of high officials possessing the right to memorialize became, in their own minds, an elite group, and in the view of the throne this uncomfortable situation needed constant attention.

Using his vermilion brush, the emperor usually commented on or "rescripted" each palace memorial before copies were returned to the sender. Naturally, given the volume of correspondence an energetic ruler read each day, these rescripts were often limited to a simple "Noted." But rulers who were keen to keep bureaucrats on their toes used the rescript to tease, cajole, threaten, or motivate officials in a highly personal and colloquial way. The following, scribbled by Qianlong on a memorial from a provincial official, was typical: "When you were serving in the Board [of Punishments] you were an outstanding official. As soon as you are posted to the provinces, however, you take on disgusting habits of indecisiveness and decadence. It is really detestable . . . You take your sweet time about sending in memorials, and there isn't a word of truth in them! You have really disappointed my trust in you, you ingrate of a *thing!*"[13] Qianlong came to feel that this cozy group of officials were becoming too comfortable in their status and too collectively orchestrated in what they revealed to him about real conditions in the provinces. He launched periodic systematic campaigns of harangue and intimidation just to shake them up.

A more thoroughgoing means of bypassing the dysfunctional clubbiness of the upper bureaucracy was by periodically opening the "pathways of words" (*yanlu*). Whenever a Qing emperor felt that palace memorials betrayed too much complacency and routine or that thinking on a central issue had stagnated, he had the option of dramatically expanding downward the pool of bureaucrats or even nonofficial literati allowed to submit memorials on a specific policy issue for a specified duration of time, in order to solicit new ideas and also to gauge the sentiment of the larger political public.

Of Money and Men

The Qing government's revenues came overwhelmingly from taxes on agricultural production, presumed to be the foundation of the empire's economy. The land tax was a hybrid assessment, combining both a tax on adult males in the household and an assessment per unit of land, evaluated according to the presumed yield of the household's cultivated fields. Up until the 1720s these two components had been separately assessed, but the third Qing emperor, Yongzheng, decided to drop the head tax and collect household taxes as a single assessment on land alone. The progressive nature of this reform, which shifted the tax burden onto property holders in proportion to their holdings, was not lost on landed elites, who resisted but to little avail.[14]

In assessing and collecting land taxes, the early Qing largely relied on Ming registers of which households owned what—registers that everyone knew to be faulty and outdated. In 1712 the Qing published its one and only empire-wide cadastral survey. Assessments were aggregated at the county level and then forwarded to the province for further upward remission to the central imperial coffers. Both the county and the province retained a portion of the take for their troubles (and at the provincial level another portion was sometimes diverted to contiguous provinces deemed to be in greater need). But neither counties nor provinces were empowered to assess land taxes for their own use: they were simply collection agents for the throne. Nevertheless, how assessments were divided up *within* a county was left in the hands of county officials—a source of much contention in local politics and society. The constitutional means of financing regional and local administration remained a critical unresolved problem in the Qing.

Although significant differences over time and space adversely affected specific local populations, for most of the Qing era the aggregate fiscal burden on the Chinese people was not excessive.[15] Indeed, the population was in all likelihood undertaxed. On repeated occasions, especially in the middle decades of the eighteenth century, the Qing court took advantage of prosperity to reduce the tax burden in specific reformist ways.

This was Confucian "benevolent governance," to be sure, but it also decreased the capability of the state to mobilize in the face of new threats or unanticipated needs. And by leaving the economic surplus in the hands of producers and market forces, the government subsidized a rate of population growth that would ultimately strain the capacities of the regime.[16] From the early eighteenth century on, Qing rulers recognized that their subject population was increasing at a dangerously rapid rate, but population growth was so universally identified as a sign of good governance that the notion of using fiscal or other means to put a brake on births was unthinkable.

Though no tax was levied on developed property per se—shops or handicraft factories, for example—local administrations collected a fee for registering property title and contracts of sale. But since titles were usually enforceable in magistrates' courts even without being formally registered with the state, most property holders simply avoided paying these fees. There were very few taxes on manufacturing, wholesale trade, and retail sales—the commercial sector was for the most part overlooked as a source of state revenue—but a number of indirect taxes were imposed on mercantile activity. The domestic and maritime customs services collected modest tolls on the long-distance transport of commercial goods, and the government licensed wholesale commodities brokers in major trans-shipment centers. These brokers charged a commission to merchants for their service in regulating the local market and then paid a percentage of their take to the state for their license. The state also received revenue from its monopoly on the production and distribution of salt—the one essential consumer item—and derived further income from the mining sector, especially the monetary metals silver and copper.

Other irregular, miscellaneous sources of revenue included confiscations of property in the form of fines, "contributions" solicited from wealthy individuals to finance various public projects, and sales of civil service degrees and official posts (most often nominal ones) to finance the state's impressive system of relief granaries in each locality. In the late eighteenth century the sale of degrees and posts accelerated to meet the costs of various military campaigns along the inland frontiers, and reached unprecedented levels to finance the suppression of domestic rebellions in the mid-nineteenth century.[17] With all of this, however, at least until the Qing's final half century, all nonagrarian sources of government revenue remained but a small fraction of the take from the land tax.

Where did government officials come from? Up through the Tang dynasty (618–906), imperial bureaucrats were recruited through recommendations from currently serving officials. This meant that the bloodlines of the official class simply reproduced themselves—that is, early imperial China was a political meritocracy superimposed on an aristocratic society. Then, in what is usually seen as one of the most fundamental transformations in Chinese history, the late Tang and early Song dynasties gradually put greater weight on the system of civil service examinations that had been on the books for many centuries. By the time of the Ming and Qing, the civil service examination system had become the primary vehicle for selecting officials, and the imperial state exerted great efforts to ensure its integrity and effectiveness.[18]

Of the three levels of examination under the Qing, the lowest was given every year and a half at the local level. The odds of passing this exam were remote, and some candidates took it dozens of times without success. But for those who passed, the rewards were great: they became *shengyuan* (novice scholars) and thus members of the gentry elite. This status entitled them to wear gentry robes, enjoy exemptions from common criminal punishments and corvée impositions, receive state stipends in some cases, and most importantly enjoy privileged access to—and status equality with—local officials.

The second level of examination was administered at the provincial level every three years. Candidates passed at a rate ranging from one out of every twenty-five to one out of a hundred, depending on the quota pertaining in the particular time and place. Those who succeeded became *juren* (selected men) theoretically eligible for appointment to office, though without a yet higher degree this was unlikely. Even so, selected men gained entry to what is sometimes called the upper gentry—the distinction between upper and lower gentry status being very real in contemporary sensibility.

The third and highest level, the metropolitan examination administered at Beijing every three years, allowed winners to call themselves *jinshi* (scholars presented to the throne, or presented scholars). These men were the true national elite and the talent pool from which most officials were drawn. Their names were inscribed on steles, lined up in ranks, class by class, in the Confucian Temple in the imperial capital (Fig. 3).

At all three levels, the civil service examinations consisted of questions on the Confucian classical texts and on poetry. Students were required to write "eight-legged essays," a form of logical argumentation on desig-

Fig. 3   Steles listing recipients of metropolitan examination *(jinshi)* degree, by year, Confucian Temple, Beijing.

nated moral issues in the classics with elaborately specified stylistic rules. There were also some policy questions on administrative techniques and economic and political issues of the day, but these were of far less consequence for passing or failing. Those who passed the exams and went on to become officials did, of course, necessarily educate themselves in administration practices, but this was an entirely separate body of literature from the examination curriculum. Vociferous arguments raged throughout the Qing over whether the examination curriculum ought to be reformed to stress more policy-oriented questions, but it was never substantially revised.[19] The exams remained above all a test of refined literacy, which, given the crucial importance of clear written communication to the task of administering so vast an empire, made a certain amount of practical sense.

Yet the examinations were written and graded by human beings with agendas of their own, and they could be subtly manipulated for political purposes. During the Ming, for example, a throne sensitive to literati criticism frequently asked questions demanding candidates to expound on the virtue of political loyalty to the imperial master. In the Qing, during the eighteenth-century heyday of the so-called "empirical research" movement, officials skilled in the comparative philology of classical texts often inserted questions along these lines on the examinations. Not coincidentally, this favored candidates hailing from Jiangnan and other regions of the country endowed with rich private book collections (the areas from which the examiners themselves usually came) over others from more remote areas whose education had concentrated on intensive study of a few canonical works. Later in the dynasty, examiners adhering to the ancient prose movement passed candidates whose answers were written in the spare classical style they themselves had mastered—a style which, theoretically at least, encoded a shared commitment to fundamentalist moral and political values.[20]

The Qing regime was very deeply committed to fair and impartial examinations. It hired an army of clerks to recopy each examination paper in order to efface the candidates' calligraphy and identity from sympathetic examiners. One way of getting around this was to place a character or phrase in a spot in an examination essay that had been pre-arranged between the candidate and examiner. The law of avoidance was applied to the exams, and special "avoidance examinations" were administered to candidates whose familial or local-origin ties to examiners might prove compromising. When violations of the examination's integrity were exposed, as they frequently were, the consequences for the implicated examiner or candidate were drastic.

The court was also strongly committed to achieving geographic distribution among the candidates who passed, indeed in some instances practicing a kind of geographic and ethnic affirmative action to make sure that socially and culturally less favored subjects had ample opportunities to prepare for, take, and pass the test. Quotas were set at all three levels of examination and continually readjusted with the goal of populating the bureaucracy with men from a variety of groups. Officials and families from the more economically prosperous and culturally advanced regions of the empire of course had precisely the opposite interests, and an elaborate cat-and-mouse game took place between the court and elite society on this score. For instance, kinship groups in wealthy areas, where competition for passing the exam was extreme, would routinely establish a member household in a remote, less educationally competitive area such as the southwest and transfer to that household via adoption or apprenticeship a particularly promising lad whose chances of examination success in his adoptive home would be much greater than in his birthplace.

Clearly, one of the regime's goals for the civil service examination system was to allow some upward mobility for talented and ambitious individuals not especially favored by place of origin or social class. It seems that they succeeded at this, within strict limits.[21] The majority of degree winners were not the sons of other winners—but a large percentage had a degree winner as a fairly close relative. That is, there was a definite social floor below which these upward mobility opportunities did not extend— a floor imposed by the costs of the intensive and protracted education demanded of examination candidates. It was less the expense of books or teaching than the simple value of lost labor. A household had to enjoy a degree of economic comfort sufficient to sacrifice the labor of a male offspring (a sturdy one, since classical study and examination training were reasonably physically demanding) and to support him for decades while he prepared to become a *candidate* for the examination; and even after years of study and sacrifice, he might still never pass the test.

There were ways around this. For example, extended kinship organizations sometimes established a collective fund to subvene the costs of educating a particularly promising young man, hoping for the bonanza in status and wealth that would accrue to the entire lineage should he actually win a degree—but this was very limited. Thus, while there was fairly regular circulation into and out of the top, say, 2 percent of the adult male population who enjoyed elite or "gentry" rank, that circulation came pretty much from within the top 10 percent or so of the population as ranked by economic level. For the lower 90 percent or so, there was no possibility whatsoever of advancement via China's most culturally approved means of getting ahead.

If the civil service examination system provided the regime with a competent pool of personnel for official service and, to a far more limited extent, allowed its subjects some prospect of upward mobility, its greatest advantage for the ruling house was something different again. Across the vast expanse of empire and its myriad local cultures, the exams produced a large group of persons who had voluntarily submitted to an intensive and common course of indoctrination in an orthodox ideology approved by the government. Still more useful was the fact that this group was also the most wealthy and influential individuals in their respective local communities. This wondrous educational institution, more than any other factor, may have held the late Qing empire together.

Local Governance

The central state's commitment to small government meant that the Qing administration was consistently forced to rely on indigenous, nonbureaucratic people and organizations (residential communities, lineages, merchant and artisanal guilds) to supplement its own personnel at the local level. These groups were seldom easy to control, and there was constant tension between the interests of the imperial state, the local society, and the functionaries who carried out most tasks.[22] The county administration had to rely on informal sources of income to cover its costs—a revenue stream that might look to us like corruption but was in fact a built-in part of the system. In other words, the functioning government at the local level was always larger than it was represented on paper.

The primary official—the county magistrate—faced a paradoxical situation. He was a centrally trained and salaried outsider serving a very short tour of duty in any given jurisdiction, and yet he was also the "father and mother" figure responsible for all aspects of life in his county and the well-being of its residents. His job got ever tougher over the course of the Qing, as it had over the entire last millennium of imperial China, as the empire's population grew steadily while the number of counties, hence the number of local administrators, grew only very marginally.

The line between the magistrate's personal finances and those of his local administration was rather hazy. For example, he might well be expected to make personal contributions to any local project that needed doing, or even to help make up tax shortfalls out of his own pocket, even as he also reimbursed himself for "entertainment" and other expenses out of public funds.[23] The magistrate drew a salary that everyone knew to be anachronistically low. Over the late imperial period, with inflation continuing apace, the central government gradually supplemented his formal salary with an annual stipend known euphemistically as "silver to nourish honesty" (yanglian)—in other words, a payoff to allow the magistrate to survive without having to steal too much.

In the late 1720s the Yongzheng emperor took a major step by allowing counties to deduct "meltage fees" from land tax revenues they forwarded up the chain of command. This fee theoretically offset the amount of silver lost in recasting the small amounts collected from taxpayers into the larger ingots that were remitted to the throne. But in reality, as everyone knew, these fees simply helped cover the general costs of local administration.[24] It was characteristic of the Qing to engage in this charade rather than to formally empower county magistrates to levy a local tax, and in any case it proved to be only a temporary palliative. Since meltage fees were not adjusted upward by Yongzheng's successors in the face of inflation, population growth, and the demands of an ever-more complex society, the major source of revenue for public projects and the personal income of local officials and their subordinates continued to be what is charmingly termed in English-language sources the "squeeze" (*lougui*)—irregular fees, kickbacks, and what-have-you that everyone condemned in principle but considered indispensable in practice.[25]

Although the county magistrate was the lowest level of territorial administrator in the Qing governmental structure, many counties also employed centrally-assigned deputy magistrates. In many localities, they seem to have done little besides absorbing what they could from their experience in the expectation of being assigned a substantive magistracy elsewhere in the future. Often, though, they assisted the magistrate by taking over a portion of the legal caseload that occupied most of his workday, and in certain counties deputy magistrates did this for a discrete territorial sector of the county. The possibility that the deputy magistrates might evolve into full-fledged multifunctional administrators in subcounty jurisdictions of their own was addressed in the 1720s, when a senior official proposed to the Yongzheng emperor that centrally-appointed officials known as township administrators (*xiangguan*) be assigned to each subcounty township or ward, perhaps six to eight per county. This idea—to confront the growing magistrate workload by essentially shifting the grid of field administration one notch lower and multiplying the density of formal officials on the landscape—was debated at court but finally rejected. In the emperor's view, since each new township official would then need a staff of his own, this would simply compound the already excessive bureaucratization of local governance.[26] As with the imposition and subsequent neglect of "meltage fees," this was both a direct acknowledgment by the regime of the inherent weaknesses in its minimalist system of local governance and an ultimate decision not to restructure it.

With further subdivision of the county rejected, the lone magistrate was left to rely on four types of assistants for aid in governing his large, more-or-less foreign jurisdiction: sub-bureaucratic clerical personnel, his own personal secretarial staff, the local elite, and appointed village headmen. The first group, the ubiquitous clerks and runners, were legally prescribed for each county in very small numbers but were far more numerous than authorized by law—in some counties numbering in the hundreds. Clerks took care of the county's proliferating tax account ledgers, legal documents, correspondence, and so on. Runners worked as guards, tax collectors, servers of subpoenas, and other nonliterate roles. Many were local men, but others came from outside, most especially from the prosperous Yangzi delta prefecture of Shaoxing, which over the late imperial era responded to its own surplus production of literate males by sending them into an empire-wide clerical diaspora.[27]

Whether or not these functionaries were natives, from the magistrate's point of view they were an entrenched local sub-bureaucracy; they came with the post, not with the incumbent. The magistrate could theoretically hire and fire them as he saw fit, but in practice their importance to his administration's success (and hence his service record) prohibited him from doing so indiscriminately. The clerks were in a highly ambivalent position. They were part of the administrative apparatus, but since they were mostly off the books they were only minimally under central control. Since only a minority of county clerks received a formal salary, and a ridiculously low one at that, collectively they lived off gratuities and self-imposed arbitrary fees. Consequently, probably no social group in Qing China was more universally reviled than they were. As agents of the state they were feared and obeyed by the local populace, but as commoners rather than gentry they were not respected. Condemned by reformers for engorging themselves at the expense of officialdom above and society below, they were vilified by nearly everyone as "rats and crows picking the flesh of the people."

Until very recently, historians took this chorus of complaints in the primary literature at face value. But we now know from one well-documented local archive in Sichuan that county clerks at least in this area had an emerging professional ethic and *esprit*. They administered systematic training to apprentices and discipline to miscreant colleagues. Most important, they conceived of the civil justice system as a cash cow whose various litigation fees could provide for not only their personal support but also the maintenance of public works and other less self-supporting areas of local administration. Often behind the magistrate's back, they were the engine that allowed the county administration to perform its necessary tasks in what was otherwise a cripplingly underfunded system of local governance.[28]

The county magistrate's personal staff seems to have evolved largely as a means to insulate and protect the official from the machinations of clerks, whom he depended on but could not trust. County magistrates, and provincial officials as well, gradually spun a "tent government" (*mufu*) around themselves—an entourage of private secretaries with expertise in litigation, military affairs, fiscal administration, and official correspondence. These specialists traveled with the incumbent and shared his sense of foreignness to the locality in which they worked. Reimbursed out of the magistrate's own personal funds, they were responsible to neither the state nor the local society but to the man who paid them.[29] They were typically civil service degree-holders, however, or at least classically trained literati, and so commanded a greater degree of respect in the local society than did the clerks.

Early nineteenth-century reformers such as Bao Shichen argued that the institution of private secretaries should be abolished altogether and the considerable savings from their financial support should be used instead to raise the unrealistically low salaries of regular bureaucrats. The number of both clerks and secretaries grew dramatically over the course of the Qing dynasty, in response to the growing complexity of governmental tasks. The fact that both groups did so without being centrally paid or regulated reflected the state's willingness to sacrifice a degree of central control at the local level in order to live up to the dictates of benevolent governance—meaning most importantly to keep taxes low.

A small formal government had to rely to an extraordinary degree on leadership generated by the local society itself, above all the gentry. To the extent that these men had, at a minimum, passed the lowest level of the civil service examination, they might be presumed to have internalized the imperatives of moral conduct, public service, and loyalty to the Son of Heaven that lay at the core of the exam curriculum. But they were also protectors of the local community, members of kinship groups often locked in intense rivalries with one another, and landholders whose agenda conflicted in many ways with those of their tenants and other poorer neighbors. How far, then, could the magistrate trust them to carry out the mission of the imperial regime he represented? This was one of the central dilemmas of local administration.

By the time of its consolidation, the Qing had come to rely on local elites to perform a wide range of quasi-governmental tasks: supervision of education, propagation of ideology through public lectures and recitation of the "Sacred Edict," leadership of state-sponsored ceremonies of community bonding and political loyalism such as the community libationer ritual, mediation of conflicts to avoid lawsuits or armed feuds, and management of local-level public works projects. With greater frequency over time, elites also served as tax-farmers and leaders of self-defense militia. For an imperial state claiming an absolute monopoly on taxation and armed defense within its borders, such activities on the part of local elites lay on, or even outside, the margins of legality. But lacking sufficient reliable personnel on their own payrolls to carry out these functions, most magistrates condoned or even encouraged the local elite to engage in such activities.

In these ways, the gentry served the magistrate's interests by helping him govern his jurisdiction, but these activities also increased the private power and social influence of elites themselves. Was the trade-off worth it, from the state's perspective? Following the seminal early Qing political thinker Gu Yanwu, some contemporaries believed that in the case of the upper gentry, it was. These men—holders of both the local and provincial degrees—had undergone more extensive training in the Confucian curriculum than the lower gentry, who had merely passed the local examination, and thus the upper gentry presumably had better internalized its moral message. They had sat for examinations and forged friendships with fellow candidates beyond the local level, and so presumably were better able to transcend the particularisms and limited concerns of their own community. And not least, they were usually wealthier and more economically secure than the lower gentry, so their interest lay less in exploiting their neighbors for a slight material advantage than in doing whatever it took to preserve social harmony. The experience of the late Ming had taught them that uprisings of aggrieved and immiserated commoners were what they had to fear most. This was, of course, a crude (and, for an upper-gentry member like Gu, self-aggrandizing) measure of local elite tractability, but it seemed to many to have some rough truth to it.

An alternative group within the society that came to the magistrates' aid in governance—a group deliberately cultivated in part because they were *not* gentry—were village headmen. Twentieth-century ethnographic accounts suggest that headmen were of two sorts: the genuinely respected and influential local farmers who managed the village's internal affairs, and persons of lesser status designated by villagers to play the headman's role in the village's relationship with the state (a job that no man of real social standing would want). Most likely this situation pertained under the Qing as well. But the Qing regime mandated yet another kind of nongentry headman through its imposition of the ancient *baojia* system—an artificial nested hierarchy of decimal groups of households (ten, a hundred, a thousand), each unit of which was supposed to be collectively responsible for the good conduct of its members. Each unit was led by one head of household who was theoretically held accountable not just for the behavior of his own kinsmen but for his neighbors as well. To that end, he maintained population registers, kept the peace, resolved disputes, reported offenses to the magistrate, and gave expert testimony in criminal trials or civil litigation.

While the notion of collective responsibility was perhaps illusory in reality, there were indeed countless individuals running around the Qing countryside exercising at least some of the real functions assigned to *baojia* headmen. These positions were legally presumed to be part-time collateral jobs for full-time farmers and agrarian heads of households, and they were intended to rotate among neighboring families. But in practice it seems likely that *baojia* headmen worked in this capacity full-time, probably as a permanent career, perhaps even a hereditary one. While they were intended to serve voluntarily without remuneration, most in practice were salaried by their constituency, or at least by some portion of it.

This was but one example of the more general trend in Qing society toward niche-seeking professionalization. The question, of course, is who selected these men, who paid them, and whose interests, ultimately, did they serve? The answer probably varied from place to place. In some localities they were likely little more than hired goons in the employ of domineering local magnates, but in others it seems they were paid by subscription of a local community that genuinely valued their services and to whom they were at least loosely accountable.[30]

Administrative Capacities of the Qing State

Probably no aspect of Chinese history has elicited more contrary generalizations from competent historians than has the size and reach of the imperial state. The two most common depictions offer essentially an all-or-nothing choice: the Ming-Qing state was either a totalizing "Oriental despotism" or a minimalist "taxing and policing agent" that otherwise left its subjects entirely to fend for themselves.[31] Our current state of knowledge would belie both of these views, although not entirely: when it chose to, the state could certainly marshal the resources to despotically terrorize its subjects, whereas on a day-to-day basis it left many of the functions we might think of as governmental to private individuals and groups. Yet there was also a substantial middle ground—certain areas of policy in which the Qing played a highly activist role in the interests of both its own survival and the well-being of its people. Among these areas, especially impressive were expansion and management of the food supply, monetary regulation, and civil litigation.

As early as the Kangxi reign, Qing rulers recognized that their empire's rapidly growing population had created a need to extend the amount of land under cultivation through reclamation and also to increase the productivity of acreage already under cultivation through more intensive farming methods.[32] The more energetic among regional and local officials vigorously disseminated new crops well suited for hillside planting, such as sweet potatoes and mulberry bushes for sericulture, along with better strains of rice and other existing crops. They also extended irrigation infrastructure to new areas. When massive regional shortages occurred, as they inevitably did, the Qing regime during its best years was capable of launching impressive campaigns of famine relief, through dispersals from emergency granaries or by rerouting tax grain held by the Grain Tribute Administration to the affected areas.

But the Qing also understood that large and growing segments of its population could never be expected to produce the food they consumed. This included urbanites, the proliferating rural workforce engaged in transport and other occupations, and the growing percentage of agrarian households who concentrated on production of nonfood or nonstaple crops. In the interest of feeding these people, the Qing strove to assure the unfettered flow and exchange of grain and other foodstuffs between regions. Grain moved in a predictable pattern from Hunan to the southwest, from Guangxi to coastal Guangdong, and from Taiwan to mountainous and maritime Fujian. But the most celebrated commercial grain shipments during the Qing were those that fed the lower Yangzi region. During the Tang and Song dynasties it was the empire's premier grain surplus area, but since the sixteenth century the lower Yangzi had become a highly urbanized region specializing in handicraft industrialization and above all shifting to cotton and other commercial crops. The delta's massive grain deficit was met with interregional imports of grain from farther upriver in the Yangzi tributary system: from the Gan River valley of Jiangxi, the Xiang river valley of Hunan, and the Red Basin of central Sichuan—each distant region assuming new agricultural importance as regions closer to the lower Yangzi progressively diversified and reduced the amount of grain available for export. All of this longdistance private commerce was encouraged and protected by the state, in part by exempting it from normal transport taxes.

But the state did much more than this. Through its "ever-normal granaries" the Qing attempted to ensure not only an adequate supply of grain in all parts of its domain but also a stable and affordable price in local markets. Such an ambitious and systematic effort to control regional and temporal price fluctuations was unprecedented not only in China but probably also in the rest of the world. Whereas historians once assumed that this massively documented price-stabilization apparatus could never, from its inception, have been more than a bureaucratic fiction, we now understand that it had real force and actually worked remarkably well in the dynasty's best days. The intent was to protect the interests of grain producers by buying up surplus grain on local markets when the price was at its lowest after the fall harvest, and simultaneously to protect the interests of consumers by selling this same grain when local market supplies were scarce in late winter and early spring. Thus, by repeatedly buying low and selling high, the granaries were self-supporting, even profitable.

Moreover—and this was crucially important in the Qing's economic logic—price stabilization would be achieved not by price controls or even giveaways of tax grain but by state participation in local markets themselves. The Qing strategy was to use the market to control the market. The system was never designed to supplant the market's ability to supply grain but rather to supplement it. Price stabilization had greatest force, by design, in regions such as northwest China where the market was less developed and needed additional prodding. The system's ultimate decline had more to do with the growing ability of the interregional commercial market to meet the empire's need for grain than with the declining capacities of the late Qing state.

Though the ever-normal granary system had much older roots in imperial history and vestiges of it had been present from the time of the Qing conquest, it was implemented most effectively under the Yongzheng emperor in the 1720s and 1730s, when active and well-stocked granaries could be found in every county of the empire. But the system came under imperial suspicion during the reign of Yongzheng's son and successor, the Qianlong emperor. Concerned with the secular trend of rising grain prices empire-wide and beset by a mounting series of local grain riots, Qianlong decided in 1748 that government programs designed to buy on local markets to restock granaries were a major contributor to rising prices. He therefore ordered a reduction in annual restocking quotas and a downsizing of granary holdings throughout the empire. Significantly, officials in many regions protested that their own jurisdictions needed these granary reserves, and one after another they succeeded in receiving "exemptions" to the general policy. Thus, the system remained of significant (though diminishing) utility well beyond the eighteenth century High Qing period, until like so much of the dynasty's institutional infrastructure it received the *coup de grâce* during the mid-nineteenth-century rebellions.

A second policy area in which the Qing state showed impressive acumen and vigor was its management of the money supply.[33] Rather than adopting a single standardized currency across its vast domains, the Qing opted for a bimetallic monetary system comprising unminted silver bullion (measured in Chinese ounces or taels) and minted copper coins (known as cash, *qianwen*). The coins, which had square holes in their centers, were customarily tied together on thousand-cash strings, and the par exchange rate was one thousand cash (one string) equaled one ounce of silver. But the administration knew well that attempts to mandate this or any other exchange rate by fiat would prove counterproductive, leading to speculation, hoarding, black-marketeering, counterfeiting, and other abuses. It thus sought to maintain monetary stability over time and across regions by creatively adjusting the relative supply of the two monetary metals in circulation—as with the granary system, effectively using the market to manage the market. Each locality was required to submit monthly reports on local currency exchange rates, just as they were on local grain production and granary activities.

Throughout most of the eighteenth century, the major problem was that copper cash became increasingly expensive, as each coin commanded a market value of well above one-thousandth of an ounce of silver. This was because the silver supply, fed primarily by New World imports, was growing while the copper supply, traditionally imported from Japan, was contracting. With the mushrooming of rural commercialization, the demand for cash increased, as did the use of copper for competing nonmonetary purposes. First Yongzheng somewhat reluctantly, and then Qianlong with greater enthusiasm, responded by lifting bans on private mining (bans that had been prompted by fears that congregations of bachelor miners would be uncontrollable) and allowed entrepreneurs to tap China's own copper resources, which were considerable. This precipitated a mid-eighteenth-century copper boom throughout many areas of the empire, but most dramatically in the tense multicultural southwest.

These central-government initiatives helped, but the major role in managing a stable money supply was left to regional and local officials.

By dumping cash on the market or withdrawing it, arranging timely shipments between adjacent jurisdictions, altering demands for payment in cash or silver in the fiscal system (and more frequently in the "contributions" made in exchange for government honors), and, under extreme circumstances, adjusting the copper content of coins to reflect the changing market value of bulk copper, these individuals collectively performed this task impressively well.

A third, noneconomic, area in which the Qing state took a remarkably hands-on role was in the resolution of civil disputes.[34] The fact that imperial China had no codified civil law and that conflicts within society over land tenure, water rights, marital affairs, and debt were dismissed in official rhetoric as "trifling affairs" not worthy of the sovereign's attention led past scholars to characterize late imperial China as judicially undeveloped, in contrast with the West. We now know that civil litigation was in fact a routine part of Qing administration. Lacking a civil code, local officials invoked substatutes of the criminal code to resolve property disputes. While these substatutes might appear to have little relevance to the issue at hand, a substantial body of Qing judicial precedent made clear to all within the system how they were to be systematically interpreted in civil matters. Imperial authorities resisted the seemingly obvious step of actually promulgating a civil code, out of concern that doing so would invite yet further litigiousness and disturb the social harmony that the Confucian state propagandized as the norm. But this by no means implied that the state did not actively proffer its services in civil conflict resolution. This was just one more area in which the formal representation of Qing governance and its actual practice systematically diverged—the state was far larger and more active than it allowed itself to appear on paper.

Adjudicating civil lawsuits almost certainly took up more than half of the average county magistrate's workday by the late eighteenth century. Private interests hardly avoided the legal process, costly as this might be; rather, plaintiffs frequently filed frivolous lawsuits simply as a means to coerce an adversary to concede advantage in an unrelated dispute. While the society's growing litigiousness was condemned by officials, the Qing state nevertheless continued to advertise itself as willing to hear such lawsuits. Not only did this act of benevolent governance, in theory, preclude more violent means of private conflict resolution, but the very act of filing a lawsuit was a *de facto* endorsement by the litigant of the state's legitimacy—no small matter for a self-conscious dynasty of alien conquest.

Methods of managing the growing civil caseload became something of a science for local magistrates and their judicial advisors. A common technique was to issue a preliminary verdict on the basis of a first hearing, likely with harsh consequences for both parties, and then invite them to seek nongovernmental mediation if they did not want to suffer such a verdict once the entire body of evidence had been heard by the court. In deciding civil matters, a complex logic was employed in which not only the letter of the law was considered but also a transcendent rational morality and an awareness of practical social consequences of the verdict— the judge's goal being to best allow the litigants to go back into their local community and live at peace with one another once the dispute was resolved.

Qing Critiques of the Local Administrative System

A continuing thread within Neo-Confucian thought since the Song dynasty emphasized techniques of practical administration, especially at the local level. This increasingly self-conscious tradition was usually known as *jingshi,* a term customarily translated into English as "statecraft" but meaning more literally "ordering the world"—a rendering that reflects the significant absence of the notion of "state" and captures a spirit of striving for cosmic as well as administrative order.[35] In the final years of the Ming dynasty, a Yangzi-delta reformist scholar named Chen Zilong (1608–1647) published a large collection of recent historical documents on these issues entitled *Collected Writings on Statecraft in the Ming Dynasty (Huang Ming jingshi wenbian),* thus introducing a generic form for organizing debate on proper governance that would be added to repeatedly during the Qing.

By the late seventeenth and eighteenth centuries, statecraft concerns had become linked to an initially separate scholarly movement promoting practical or substantive learning (*shixue*), emphasizing ritual-moral correctness and, somewhat incongruously, managerial technique that often appeared amorally pragmatic. What substantive-learning adherents shared was their common distaste for the intellectual sterility of writing eight-legged essays and cramming for exams, the refined aestheticism of literary style, any type of metaphysical speculation, detached moral contemplation of the sort associated with the Wang Yangming "school of the mind" (*xinxue*), and the pedantic textual scholarship championed by the ascendant "philological" school of their own day. Intensive study of history and geography, and of such technical subjects as hydraulic engineering and military science, they argued, far better equipped literati to confront the pressing political and economic issues of the times and indeed to justify their own status as cultural elites.[36]

By at least the early Qing, both statecraft and substantive learning had become linked, at least for some, with a persistent reformist critique of imperial bureaucratic administration encapsulated in the term *fengjian*— the modern Chinese word for "feudal" but with few of the specific connotations this word carries in Western historiography or Marxist theory. *Fengjian* was juxtaposed to *junxian,* which referred to the division of the empire into artificial administrative jurisdictions such as prefectures and counties and their governance by centrally appointed, salaried, and rotated professional officials. To avoid the dysfunctions of *junxian, fengjian* would leave governance of localities in the hands of local elites, sanctioned and more or less enfeoffed by the state.[37]

No individual better epitomized the conjoining of *jingshi, shixue,* and *fengjian* concerns than the Suzhou landowner, discreet Ming loyalist, and brilliant polymath Gu Yanwu. In a widely circulated series of essays written around 1660 and known as the *Junxian lun (The Prefectural System),* Gu suggested that the imposition of a bureaucratic field administration by China's First Emperor in the third century B.C. was something of an original sin in Chinese administrative history but one which could no longer be completely avoided. Instead, Gu proposed "infusing the spirit of the *fengjian* system back into the body of the *junxian* system," a bold move that would "allow the empire to be well governed." Gu railed against the proliferation of parasitic clerks and runners, the lack of initiative and genuine concern for his jurisdiction displayed by careerist outsider officials, the excessive costs of a large central administration exercising undue regulatory oversight, and—not surprisingly, coming from an elite native of the empire's most prosperous region—against extracting revenues from one favored locality to spend on needier areas elsewhere: "No abuse of law is so extreme as that of taking rations from the eastern regions in order to supply troops on the western frontiers, and taking grain from the south in order to support courier stations in the north. My plan calls for all of a county's produce to remain within that county."[38]

Gu's solution was to appoint a member of the local elite itself to serve as the county magistrate. As a precaution against the possibility that such a magistrate would act corruptly or incompetently, his initial appointment would be a three-year probation. With satisfactory performance, he would be granted a second term, and with further good work the post would be declared his for life. Assuming that he continued his good conduct, the magistracy would become hereditary. Superfluous supervisory posts such as governor-general, governor, provincial treasurers, provincial judges, and grain and salt commissioners would be abolished. To counter his critics, Gu argued that:

> It is every man's natural disposition to cherish his own family and love his own children. His feelings toward the emperor, and toward all other men, are invariably not as strong as his feelings toward his own kin . . . Now, if we allow the county magistrate to have this personal interest in his jurisdiction, then all the people in the county will become in effect his own children and kin, all the lands of the county in effect his own fields, all its walls his own defenses, and all its granaries his own storehouses. His own children and kin he will of course love rather than injure; his own fields he will of course manage well rather than abandon; his own defenses and storehouses he will maintain rather than destroy. Thus, what the magistrate thinks of as "looking out for my own" will be seen by the emperor as "acting responsibly," will it not? The proper governance of the empire lies in this and in nothing else.

Gu's proposal obviously evidenced an enormous faith in enlightened self-interest on the part of at least certain members of the upper gentry. His suspicions of both the lower gentry and the clerical sub-bureaucracy stood in stark relief against his conviction that men of superior wealth and cultural attainment, men of his own class and breeding, could be relied upon, by his own version of an "invisible hand," to serve the interests of all. Was he simply naive in this assumption? Had the plan been enacted and magistracies filled with men such as Gu Yanwu himself—who once beat to death a third-generation servant of his family whom he suspected of infidelity—would the empire truly have been better governed?[39]

It would be easy, on the basis of the *Junxian lun* alone, to see Gu Yanwu as a simple champion of private elite self-interest. But in his larger work, the *Record of Knowledge Acquired Day-by-Day (Rizhi lu)*, Gu's political views were more nuanced.[40] The crux of his argument was a systematic distinction between the two categories "above" (*shang*) and "below" (*xia*), which, depending on context, might mean central versus local administration, or state versus society, or wealthy versus poor. Maintaining a hierarchical distinction between above and below was the bedrock of civilization itself, but at the same time it was a necessary check on the natural tendency to concentrate political power and economic resources at either pole. The persistent threat was monopolization at the top, but there existed also the less obvious danger of petty despotism below, in the hands of clerks or local strongmen.[41]

In Gu's ideal world, wealth would circulate freely at all levels, and political authority would be delegated by the throne to competent, locally responsive county administrators. Attempts at micromanagement via excessive regulation or scrutiny by the throne only undermined the authority of local officials and empowered petty clerks, who—in collusion with "evil gentry"—manipulated these regulations in their own interest. Gu's proposal to enfeoff certain public-minded local elites as county magistrates seemed to be designed to rein in local gentry rather than to cede power to them, and to achieve a true, anti-despotic "rule of many."

Having refused appointment as a Qing official because of his pledge to his dying mother and his loyalty to the departed Ming dynasty under which his forebears had served, Gu never submitted his plan to the throne. It is unlikely he ever thought it stood a chance of implementation. But his treatise circulated widely, along with his other voluminous scholarly publications, and its bold outlines inspired political reformers throughout the remainder of the imperial era. It is both ironic and significant that scholars in the last Qing decades and well into the Republican era, influenced by Western ideas of representative government and popular sovereignty and looking for an indigenous Chinese tradition on which to graft them, found that tradition in the "feudal" proposals of Gu Yanwu.[42]

3

HIGH QING

THE SHUNZHI emperor died suddenly of smallpox on February 5, 1661, at the age of twenty-three. Fulin had formally exercised personal rule for eight years but had never been a very forceful monarch. At his death, a power struggle ensued at court, featuring the suspiciously quick cremation of the emperor's remains, the alleged forging of his will, and the execution of his favorite eunuch. Shunzhi's seven-year-old third son, Aisin Gioro Xuanye, was placed on the throne as the Kangxi emperor, chosen on the somewhat flimsy grounds that he had already survived an infantile bout with the disease that killed his father. With the Qing consolidation still very far from complete, the prospects for the new dynasty's survival did not look promising.

And yet it survived, shortly to enter a period celebrated in Chinese-language historical writing as the "prosperous age" (*shengshi*) and in the West as the High Qing.[1] No small reason for this success was the Qing's astonishing good fortune to have on the throne over the "long eighteenth century"[2] three remarkably capable, hard-working, and (not least) long-lived men—two of whom ruled for sixty years each—reigning under the titles Kangxi, Yongzheng, and Qianlong.

Kangxi (r. 1662–1722) is widely acknowledged as one of the greatest emperors in Chinese history (Fig. 4). In 1669 at the age of sixteen he moved decisively against the regents who had put him on the throne, arresting chief regent Ebai for a detailed list of crimes and throwing him in prison, where he shortly died. A passionate devotee of the Manchu-style hunt, Kangxi was an extremely successful military commander, personally leading the suppression of the Three Feudatories rebellion and Qing

Fig. 4   The Kangxi emperor, with a writing brush. Courtesy of the Palace Museum, Beijing.

incursions into Inner Asia, as well as a brilliant and innovative civil administrator.[3] He had a broadly curious and complex mind and was eager
to sit through long lectures and debates by advocates of differing schools
of thought, including Jesuit missionaries from the West. He held public
demonstrations of scientific and mathematical principles and was fond
of showing off the degree to which he grasped their significance or re-
membered their details.[4] Through his patronage of Jesuit scholars, he
absorbed Western pharmacology and anatomical study.[5] He sponsored
grand collections of Tang poetry and other massive literary anthologies,
as well as guiding the compilation of a standard dictionary of the Chinese
language.

Added to all this, Kangxi was a man of extraordinary sensibilities—
sensitive to the concerns of his subjects, to the joys and pains of raising
his sixty or so children (who, it seems, regularly disappointed him), and
to his own emotions. On the consideration to be shown to the old and
dying, he wrote:

> It's really unbearable not to look after the old when they grow ill; as
> well as money for their support, and doctors, we should send their
> old friends to talk with them, no matter whether the sick person is
> an old and loyal official, or one of my brother's slaves, or the Jesuit
> Dolzé bloated with dropsy north of the Wall, or an old princess in
> her palace. Like my aunt, the Barin Princess Shu-hui, daughter of
> [Hong Taiji]: I visited her regularly as she was dying in [Beijing], and
> gave her all she needed; and she *did* die with a smile on her face . . .
> We can cheer old people up with presents, too. Every year Princess
> Shu-hui used to send cakes of fat, and dried mutton, to my grand-
> mother and me, and we would send her sable, black fox, and satin. I
> would always try to make my presents something needed, or some-
> thing that I knew would bring pleasure, for if you just give an object
> at random it might just as easily be given back—then all you have is
> an exchange of items, something with no real feeling behind it . . .
> The affections and filial piety are a matter of spontaneity and natu-
> ralness, not of fixed rules and formal visits.[6]

Probably Kangxi's most celebrated and far-reaching policy decision
came toward the end of his long reign. In 1713 the emperor announced
his belief that the economic production of the empire had been fully restored to what it had been at the height of the Ming and that the cadas-

tral survey his ministers had been working on for some time was now completed. The fiscal base for his regime was thus permanently and comfortably secure. Although new lands might continue to be brought under cultivation to meet the needs of his growing population, and these might be taxed accordingly, there would be no need ever in the future to raise the basic tax rate on agricultural land—even though, with new technologies, crop selection, and commercialization the productivity of that land might well increase.

With this declaration, Kangxi committed his successors to governing with a declining share of the realm's bounty, despite facing an inflationary economy, an ever more complex society, and a dramatic range of new challenges. They would find means of augmenting the government's take from agriculture through the imposition of various surtaxes, and they would discover other sectors of the economy to tax. But filial piety dictated that they would never violate Kangxi's pledge to keep the basic land tax as it was in 1713. By the nineteenth century the Qing central administration would find itself permanently impoverished.

Aisin Gioro Yinzhen, the Yongzheng emperor (r. 1723–35), was quite a different man from his father (Fig. 5). Of the fifteen elder sons of Kangxi who might have claimed the throne, Yinzhen, the fourth, was not the obvious favorite. He ruthlessly eliminated any of his brothers who opposed his succession and endured rumors that he was a usurper throughout his reign.[7] Nearly forty-five years old at the time he ascended the throne, Yinzhen already had a well-formed idea of problems in his father's later reign that needed correction and, though his own reign lasted a mere thirteen years, he used that time to leave an indelible mark on the Qing empire's—and China's—subsequent history. He was by all accounts a blunt man, with little of his father's bravado, showmanship, or refined intellectual and aesthetic tastes. Yongzheng surrounded himself with similarly plain-talking officials drawn from lower rungs of the Manchu peerage, and Chinese from obscure, often frontier, backgrounds. He routinely invited their criticisms of his own initiatives, in a collegial, pragmatic spirit of getting things done.

The basic tenor of Yongzheng's reign was said to be "strict" or "severe" (yan). But he was not aggressive or brutal—he was by no means adventurous in his military policies, and he could be remarkably lenient in his treatment of criminal offenders. The term referred instead to a hardheaded drive to rationalize bureaucratic administration and centralize imperial control, no matter the cost or the opposition. His initiative

Fig. 5   The Yongzheng emperor, formal portrait. Courtesy of the
Palace Museum, Beijing.

to make counties more self-supporting by allowing them to collect a meltage fee was emblematic of this concern. So too were his efforts to bureaucratize the Eight Banners, to eliminate certain gentry tax breaks, and to fold the head tax into the land tax for simplification. He sought to establish orphanages, poorhouses, and elementary schools in every county of his empire. Briefly and ineffectively, he also campaigned to make a uniform vernacular Chinese (what we sometimes call Mandarin) the standard spoken language throughout his realm.[8]

As part of a crackdown on sectarian deviance, Yongzheng ordered the expulsion of Christian missionaries from all parts of the empire outside of Beijing. He was the prime mover in the ambitious scheme to centrally control local grain reserves through the ever-normal granary system, and he was also behind visionary programs to bring as much land as possible under productive cultivation and to emancipate servile tenants and agricultural laborers and other debased status groups. In short, Yongzheng was an early-modern state-maker of the first order.[9]

Upon his death in 1735 the Yongzheng emperor was succeeded by his son Aisin Gioro Hongli, who as the Qianlong emperor came to embody what the wider world understood as "China." Hongli was twenty-five years old at the time of his succession—neither a young boy like his grandfather nor a middle-aged adult like his father.[10] Mindful of his own baggage of illegitimacy, Yongzheng had selected his heir apparent in early adolescence and had carefully tutored him in the craft of imperial rule. But as his father had done two decades earlier, the young Hongli monitored with some concern the shortcomings of his predecessor, and after he ascended the throne he formulated his own strategy for correcting these policy excesses and mistakes. One of his first acts was to recall his childhood tutor, the venerable Chinese minister Zhu Shi, to assist him during the transition. In the last years of Yongzheng's reign, Zhu had served as a sounding board for literati grumblings about the emperor's "strict" policy initiatives. Empowered now to advise the newly enthroned Qianlong emperor, he offered counsel to the new ruler on how to address these criticisms.

Announcing that the hallmark of his reign would be liberal magnanimity, in contrast with his father's severity, Qianlong reversed many policies of the Yongzheng era during his first fifteen or so years on the throne. He backed off from his predecessor's frenetic drive for reclamation of new farmland and in 1748 scaled back the holdings of state granaries at the local level. Restating the belief that the wealth of the empire was fixed and that mobilization of this wealth in the hands of the state ran counter to the preferred strategy of "storing wealth among the people," he portrayed his father's two major fiscal initiatives—imposing the meltage fee and folding the head tax into the land tax—as unseemly greed counter to the dictates of benevolent governance. He quietly let these practices atrophy by not raising surtaxes commensurate with inflation. Qianlong engaged in a series of piecemeal tax reductions throughout the first part of his reign—cutting back on local grain assessments, extractions for military-agricultural colonies, real estate transfer and title registration fees, and numerous other local levies—until the spiraling cost of his own military adventures made this no longer feasible.

In 1745, to celebrate the ten-year anniversary of his accession, Qianlong declared a general remission of the land tax amounting to some twenty-eight million taels of silver. In effect, he ended his father's unfinished experiment to create a financially capable, significantly interventionist state apparatus.[11] Whether or not this policy reversal was wise in the context of its own time, its legacy would haunt the Qing in the late nineteenth century when it was suddenly thrust into competition with predatory nation-states from both Europe and East Asia.

Far more sympathetic to the interests of the Chinese literati than his father had been, Qianlong seemed to view these men as partners in rule rather than as brakes on centralized authority. He restored a number of the gentry's tax privileges and exemptions from criminal punishments that Yongzheng had abolished. His preferred ministers were far more likely to be highly polished aesthetes than the rough-and-ready can-do technocrats favored by Yongzheng. During Qianlong's reign the examination curriculum gradually shifted to place greater emphasis on mastery of prose and poetic style and on philological erudition. At the lower end of the literary scale, Qianlong abandoned the drive for mass education, especially in frontier areas, on the belief that endowing untrustworthy minority groups with the advantages of literacy was politically unwise and financially wasteful.[12] Lying behind all such decisions was Qianlong's distaste for his father's crusade to reduce social stratification and cultural differentiation within the empire and create a relatively homogeneous population of subjects to an absolutist throne. Qianlong was quite content to wear many hats as he ruled over a universal empire comprised of multiple distinct corporate groups defined by status and ethnicity.[13]

Nothing epitomized the differences between the two emperor's conceptions of the Qing domain more neatly than the Zeng Jing case of 1728.[14]

Zeng was an obscure schoolteacher who interpreted severe flooding in his native Hunan as a sign of Heaven's displeasure with Yongzheng's rule and a mandate for dynastic change. When he tried to enlist the aid of the Shaanxi-Sichuan viceroy—a descendent of the martyred Southern Song general Yue Fei, heroic defender of Chinese culture and independence from alien conquerors—his treasonous plot was betrayed. Zeng's antipathy to Yongzheng was based in part on claims of the emperor's usurpation of the throne and in part on rumors of his debauched personal conduct. But mostly it reflected an essentialist tradition that viewed the Han Chinese as biologically superior to alien "races." Domination by inferiors such as the Manchus must be resisted to the death. Zeng explicitly cited the seventeenth-century Zhejiang scholar Lü Liuliang as the source of these ideas, but they were even more apparent in the manuscript writings of Zeng's fellow provincial Wang Fuzhi. This underground vein of Hunanese nativism would come into the open more forcefully in the Qing's final century.

Yongzheng's response to the discovery of Zeng's plot was remarkable. He had the bones of Lü Liuliang exhumed and pulverized but, as a gesture of imperial grace, he allowed the repentant Zeng himself to return home, where he became something of a local hero. The emperor then compiled and widely promulgated his own record of the case, in which he argued at length against the theories that had prompted Zeng's crimes. In his *Record of Great Righteousness Dispelling Superstition* (*Dayi juemi lu*), Yongzheng explained that "Manchu" was really only a native-place designation—like northern, southern, western, and so on—not a racial marker. Indeed, he came quite close to arguing that ethnic distinctions in general had no reality at all.

But for Yongzheng's successor, with his corporatist concept of rule, this attitude was totally unacceptable. In January 1736, as one of the first acts of his reign, Qianlong had Zeng Jing rearrested and executed by "lingering death" and then launched a search-and-destroy mission against all copies of his father's heretical tract. Implicitly agreeing with Wang Fuzhi on the essential reality of races, Qianlong placed high value on his Manchu heritage and made strenuous efforts to preserve its language, horsemanship, archery, and hunt, to clarify ethnic lines within the banners, to trace the geographical and genealogical origins of his people, and to commission the writing of a national epic, the *Ode to Mukden*. Qianlong's grand mission to invent the Manchus as a national group decisively ended Yongzheng's project of cultural homogenization.[15]

Even as he backed away from Yongzheng's policies, however, Qianlong by no means presented himself as reversing his father's intent. To do so would be unfilial, and Qianlong was ostentatiously observant of ritual propriety. Instead, he presented himself as retrenching in ways that his father himself would certainly have endorsed had he lived longer. Qianlong was, in fact, an unrivaled master of display, the ever-visible "exemplary center" of the empire, the famously hard-working, stabilizing force of the High Qing. His various military adventures—of variable significance for shoring up or expanding the boundaries of empire—were neatly rounded off and packaged for posterity by the emperor himself as his Ten Great Campaigns.[16] He was fond of having himself drawn or painted in different costumes—as a Buddhist bodhisattva to appeal to his Lamaist constituents, for example, or on horseback in European-style military armor by the Jesuit court painter Giuseppe Castiglione (Fig. 6).

At his summer retreat just outside the Great Wall in the city of Chengde, Qianlong constructed a grand theme park representing the public architecture of the vast Qing domain—a mini-Potala to exemplify Tibet, a southern Chinese temple in the Jiangnan style, and other buildings.[17] Whereas his prosaic father had eschewed the practice of making ceremonial visits throughout his realm, Qianlong delighted in his "southern tours," and no expense was spared in making everything look just right. Large sections of the wealthy commercial city of Yangzhou were entirely rebuilt prior to one of his visits in order to make them conform to the emperor's imaginings of what the city must be like. He also sponsored elaborate jubilees on ten-year anniversaries of his reign.[18] Probably Qianlong's single grandest act of showmanship, though, came with his retirement in 1795. After sixty years on the throne, he ended his rule one day short of the length of his grandfather Kangxi's reign, in the ultimate display of filial respect.

Imperial Expansion

Chinese nationalist historiography, at least since the May Fourth era of the late 1910s, has portrayed Qing China essentially as a victim of intensifying imperialist aggression on the part of Western nations and eventually Japan. There is of course good reason to accept this portrayal, as far as it goes. But what it tends to gloss over is the extent to which the Qing itself played the imperialist game, and did so very well—at least until the end of the eighteenth century. In the West, historians no longer depict

Fig. 6 The Qianlong emperor, in armor on horseback. Painting by Giuseppe Castiglione. Courtesy of the Palace Museum, Beijing.

Qing China as a victim or an anomaly but as of one of several early modern empires that arose on the Eurasian continent in roughly the same era, including the Mughal, the Muscovy-Romanov, the Ottoman, and the British empires. We are now struck less by the differences than by the common features of their imperial ambitions: a new capacity for administrative centralization across vast distances, a deliberate multi-ethnicity and transcendence of national borders, and, not least, an aggressive spatial expansionism.[19]

In its first century and a half on the throne, the Qing more than doubled the spatial expanse of the Ming empire and bequeathed to its twentieth-century successors most of the boundaries claimed today as China. For the many Qing soldiers, statesmen, and ideologists involved in this expansion, a "civilizing mission" not all that different from the European experience was associated with conquest. Such particular products of China's own history as the patrilineal-patrilocal family system, partible male inheritance, incest taboos, marriage and funerary practice, sedentary agriculture, proprietorship of agrarian land by registered and tax-paying households, and literacy in the Chinese language were vigorously implanted in frontier or colonial areas as the norms of civilized human society. Like their subjects, Qing rulers also tapped into these ideas when they were useful for the dynasty's own purposes. But for the most part the expansionist agenda of the Qing was quite different: it drew upon Inner Asian notions of historical mission, on the perceived needs for different peoples for imperial security, and at times on the personal bravado of individual monarchs.

The Zunghar Mongols, a semi-nomadic people of the steppes of central Eurasia, fiercely resisted incorporation into the Qing empire and the divide-and-rule fragmentation that was a staple of Qing frontier policy, as it had been for the Ming. Instead, under the enterprising khans Batur Hongtaiji (d. 1653) and his son Galdan (d. 1697), the Zunghars busied themselves with a project of alliance formation and state building analogous to that undertaken by that other Hong Taiji who had played such a pivotal role in the formation of the Qing itself.[20] By around 1660 they had created a formidable inland empire bordered by Muscovy-Russia to their north and west and the Qing to their south and east. But as early as 1689 the Treaty of Nerchinsk between Muscovy-Russia and the Qing stabilized for the time being the eastern (Manchurian) sector of their joint frontier. Over the next century, this triad of empires would be gradually reduced to a pair, as the two agrarian empires on the Zunghars' flanks progressively extended and hardened their borders to squeeze out their pastoralist neighbor.

The very year after concluding the Nerchinsk accord, the Kangxi emperor declared his own personal campaign to eliminate the khan Galdan. He marched into the steppe and engaged the Zunghars at the great battle of Ulan Butong, where Kangxi's chief general and uncle, Tong Guogang, met his end. Despite a Qing declaration of victory, the campaign and its successors dragged on for decades. In 1697 Kangxi's war of attrition on Galdan's allies and food supplies finally brought about the khan's death, under uncertain circumstances. His remains were presented to the triumphant Qing emperor, who had them pulverized and scattered to the winds. But under a succession of khans the Zunghars continued to hold out, and the war slogged on.

When Kangxi himself died in 1722, Yongzheng traded in his father's personal vendetta for various initiatives to pacify the Mongols through negotiated truces and offers of trade. But another round of open revolt in the late 1750s prompted the professedly magnanimous Qianlong emperor to launch a genocidal campaign against the Zunghar survivors, who numbered more than half a million. It was successful, and the depopulated steppes were quickly resettled with millions of Qing subjects.

Piggybacking on his success against the Zunghar Mongols, in 1757–1759 Qianlong invaded the territories around the Tarim Basin to the south and west of Zungharia, an area populated by Turkic, Uighur, and other Muslim peoples.[21] The campaigns in the field proved much easier than the task of selling the adventure to high-level Han literati at home, who saw no need to conquer this huge pastureland, whose peoples had not traditionally threatened the Chinese homeland. The trusted grand councilor Liu Tongxun, the long-serving northwest governor Chen Hongmou, and other officials one by one cautioned against the project, and in 1760 a seemingly orchestrated chorus of answers on the metropolitan examination subtly condemned the campaigns as a vain and wasteful display of imperial arrogance. Qianlong brushed these criticisms aside and in 1768 announced the formal annexation of the region under the name Xinjiang (New Dominion). With this one gesture, he expanded the empire into a vast territory that China still claims today, and bequeathed to his heirs a morass of lingering ethnic-nationalist tensions.

Though he ignored the advice of his councilors not to invade, Qianlong solicitously tried to blunt their criticisms by making the New Dominion pay for the cost of its conquest. He never succeeded, and the maintenance of the territory remained a financial burden throughout the dynasty. The system of theoretically self-supporting military-agricultural colonies implanted throughout Xinjiang never remotely provided for their own maintenance, necessitating continuing grain imports from the interior. The mining of newly discovered silver deposits, the establishment of horse farms, the settlement of semi-conscripted farmers with state-supplied seed and tools (along with liberal start-up tax holidays), and the selective opening of the area's trade routes to Han merchants all helped but were never enough to offset the territory's spiraling military and administrative costs. The most successful use made of Xinjiang was as a penal colony. An estimated 10 percent of the empire's governor-generals who served from 1758 to 1820 spent time there in punitive banishment, as did a considerably larger number of local officials and many thousands of common convicts.[22]

In 1768 when a community of such exiles rebelled against mistreatment by a drunken commander and were massacred in response, the New Dominion revealed itself as a troublesome locus of violence. Jihads by indigenous and immigrant Muslim populations against their Manchu and Han overlords recurred with gathering intensity. Attempts to administer the area indirectly and on the cheap through indigenous chieftains of uncertain loyalties enjoyed mixed success at best. And frontier conflicts with the expanding Russian empire never went away, despite periodic rounds of negotiation to settle imperial borders. By the third quarter of the nineteenth century, when massive internal rebellion and predatory invasion from overseas rendered the Qing dynasty unable to respond effectively, defense of the New Dominion reached a point of crisis.

With encouragement from the British in India, a Muslim militarist named Ya'qub Beg (1820–1877) entered Xinjiang in 1865 and carved out an expanding autonomous state. In 1871 the Russians, supposedly to protect their own borders from Ya'qub Beg's incursions but more importantly to counter the British, moved in and occupied northeast Xinjiang. The Qing was slow to respond, in large part because its most effective military leader in the region, the anti-Taiping hero Zuo Zongtang, was busy suppressing a separate Muslim uprising in the adjacent provinces of Shaanxi and Gansu. Zuo completed this task in 1873, and four years later—as British mediation proceeded too slowly to rescue their client—he moved into Xinjiang and extinguished Ya'qub Beg's regime. The territory was almost entirely recovered for the Qing empire (a small chunk of Ili remained in Russian hands), and in 1884 the New Dominion was declared a province, administered bureaucratically like any other. The crisis was resolved—for the moment. But the costs of colonization continued to rise, and the Muslim separatist movement never went away.

Another Qing imperial legacy that continued to haunt China into the twenty-first century was Tibet.[23] The Ming neither claimed nor sought to intervene directly in that vast territory, preferring simply to exercise the traditional Chinese divide-and-rule policy toward the various sects and tribal communities there. The preconquest Qing likewise initially had little interest in Tibet, until its relations with its Mongol allies and rivals raised its awareness of Tibet's religious significance. Accordingly, in 1639 Hong Taiji invited the Dalai Lama to visit the imperial court. He declined but sent a reply identifying Hong Taiji as a bodhisattva and Manjusri (Great Lord). The Lama eventually visited Beijing after the conquest, in 1652, where he received various high honors from the Shunzhi emperor. Qing historical records identified these ceremonial exchanges as Tibetan acceptance of Qing suzerainty, but that does not seem to have been the Tibetan understanding. The fifth Dalai Lama had proudly forged the first effectively unified Tibetan state at around the same time that the Qing invaders were dispatching the Ming, and Qing influence in domestic Tibetan affairs remained negligible throughout most of the eighteenth century.

That situation changed toward the century's end when Tibet was thrown into domestic turmoil by feuding aristocratic lineages. The usurper, Samgye Gyamtso (1653–1705), allied himself with the Qing's enemies, the Zunghar Mongols, prompting the Kangxi emperor to collude in his assassination. When Zunghars invaded politically-divided Tibet in 1717, Kangxi responded in kind, occupying Llasa in 1720. Upon his succession, the Yongzheng emperor sought to pull the Qing forces out, but further eruptions of domestic unrest in Tibet convinced him to send in more troops in 1728. Later waves of Qing invasion followed in 1750 and in 1791. Gradually the empire took over local administration in Tibet under the control of a caretaker official known as an *amban*. At the same time, in its self-proclaimed role as protector of the Buddhist world and in accord with the maxim taken from the *Book of Rites* to control diverse populations by using their own cultural characteristics, the Qing did little to sinicize or otherwise alter Tibetan local society.

In Taiwan, following the Kangxi emperor's suppression of the Zheng regime in 1683, the Qing sought to have the claimed territory pay for the costs of its own administration, principally through the land tax.

Kangxi's eighteenth-century successors were aware of course, from the experiences of Zheng Chenggong and the Dutch before him, that for security reasons they needed a stronger colonial presence than the Ming had established there. But through most of the century the court's cost-benefit calculus dictated that the expense of keeping peace between Han settlers and indigenous Taiwanese tribes, and among the settlers themselves, would not repay the benefits of systematic land development on the island. Consequently, despite the advocacy of radical expansionists such as the highly prolific local official Lan Dingyuan, the court consistently legislated against Han migration across the straits. In 1684, right after the suppression, the Kangxi emperor announced a quarantine policy, and for the first decades of Qing rule the Chinese population of the island was lower than it had been under the Zheng regime. Though the Kangxi quarantine was relaxed somewhat under Yongzheng, the mid-Qing court never conducted the state-sponsored settlement drives in Taiwan that it did in both Zungharia and Xinjiang.[24]

As it turned out, it did not have to. Population growth in land-starved southern Fujian province prompted pioneering emigration to Taiwan in defiance of the central government's fiat. Even more dramatically, grain shortages in areas along the coast where local populations were increasingly engaged in maritime trade and other nonagrarian livelihoods created a strong demand for the rice that commercial farmers of northern and central Taiwan's coastal plains could produce in abundance. The commercial possibility of lucrative sugar exports attracted further settlers. Despite intermittent maritime bans, governors of coastal provinces, mindful of provisioning concerns, managed to have the cross-straits trade exempted, though in theory it was regulated by permit. Consequently, Han Chinese colonization of the Taiwan frontier proceeded apace.

One government response, undertaken in the wake of a local uprising in 1722, was to draw a boundary line between the area allowable to Chinese settlement and the area legally reserved for the indigenous "savages." This line was expansively redrawn several times in the eighteenth century. It was only in 1875, after Danshui and Anping had been opened to foreign traders as treaty ports and Qing possession of Taiwan as a whole was challenged by Meiji Japan, that the court moved to an aggressive "open the mountains and pacify the savages" policy throughout the island.

The eighteenth-century court's fears of costly security bills proved well founded. In the absence of a dense bureaucratic and military presence, the elite that emerged in mid-Qing Taiwan was largely comprised of wealthy strongmen who combined planting with command of their own paramilitary forces. Over time these men and their heirs became gentrified, seeking and winning civil service degrees and adopting more refined lifestyles. Moreover, skillful Qing local administrators in Taiwan, as elsewhere throughout the empire, adroitly co-opted selected strongmen to suppress others who from time to time rose in defiance of the throne. But the growing complexity of Taiwan's society eventually frustrated the Qing design to govern the island on the cheap.

In 1786 Lin Shuangwen rose up and seized several county seats. The Qianlong emperor responded with a massive force of a hundred thousand troops, led by the seasoned general Fukang'an, and the rebellion was crushed within two years. In retrospect, the Jiaqing emperor identified this "great campaign" orchestrated by his father as marking a turning point in the empire's string of glorious expansionist victories: it was the first campaign, Jiaqing noted, in which regular troops needed to be augmented with "local braves." The failure to develop a plan to demobilize these forces when they were no longer needed would haunt the dynasty during the White Lotus rebellion of the subsequent decade, and indeed until the dynasty's collapse.[25]

In the southwest, in the provinces of Yunnan and Guizhou, and in adjacent portions of Sichuan, Hunan, and Guangxi, the Qing faced a similar dilemma with regard to the multitude of indigenous peoples. While increasingly recognizing the diversity of these linguistic and cultural groups—and studying them with ever greater ethnographic precision—Qing observers simultaneously tended to reduce them to a homogenized cultural construction, called the "Miao," a savage "other" in contrast with their civilized selves.[26] Policy toward the Miao in the eighteenth century included both quarantine and enforced acculturation, sometimes alternating but also expressed simultaneously by different officials. In one center of non-Han population in mountainous western Hunan, for example, a "Miao pale" (*Miaojiang*) was sometimes cordoned off to limit or prohibit Han migration, and yet at other times the same area was under active commercial-agricultural development.

Settlement of criminal cases involving the Miao similarly varied between separate judgments under a special set of statutes reflecting indigenous customary law—a forerunner to the extra-territorial judicial privileges later granted to Europeans along the coast—and prosecution and punishment of Miao criminals as ordinary Qing subjects. Acculturation of the west Hunan population to Qing norms gradually occurred over the eighteenth century, largely through intensified commercial relations, but acculturation was hardly assimilation or still less sinicization. At century's end, when resistance broke into the open, prompted by the predations of Qing military forces, self-consciously non-Han peoples of the five-prefecture region united as one in the Great Miao rebellion of 1795.[27]

Han Chinese had been present in Yunnan and Guizhou for millennia, and the area had been generally claimed as part of the Chinese empire since the earliest dynasties. But Han immigration into these regions in the Ming, and even more so in the first century of the Qing, was unprecedented, prompted by land hunger, trade opportunities, and—especially after the 1720s—a rush to mine the region's rich deposits of copper and other monetary metals. As the home base of Wu Sangui, moreover, the southwest had been disrupted by the Three Feudatories rebellion of the 1670s and 1680s, and during the reconstruction period the government intensified its effort to integrate the area administratively in order to reduce any future threat.[28] But Qing authorities seem never to have sought a wholesale dispossession or displacement of indigenous populations. As conflicts arose with increasing frequency and ferocity, they were seldom simply two-sided disputes. Aggrieved parties resorted to arms to defend highly complex and specific local interests, and not necessarily along strict ethnic lines.

As in Taiwan, the early Qing sought to administer this area without great expense, through a selective enfeoffment of native chieftains as its agents. But with the gradual introduction of Han-style patrilineal inheritance practices, new disputes arose over succession to chieftainships. When the Qing announced in 1705 that it would only recognize as chieftains individuals educated in Chinese-language schools, these disputes regularly erupted into factional warfare. The Qing's decision in the 1720s to enforce a transition from native chieftainships to direct bureaucratic administration was in large part a response to the political anarchy already under way in the region.

Bureaucratic administration had been tried in the sixteenth century by the Ming but with little real effect. The initiative was revived under Wu Sangui in the 1660s and 1670s, but the outcome was a multiplication of native chieftaincies rather than their elimination. As the largest domains were broken up into prefectures, effective administration was simply passed down one level, to jurisdictions below the prefecture.

In contrast with the northwest, where Yongzheng was notably less bellicose than either his predecessor or successor, in the southwest he was by far the most aggressive colonizer. His Yunnan-Guizhou governor-general Ortai launched vigorous land reforms, including reclamation, private ownership, and household registration for tax purposes. Local resistance to each of these policies required an ever-growing military presence in the region. When Chinese literati in the heartland predictably complained about the cost, Yongzheng defended his incorporationist policies in 1728 as follows: "I take this action only because the unfortunate people living in these frontier areas are my innocent children. I hope to free them of such hardship and make their lives safe and happy. Under no circumstances am I expanding the size of my empire simply because of some misguided notion that there are people and land in these areas that I can use."[29] But the violence escalated, culminating in the near genocidal Guzhou rebellion of 1735–1736 in which by the Qing's own accounts nearly 18,000 local people were massacred and some 1,224 villages torched. This bloody catharsis, which coincided with the succession of the Qianlong emperor (whose ambitions lay elsewhere), effectively brought to an end the first phase of expanding Qing hegemony in the southwest.

The sinicization process was yet more problematic in the Sino-Burmese borderland encompassing western Yunnan and the upper valleys of the Mekong and Irrawaddy rivers.[30] A significant Chinese presence there dated only from the arrival of Wu Sangui and his Green Standard armies in 1659, but it grew rapidly. Wu and his Qing superiors attempted to impose an administrative structure built on enfeoffed native chiefdoms, but indigenous local aristocrats—a complex cultural mélange of Tai and other language groups—more often managed to accept and balance appointments from several adjoining polities, of which the Qing was but one. Similarly, cultural elements were selectively adopted from several regional metropoles. In the prosperous border towns, for example, Confucian schools sprang up adjacent to older Theravada Buddhist temples.

This region of fluid identities, bloodlines, and political loyalties was also a great commercial crossroads, with Chinese manufactures traded alongside indigenous products such as smoked hams, rhino horns, and specialty woods, as well as cotton and tea from newly carved-out plantations. Chinese merchants, with their tight networks organized by lineage, guild, and native place, seized the dominant role in this commerce, which ran in several directions throughout China and Southeast Asia, according to demand. The Qing authorities alternately encouraged this trade and imposed embargoes, depending on their fluctuating security concerns. One major ban came in the 1760s during the Qing's Burmese campaigns. Though Qianlong lauded this as yet another victory in his string of Ten Great Campaigns, in fact it was something of a debacle, as thousands of Manchu and Chinese troops succumbed to tropical diseases, with very little payoff. In the wake of the campaign and the lifting of the embargo, trade grew at an even more rapid pace.

Elimination of petty principalities and the consolidation of the Burmese and Siamese monarchies in the late eighteenth and early nineteenth centuries led to a more multipolar political, cultural, and economic scene in the borderlands. But as elsewhere, the hardening of boundaries between early modern states gradually closed off the ambiguous frontier zones of the past, and growing cultural tensions would eventually culminate in the Panthay rebellion of the mid-nineteenth century.

High Qing Culture

Compared with the intellectual license and aesthetic experimentation of the late Ming, the early Qing represented in many ways a return to discipline and control. In the area of Confucian scholarship, for example, the radical freethinking of the late Ming Taizhou school was soundly repudiated by the Kangxi court, which revived the Neo-Confucian learning (*lixue*) of the Song dynasty, with its emphasis on social hierarchy and ritual conformity. The culmination of this was the court's publication of *The Complete Works of Master Zhu Xi* (*Zhuzi quanshu*) and *Essential Ideas of Nature and Principle* (*Xingli jingyi*) in 1713 and 1715, compiled by the establishment intellectual Li Guangdi. Yet this recycling of Neo-Confucian scholarship was in its own way innovative. It dramatically downplayed the speculative cosmological elements and the search for personal sagehood of the Song tradition and emphasized instead the Neo-Confucians' creative quest for practical solutions to social, economic, and administrative problems—what would later come to be promoted as substantive learning (*shixue*) or statecraft (*jingshi*).[31]

By the time of the Yongzheng and Qianlong reigns, the rising prosperity of a broad urban class had revived and expanded the middle-brow culture that had emerged in the late Ming. The tastes of these merchants and artisans bridged the gap between the fairly rigid, homogeneous philosophical, literary, and artistic traditions of the elite and the vibrant, infinitely varied popular culture that elites routinely condemned.[32] But just how independent from court-dominated orthodoxy was this mid-Qing urban culture? Scholars have debated this question by considering the case of Yuan Mei (1716–1798), perhaps the Qing's greatest eighteenth-century poet. Yuan was also a highly popular and financially successful professional writer of fiction, nonfiction, and quasi-fiction prose, and a commentator on socioeconomic policy whose views were respectfully considered, if not necessarily followed, by many high officials. Some historians have emphasized Yuan Mei's freewheeling bohemianism and alienation from orthodox values, while others have pointed out that most of his work lay firmly within the classical literati tradition. At a minimum, Yuan's case shows how even an orthodox member of the urban literati could be influenced by the distinct bourgeois culture thriving in cities across the empire.[33]

This influence emerged most strikingly in the literary and performing arts, as literacy seeped into the lower registers of the social order.[34] The rapidly growing market for commercial publications was noted with some irony by the classicist Qian Daxin (1728–1804): "In ancient times, there were three teachings: Confucianism, Buddhism, and Daoism. Since the Ming dynasty, there has been one more, called popular fiction. It does not call itself a teaching, but among all classes of society there is no one who does not practice it. Even illiterate women and children frequently see and hear it performed; for such persons it is the *only* teaching. Thus, compared with Confucianism, Buddhism, and Daoism, it is yet more widespread."[35] As Qian suggested, there was a considerable interface between the rapidly expanding print culture and the older oral culture, occupied by such media as popular story-telling and public recitations, even those of the supposedly sacrosanct Sacred Edict.[36]

The new fiction included short stories, such as the supernatural tales of the Shandong writer Pu Songling (1640–1715).[37] But Qing readers, much like their contemporaries in early modern Europe, developed a taste for longer fictional forms. The greatest "novel" from the High Qing was unquestionably *The Scholars* (*Rulin waishi*), a sprawling, satirical take on the values and aspirations of the examination elite, who were portrayed as increasingly out of step with the realities of social and economic change. The work's author, Wu Jingzi (1701–1754), the scion of a declining official family, was a lower degree-holder who repeatedly failed the two higher examinations and eked out a livelihood in Nanjing and Yangzhou as a semi-dissolute writer. His novel circulated in manuscript around midcentury and was first printed two decades after his death. It became enormously popular in the nineteenth century and was republished many times.

The Qing empire saw a great variety of theatrical genres, spanning a wide range of formality and literary quality, from plebeian puppet and shadow puppet shows to the slyly sophisticated and often explicitly erotic dramas of Hangzhou's Li Yu (1611–1680), perhaps the first member of the Chinese literati to derive a comfortable living as a writer for the stage.[38] In the countryside, ritual and historical plays and pageants, with centuries-old scripts, were performed at village and temple fairs, sometimes continuing over several days and drawing enormous crowds from many miles around.[39] In cities from Jiangnan to Sichuan, guilds or neighborhood associations sponsored regional operas for the general urban public, often performed on the streets without benefit of a stage.[40]

The more refined operatic traditions of private theatrical troupes were supported by urban elites, such as the thirty or so troupes patronized by the newly ascendant "merchant princes" of Yangzhou's salt trade, or those sponsored by the court and officials in Beijing. Individual star actors, and sometimes whole troupes, moved from patron to patron, continually negotiating better deals for themselves. In a number of cosmopolitan cities, multiple regional operatic traditions existed side by side, with much mutual influence. In the capital, the hybrid form known as Peking Opera gradually took shape in the late eighteenth century and would be appropriated to serve as China's national art form in the late Qing and Republican eras.[41]

The rise of a middle-brow culture was somewhat less pronounced in the visual arts, but change was evident there as well. By the late Ming, the court's patronage of academic painting was already being displaced by a highly diversified urban art market. Interrupted by the dynastic transition, this market vigorously revived by the final decade of the seventeenth century. It was governed by a fashion-conscious literati taste, as the commercial gentry in Qing cities sought to establish their cultural superiority through connoisseurship of luxury commodities. Just as localized specialties developed in the decorative arts (Suzhou jade carving, Jiading bamboo carving, Songjiang metalwork, Yangzhou lacquerware), particular places came to be associated with different schools of literati painting— the Wu painting of Suzhou, the Zhe painting of Hangzhou, and the school of Yangzhou.

One of the greatest Yangzhou painters was Shitao (birth name Zhu

Ruoji, 1642–1707), a descendent of the Ming imperial house who emerged from a peripatetic life as a Buddhist monk in the late 1690s to become a professional artist-entrepreneur, producing paintings and calligraphy for sale in the lower Yangzi's booming metropolis, where fortunes were being made in the salt trade. Along with another Ming prince, Bada Shanren (Zhu Da, 1626–1705), Shitao created a school of painting known in his own day as "the originals" (*qishi*) and by art historians today as "the individualists." Shitao's work was characterized by an aggressive rejection of traditional norms ("I have been taught by Heaven itself"), a revived and transformed concentration on subjective response, a multiplicity of viewpoints, an alienation between artist and viewer, and a sense of doubt (Fig. 7). In the urban-commercial world of the emerging High Qing, these sensibilities sold well.[42]

Throughout imperial history, the foremost area of China's artistic greatness was porcelain, and in the Kangxi era it reached its pinnacle of technical achievement. By the late seventeenth century the production of the great ceramic manufacturing city of Jingdezhen in northeastern Jiangxi had regained and surpassed its previous height in the late Ming. The imperial kilns there were wholly rebuilt in 1677, and they were joined by many others operated by private capitalists. During the mid-Qing, Jingdezhen's booming output was destined in large part for European and North American markets, feeding the growing Western taste for *chinoiserie*. Much of this "china" was directly commissioned by Western buyers and featured European family crests and scenes from Western classical antiquity or the Bible (Fig. 8). This booming export trade in porcelain seems to have had relatively little effect on domestic tastes, which in ceramics far more than in painting remained dominated by the court.

By the late Qianlong reign, the export market for porcelain began to shrink dramatically, owing to competition from manufacturers in Europe, who took advantage of newly discovered clay deposits at home and technology stolen from China by industrial spies such as the Jesuit François Xavier d'Entrecolles.[43]

If exported porcelain did not spawn much domestic imitation of European taste, by the last decades of the eighteenth century *"euroiserie"* came into vogue in China, reciprocating the vogue on the other side of the Eurasian continent. Clocks and watches, tobacco and tobacco containers, English woolens and cotton broadcloth all arrived through port cities such as Guangzhou and came into routine use among the urban elite. *Fin de siècle* Yangzhou and other major cities exhibited a character-

Fig. 7 *Lotus Pond*, by Shitao. Courtesy of Palace Museum, Beijing.

Fig. 8   Export porcelain bowl from Jingdezhen, with painting of a cricket match. Courtesy of Marylebone Cricket Club, London.

istically modern consciousness of participation in a global community of taste, and each one also competed to develop its own distinctive fashion sense for imitation elsewhere. In the domain of clothing and other consumer items, the major commercial cities of the High Qing exhibited a feverish passion for the newest or most up-to-date styles. Wigs, household pets, gowns, jackets, trousers, and pleated skirts enjoyed sudden waves of popularity and then disappeared overnight.[44]

Even in the realm of classical scholarship, the High Qing saw major innovations. By the mid-eighteenth century, the dominant trend was the critical application of techniques such as phonetics, epigraphy, geography, and comparative philology to the classical canon. The influences on this movement—known variously as evidential research (*kaozheng* or *kaoju*) or Han Learning (*Hanxue*)—included Jesuit-imported Western sciences and mathematics and also the pioneering linguistic studies of Gu Yanwu.[45] Although the Hanxue scholars condemned the late-Ming Taizhou school's stress on innate moral autonomy as being a major reason for that dynasty's collapse, partisans of evidential research clearly derived some of their own skeptical attitude from Li Zhi and others affiliated with the Taizhou school.

Han Learning adherents used philological methods to bring to light and purge interpolations and copyists' errors from canonical texts. Major studies such as the *Critical Investigation of the Old Text Book of Documents* (*Shangshu guwen shuzheng*) by Yan Ruoju (1636–1704), which circulated in manuscript form during Yan's lifetime but was first printed only in 1743, and the *Analysis of the Old Text Book of Documents* (*Guwen shangshu gao*) by Hui Dong (1692–1758) exposed as forgeries existing versions of this urtext of Chinese culture. Early Hanxue scholars paid polite respect to the contributions of Zhu Xi and other Song Neo-Confucians, but by the heyday of the Hanxue movement Song scholarship had been identified as a major part of the problem. Dai Zhen's (1724–1777) controversial *Critical Investigation of the Meanings of Terms in the Mencius* (*Mengzi ziyi shuzheng*) of 1768, for example, argued that Zhu Xi had flatly misunderstood the meanings of such key terms as *li* (principle), *qi* (material force), *xing* (nature), and *qing* (circumstances or emotional response) as they were used in ancient times.

The evidential research movement was a collective project undertaken in the urbanized and commercialized lower Yangzi. It benefited from the same boom in publishing that spurred the growth of pulp fiction and other middle-brow reading materials of the time.[46] In challenging the authority of Zhu Xi, these southern philologists were rebelling against the readings of the classics that the Qing court in Beijing had just declared to be orthodox, but for whatever reason the regime proved exceptionally tolerant of this behavior. Over time, the movement itself became orthodoxy, as men trained in philological scholarship gained access to high office, took charge of the writing and grading of civil service examinations, and systematically allowed candidates who thought as they did to pass the tests. To some extent this meant a systematic favoritism toward scholars of the lower Yangzi, who enjoyed disproportionate access to the large private collections of rare books that dotted that region and without which comparative philological research was impossible. It was just this kind of regional partisanship that the Qianlong emperor sought to counter in 1761 by personally re-ranking the order of passes on that year's metropolitan examination, bouncing a Jiangnan scholar from the top position and replacing him with a more rustic Shaanxi native.[47]

While twentieth-century nationalist Chinese historians celebrated the evidential research movement as evidence of a proto-scientific strain in late imperial culture, some revisionist studies have emphasized the *kaozheng*'s more reactionary, fundamentalist side. These studies have noted that even while eighteenth-century scholars employed increasingly sophisticated techniques to purge the classics of forgery and interpolation, the actual goal of this endeavor for many—including such brilliant minds as Dai Zhen—was recovering the authentic classics, which were seen as repositories of revealed truth, and reinstituting their prescribed social and moral orders.[48]

The culminating intellectual project of the High Qing was the decade-long compilation of the *Imperial Library in Four Treasuries* (*Siku quanshu*), inaugurated by the Qianlong emperor in an edict of February 1772. All published books and unpublished manuscripts in the empire were submitted to an imperial commission at Beijing, which altogether reviewed over ten thousand works. About 3,450 of these were copied into a standardized set of 36,000 volumes, copies of which were housed in the Imperial Palace at Beijing, the Summer Palace north of the capital (this set was destroyed, along with the Summer Palace, by Lord Elgin in 1860), and the palaces at Chengde and Mukden (Shenyang). Later copies were installed at Yangzhou, Zhenjiang, and Hangzhou. An annotated catalogue of these works was presented to the throne in February 1781.[49]

Actual control of the editing project was effectively captured by the circle surrounding the philologist and Hanlin academician Zhu Yun (1729–1781). Though native to Hangzhou, Zhu's family had resided for three generations in Beijing. His intellectual rise thus reflected the stature of Beijing itself as an alternative cultural center to Jiangnan. Zhu and his circle imposed their own Han Learning agenda on the empire's intellectual world, challenging Song dynasty Neo-Confucian readings of classical texts at every opportunity. Thus, one legacy of the Imperial Library project was to intensify factionalism among the literati, which contributed in turn to the deterioration of bureaucratic morale in the final decades of the eighteenth century.[50]

Warning Signs

The High Qing is assumed by most scholars to have ended with the formal abdication in 1795 of the Qianlong emperor in favor of his son, Jiaqing. A range of critical dysfunctions that appeared, more or less dramatically, around the turn of the century collectively justify this periodization. But in the area of bureaucratic initiative and morale, troubling signs appeared well before this date.

In 1774 an uprising led by Wang Lun, an itinerant preacher of a millenarian Buddhist sect, broke out along the Grand Canal in western Shandong province. Seemingly motivated not by economic distress but by genuine religious conviction, the rebels managed to capture several county seats and eventually threatened the major canal port of Linqing. A truly alarmed Qianlong court was able to send sufficient troops to put down the rebellion handily, but the fact that the it had managed to get off the ground at all, still less to capture county seats, was a shocking indication of the regime's weakening social control.[51]

Some seven years later, a widely publicized scandal erupted in the management of what might be considered the masterpiece of Qing statecraft, the ever-normal granaries system. These county-level repositories had shown remarkable success during the preceding half-century in controlling regional food shortages and achieving price stability over the annual agrarian cycle and across the territorial breadth of the empire. One of the principal means of stocking granaries was by selling civil service degrees for contributions in either grain or silver. But over the course of the 1770s, a racket headed by Gansu's provincial treasurer, Wang Ganwang, had pocketed huge amounts of silver collected for the purpose of purchasing grain and had then falsely reported famine relief distributions to account for the grain's nonexistence. By 1781 when the throne was accidentally tipped off about the scheme, Wang had been promoted to Zhejiang governor, and his personal assets were found to exceed a million taels of silver. As the eighteenth century drew to a close, the ever-normal granary system—the crowning achievement of Qing bureaucratic governance—was becoming decidedly abnormal, as the "prosperous age" drew to a close.[52]

4

SOCIETY

EUROPEANS and Americans encountering China in the nineteenth century frequently described its society and culture as "stable" over long periods of historical time, or, more perniciously, as "stagnant."[1] For Western civilization—on a mission to bring its unique experience of progress to the vast backwaters of the world—this was a convenient myth. Stagnation, unfortunately, found its way into standard histories of late imperial China during the last half of the twentieth century not only in the West but also in China. In the People's Republic, "stagnation" dovetailed nicely with "feudalism," while in Taiwan it supplied a suitable contrast with American "modernization" that so enamored the Nationalists. This view of late imperial stagnation still finds adherents today.

To be sure, many elements of society remained relatively constant or were even strengthened during the Qing, providing continuity with China's imperial past. These included patrilocal marriage, patrilineal kinship, partible male inheritance, the centrality of the household unit, sedentary agrarianism, land ownership, and the civil service examination system—the fundamental dividing line between elite and commoner. And Western observers who increasingly took "machines as the measure of men" were probably not wrong to find in the Great Qing empire little evidence of basic technological innovation. Yet the notion of Qing stagnation was illusory. Within a time frame paralleling the "early modern" period in the West, Qing society experienced many small and not so small changes that amounted, altogether, to a structural transformation. By the fall of the dynasty in 1911, and even by the Opium War of 1839–1842, China was a different society from the one that experienced the crisis and conquest of the mid-seventeenth century.

Population Growth and Movement

The most striking change from the beginning to the end of the Qing empire was increasing population density. Both sides of the Eurasian continent began to experience "modern population growth" in the fifteenth and sixteenth centuries, due in part to the introduction of hardy New World food crops such as potatoes, sweet potatoes, and peanuts. These countercyclical crops served as brakes on starvation during harvest failures of the more preferred staples, rice and wheat. Following the seventeenth-century crisis, China's population growth resumed and shortly began to accelerate. A consensus estimate might place the population in 1700 at about 150 million, roughly the same as it had been a century earlier under the Ming. By 1800 it had reached 300 million or more, and then rose further to perhaps 450 million at the outbreak of the Taiping rebellion around 1850. By 2000 China's population exceeded 1.25 billion.[2]

Like its late-Ming antecedent and its European counterpart, the early Qing's rapid growth certainly owed something to declining mortality. The spread of potatoes and peanuts to the interior, aided by zealous local and provincial officials, staved off death from malnutrition. Smallpox, the great killer of the seventeenth century, was controlled through widespread inoculation. And improved birthing techniques and childcare practices, disseminated by a professionalized cadre of doctors and midwives and by commercially published medical handbooks, played some role in reducing infant mortality. But probably the most important element in China's population growth was a drop in the rate of infanticide, which had been largely but not exclusively applied to girls. Beginning in the late seventeenth century, with the establishment of domestic peace and the opening of new lands and opportunities for livelihood, Qing subjects deliberately relaxed their practice of killing or abandoning newborns, though they returned to it again some time in the nineteenth century. While intensified contraception practices were slowing population growth in Europe during the twentieth century, ever more successful government anti-infanticide campaigns in China during the same time removed this traditional "preventive check" on the size of the population, with dramatic consequences.[3]

In Europe, which underwent structural changes in the economy from agriculture to manufacture, the areas of greatest population growth were major cities and the surrounding countryside. In China it was the reverse. Population growth was negligible in the Qing's most urbanized and populous region, the Yangzi delta, even in periods when the rest of the empire was growing rapidly.[4] But settlement burgeoned in remote borderlands and highland areas, because these regions offered the best opportunities to improve one's livelihood by clearing and farming large tracts.

What this suggests, of course, is not merely population growth but also movement out of already crowded regions and into new lands of opportunity. The Qing regime deliberately contributed to an unprecedented westward migration by abrogating most of the Ming's legal prohibitions on geographic mobility (prohibitions already ignored for the most part during the Ming's last century or so) and providing positive incentives such as tax holidays, seed grain, and livestock. Sichuan's fertile Red Basin, which had been greatly depopulated by the bloodbaths of Zhang Xianzhong in the late Ming, produced a vacuum effect: "Huguang filled up Sichuan, and Jiangxi in turn filled up Huguang," in the words of the early nineteenth-century scholar Wei Yuan. By the 1720s the province's population was 70–80 percent non-native, and as much as 85 percent a century later. The social-cultural mix within Qing Sichuan was consequently complex and fraught with tension.[5]

Once long-inhabited areas of China proper had been resettled by the early eighteenth century, Qing subjects began streaming into the empire's frontiers, converting marshland and forests into Chinese-style sedentary farmland. As we have seen, throughout most of the 1700s millions of Han Chinese moved into the southwest (today's Yunnan and Guizhou provinces), braving tropical diseases to which they lacked immunity in order to farm the region's fertile valleys and mine its mountains for copper and other valuable metals.[6] In eighteenth-century Taiwan as well, Qing constraints on colonization were frustrated by an intense land hunger, aggravated by profit-making opportunities for commercial rice cultivation to feed the chronically grain-deficit mainland areas just across the straits. Effectively, over the course of the mid-Qing, Taiwan became socially and economically incorporated into Fujian province.[7]

After the Qing's conquest of the northwest New Dominion (Xinjiang) in the 1750s and 1760s, the Qianlong court launched a deliberate policy of agricultural colonization, in part to guarantee a stable grain supply for the large contingent of troops stationed there and in part to alleviate population pressure on the central provinces. The colonies came in many forms: East Turkestani Muslims, bannermen, and Han Chinese; military colonies, penal colonies, and colonies of free civilians. Government incentives to homesteaders consisted of land grants, free tools and seeds, loans of cash, and livestock. By the middle of the nineteenth century, some 3,600,000 *mou* (approximately 600,000 acres) of land in Xinjiang had been converted to settled agriculture.[8]

In the Jurchen ancestral homeland in the northeast, Han migration was at first much slower than in the northwest. Prior to 1668 the court promoted colonization of Liaodong, and in the 1670s and 1680s sent some colonists into the frontier territories of Qilin and Heilongjiang. But most migration into Manchuria came about in defiance of imperial law. In the first year of his reign, Qianlong—acknowledging the scope of the problem—declared the leasing of Jurchen lands to Han civilians illegal. But by the late nineteenth century, even minimal attempts to enforce this edict were abandoned, and from the 1890s through the early twentieth century 25 million people migrated from Shandong and Hebei to Manchuria—one of the greatest movements of people in modern times.[9]

The Qing migration into frontier regions was paralleled by movement into newly reclaimed environments within China proper. The traditional pattern of Chinese agriculture, which favored cultivation of plains and river valleys, had left the empire's considerable highlands to indigenous peoples or to bandits, smugglers, and other marginal types. A Ming prohibition on highland residence had carried over into the early Qing, but like other bans on geographic mobility, it was honored more in the breach than the observance and was gradually revoked under the Qing. Consequently, the eighteenth century was the period when Chinese civilization moved decisively uphill. One attraction of the mountains was their metal deposits, particularly copper and lead to meet the rapidly commercializing economy's demand for coin. The result was a full-fledged mineral rush throughout the empire in the second quarter of the eighteenth century. But a more pervasive compulsion was, again, the hunger for new farmland.

The early settlers who moved into highland areas along provincial borders in central and south China and flanking the Han River in the northwest often practiced a shifting agriculture—they cut down trees and sold them for timber or charcoal, burned the remaining vegetation in place for fertilizer, and then moved on to adjacent areas for the next growing season. Their slash-and-burn practices and other forms of mountain livelihood progressively distinguished upland settlers from their lowland neighbors, with whom they lived in a tense reciprocity. They became known as "shed people" (*pengmin*), because of the mats they carried on their backs and erected as temporary shelters. Though ethnically Han, they were something of a denigrated social caste.[10]

Another wave of migration was made possible by wealthy land developers who contracted with the administration to reclaim very large swaths of highland and then subcontracted with smaller entrepreneurs to strip the tract into sections and prepare it for cultivation. The same parcel of farmland might thus acquire multiple layers of ownership with multiple collectors of rent.[11] Individual households were recruited to do the actual farming. Dry-field crops such as sweet potatoes were usually the first to be grown because they were well suited for hillsides, but wherever possible flat terraces were eventually cut into the slopes to allow wet rice cultivation (Fig. 9).

The impetus for land reclamation came essentially from the private sector, but around 1730 the Yongzheng emperor—justifiably alarmed by the need to expand the food supply to feed a growing population—launched a campaign designed to motivate his field officials to compete with one another to reclaim new land. With five- or ten-year tax holidays as an incentive, these officials added over a million new arable acres

Fig. 9   Terraced hillsides.

to the registers during Yongzheng's reign. One predictable result was a flurry of false reporting and the assignment of uncultivable land to local households in order to record it as reclaimed. When the tax holidays expired, a further crisis arose because the new tax burden (made heavier by nonexistent or nonproductive lands on the registers) had to be distributed among the jurisdiction's farm households.

One attempted solution was to ferret out genuinely productive land that had been illicitly reclaimed by these farmers in the past and then assign the new tax burden to these formerly untaxed parcels. But this, of course, set into motion another round of corrupt practices. With the accession of the more cautious and self-consciously "magnanimous" Qianlong emperor in 1735, the court decided to strike a large percentage of the new acreage from the tax registers altogether. Several officials, including the governor of Henan province, were dismissed for their imprudence in the reclamation campaign. But the court announced its continued support for legitimate land reclamation, offering in some cases permanent tax exemptions for newly cultivated small parcels of land within existing settlements.[12]

Without question, the frenzy of agrarian land reclamation greatly increased the empire's food output, and to the end of the eighteenth century supported a population growth spurt without a per capita decline in food consumption. But an unanticipated and disastrous consequence of land reclamation was ecological decay. Deforestation led to massive topsoil runoff, which not only made the land progressively less fertile but silted up river channels, raising the riverbed, constricting the banks, and causing floods. Although the Yellow River and other waterways running through the sandy soil of the north China plain had presented a chronic flood threat for millennia, the well-channeled Yangzi and other rivers of central and south China had not. But the wholesale ecological deterioration of the mid and late Qing changed this for all time. The problem was compounded by the dramatic constriction of central China's two largest lakes, the Dongting in Hunan and the Boyang in Jiangxi. These and other lakes historically served as floodwater receptacles for torrential snowmelt from the highlands, when the river channels could not handle the sudden volume of water. Over the course of the Qing, as land-hungry farmers constructed polders (dikes) in order to claim parts of the lake bed for rice cultivation, the capacity of these natural receptacles to mitigate flood damage was greatly reduced.

From the late eighteenth century on, the administration was aware of its growing ecological problem and periodically—following a major flood—would condemn and destroy the new reclamation projects thought to have caused the catastrophe. One of the first instances came in 1788, when the Yangzi's dikes burst in western Hubei, prompting the Qing administration to seize and destroy a privately reclaimed island in the river. But over time the compulsive drive for new arable outstripped any government efforts to constrain it.[13]

Land and Labor, Debasement and Servitude

Generally speaking, and without making allowance for the considerable regional variation that certainly existed, we can posit some broad trends in the concentration of landholding during the late imperial period. At the beginning of the Ming, land was held in the form of large manorial units. The first Ming emperor, who had come to the throne in part as an agrarian reformer, broke these estates up under a "land to the tiller" policy that ushered in an era of small freeholding proprietorship. But over the course of the Ming, the trend was toward reconcentration in the hands of fewer owners, though not in the same form as before. One key method was commendation, whereby a small farm household, unable to meet the increasing tax burden on its land, would sign over ownership to a more prosperous neighbor (or one enjoying gentry tax breaks) in exchange for freedom from tax obligations and a permanent lease on its former property. By the early seventeenth century, perhaps the majority of the empire's farmland was owned by what modern scholars call "rentier landlords" and was worked and managed by small households of commoners.

The conquering Qing declined to follow the Ming founder's example in undertaking systematic land reform, ultimately choosing instead to acknowledge the Han elite's economic dominance in exchange for their acceptance of the Qing conquerors' political legitimacy. However, the peasant wars of the Ming-Qing transition had done their part to improve the position of tenant farmers. Many landlords, fleeing the volatile countryside, abandoned their holdings or sold them off cheaply. By reducing population pressure, warfare increased the value of labor relative to land. One result was a revival of small freeholding proprietorship. Another was that labor-hungry landlords granted willing and capable tenants permanent tenancy rights or surface ownership of land, conditional only on payment of rent. This arrangement gave tenants a sense of security and an incentive to make capital improvements and experiment with new crops. The resulting agricultural productivity over the course of the Qing kept pace (roughly) with the era's rapid population growth.

The continual movement of rural elites into towns and cities and into various professions allowed many tenant households to exercise a great deal of autonomy in crop selection and other managerial decisions. In certain prefectures of the lower Yangzi region, and perhaps elsewhere, an agency known as the landlord bursary found tenants and collected rents for urbanized landlords, who often had no idea who was actually farming their land or even where those properties were located.[14] The benefits to tenants of this relative freedom may have been largely offset by the impact of population growth, however, which once again raised the value of land relative to labor and consequently drove rents ever higher. In certain especially hard-hit regions, the mid-nineteenth-century rebellions and their associated depopulation may have reversed this effect, recreating the conditions of the early Qing and inclining labor-starved landlords to offer very favorable terms to capable tenants. One scholar has argued that a labor shortage in the wake of the Taiping rebellion of 1851–1864 may have had repercussions as late as the 1920s and 1930s, impeding the efforts of the Communists to incite tenant rebellion in the lower Yangzi region.[15]

The economic realities of landlordism and tenancy were complicated by issues of personal status. While the vast majority of ordinary subjects of the Great Qing empire were free commoners (*liangmin*), not everyone enjoyed this standing.[16] There existed two basic alternatives to "free" or "good" (*liang*) status: membership in a debased status group, and one or another form of personal servitude. Both debased and servile persons were legally ineligible to sit for the civil service examinations like ordinary commoners, and in judicial hearings their rights and obligations were differently understood by the court (though even servile individuals, despite their status as "half-human, half-chattel," were held personally competent to obey the law). In customary practice, debased and servile persons were excluded from marriage with free commoners and were obliged to bow or otherwise acknowledge their inferiority in social situations. Over the course of the Qing, the imperial court and the bureaucracy moved to merge more of debased and servile people into the broad population of free subjects of the throne, but it did so in fits and starts, and by the end of the imperial era it had still not eliminated the two categories altogether.

The caste-like status of debasement was assigned to tattooed criminals, prostitutes, female adulterers, the penetrated party in homosexual male unions, and other individuals identified as social deviants. But certain hereditary groups, most of them occupation-specific, existed in various discrete localities which were also classed as impure. These included the professional musician-dancer families of Shanxi, the beggars of Suzhou, and various boat-dwelling fisherman households along the southeast coast. Altogether, the number of debased subjects was probably never more than a minute segment of the Qing population, and membership was often quite negotiable. Economically successful households could buy their way out of this category over the course of several generations.

The number of imperial subjects living in some condition of servility was certainly much greater, the true percentage being obscured by the fact that the category itself was nebulous, with many kinds of servitude being outright illegal under Qing statute. Servile status existed at every level of the economic hierarchy. For example, all members of the Eight Banners—including many of the highest officials in the empire—were by definition slaves of their banner headman and ultimately of the emperor. In the process of conquering north China, moreover, as the Qing carved out imperial, princely, or official manors out of lands left fallow during the late Ming rebellions, workers on these estates all became bondservants—but so too did the estate overseers, who could be very wealthy and powerful individuals indeed. Over the first century and a half of the dynasty, much of the land belonging to these manors became effectively privatized and often fell into possession of the overseers. Former estates gradually grew into agrarian villages, and resident households became in practice free owner-cultivator or tenant households.[17]

Probably a still greater number of servile persons were products of indigenous Han Chinese arrangements inherited from the Ming or even earlier. Among these were a relatively small number of household slaves, plus much larger numbers of hereditarily unfree farm laborers and enserfed tenant farmers. Rebellions of just such groups had contributed to the Ming collapse, but they were still around in the early Qing, although substantially reduced in number. Rumors that the new regime was committed to their universal liberation spawned the occasional local bondservant rebellion in the Qing's first decades. Such rumors were false, and indeed the forging of the new regime's throne-gentry alliance grew in part out of its demonstrated willingness to help landlords suppress uprisings of their servile labor force. Nevertheless, the early Qing reigns were dotted by government efforts to manumit various segments of the empire's unfree population.

In the 1680s, for example, the Kangxi emperor launched a program whereby indentured servants on government estates might purchase their freedom and become commoners. Throughout the late seventeenth and early eighteenth centuries, judicial officials at all levels of the bureaucracy, with court approval, moved progressively to narrow the categories of agrarian hirelings whose personal freedom might legally be restricted by their employers. Various formulas were experimented with to distinguish the free from the unfree: how many years the worker had been in the master's employ, whether the worker lived in a separate household or lodged in the master's own house, whether the workers' forebears were interred in the master's family cemetery, whether or not an employment contract existed, and, if so, whether it stipulated a date for the expiration of service.[18]

But it was the vigorously state-making Yongzheng emperor who most directly attacked the problem of debasement and servitude. During the first years of his reign in the late 1720s, he legislated aggressively to have various local pariah groups such as musicians and fishermen accorded full legal rights as Qing subjects, and also to manumit agrarian bondservants. Much has been written about the Yongzheng emancipation campaigns, and their breadth has sometimes been overstated. What the emperor himself said was that he wanted to *protect* the sanctity of the bond between master and servant—the canonically approved differentiation between superior and subordinate—but that to uphold such relationships where they were legitimate it was first necessary to identify and correct instances where such servile arrangements were improperly imposed.

Chief among the latter, in Yongzheng's view, was agrarian tenancy, which in the vast majority of cases was and ought to be a freely contracted arrangement allowing farm households to acquire managerial rights over a leasehold and to leave that leasehold upon the expiration of their contract if a more favorable situation arose. In other words, tenancy was less a status arrangement than a pragmatic device that allowed land and labor to consistently be put to their most productive use. How effectively Yongzheng was able to enforce his views throughout the empire remains unclear. In the reigns of Qianlong and his successors, in any case, there was little follow-up action. In scattered pockets such as Anhui's Huizhou prefecture, servile tenancy remained significantly widespread.[19]

Ethnicity

In the multinational Qing empire, ethnic identities were matters of open debate to an extent they had likely not been at any previous time in imperial history. Among the many reasons for this, foremost was the fact of rule by an avowedly non-Chinese house, along with very public disagreement within the court itself on the rulers' own ethnic character. Second was the tremendous imperialist expansion undertaken by the Qing, which more than doubled the Ming territory and bequeathed to postimperial China the headaches of ethnic separatism. And third was the filling in of peripheral and marginal areas within the inner heartland, which had been claimed as part of the empire for nearly two millennia but which had until the early modern era been only sparsely populated by persons who understood themselves to be Han Chinese.

The new necessity of confronting culturally diverse populations within the expanding confines of "our empire" presented Qing subjects with a profound challenge of alterity ("otherness") not unlike that experienced by early modern Europeans encountering the peoples of the New World. Was what distinguished the Chinese from the barbarian or savage simply a package of cultural practices—such as eating with chopsticks, practicing sedentary intensive agriculture, living in a patrilineal-patrilocal family system, properly burying one's dead and offering them ancestral sacrifice, and (at least for the elite) striving to achieve literacy in the Chinese written language—or were there, as Wang Fuzhi had argued in the era of the dynastic transition, more essential biological ("racial") differences between us and them?

This question of course had profound implications for the possibility of assimilating or "civilizing" these exotic populations. Should one attempt to educate them through intensive elementary education programs, such as that introduced in Yunnan in the second quarter of the eighteenth century, or was this project fruitless or even undesirable? Was intermarriage to be encouraged or rather prohibited, on the grounds that devolution of Chinese into renegade half-breeds or racial traitors was the more likely outcome than elevation of the savage? Were indigenous peoples infinitely diverse, as the ever more sophisticated Qing ethnographies seemed to suggest, or were they effectively all alike, an undifferentiated "other" that could be homogenized into the category of Miao?

Just who were these bizarre creatures: were they truly "people" (*min*) or another species altogether, as hinted at by the use of snake, dog, or other animal radicals in the Chinese characters invented to transcribe their names? If they were indeed people, albeit primitive ones, did this suggest, as the sixteenth-century Yunnanese exile Yang Shen had proposed with a radical hint of cultural relativism, that *min* was not really a singular category—there were actually multiple *min,* some presumably yet to be discovered? Or did their existence argue instead for a single scale of human evolution, in which case these primitive peoples must resemble the way we Chinese had looked in the distant past? Were their cultural practices simply pitiful or contemptible, or was there something in them of the "noble savage," to be wistfully admired if not emulated? The proliferation of illustrated albums of aboriginals (a Qing equivalent of *National Geographic*) seemed to suggest that this might be the case.[20]

And, if these savages were indeed the ancestors of Han Chinese, was it not remotely possible that something had been lost as well as gained in the course of the civilizing process? This was suggested by one Chinese observer of Taiwanese aborigines in the 1820s. Deeply affected by the cultural malaise of the troubled Daoguang era, with its economic depression, recurrent natural disasters, and ominous threat of European expansion, he argued that the rampant commercialization of contemporary society had corrupted our inherent propriety and that we should "get back to fundamentals, like the ancients," along the model presented by these noble primitives.[21]

Even among populations that all agreed were essentially Han Chinese, there was debate about whether certain of them were truly *min*—persons of full competence. One such group, comprised largely of boat-dwelling fishermen and peddlers along the Fujian and Guangdong coasts, were known as Dan. Although physiologically and linguistically indistinguishable from their agrarian neighbors, the fact that they did not have title to onshore property, did not possess graveyards to properly inter their ancestors, and were popularly associated with female prostitution made them unsuitable marriage partners for members of polite local society, and had gradually forced them into the status of a distinct and despised cultural group. It was said that the Dan were descendents of a later wave of the prolonged southern migration from north and central China that had occurred over the early and mid-imperial eras, but more recent scholarship suggests that it was less the date of arrival than the simple matter of relative success or failure at acquiring good farmland when they got there that initially determined whether or not a given household would be labeled Dan.

Yet Dan status, too, was mutable and negotiable. If a boat-dwelling household through its economic success in commerce or even piracy succeeded in acquiring property—"getting landed"—it might be only a matter of a generation or two before it shed its Dan label. Close inspection of elite genealogies in the Fuzhou area suggests that at least some lineages emerged from Dan roots during the Qing. Grafting their own patriline onto another one of impeccable *min*-hood, and even explaining away the awkward fact of a differing surname by positing male adoption of a forebear several generations earlier, newly wealthy families were able to claim descent from the earliest southern migrants from China's prestigious central plain; as such, they could not possibly have been Dan. Like other identities in the culturally fluid Qing empire, this was at bottom a product of local consensus; if you could convince your neighbors you were not Dan but *min,* then that was what you were.[22]

Somewhat comparable was the case of the Hakka ("guest households"), so named to distinguish them from the "host people" (*bendi ren*) among whom they lived in south China. The Hakka probably did descend from a later wave of southern migrants, and through centuries of intermarriage and isolated living gradually developed a somewhat distinctive physical appearance and cultural identity based on dialect, cuisine, and social practices such as the rejection of female footbinding. Having settled largely in the highlands (the only land readily available in the south at that late date), they developed technologies suitable to their ecological niche, including forestry and the cultivation of tea, indigo, and tobacco. They lived in tense mutual accommodation with their lowland neighbors, with whom they traded for grain.

The mid-Qing was a favorable era for the Hakka. Not only were their products in demand, but the mining boom of the Yongzheng and early Qianlong reigns opened new livelihoods for those already long-adapted to highland living. A Hakka diaspora thus fanned out from its initial center in Guangdong's Mei County to upland areas throughout the southeast, including Taiwan, and newly wealthy Hakka men began to acquire examination degrees and enter the empire's cultural elite. Though the group had been around for centuries before this, it seems to have been only in the eighteenth century that the label "Hakka" itself began to acquire broad currency, and only in the early nineteenth century, under the leadership of the new Hakka literati, that a transcendent and proud cultural identity was forged among the geographically dispersed Hakka population as a whole. They became politically active and eventually played a central role in both the Taiping rebellion and the Republican Revolution of 1911.[23]

Of course, in the geographically mobile Chinese society of the Qing era, ethnicity could be based on nothing more than local origin and, under the right circumstances, could lead to social marginalization. In the great middle Yangzi entrepôt of Hankou, merchants from Shaanxi, though among the richest men in town, were marked off by costume, cuisine, and ghettolike residence patterns and were held in suspicion by their neighbors for their dour and reclusive conduct. In the riverport city of Xiangtan, "guest merchants" from Jiangxi were attacked by crowds of local Hunanese in 1819 during a performance of their distinctive Jiangxi-style opera. And in the rapidly growing treaty port of Shanghai, in which migrants from well-off Jiangnan areas such as Ningbo, Wuxi, and Suzhou made up the urban elite, poorer immigrants from northern Jiangsu province were identified as an inferior cultural group. Denigrated because of their coarse "Subei" dialect and rustic ways, they were systematically channeled into the most menial and ill-paying jobs and suspected of sedition and collaboration with the Taiping and later the Japanese. Though "Subei" identity had no significance in northern Jiangsu itself, once it had been constructed by others in Shanghai, it became a unit of collective identity and eventually collective pride.[24]

One of the most objective markers of ethnic marginalization in the Qing empire was reduced access to the examination system. The distribution of scarce examination passes provoked as much conflict between settled mainstream populations and their culturally stigmatized neighbors as did major economic disagreements. This particular issue was consequently a special focus of imperial ethnic policy. The assimilation-minded Yongzheng emperor, for instance, set up special Miao exams in Yunnan in the 1720s in order to foster an indigenous literati elite, and in 1734 he set aside special quotas for non-Han peoples on exams in Guizhou. In the wake of a 1723 rebellion in Jiangxi of shed people—largely but not exclusively Hakka—over their exclusion from local examinations, Yongzheng declared that landholding shed people were fully eligible to sit for the exams. In the hope of assuaging the hostility between them and the host population, however, he designated separate quotas for passes by the two groups—in effect reifying the notion that shed people were somehow distinctive.

In an edict of 1729 the emperor declared Dan and other stigmatized populations to be ordinary commoners (*fanmin*), with all the privileges that accrued to this status, including examination candidacy. But over the first decades of his reign, Yongzheng's successor gradually eliminated nearly all such affirmative action policies. In 1771 Qianlong went so far as to modify his father's 1729 *fanmin* edict to specify that the right to sit for the examinations would accrue to formerly stigmatized groups only four generations after they became taxpaying property holders.[25]

Women and Men

Gender roles in the Great Qing Empire were in constant flux. Discussing his married life in the late eighteenth century, for instance, a government secretary from Suzhou named Shen Fu wrote:

> It was almost three in the morning when I returned [home]. The candles had burned low and the house was silent. I stole quietly into our room to find my wife's servant dozing beside the bed and Yün herself with her make-up off but not yet asleep. A candle burned brightly beside her; she was bent intently over a book, but I could not tell what it was that she was reading with such concentration. I went up to her, rubbed her shoulder, and said, "You've been so busy these past few days, why are you reading so late?" Yün turned and stood up. "I was just thinking of going to sleep, but I opened the bookcase and found this book, *The Romance of the Western Chamber*. I had often heard it spoken of, but this is really the first time I had had a chance to read it. The author really is as talented as people say" . . .
>
> Yün's habits and tastes were the same as mine. She understood what my eyes said, and the language of my brows. She did everything according to my expression, and everything she did was as I wished it. Once I said to her, "It's a pity that you are a woman and have to remain hidden away at home. If only you could become a man we could visit famous mountains and search out magnificent ruins. We could travel the whole world together. Wouldn't that be wonderful?"[26]

The relationship of Shen Fu and his wife was far from the coldly instrumental form of marriage often taken as typical of Chinese society in past times. Expressed most simply, they were "in love," and in the kind of companionate marriage that emerged during the late Ming. But they were probably not typical of married couples in the mid-Qing.[27] In the

predominant form of spousal union at that time, women were systematically subjected to the many restraints embodied in a Confucian moral
system designed by and for men. They were more likely to suffer infanticide; they were severed from their natal family at marriage and became
effectively the property of their husband's parent's household; their only
legal grounds for divorcing their husbands were severe physical mutila-
tion or the attempt to sell them into prostitution, while husbands could
dismiss their wives for such failures as excessive talkativeness; their rights
of inheritance and property ownership were severely restricted; they were
confined to the inner quarters of their homes and denied mobility and sociability; their practice of binding their daughters' feet to make them
more marriageable caused severe pain and restricted physical movement
throughout life; and so on (Fig. 10).[28] But Shen Fu and Yün's marriage
had itself been an arranged one (at age fourteen for both of them), and
though they were urban, literate, and of the gentry class, they were by no
means part of the economic elite. Yet they enjoyed a romantic union of
the kind we usually think of as Western and middle-class.

One thing conspicuously absent from Qing companionate marriage,
by comparison with its earlier manifestation in the late Ming, was the inspiration provided by the courtesan culture. In famous late-Ming pleasure quarters such as the Qinhuai riverfront in Nanjing, sojourning males
encountered a model of refined, literate female companion that some
sought to emulate in their marriage partners. But by the early Qing the
romanticized courtesan culture had gone underground, if not departed
altogether. As part of its defense of fundamentalist Confucian family values and its attempt to put the genie of "cultural revolution" back into the
bottle, the Qing court in the late seventeenth and early eighteenth centuries cracked down hard on sexual permissiveness as manifested in prostitution, pornography, homosexuality, and rape. In this project it enjoyed
real but only temporary success.[29] By the Qianlong reign, if not before,
red-light districts such as the "flower boats" on the canals of the wealthy
salt-trade city of Yangzhou had once again become empire-wide meccas
of courtesanship in its most elegant and fashionable form.

Meanwhile, in more economically diverse port cities such as Tianjin,
Hankou, and Chongqing, the recovering sex trade became big business,
serving all strata of the commercial and transport male labor force with a
finely-graded hierarchy of prostitutes. Eventually, with the mushrooming growth of Shanghai in the late nineteenth century, the two trends
overlapped. This treaty port became a city of prostitutes, ranging from

Fig. 10　A Chinese woman, 1870s. Courtesy of Peabody Essex Museum, Salem, Massachusetts.

immiserated streetwalkers to nationally famous emblems of femininity, sophistication, and cultural cosmopolitanism, whom male patrons worshipped, compulsively gossiped over, and treated with elaborate ritual deference.[30]

A particular flashpoint in the shifting terrain of gender roles in the Qing empire, especially in the eighteenth century, was the cult of widow chastity. The practice of child or early adolescent betrothal, combined with a high incidence of early mortality, added up to a significant population of youngish widows. Usually, these women had already moved into their husband's parental household prior to his death, and this family now bore the burden of supporting an individual who could never fulfill her intended function, which was to bear her husband and his patriline a male heir. On the other hand, given the society's unbalanced sex ratio (owing mostly to infanticide but also to death in childbirth), a still-attractive female, regardless of whether she had been betrothed in the past, might command a hefty brideprice were she sold to a new husband.

Mindful of this powerful incentive to commodify young widows, and viewing widow chastity as a synecdoche for all other relationships of devout filiality (including loyalty to the throne), the Qing court launched a program to bestow honors (such as the right to erect a ceremonial arch) on those families who resisted the temptation to sell off their superfluous daughter-in-law and chose instead to underwrite her virtuous widowhood. In culturally marginal areas such as the southwest, imperial officials used widow-chastity campaigns as a vehicle of civilization and a means to eradicate "barbaric" marriage practices such as the levirate (according to which a man is obligated to marry the childless widow of his dead brother in order to father children and preserve his brother's line). But in wealthy central regions such as Jiangnan, many elite families began to use imperial acknowledgment of widow chastity in the social competition with their neighbors for status, and the throne came to view this behavior as unseemly. Especially in cases where honors were extended to families of chaste widows who committed suicide at the time of their husband's death, the authorities increasingly suspected that such actions might have been coerced and argued that widow suicide, however selfless, still showed an immoral lack of respect for human life. Gradually, then, the court tempered its enthusiasm for the widow-chastity cult and offered awards more sparingly.[31]

New intellectual trends such as the evidential research movement contributed to doubts about what constituted virtuous widowhood. Skeptical of Song Neo-Confucianism in general, scholars such as Wang Zhong began to challenge Cheng Yi's famous dictum that it would be better for a widow to starve to death rather than remarry. Noting that such sentiments were not backed up by new research into the realities of classical antiquity, they contrasted the excessive demands of ritual propriety with commonsense human compassion and came down more often than not on the side of the latter.[32]

A major stimulus to the changing and contested constructions of gender during the Qing was the historically unprecedented incidence of male sojourning. In a variety of ways, being left alone at home for extended periods gave women considerable leeway for action.[33] Wives of absent husbands expanded their role as household financial managers. Elite women continued the kinds of artistic pursuits that had become fashionable in the late Ming, especially writing (and occasionally publishing) poetry. And new arenas of female sociability continued to open up. The conventional norms that prevented Shen Fu and his wife from getting out together and seeing the world (constraints they both lamented) still pertained but were also increasingly violated in practice, as conservative reformers repeatedly noted with alarm. Women left the inner quarters to attend local opera performances and temple festivals and, worse, they increasingly formed pilgrimage societies to tour famous sacred sites in the company of other restless women like themselves.[34]

While Shen Fu welcomed the opportunity to read and discuss popular novels like *Romance of the Western Chamber* with his wife, other males were far more skeptical of female literacy. The eighteenth-century debate over education for women ran along strikingly similar lines to that over education for non-Han peoples at the frontiers, and indeed featured some of the same individuals. Critics claimed that educating women was a waste because their minds were too unsophisticated to grasp the essential meaning of the classics. Educated females would in fact prove more of a liability to society than a benefit, since they would just read pulp fiction and other trivia and have their horizons needlessly broadened beyond their proper domestic sphere.

Advocates of literacy held that all human beings were imbued with rational principle (*li*) and hence educable, and thus it was an offense against Heaven to systematically exclude any category of persons from educational opportunity. Since in the contemporary world women were rapidly becoming literate anyway, the best way to channel their reading tastes in a productive direction would be to afford them full access to the classical curriculum. And in an argument strangely echoing that for "Republican motherhood" in the antebellum United States, Qing reformists pointed out that in most cases it was the mother who provided her son his formative literary and moral training, and that educated mothers produced better-educated sons. As the activist official Chen Hongmou (1696–1771) concluded, "The process of civilization begins in the women's quarters."[35]

Around the same time, the ideal of the "talented woman," which had been out of favor since early Qing rulers and elites repudiated the socio-cultural permissiveness of the late Ming, gradually regained public acceptability. A probable turning point came with the notoriety of Yuan Mei (1716–1797), a highly successful professional writer and celebrated libertine who energetically promoted the poetry of the various female members of his circle at Nanjing. By the early nineteenth century, the highly educated woman had become a noncontroversial staple of at least some segments of elite society, modestly but confidently discussing both cultural and political issues with prominent male scholars. And over the course of the century women reasserted their position in literature, as writers, critics, and readers within an expanding sphere of prose fiction.[36]

Another arena of gender contestation was female footbinding. Shortly after the Qing conquest, the new regime prohibited this centuries-old Chinese practice, as a counterpart to its mandate that Chinese men and boys adopt the queue. Meeting social resistance on both fronts, the court decided that the queue fight was worth the cost, but footbinding was not. In fact, this mutilating practice probably became more widespread over the course of the Qing, working its way down the economic spectrum from its initial confinement to the leisured class. Whereas some families viewed the education of their daughter as a means of attracting a more desirable husband, many more families saw footbinding as an essential practice to secure a good marriage partner.

Certain groups such as the Hakka and—in apparently declining numbers—Manchus themselves eschewed footbinding as alien to their own cultural tradition. By the time the Qing empire entered its final decade, however, antipathy to footbinding had become a *cause célèbre,* and Natural Foot Societies began to spring up in many localities. Kang Youwei and other reformers—almost exclusively male—identified the practice not only as uncivilized but also as an enormous waste of the labor and energies of half the population, a perfect emblem of the dysfunctional nature of all of "old China."[37]

The Qing Gentry

In the classic mid-twentieth-century rendition of traditional Chinese rural society, class structure in the countryside consisted of but two contrasting groups: "peasants" (*nongmin*) and "gentry" (*shenshi*).[38] Beguiling as this simple picture might be, there were in fact a great many other social groups out there—merchants, peddlers, artisans, clerics, and especially transport workers. Even within these two major "classes," the interests of individuals and subsets were as often at odds as they were in harmony with one another. And this complexity within each group was increasingly exacerbated over the course of the Qing.

The English term "gentry" is misleading, calling to mind the red-coated fox hunters in novels by Henry Fielding and Jane Austen. But the term's application to China is not entirely without reason. Though the Qing gentry were not in possession of hereditary noble rank, they—like the British social group from which the name was drawn—were a landed elite upon whom imperial privileges were conferred and from whom a commitment to the management of local affairs was expected. In China as in England there had once been a true peerage or aristocracy, traces of which remained into the early modern period, but this group had been largely replaced by these newcomers as the dominant social force in the countryside. The displacement of an aristocracy of birth by a gentry based on personal educational achievement was initially a function of the late Tang and Song court's decision to grant the civil service examination system the decisive role in access to bureaucratic office and hence upward mobility.[39] But a more dramatic rise of the gentry may have come in the sixteenth century, when they stepped up their involvement with economic commercialization and local management. This development made them unquestionably the dominant rural class.[40]

Like their British counterparts, the Qing gentry were practitioners of a cultural-political style that was equally at home in the countryside and in the city. In his public role, a member of the Qing gentry was an imperially recognized male scholar and civil servant who had passed at least one level of the civil service examinations, held a degree, was legally entitled to wear gentry robes, was eligible for official service, and, though not necessarily an official himself, could talk to officials as an equal. Not infrequently in the Qing, the gentry were "retired" officials who had served in one or two brief appointments in their youth and then returned home for the bulk of their adult life to bask in the glory of this status. In his much broader private role, a member of the rural gentry was a large-scale landholder and part of a "great household"—he was, in other words, the local elite. In this private realm the term "gentry" included not just adult male degree-holders but their wives, descendents, and certain of their collateral relatives, as well as many patrilines that had at one time in the past (or perhaps never) produced a degree-holder.[41]

The Qing gentry were defined primarily by their lifestyle—they were more refined and leisured than commoners, and more likely to be carried in a sedan-chair than to travel any significant distance on foot. They were usually more literate, and by the late Qing they regularly wore eyeglasses to prove it. They could afford to have art objects in their homes—a piece of porcelain, for example, with no practical utility other than to be admired for its beauty. For the upper gentry, connoisseurship of these "superfluous things" was an emblem of status.

Though many people in the local community might belong to common surname groups, gentry were far more inclined than their neighbors to participate in formal lineage organizations. For the major rituals of life passage—weddings, funerals, burials, ancestral sacrifices—they were more likely to adhere to the orthodox (and expensive) dictates of the twelfth-century Neo-Confucian Zhu Xi. Where commoners might engage in the cremation of deceased family members or invite an indecorous (but often highly entertaining) shaman or exorcist to officiate over a funeral, the gentry used these occasions to bolster their cultural hegemony—we are more orthodox and straitlaced than you and so have the right to enjoy a greater degree of wealth, along with your deference and obedience. Funerary and wedding ritual handbooks prescribed ceremonies of varying levels of complexity and expense, allowing households to calculate just what degree of ritual propriety they could afford. The performance of these family rituals also allowed gentry lineages to solidify their boundaries and establish internal hierarchies by deciding whom among those with the same surname to invite and where to place them in the seating arrangement. A major reason for the heated debates among Qing philologists over the authenticity of ancient ritual texts was precisely such practical issues as how to organize and stratify local society.[42]

Over time, the narrower category of civil service degree-holder and the broader category of local elite merged. One reason was that those who passed the exams and secured official appointment often did well financially by this—that was the idea, of course—and invested their new wealth in land near their native home. Another reason was that degree-winners were nearly exclusively drawn from the leisured and economically comfortable group in the first place, since these families could afford to invest years in the education of their sons. And when a poorer household happened to produce a successful examination candidate, he would quickly marry into a wealthy neighboring family that may not have enjoyed this precise asset. A final commonality of interest that further cemented the two groups, if they did not overlap sufficiently beforehand, was the system of tax breaks given to both degree-holders (legally, as a mark of status distinction) and to great households (extra-legally, by local authorities, as a means of enlisting their aid as tax farmers).

The examination system was founded on the myth that diligence in farming, combined with assiduous study, was the formula for examination success. But far more frequently than they admitted, the degree-holding gentry who were not drawn from the literati class itself had a family origin in trade rather than agriculture, which is why, for example, the commercial diaspora headquarters of Huizhou prefecture, Anhui, or the silk-producing town of Nanxun, Jiangsu, did unusually well in the examination sweepstakes. In not a few cases, the gentry's forebears were powerful local "strongmen"—militia and vigilante leaders who parlayed their entrepreneurship of violence into success for their descendents as civil literati.[43]

The best idea of just who the gentry were as a social class—and a useful guide to where some of the fault lines within the group may have been drawn—can be derived from examining their sources of income.[44] The largest resource was private investments, first and foremost in land but also in pawnshops and other forms of usury (as the lending of money with interest became increasingly important over the course of the Qing) and in the growing commercial sector, where participation by degree-holders was formally illegal. Then came what might be termed their "official" income. If they were serving as bureaucrats, this included their salary, *yanglian* supplement, and various forms of "squeeze." If they were students in a county or prefectural school, it included a possible state stipend. But of growing importance over the course of the late imperial period were varying types of income-producing jobs that exploited the gentry's primary capital asset, its literacy.

Members of the local elite might serve as family tutors or schoolteachers. This had long been a means for a failed office-seeker to eke out an income, and in Ming and Qing fiction the impoverished village schoolmaster was a stock, often comic, figure.[45] In the booming nineteenth-century port of Hankou, a popular joke claimed that hanging out a shingle over one's door with the word "Teacher" had a double benefit: it was sure to attract students, plus, as an advertisement of the occupant's poverty, it kept beggars away. Nevertheless, with the rise in popular literacy from the late Ming on, there was a growing economic niche for this profession. More eminent scholars might sell their literary skills in the expanding marketplace of commercial publishing: as authors or ghostwriters, compilers of examination aids, writers of prefaces that served a function similar to today's book-jacket blurbs. They might even sell their name to a list of reputable "proofreaders" for potential best-sellers.[46]

A growing number of gentry served as private secretaries in the entourages of sitting officials. Larger numbers derived incomes from service as managers of lineages, temples, guilds, or long- or short-term local community enterprises such as irrigation systems, relief dispensation agencies, and various civil construction projects. Especially in the late nineteenth century, they filled managerial posts in the mushrooming number of bureaus that collected and dispensed irregular taxes, contributions, and solicitations to finance peacekeeping and postrebellion reconstruction.[47]

Certain of these gentry-managers looked more and more like professional engineers, most notably in hydraulics. Other gentry members involved themselves in the increasingly professionalized fields of medicine and law. Private legal advisors—a great many of them, if one believes the complaints of contemporary officials—were referred to as "litigation masters" or "litigation thugs," depending less on the agenda of the individual litigator than on the attitude of the speaker. While the Qing legal code did not contain any explicit reference to civil litigation and officials nearly universally condemned it, civil lawsuits gradually became routine, and the Qing state grudgingly advertised itself as willing to hear them, for a price. Not only did this act of "benevolent governance" preclude more violent means of private conflict resolution, but the very act of filing a legal complaint was a *de facto* endorsement by the litigant of the state's legitimacy. Acting as a "litigation master" was formally illegal after 1725—in the view of most bureaucrats the chief intent of such persons was to prolong the suit until all parties were bankrupted and no longer able to pay—but the state's own actions turned it into a growth industry.[48]

All of this incipient professionalization was an elite counterpart of the occupational niche-seeking that commoners likewise pursued with ever greater specialization over the course of the Qing. The interest-orientation of the individual might vary greatly, depending on the particular mix of income sources upon which he drew. By the end of the dynasty, if not well before, it was probably unreasonable to speak of a coherent gentry "class."[49]

For those who wished to sidestep the rigors of examination on their way to elite status, an alternative path was to purchase their degrees outright. The sale of gentry rank to wealthy commoners for a "contribution" of cash or grain was first systematically employed by the Kangxi emperor during the early years of his rule in the 1680s. Under his successor, Yongzheng, the sale of degrees became a regular method not only of financing the government's response to natural disasters or pressing military needs but also of restocking the expanding system of ever-normal granaries. Many Qing literati applauded this system, not only as a means of underwriting legitimate administrative costs without raising taxes but also as a way of facilitating the upward mobility aspirations of manifestly successful subjects. A still larger number, however, decried the trading of degrees for contributions as diluting the moral integrity of the literati class. Responding to these critics, the Qianlong emperor severely curtailed the practice during the first decades of his reign, as part of his systematic reversal of the overly strict state-making initiatives of his father. However, by the second half of the eighteenth century the mushrooming expenses of Qianlong's military adventures persuaded him to resurrect the auction of degrees with unprecedented vigor. By 1800 there were an estimated 350,000 holders of purchased degrees in the empire, and that number would spiral upward as the government became more fiscally strapped in the nineteenth century.[50]

Similar oscillations marked the throne's policies toward the privileges of gentry rank. As part of his program to reaffirm the throne-gentry alliance, the Kangxi emperor ordered that degree-holders accused of crimes be exempt from local criminal prosecution and turned over instead to the county education commissioner for "counseling." Yongzheng eliminated this practice, but Qianlong reinstated it. On the fiscal front, the Yongzheng emperor in the mid-1720s eliminated the privileged tax categories of "official household" and "scholar household" and restricted the gentry exemption from corvée obligations to members of the degree-holder's immediate household, rather than a wider circle of relatives. Again, his successor—who consistently saw local literati less as challengers to centralized authority than as partners in its exercise—with self-conscious "magnanimity" reversed these decisions. The Qianlong emperor's reinstatement of gentry privileges remained Qing policy throughout the rest of the dynasty.

Family and Kinship

One of the most striking features of the Qing period is the compelling power of patrilineal kinship, both culturally and socially. People deeply believed that the success or failure of any individual was centrally determined by the paternal guidance he received. In northeastern Hubei, for example, local sources throughout the Qing reprinted over and over the letter written to his son by a local Ming-era patriarch, away in official service at Beijing. He wrote in part:

To Zou Han, son of my principal wife, Madame Yang:
I have been away from home now for nearly two years. The affairs of our home area; our relatives, neighbors, and friends; the comings and goings of people; our houses, irrigation works, trees, and crops; the prosperity of your elder brother's family; the health of the younger children—about all of these things I have heard very little. Although you have written me once or twice, you only give me the general picture of things . . . Your conduct is so slovenly and lackadaisical! A young man who treats his own parents this way will certainly not know how to behave toward relatives and neighbors . . .

You read almost nothing, and your experience of life is terribly shallow . . . You do not know how to live harmoniously with our neighbors, nor how to treat the aged with veneration, nor to show consideration to those in distress, nor to show compassion to those stricken with grief. You don't know how to reject those who would be bad examples for you, nor how to emulate those who are good. Neither do you know how to reciprocate those who are gracious to you, nor how to shun those who would do you harm . . . When you drink wine you don't know your limit. Your words on such occasions are wild and reckless, without either courtesy or forethought. When drunk, you act without regard for who is watching, and spend money heedless of what is reasonable and proper . . . You eat without proper etiquette, making yourself a laughingstock among polite society . . .

You fail to grasp the essentials of what is necessary to raise our family fortunes and status. Don't you understand that success in agriculture requires hard work—that raising farm animals requires feed and water, and raising crops requires planting and sowing? In the same way, raising children requires education and moral instruction. Our home must by kept clean and in good repair, the inner and outer must be kept segregated, and entering and leaving properly regulated. At nighttime, avoid gambling. In bountiful years, avoid extravagance. Avoid wasting time. Ensure that our hired workers are warm and well-fed, and that our household retainers are treated with compassion and respect . . .

In financial matters you must watch what other households do, and pay your taxes accordingly. Pay hired laborers according to the dictates of compassion. In every single matter you must match expenditures to income. You cannot give too much thought to this! You must always keep the improvement of family fortunes foremost in your mind, lay aside what will be needed to pay our taxes, and anticipate the possibility of harvest shortfalls. Always calculate for the long-term, not simply on the basis of present conditions![51]

According to local people, this kind of parental oversight was the formula for a family's, and the entire locality's, continued prosperity.

To further aid in this project, the Qing witnessed the full triumph of the type of kinship group known as the patrilineage—in older English-language sources often translated "clan"—as the major organizational device for local society. It was initially the outgrowth of a transformation in Chinese society during the Song dynasty that historians term the "localist turn." When the civil service examination replaced aristocratic preferment as the major vehicle for staffing the imperial bureaucracy, elites gradually responded by altering their marital practices, their identity, and their loyalties. Instead of intermarrying within a broad quasi-aristocratic empire-wide elite, they forged systematic marital alliances with other wealthy families within their own native place, and in the process established the interests of the locality as paramount in their consciousness. What emerged were tightly intermarried township or county-level lineages that either individually or collectively sought to patronize, protect, and dominate their native turf. The construction of local lineages of this sort took place over a long period of time but reached a frenzy during the Qing era, when these prominent families became the basic building blocks of local society.[52]

Why such a heavy emphasis at this particular time? One factor was intellectual. Following the wave of experimental free-thinking exemplified by Li Zhi and the social vogue of Buddhist and Daoist piety during the late Ming, the early Qing witnessed a zealous (and often competitive) return to Confucian orthodoxy. Whether this took the form of adhering to the prescriptions of the ancient Five Classics or the competing Four Books of the Song, lineage organization seemed to be a Confucian mandate. The elite's recoil from the social liberalism of the late Ming, along with the bloody class warfare that seemed to have been its outcome, led them to search for more effective means of imposing social discipline on their neighbors, and lineage-building provided one answer. But kinship organization was not merely a reactive or defensive social strategy, it was an aggressive one as well. The Qing consolidation, with its demographic explosion and economic boom, seemed to offer both greater competition for resources and enormous opportunities for advancement to those who had effective organizational means to secure them.

Though ostensibly based on biological descent, Qing lineages were by no means facts of nature: they were deliberately crafted human artifacts. The first act in their creation, usually on the part of a later-generation member who had made good economically or in official service, was to identify an older "founding ancestor"—often but not always the first forebear of the surname group who had moved into the family's present locale of residence. Precisely how far back in time one went to find this man, and how many of the branch lines of his descendents one chose to include in the organized lineage, was not specified, allowing for considerable flexibility in designing the parameters of membership. Not infrequently, lineages through some process of internal negotiation continually redefined these limits more broadly or more narrowly, depending on just whom they wanted to acknowledge as kinsmen.

Lineage leaders could be highly creative in selecting their founding ancestor, even postulating changes of surname along the way in order to stake their claim to prestigious origins.[53] Once the founder had been agreed upon, specific generational characters were assigned to each successive male generation: the character *hong*, for example, might be included in the given name of all males ten generations after the founder, the character *chuan* in all of the eleventh generation, and so on. A written genealogy was compiled, and often but not always professionally printed, to include the lineage's history, biographies of illustrious ancestors, a chart of all members in each generation, regulations to govern members' behavior, and often sitemaps and copies of title contracts for collective property. Finally, an ancestral hall was built to serve as lineage headquarters and locus of the annual ancestral sacrifice, at which time all members would be present and seated in finely differentiated hierarchical order.

Besides serving as an instrument for elites' control over their commoner neighbors, lineage organization offered many additional attractions. One was to diversify the membership geographically and occupationally. Though rooted in one locality, for example, lineages might choose to keep as members households who had migrated or sojourned to other areas, if having representation in that area appeared beneficial for commercial or other reasons. The ownership of collective property was another benefit of lineage organization. Although some very prominent lineages held little collective property beyond the ancestral hall itself, for others the lineage was important first and foremost as a vehicle for capital mobilization and management. In some Guangdong lineages, the lineage operated as an inheritance scheme equivalent to the European entail. To avoid the downward mobility of partible inheritance over successive generations, the lineage held title to virtually all the property of its member households, and shares in the collective, income-generating lineage estate rather than real property itself were divided by sons upon their father's death.

In many parts of the empire, lineage trusts were established to provide endowment income for maintenance of the ancestral hall and conduct of ancestral sacrifices, but very frequently their actual purposes went well beyond this. In some places they took the form of charitable estates that provided poor relief for indigent members of the lineage, or, in portions of the Yangzi delta, for the entire residential community regardless of surname.[54] In extreme cases such estates were established by multiple surname groups acting collectively. In the absence of an effective system of bank credit, lineage trusts were also probably the single most important means of mobilizing capital for large investments. With the lack of a limited liability incorporation law, these well-endowed funds usually did not operate businesses themselves but instead extended credit to individual entrepreneurs, usually members of the lineage.

In the eighteenth and nineteenth centuries, lineage trusts financed the capital-intensive reclamation of coastal rice paddy land in Guangdong's Pearl River delta and the very large and complex salt mining enterprises in southern Sichuan.[55] The trusts involved in operations such as these usually did not represent all members of the lineage but rather a specific group of investors who set aside capital in the name of a selected ancestor within the descent group (there could be many such trusts within a single lineage) and bought and sold shares in this trust much like any security within a modern capital market. Ancestral piety, in other words, acted with increasing transparency as moral cover for ideologically suspect speculative investments.

Qing officialdom held an ambivalent view of lineage organization. Because lineages were so supportive of the Confucian orthodoxy that was the bulwark of the imperial state's own legitimacy, they had to be applauded in theory; and in practice, regional officials often depended on lineages' charitable and even entrepreneurial activities to maintain the welfare and livelihoods of people in their jurisdiction. In some cases during the Yongzheng and early Qianlong reigns, provincial officials even delegated juridical authority to lineage headmen as a means of relieving the strain on county magistrates of excessive criminal proceedings. But lineage power was at best a mixed blessing. Left unchecked, lineages could bully or even enslave their neighbors, as they routinely did in Guangdong, or they could engage in escalatingly violent feuds with one another, as they did in Fujian. Their entrepreneurial activity could be counterproductive to the larger economy, as when one western Hubei lineage's collective reclamation of a riverine sandbar for a rice paddy led to calamitous flooding throughout the middle Yangzi valley.[56]

Sometimes descent groups simply grew too large for the central government's comfort, setting up multitownship or even multicounty higher-level lineage organizations, as they did in Jiangxi and Hunan. In such cases Qing officials might set aside their support for ancestral piety and break up kin groups, confiscating their collective assets on the grounds that the groups were not legitimate products of common descent but rather "unrelated households that happen to share a common surname."

Philanthropy

The Qing passion for founding lineages was but one manifestation of the remarkable wave of popular organization-building that characterized the early modern era in China. This was seen in new kinds of business enterprises, merchant and artisanal guilds, and native-place associations for sojourners. It encompassed revived scholarly academies, fraternal societies, and religious organizations spanning the gamut from orthodox to heterodox. All of these responded in their own ways to the greater competitiveness for scarce resources in a densely populated society, to the anomie generated by greater personal mobility and the Qing admixture of cultures, and also to the sense of opportunity afforded by the economic complexity of the times.

One of the most distinctive Qing-era expressions of the passion for organization-building was in the area of philanthropy.[57] Turning away from Buddhist and toward orthodox Confucian ideologies to underpin this activity, Qing society clearly articulated the concept of a "public" or "communal" sphere, as opposed to a "state" or "private" sphere, as both the agent and the beneficiary of philanthropic activism. Its increasingly sophisticated, depersonalized, and bureaucratized forms of charitable organization represented a shift in goals from moralistic or exemplary action to practical ministration to the manifestly serious needs of a growing and complex population.

Perhaps the pioneering model of local charitable activity, dating from the Ming but surviving into the early Qing, was the Buddhist *fangsheng hui,* an association formed to accord its members karmic merit by purchasing and liberating captive fish, birds, or other small animals. A more functionally expansive type of organization constructed on this model, which enjoyed a wide vogue during the late Ming especially in lower Yangzi commercial cities, was known as the benevolent society (*tongshan hui*). The expressed purpose of such societies was to minister to the moral well-being of their members, known as "friends of the association," rather than to cure the ills of the society as a whole, but they often took on such social missions as poor relief as a way to cultivate Buddhist or, increasingly, Confucian virtue.

With the return of competent government during the High Qing, the court vigorously sought to enter the arena of local charity. The Yongzheng emperor made mandatory in all counties the kinds of orphanages and poorhouses that had begun to appear on local initiative, and he also tried to standardize their activities. Though their finances might fall under the "public funding" entries in the county government's account ledgers, actual support came most often from private contributions or bequests rather than from fiscal collections. Though these organizations served a very real social need by providing poor relief, they made no attempt to take full responsibility for the local indigent population but instead tried to provide an official model of how private interests ought to act toward the less fortunate in their midst.

A new style of organization gradually emerged in the early nineteenth century that would come to be known generically as the benevolent hall (*shantang*). Unlike orphanages and poorhouses, these institutions were fundamentally nongovernmental organizations, though they were usually registered with the local administration. They emerged in commercial cities of the Yangzi valley and along the coast, first in the 1820s but with much greater frequency in the turbulent years of post-Taiping reconstruction. Financed and managed by local merchants and urban property-holders, benevolent halls originated in local firefighting associations, lifeboat agencies, and societies to gather and inter corpses found on city streets. They added to these functions others such as operating gruel kitchens (initially in the wake of floods or other natural calamities but increasingly during normal winters), dispensing medical aid, and in some localities sponsoring local peace-keeping militia.

Shantang were financed by scheduled subscriptions of their sponsors and by the proceeds from their endowment portfolios of urban rental properties. Management moved from voluntary service on the part of sponsors themselves into the hands of quasi-professionals. The benevolent halls' clear goal was to take care of all who needed their services so that the very profitable local commerce could function smoothly the growing presence of an underemployed class of urban poor. Although most benevolent halls took a specific neighborhood of the city as their operational horizon—frequently a neighborhood dominated by sojourners from a particular area of origin—in many cities they gradually worked out a means of mutually coordinating their activities and ultimately formed umbrella organizations on a municipality-wide level during the final decades of the century. This was Qing organization-building at its most impressive and dynamic.

5

COMMERCE

ALTHOUGH China's population has always been overwhelmingly comprised of farmers, and although China was long thought of in the West as the very model of an agrarian society, by the mid-Qing era it was possibly the most commercialized country in the world. Chinese elites who claimed to live the idealized gentleman-farmer life of "ploughing and reading" more often than not were subsidized by a family fortune made from trade. And Western self-professed "pioneers of commerce" who came to China in the nineteenth century thinking they were teaching the natives the virtues of exchange were simply deluding themselves.[1] Of course, the total amount of the empire's commerce increased with the rising volume of overseas trade from the sixteenth to the nineteenth centuries, and even more with Western mercantile penetration of inland cities following the Opium Wars. But this commerce never remotely approached the scale of the Qing empire's own vast and thriving domestic trade.

China's domestic trade developed well before the arrival of Westerners. If we can posit something like a "natural economy" of self-sufficiency as the norm in the early imperial period (this in itself may be something of a stretch), that economy can be divided into two fundamental periods of change. The first was the commercial revolution of the Song, from roughly the eleventh to the thirteenth century. This period saw long-distance interregional trade on a large scale, as well as the beginnings of an overseas trade with Southeast Asia. Improved transport routes (especially canals and other waterways) moved goods throughout China, causing large cities such as Hangzhou, whose *raison d'être* was commerce, to rise and flourish. A relatively small but very wealthy merchant class emerged to create innovative partnerships for capital mobilization. The Song commercial revolution was without a doubt a major transformation of the Chinese economy.

Still, it had significant limits. Interregional trade was largely in luxury goods, mostly produced and consumed by urbanites—silks, spices, medicinal herbs, and artistic manufactures such as porcelain, lacquerware, and metalware. As early as the Tang dynasty, there had been substantial movement of grain and other staples from the countryside to the city and from the fertile southeast region to the capital in the northwest, to feed a growing urban population, provision armies, and relieve shortages. But for the most part the shipment of staples was accomplished by commandist means—rents and taxes—rather than through vagaries of the commercial market.[2]

Draconian restrictions on trade, occupational activities, and geographic mobility imposed by the Ming founder in the late fourteenth century slowed the development of China's domestic trade considerably.[3] But from the mid-sixteenth century to the end of the eighteenth, the empire underwent a second commercial revolution even more transformative than the first.[4] This period saw the development of what historians sometimes call a "circulation economy" or "commodity economy" in which commercialization penetrated local rural society to an unprecedented degree. For the first time, a large percentage of China's farm households began to produce a significant percentage of their crop for sale and to rely on market exchange for items of daily consumption. Interregional trade included staple, low-cost-per-bulk items such as cotton, grain, beans, vegetable oils, forest products, animal products, and fertilizer. While most farm products continued to be consumed by their producers, by the end of the eighteenth century more than a tenth of the empire's grain, more than a quarter of its raw cotton, more than half of its cotton cloth, over nine-tenths of its raw silk, and nearly all of its tea was produced for sale in the marketplace.[5]

Regions began to specialize in particular export crops, the first perhaps being the lower Yangzi valley (Jiangnan), which focused on the cultivation of cotton. From a virtually unknown commodity in the early Ming, cotton became the most common clothing material throughout China by the late Qing. When Jiangnan could no longer produce enough to satisfy the market, cotton cultivation spread northward along the Grand Canal into Shandong and Hebei, then westward up the Yangzi into Hubei. The intense demand for grain in the Yangzi delta, which was formerly the empire's premier rice producer but was now suddenly a grain-deficit producer of cotton, opened the door for export-oriented commercial rice farming in other regions. The first to respond was Jiangxi's Gan River valley. When this region's production proved insufficient, the Xiang valley of Hunan farther upriver and eventually the Red Basin of Sichuan came to the rescue. By the 1730s, an estimated 1 to 1.5 billion pounds (8 to 13 million *shi*) of rice moved down the Yangzi into Jiangnan every year.[6] From the perspective of the new middle-Yangzi port of Hankou, which in the seventeenth century became the central entrepôt in this massive interregional trade, we can see scores of other bulk commodities moving great distances throughout the empire: tea from Hunan and Fujian, salt from Anhui, medicinal herbs from Sichuan, timber and lacquer from the southwest, millet and hemp from the northeast, hides and tobacco from the northwest, and sugar, marine products, and other semitropical foodstuffs from the southeast.[7]

This second commercial transformation came about as a logical progression from the first one, whose inception point in the late Tang and Song had been the Yangzi delta. In fits and starts, commercialization spread out from there to the rest of the empire. During the late Ming, the state's declining ability to enforce its earlier anticommercial policies—coupled with actively pro-trade innovations, such as a sixteenth-century program that rewarded merchants with salt monopoly franchises and other commercial benefits in return for shipping food and war matériel to troops on the beleaguered northern frontiers—laid the groundwork for rapid further commercial development under the Qing. The new regime actively promoted the efficiency of markets by abrogating statutes against personal mobility, enforcing commercial contracts and property rights, and eliminating cartels (*bachi*) and other restraints on the maximum circulation of goods.

But perhaps the most important factor in the second commercial revolution was the sudden influx, via Manila, of massive amounts of silver shipped from the New World mines of Oaxaca and Potosí in Mexico. The empire had gradually shifted to the silver standard in the mid-Ming and incrementally adopted the so-called Single Whip tax reforms. The key feature of this complex set of fiscal policies, which culminated in the late Kangxi reign, was the assessment and collection of the land tax in silver. Needing cash to pay their taxes, landlords began to demand rent payments in cash as well, and this in turn gave tenant farmers a powerful incentive to shift to crops grown for cash sale rather than personal consumption or barter.

Entrepreneurial Innovation and Urbanization

In the typical form of land ownership in late imperial China—rentier landlordism—a proprietor with more arable land than he could cultivate efficiently using household labor would lease small plots to tenant-farmer households. But where the land was adaptable to cultivation of cash crops and markets were accessible, some larger landholders increasingly opted not to subdivide their property into household-scale tenant farms but instead to manage their entire estate as a profit-driven agro-enterprise. An obvious comparison would be to cotton and tobacco plantations in the antebellum American South, except that Chinese plantations were operated by wage workers rather than slaves, which meant that their profitability was dependent on the growing availability of free, mobile labor.

This sort of managerial landlordism probably first developed in the lower Yangzi during the seventeenth century, but the best documented cases have been drawn from the northern stretches of the Grand Canal in western Shandong and eastern Hebei, where commercial cotton cultivation began to boom in the late eighteenth century. Here, entrepreneurial planters were able to take advantage of the cheap freight rates offered by grain-tribute boats on their return trip south to profitably sell raw cotton to spinners and weavers in Jiangnan.[8] How widespread this capitalist-style agriculture became in the course of the Qing is subject to debate—it clearly never displaced rentierism as the more customary practice. And even in north China where managerial landlordism incontestably emerged, constraints imposed by the quality of land and the practical limits of personal supervision kept the number of landholders who could afford to farm this way to a small number.[9]

In the refining and processing of these newly expanding cash crops, however, the first century and a half of the Qing dynasty saw an explosion of handicraft goods. Most of this artisanal production—the spinning and weaving of cotton and silk textiles, for example—was probably accomplished as a sideline occupation of rural cultivators. Yet a small but increasing share was undertaken by larger-scale handicraft workshops using wage or piecework labor. Suzhou in the mid-eighteenth century, for instance, hosted 33 papermaking workshops and no fewer than 450 textile dyeshops, averaging upward of two dozen workers apiece under a single entrepreneur. As Marxist historians would stress, these enterprises were "sprouts of capitalism" and those who worked there represented the beginning of the Chinese urban proletariat.[10]

Capitalist enterprise took hold perhaps most dramatically in the area of mining. In the first half of the eighteenth century a boom in copper and related monetary metals began in the pioneer regions of Yunnan and Guizhou and spread to other provinces. The reluctant Yongzheng and Qianlong courts, persuaded by the consumer economy's demand for copper cash, overcame their fears of proletarianized, family-less, rowdy miners and progressively allowed merchants to open new and larger mines. Lacking bank credit or an established company law but building on a highly refined regime of property rights and legally enforceable written contracts, these entrepreneurs developed innovative means to raise capital and expand their scale of operations. By the eighteenth century in the environs of Beijing, for example, operators of coal mines had devised a system of financing that looked a great deal like the sale of common stock. Merchants operating salt mines in southern Sichuan mobilized capital through lineage trusts, set up partnerships of great scale and flexibility, created professionalized management bureaus to oversee diverse operations, and, mostly through interlocking investments, achieved considerable vertical integration of various stages of production and interregional marketing.[11]

One of the most significant effects of the second commercial revolution was urbanization. Imperial China had always had very large cities that doubled as regional administrative centers and military garrisons. In the middle period these were joined by large commercial metropolises such as Hangzhou, which Marco Polo in the thirteenth century claimed was larger than his native Venice. But both types of city were very much urban islands in a rural sea. There were very few small or mid-sized cities to mediate between the large metropolises and the countryside. Smaller urban places were not really necessary since extraction of rural surplus to feed the cities had historically not been accomplished by commercial but by government means. But in the late Ming and early to mid-Qing, as rural-urban economic exchange became more marketized and larger amounts of produce flowed through the channels of domestic trade, a more fully fleshed-out hierarchy of towns and cities grew up in most regions to manage the exchange of goods between the countryside and the great metropolises. Beijing, Suzhou, Guangzhou, Nanjing, and Wuchang

were probably no larger in the Qing than they had been under the Song—
the real action of urbanization was taking place elsewhere.

As periodic markets in the countryside proliferated and intensified
their schedules, some gradually promoted themselves into genuine market towns. The more active of these became multifunctional small cities,
mediating between the market towns and the larger regional cities above
them.[12] This hierarchy was most pronounced in Jiangnan, which by the
eighteenth century was an urban region not unlike Tuscany or the Low
Countries in the early modern era or the Northeast Corridor in the United
States today. No rural household was more than a day's travel from a
town of considerable size. Other regions of the empire saw similar developments, including Guangdong's Pearl River delta, Sichuan's Red Basin,
and Hunan's Xiang River valley, among others. In the Xiang valley's rice-
exporting Xiangtan county, for example, the number of recorded market
towns grew from three in 1685 to more than a hundred in 1818.[13]

These new market towns and small commercial cities developed a distinctive culture of their own, part of a broader bourgeois identity and
consciousness. Their street plans grew more complex, with whole streets
devoted to specific trades. Merchants frequented the town's teahouses,
side by side with shop clerks and artisans, to hear recitations of the martial and romantic stories they loved. But the *nouveaux riches* merchants
did not abandon aspirations to join the literati elite nor neglect classical
education for their sons: the silk town of Nanxun in Zhejiang, for instance, produced no fewer than 58 upper degree holders, as well as 69
purchasers of lower degrees, in the first century or so of Qing rule.[14]

The Conduct of Trade

The commercial marketing hierarchy of late imperial China was divided
into some ten macroregions, as G. William Skinner has demonstrated
(Map 5).[15] Within each macroregion the urban system was more integrated and coherent than it was over the empire as a whole, and the flow
of commercial goods, along with the movement of people and information, was considerably more intense. Still, interregional trade grew remarkably, especially during the prosperous High Qing. Urban hierarchies
within the macroregions largely shaped the flow of this trade. That is,
goods moving from a relatively peripheral portion of one macroregion to
a relatively peripheral area of another would move up the collection hierarchy of the producing region, be shipped to the regional metropolis of

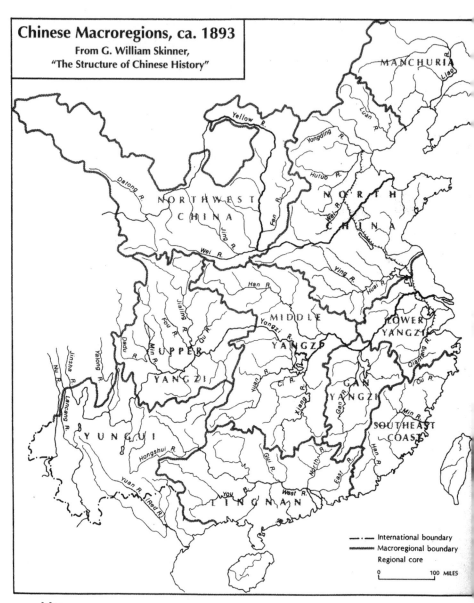

Chinese Macroregions, ca. 1893
From G. William Skinner,
"The Structure of Chinese History"

MANCHURIA

Liao R.

Yellow R.

Luan R.

Yongding R.

NORTHWEST
CHINA

Datong R.

Fen R.

Jing R.

NORTH
CHINA

Hutuo R.

Wei R.

Wei R.

Ying R.

Han R.

Huai R.

Yangzi R.

MIDDLE
YANGZI

LOWER
YANGZI

Jialing R.

Fou R.

Ou R.

UPPER
YANGZI

Dadu R.

MIN

Yalong R.

Yuan R.

Ci R.

Xiang R.

GAN
YANGZI

Gan R.

Qiantang R.

Ou R.

Jinsha R.

Nu R.

Lancang R.

YUNGUI

Hongshui R.

Gui R.

North R.

East R.

Han R.

Min R.

SOUTHEAST
COAST

Yuan R. (Red R.)

You R.

LINGNAN

West R.

—·—· International boundary
━━━ Macroregional boundary
Regional core

0   100 MILES

MAP 5

the consuming region, and then be distributed downward to the consumption areas via that region's own marketing hierarchy.[16]

The intensification of China's domestic commerce brought with it the
growth of an unprecedentedly large class of professional merchants (Fig.
11). Like the marketing system itself, the roles assumed by these mer-

Fig. 11   A Chinese merchant and his family, 1860–64. Photograph by Milton
M. Miller. Courtesy of Peabody Essex Museum, Salem, Massachusetts.

chants were both regionally and hierarchically differentiated. Goods passing from local producers to local consumers would not be carried by a
single merchant but would pass through a very large number of hands.
Different merchants tended to carry goods between each separate point
upward in the hierarchy of extraction and downward in the hierarchy of
distribution. Some of these merchants were merely commission agents,
but many of them bought and sold goods on their own account.

The unusually diffuse character of Qing interregional trade had both
positive and negative effects on commerce. The fact that so many separate merchants were able to enter the trade with a low level of capitalization and handle shipments of job lots over short distances must
have helped to stimulate the economy. The wide distribution of profits
contributed to the ease of entry by petty merchants and to the continued
expansion of the domestic market. On the other hand, the need for continual price markups at each stage of the collection process, as well as
the problem of quality control in a system where the urge to adulterate
goods prior to each change of ownership was nearly irrepressible, reduced the competitiveness of Chinese commodities at just the time when

they were being forced to compete—on the domestic as well as international market—with Indian cotton, Japanese tea, Ceylonese silk, and American tobacco. As long as the Qing's long-distance trade was contained within a relatively closed system, its diffuse character worked to positive effect; but when Chinese merchants entered the global economy, this asset became a liability.

The big boys in domestic interregional trade were the large wholesale merchants who handled the longest leg of the commodity's journey from producer to consumer—the one between the major metropolises of the producing and consuming macroregions. Very seldom did they penetrate a regional economy below this level. When foreigners began to participate directly in this trade—at Guangzhou in the eighteenth century and at Shanghai, Hankou, Tianjin, and other ports during the nineteenth—they simply added yet one more layer to the extraction network, inserting themselves at the top—the transoceanic stage of transport. But like Chinese interregional shippers, they seldom ventured personally below the major city level or disrupted existing intraregional merchant hierarchies.[17]

Large-scale wholesale merchants did, however, exert indirect control over the regional production and extraction network in a given commodity through the system of pre-purchase. Capital advances were issued by the interregional merchant to his suppliers at the regional metropolis prior to the growing season, in exchange for first rights to buy the produce when it came to the market. Often this cash advance would be reissued downward at each stage of the collection hierarchy, ultimately allowing the producer to acquire seeds or to subsist through the growing season. When Westerners entered this trade at the top, they too participated in the downward flow of credit and capital, eventually through foreign banks. Western "economic imperialism" and its associated economic dependency simply represented an expansion of processes familiar from the pre-existing domestic interregional trade.

To guarantee the good faith of their trading partners at each stage of the hierarchy, Chinese merchants relied above all on *guanxi* (connections), ties based on extended kinship or a common local origin. Although there were many such diasporic local-origin groups, in the eighteenth century the pre-eminent merchants throughout the empire were those from Huizhou prefecture (Anhui) and Shanxi province. In the nineteenth century they were joined and eventually eclipsed by groups from

Ningbo (Zhejiang) and Guangzhou, with long-cultivated ties in the overseas trade.

"Guest merchants" united by bonds of common native place fanned
out into targeted host regions to concentrate on developing a specific
commodity for extra-regional marketing. This "internal colonialism"
sometimes led to intense conflict with local populations. In 1819, for example, riots broke out against Jiangxi rice exporters in the Hunanese
river port of Xiangtan.[18] For the most part, however, the commodity-spe-
cific nature of this "colonization," as well as the complex layering and
overlap of merchant diasporas, tended to blunt the locals' sense of exploitation.

At major entrepôts where merchants of differing scales or of differing
local origins met to exchange commodities, commercial relations were
mediated by brokers. Transcending the barriers of local dialect, these
men brought together buyers and sellers, guaranteed the good faith of
both parties, standardized weights and measures and transactional procedures, collected indirect commercial taxes for the government, and
operated warehouses, stables, and inns. As early as the medieval commercial revolution in the ninth century, oversight of the market in individual commodities had begun to pass from market bureaucrats to
groups of private merchants operating as quasi-agents of the imperial
government.[19] As these guilds took on distinctive forms in the late imperial period, they began to assume a new prominence on the urban landscape. Going by a variety of names (*bang, hang, gongsuo*) and constituted along a variety of membership criteria (usually some combination
of common trade and common local origin), they were increasingly ubiquitous in commercial towns both large and small, where they served different purposes depending on the economic setting.

The rise of the guild to a position of dominance within the empire's domestic trade was a key distinguishing feature of Qing commerce. The first
recorded founding of a guild in the interregional entrepôt of Hankou was
in 1656. Published collections of guild documents from Beijing, Suzhou,
Foshan (near Guangzhou), Chongqing, and Shanghai testify to a wave of
guildhall construction, solicitation by guilds of official recognition, and
issuance of regulatory codes and price schedules in the early Qing.[20]
Something qualitatively new seems to have been going on: interregional
domestic trade had become so routinized by the early eighteenth century
that permanent and tightly organized communities of sojourning mer-

chants from various localities were now required in all major imperial cities, transforming these cities into intensely cosmopolitan, multicultural, market-driven, consumer-oriented centers of urban life.

By the nineteenth century, guilds were powerful forces in urban society in a wide variety of areas outside the economic arena. They staged theatrical performances, particularly operas from their native region, that were open to the broader population. Like lineage trusts, they became major landlords and real estate developers, and alongside the well-endowed benevolent halls they became entrepreneurs in philanthropy and other social services. For example, in the Manchurian treaty port of Yingkou in the 1880s, an alliance of major merchant guilds collected taxes on shops and transactions, imposed tolls on bridges, and managed the local grain and money markets. They used the proceeds in part to maintain the city's streets, water supply, drainage and sewage facilities, and a wide range of welfare and relief operations.[21]

Not long ago, leading Western scholars—taking at face value Confucian prescriptions for the primacy of agriculture and the moral contamination of profit-seeking—argued that the Qing administration, far from encouraging commerce, treated merchants with contempt and routinely adopted policies knowingly injurious to trade.[22] Few scholars today would see things that way. The Aisin Gioro and their allies in the preconquest northeast had, after all, risen to power precisely on the profits of their mercantile activities. Unlike their Ming predecessors, whose commandist policies eventually broke down, creating a vacuum that market forces moved in to fill, the Qing from the outset was committed to active promotion of the *minsheng* (popular livelihoods). Its mushrooming population demanded that the government nurture all sectors of the economy, and as a result the Qing was more energetically solicitous of trade than nearly any of China's preceding empires.

Rulers and bureaucrats alike strove to realize the potential of the empire's natural resources and human productive capacities, while leaving the surplus in societal rather than governmental hands—a notion expressed in the oft-repeated formula "store wealth among the people." To the extent possible they sought to uphold the principles of maximum circulation of commercial goods and of commodity pricing by market means alone. They shunned commandist policies such as price-fixing, acknowledging the existence of Heavenly-mandated laws of commerce that state fiat could not reverse. And, at least within limits, they viewed mercantile profit-seeking as a manifestation of Heavenly-endowed human rationality. This by no means suggested that the state should avoid intervention in the market to achieve imperial purposes and the public good, but the government most often chose to do this by working through, rather than against, market forces (the ever-normal granary system was a prime example). Officials regularly labored to develop new sectors of the empire's commercial economy by offering incentive packages for prospective entrepreneurs (*zhaoshang*) in areas targeted for development.[23]

This positive attitude toward the operation of the market in the mid-Qing was summed up by no less conservative a Neo-Confucian than the eminent scholar Fang Bao (1668–1749): "In general, as soon as merchants have converged on a place where the . . . price is soaring, that price is bound to fall off somewhat. Once the price has fallen off somewhat in one place, the merchants will vie to betake themselves elsewhere. If one lets them do as suits themselves, the circulation will be that much swifter."[24] Fang was speaking of the long-distance domestic trade, not the empire's overseas trade, and the consensus he expressed on the positive virtues of the circulation economy did not necessarily extend to foreign commerce. But by his later years foreign trade was rapidly gaining in importance, and it too had its advocates.

The Tribute Trade

Until very recently, our governing model of the way late imperial China conducted both its international diplomacy and foreign trade was the scheme laid out by John King Fairbank and his collaborators in a seminal 1968 book entitled *The Chinese World Order*.[25] According to this view, the human world was seen by the Chinese as "All under Heaven" and, since the Chinese emperor was the Son of Heaven, he was the mediator between the first legitimating principle of the universe and all human beings; hence he was their true governor. China was the Middle Kingdom (*Zhongguo*), the *axis mundi,* and the cultural practices of the Chinese elite were the universal norms of civilization. Those peoples who lived around the fringes of the Middle Kingdom were all, in some form, barbarians.

This distinction was not (or not primarily) racial but cultural: all barbarians could, and in time inevitably would, become civilized (or assimilated), after sufficiently long exposure to enlightening Chinese influence. Indeed, some had already become more civilized than others. These more civilized, or "cooked" (*shu*) barbarians, including the Koreans, the Vietnamese, and at certain times the Japanese, had adopted such Chinese cultural practices as sedentary agriculture, patrilineal and patrilocal family systems, proper burial of the dead, proper cooking and eating of food (with chopsticks), and familiarity with the Chinese written language. These traits made them capable of governing themselves through monarchical bureaucratic regimes, though their kings would have to be approved and invested by the Chinese Son of Heaven. Less civilized, or "raw" (*sheng*) barbarians, such as the various tribal peoples of the southwest, at times the Japanese, and perhaps the Europeans, still had a long way to go and required yet more condescending treatment.

Regularized diplomatic contact was maintained between the Chinese court and its bordering polities, but on a footing of systematic inequality and hegemony. Only the Chinese language and Chinese calendar were used in diplomatic exchanges, and the rhetoric expressed abject deference toward the empire. There were no permanent resident ambassadors in either direction, but the peripheral states routinely sent embassies to China, where they were required to prostrate themselves obsequiously ("kowtow") before the throne. In addition, vassal states acknowledged their subordinate status by sending annual tribute to the Chinese court, which consisted of native products in stipulated quantities, following stipulated schedules and routes, and magnanimously reciprocated by (presumably infinitely more valuable) imperial bequests of Chinese goods. As Fairbank saw it, the Qing sought to fit all foreigners, Europeans and Americans included, into this "tribute system" (*chaogong tizhi*).

On top of the prescribed items and quantities of tribute goods, tribute missions were graciously allowed to carry modest additional amounts of commercial goods, which they might exchange with designated Chinese merchants at the port of trade to which each tributary nation was individually assigned (presumably to protect the bulk of the empire's domestic population from contamination by foreign contact or commercial impulses). There was of course ample opportunity to stretch the boundaries of this arrangement, as both Chinese and foreign merchants hungry for profits exceeded the numbers of missions and the quantity and variety of goods allowable under the regulations. On occasion, enterprising foreign merchants might even appear bearing tribute from wholly invented polities or regimes, so as to claim a share of the lucrative China trade. The Chinese court could not have been so naive that it failed to see how the prescribed arrangements were being manipulated for private gain, but in general it was content to insist that the formalities of this so-called tribute-trade system were honored by all participants. In Fairbank's view (elaborated in far greater detail by the Japanese historian Hamashita Takeshi), this tribute-trade institution governed the entirety of the late Chinese empire's international exchange, along with that of the entire East Asian region.[26]

This Chinese World Order model implied that China was isolationist, xenophobic, incapable of adapting to a nation-state system based on mutual sovereignty and respect, and fundamentally bound by the demands of culture and ritual rather than responsive to pragmatic national interest. Identifying tribute-trade as the basis of China's foreign commerce implied that China stubbornly disparaged free trade and the profit motive, which—the model confidently assumed—were forces of rationality and progress. Most insidiously, as indicated by Fairbank's subtitle, this stagnant and inflexible culture subsumed not just the Qing but all of "Traditional China."[27]

In the decades after its most forceful enunciation, however, Western historians of China, including Fairbank's own students, gradually became uncomfortable with the eurocentric bias of the Chinese World Order model and had difficulty squaring it with empirical investigations of the historical record. For example, they showed how extradition and border control between the Qing and neighbors such as Korea and Vietnam were handled based on a model of coequal sovereign states, and how early Qing relations with the Portuguese and Dutch involved motives of *realpolitik* on the part of the Chinese.[28] The tribute-trade mode was not necessarily wrong, but it was certainly overdetermined, and historians continue to sort out precisely where it is valid and where it is not.

The reality of the tribute-trade system was far more historically contingent than the Chinese World Order model allowed. Trade had been conducted in association with the payment of tribute as far back as the Han dynasty. But over the millennia, tribute-related commerce had made up only a very small percentage of the empire's overall foreign trade. The Ming founder Zhu Yuanzhang, however, sought to make state-monopolized tribute trade the sole avenue of Sino-foreign exchange. Mindful of the economic necessity of some foreign trade but politically wary of both foreigners and Chinese merchants, Zhu in the 1370s and 1380s coupled his increasingly strident prohibitions on private maritime navigation (the so-called sea ban) with solicitous promotion of the tribute-trade channel. By the early fifteenth century it had become in fact the primary conduit for China's overall foreign trade.

But the tribute-trade system had already lost its dominant position a century or more before the Qing conquest. Not only did it prove impossible to suppress all smuggling, but the cost of maintaining the tribute-trade system itself became a growing burden on state treasuries. When the Portuguese showed up along the southeast coast in the early 1500s, the court initially sought to approach their commercial dealings under the tribute-trade rubric, but within a few decades this had proven to be infeasible. Over the course of the sixteenth century, the Ming court tacitly allowed the Portuguese to occupy the Macau peninsula in southern Guangdong and establish it as a center of private trade, and also, through a process of fits and starts, opened the Fujianese port of Yuegang to officially supervised private maritime trade by Chinese merchants. Still, these were viewed as mere concessions of convenience to the reality of a flourishing foreign trade still legally channeled through the tribute-trade system.

It was left to the Qing to abandon once and for all Zhu Yuanzhang's quixotic and historically anomalous trade policy. A year after his decisive victory over the Zheng Chenggong regime on Taiwan in 1683, the Kangxi emperor declared his own sea ban and coastal evacuation program at an end. Invoking the interests of both state finance and popular livelihoods, he dramatically proclaimed the opening of all coastal ports to private—though licensed and regulated—maritime trade and established a network of customs stations to collect taxes. The tribute system as an organizing device for intra-Asian diplomatic relations remained in place, but Kangxi reduced its economic significance to virtually nil. Foreign polities that legally enjoyed tributary status were encouraged to decrease the goods exchanged with the Qing through tribute missions and to increase the levels of trade outside this channel. After 1684, a larger and growing percentage of the empire's maritime trade was conducted with nations such as the Portuguese and eventually the English who had never held or sought the status of tributaries. Private Chinese maritime trade not only flourished but did so legally and openly.[29]

A comparable development occurred in the Qing's overland commerce with its continental trading partners. The Ming had cultivated tributary relations with various Mongol regimes and with Tibet, and the Qing, which had begun to do the same well before the conquest, inherited these relationships. Tribute trade accompanied these embassies to Beijing, and during the Ming the sheep, horses, camels, spices, and textiles it brought were of real economic significance. In the sixteenth century the Ming also

established border markets to handle overflow trade with Inner Asian societies, but, in keeping with its general goal of making tribute-trade the
central channel of foreign commerce, its commitment to these markets
was inconstant, and when they became disturbingly active the Ming shut
them down.

Over its first century, the Qing, by contrast, worked progressively to
segregate Inner Asian trade from tribute, making the latter a purely sym-
bolic expression of vassalage and diplomacy. In 1683—a year before
he lifted the maritime ban—Kangxi ordered the diversion of a growing
number of Beijing-bound tribute traders to the border markets, where
they were to conduct a deritualized exchange. Two years later he issued
the first of successive edicts (others followed in 1702 and 1713) strictly
limiting the amount of goods that Inner Asian tribute missions could
carry to the imperial capital. This by no means indicated a Qing devalua-
tion of the Inner Asian trade; indeed, the court established a new string of
border markets in Ningxia in 1689, and many more over the following
years, to encourage private (though regulated) trade. In the continental as
in the maritime world, by the early eighteenth century the *tribute system*
remained in place and *private foreign trade* was actively promoted, but
tribute trade had become little more than a historical relic.[30]

During the four decades following Kangxi's open trade edicts of 1684,
well over a thousand Chinese merchant vessels called at Nagasaki, ply-
ing routes between there, the China coast, and various Southeast Asian
ports, according to a recently discovered Japanese documentary collection.[31] But this, of course, was nothing very new. The Chinese diaspora
throughout Southeast Asia had roots stretching back at least to the Tang
dynasty. By the late Ming, sizable Chinese colonies had sprouted up
throughout the region, and expansion continued rapidly throughout the
early Qing. European colonization of Southeast Asia in the early modern
era was an active stimulus to Chinese emigration there, as Hokkienese
and Cantonese, united by ties of a common dialect and linked by personal networks back to the mainland, successfully carved out niches in
the colonial economy as maritime carriers and as middlemen between native populations and their European overlords or (as in Siam) indigenous
royal houses.[32]

By 1639 approximately 33,000 Chinese lived in Manila. Genocidal riots in that year cut it by more than half, but the population recovered quickly. An expatriate Chinese community was already present in
Batavia (Jakarta) when the town was formally founded by the Dutch

in 1619. The Chinese engaged primarily in sugar planting and export, which Dutch authorities governed indirectly through Chinese merchant-headmen. Over the seventeenth century, the Chinese community set up temples, cemeteries, schools, and hospitals to minister to its needs, centrally organized by a quasi-chamber of commerce known as the Kong Koan. In 1740 an ethnic pogrom claimed the lives of over 8,000 Chinese, but by the nineteenth century the population was many times this number.[33]

In 1717 the Kangxi emperor became alarmed at the potential for Qing subjects to travel abroad and involve themselves in subversive activities. He was particularly concerned lest Chinese accept official service under other states or regimes, as had Batavia's Chinese headmen. He therefore imposed strict limits on the amount of time merchants and their families could spend overseas, forbade repatriation to any who exceeded these limits, and ordered Chinese currently residing in Nanyang (Southeast Asia) to return within three years or forfeit their right of return forever. Officials along the southeast coast, mindful of the importance of the maritime trade to their region and acknowledging the need for prolonged sojourns abroad, consistently dragged their feet in enforcing these provisions. In 1727 they prevailed upon the Yongzheng emperor to allow overseas sojourns of two years, and in 1742 Qianlong added a grace period of a year. In 1754 the court made the entire issue of foreign residence and return a matter of provincial discretion, after which enforcement in most cases became a dead letter.[34]

Foreigners in China

Europeans were physically present in the early and mid-Qing empire in modest but hardly negligible numbers. Most prominent during the seventeenth century were Jesuit missionaries.[35] In 1601, the remarkable Italian Jesuit Matteo Ricci (Li Madou, 1552–1610) secured permission to establish a permanent Jesuit residence in Beijing and traded on his expertise in Western astronomy, mathematics, and engineering to become a favorite of the Ming court. Highly accomplished in classical Chinese, Ricci's writings had a significant impact on late Ming literati culture. *On Friendship* (*Jiaoyou lun*, 1595)—a compilation of Western writings from Cicero and others—expanded Neo-Confucian notions of personal relationships and helped provide an ideological underpinning for late Ming reformist factionalism.[36] *The True Meaning of the Lord of Heaven* (*Tianzhu shiyi*), a highly sinicized introduction to basic Christian doctrine, helped convert several high officials. Most famous among these was Xu Guangqi (1562–1633), the Shanghai-born agronomist, reform leader, and, in the last years of his life, grand secretary.

The Jesuit impact diminished somewhat during the early Qing, both at court and among the literati, but did not disappear. Translations of Western scripture into Manchu, with its phonetic script, were easier for European proselytizers than translations into Chinese, and proliferated accordingly. The German Johann Adam Schall von Bell (Tang Ruowang, 1592–1666), the Belgian Ferdinand Verbiest (Nan Huairen, 1623–1688), the Portuguese Tomé Pereira (Xu Moude, 1645–1708), and the Neapolitan artist-priest Matteo Ripa (Ma Guozhen, 1682–1746) were all in their day favorites at court. The Shunzhi emperor reportedly came very close to Christian conversion himself, while the more skeptical Kangxi was deeply intrigued by Jesuit science and liked to show off publicly what he had learned of this. The brilliant Jesuit painter Giuseppe Castiglione (Lang Shining, 1688–1766) served and painted every emperor from Kangxi to Qianlong. He also helped design the Western mansions (*Xiyang lou*) in the Summer Palace, north of Beijing, a series of buildings, fountains, and labyrinths in grand Italian baroque style.

But problems quickly developed. In 1664 anti-Christian officials at court, alarmed by the apparent influence the Jesuits had exerted over the recently deceased Shunzhi emperor, accused Schall of having caused the emperor's death, along with that of his favorite consort, by having chosen—in his capacity as head of the Bureau of Astronomy—an inauspicious day for the burial of their infant son. The following year Schall, who in the interim had become paralyzed by a stroke, was sentenced to a lingering death; however, when an earthquake the next day convinced the court of Heaven's displeasure with this verdict, he was released. Nevertheless, most Christian churches in the capital were closed down. Then, around 1720, Ripa's public closeness with the several Chinese boys whom he recruited as acolytes left him open to charges of sodomy.

But perhaps the most serious problem besetting Catholic missionaries at the early Qing court was their own sectarian infighting. Many members of other orders, including Ripa, hated the Jesuits and bitterly resented their prestige. This enmity in part contributed to the so-called rites controversy. Ricci and his Jesuit successors held Confucian culture in high regard and hoped to accommodate Christian belief with it as much as possible. In their earliest translations from Christian texts, for example, they used such familiar Chinese names as *Shangdi* (Lord on High) and *Tian* (Heaven) to render the Christian term God. Moreover, they argued that sacrifice to ancestors and to Confucius were not idolatrous rituals but civil ceremonies and thus need not be prohibited to Christian converts. Other Catholics disagreed, and in a series of decisions over the course of the early eighteenth century the papacy was persuaded to declare Jesuit "accommodationism" heretical. This fatally undercut the position of the Christian order that had labored most lengthily and strenuously to win elite approval in China.

Toward the end of his reign, Kangxi himself became increasingly suspicious of the Christian presence in the provinces and issued several prohibitions against missionary activity. Beset by a growing number of disturbances on the part of White Lotus and millenarian Buddhist sects, with whom the Christians shared an apocalyptic vision and a congregational solidarity against the outside world of nonbelievers, the Yongzheng emperor in the early 1720s conflated the two and strengthened his father's ban on foreign missions outside of Beijing and Guangzhou. Foreign priests were to be treated respectfully but expelled; Christian churches were to be appropriated for use as local public offices or reconsecrated to orthodox deities such as the Empress of Heaven (Tianhou). This policy went hand in hand with Yongzheng's more general campaign to "civilize" local religious practice and establish an infrastructure of community rituals more acceptable to the state.[37]

The Qianlong emperor conducted periodic anti-Christian campaigns throughout the 1740s and 1750s, with some success. According to one estimate, the number of Roman Catholics throughout China declined from around 300,000 at the start of the eighteenth century to 200,000 by century's end. Some 40,000 of these were concentrated in southeastern Sichuan, where the religion had spawned, among other things, a marriage-resistance movement among Chinese women known as the Institute of Christian Virgins. While the Catholic communities in Sichuan and elsewhere were fully indigenized, foreign missionaries continued to traverse the empire and visit congregations sporadically. From their base in Macau, for example, the Franciscans routinely sent Portuguese and Italian priests to their well-developed network of underground missions in Sichuan, Hunan, Shaanxi, Shandong, and Zhili. Suddenly discovering this network in 1784 and suspicious of its links to an Islamic uprising in Shaanxi and Gansu that his armies had only recently suppressed, Qianlong launched a ten-month dragnet that arrested some nineteen foreign missionaries along with dozens of Chinese priests.[38]

If no Chinese Christian convert during the Qing was quite as eminent and influential as Xu Guangqi in the late Ming, such individuals were not altogether absent. One was Wei Yijie (1616–1686), a censor and eventually grand secretary from Zhili who combined his private Christian faith with a more publicly championed Confucian moral fervor associated with the late seventeenth-century "Song learning" revival. Another was Depei (1688–1752), a Manchu imperial prince who earned a reputation as a model provincial official in Huguang, Fujian, and the lower Yangzi. Active in the years following the Yongzheng proscriptions of the 1720s, Depei practiced his religion in secret, combining it with a devotion to Western missionary science. To certain searching minds among the empire's upper elite, the foreign faith clearly retained a highly selective and individual appeal.

The Canton System

For Westerners, personal access to most parts of the Qing empire was dramatically restricted during the early eighteenth century by the ban on missionary proselytizing and was further diminished by the imposition of the so-called "Canton system" governing Sino-Western trade.[39] In 1685, immediately upon his legalization of private maritime commerce along most of the empire's coast, Kangxi established a network of maritime customs stations in major coastal ports. Each arriving vessel had to register at the customs house and pay duty on its cargo prior to sale. The station at Canton (Guangzhou) quickly became one of the most active and was known to the Europeans as the Hoppo, apparently out of a mistaken impression that it was an agency of the Board of Revenue (Hubu) at Beijing (though in fact, like all the other customs stations, it was directly subordinate to the Imperial Household Department).

Chinese mercantile houses that specialized in dealing with foreign traders quickly proliferated in Canton, numbering more than forty by the late Kangxi reign. In 1725 the Yongzheng emperor made the umbrella organization to which these merchants belonged, known to foreigners as the Cohong, legally responsible for policing the trade. While simultaneously moving to confine all Christian missionary activity outside the capital to Canton, Yongzheng apparently considered restricting the Sino-foreign commerce to that port as well but was persuaded against doing so by provincial officials in Fujian and elsewhere, who saw foreign trade as essential to their own jurisdictions' livelihoods. International commerce as a whole continued to grow steadily, without significant incident.

The Canton system was the outcome of three separate decisions on the part of Yongzheng's successor, the Qianlong emperor. In 1757 the court announced that Canton would thereafter be the sole port open for Western trade with the Qing empire. Second, the court endorsed the security-merchant system, which had been in place since about 1745 at the initiative of local Cantonese authorities, under which each arriving Western vessel was guaranteed and overseen by a Chinese merchant house. Finally, in 1760 the court issued a detailed set of regulations prescribing the allowable times during the year that foreign "barbarians" could call in China, where they might be permitted to reside while there, and with whom they might trade. Foreign wives and dependents were prohibited altogether from accompanying their spouses to China, and the merchants' personal mobility was extremely limited.[40]

The Qianlong court instituted these restrictions in part as a legal acknowledgment of what had been going on in practice anyway. Western traders had "voted with their feet" to make Canton the dominant port of Sino-Western trade: though other ports up the coast such as Zhejiang's Ningbo and Fujian's Xiamen had been active sites of that trade since the late Ming, after the Yongzheng reign they had been progressively abandoned by Westerners as ports of call, since Canton's better access to the interior via the Pearl River system, as well as other factors, ensured more reliable supplies of the Chinese goods—especially tea—that foreigners sought. The system of security merchants had already been put in place on the initiative of officials at Canton prior to the court's announcements. This was not indicative of local and provincial animosity toward the maritime trade but rather the reverse: customs, prefectural, and even provincial officials had increasingly joined with Chinese merchants in Canton to lobby the throne to promote their city as the center of overseas trade with the West. (This contrasted, for example, with the performance of Zhejiangese provincial officials at Hangzhou, who were physically removed from, and somewhat skeptical about, maritime trade at Ningbo.) Canton simply made sense (Fig. 12).

It seems in retrospect that the precise timing of the crackdown on foreigners' personal mobility was far from accidental. The Canton system initiative of 1757–1760 coincided precisely with the literati outcry against Qing incorporation of the New Dominions in the northwest. This

Fig. 12   Treasury Street, Guangzhou, 1860. Photograph by Felix Beato. Courtesy of Peabody Essex Museum, Salem, Massachusetts.

expression of disapproval probably invited Qianlong to think in new ways about the boundaries of his empire and its relations with foreign powers.[41] Perhaps more significant still was the coincidence of the court's action with the discovery of new pockets of illegal Christian missionaries in the late 1750s, and Qianlong's fear—apparently fueled by reports from Zhejiang officials about infiltration of missionaries via Ningbo—of a renewed wave of heterodox proselytizing in his realm. Now turning fifty and some twenty-five years into a reign that all around him understood to be a nearly unprecedented prosperous age, Qianlong was not unreasonably nervous lest something unpredictable, such as a massive influx of foreigners with wild and unconventional ideas, undermine what he and his forebears had so gloriously achieved.

Though the English East India Company and the British crown had readily acquiesced to the Canton system at the start, within just a few decades they began to chafe at its restrictions. And they were especially upset that foreign nationals accused of crimes on Qing soil were tried under Qing law. This became a particular irritant after 1785, when the British ship *Lady Hughes* accidentally killed two minor Qing officials while firing a gun salute. A British commercial officer on the scene was arrested by local Chinese authorities, pending surrender of the gunner who had fired the shot. Once surrendered, the gunner was strangled. The British also thought it would be nice to have a depot on the China coast where they might store their goods and conduct trade. They suspected they might rather easily wrest Macau from the Portuguese for this purpose but only if the Qing first indicated compliance. The island of Xiamen (Amoy) off the Fujian coast, near the most attractive tea districts, also caught their eye.

With these issues in mind, in 1787 the British crown dispatched an embassy under Lieutenant Colonel Charles Cathcart, a member of Parliament and quartermaster-general of the Bengal Army, to the Qianlong emperor. King George III sent a personal letter, reading in part:

> It is a truth established by the practice of Your Majesty's Imperial Predecessors, and confirmed by the experience of Your long and Prosperous Reign over the extensive Empire of China, that the Establishment of a well regulated Trade between Nations distantly situated, tends to Their mutual happiness, invention, industry and Wealth; and that the Blessings which the Great God of Heaven hath

conferred upon various Soils and Climates are thus distributed among His Creatures scattered over the whole Earth.

Though his letter rings with the rhetoric of economic liberalism (Adam Smith's *The Wealth of Nations* had been published to wide acclaim just eleven years earlier), it is significant that the British monarch offered no hint that his Qing counterpart did not in fact share his views. Rather: "We are persuaded that Your Royal Mind has long ago been convinced of the Policy of encouraging such an interchange of Commodities between Our respective Subjects, conducted upon fair and equitable principles, consistent with the honor and safety of both Sovereigns."[42] As it happened, Cathcart died of consumption while still at sea, and King George's letter never reached Qianlong.

Five years later he and the East India Company tried again. This time the emissary was the very able George Lord Viscount Macartney, Baron of Lissanoure, former ambassador to Russia, chief secretary for Ireland, and colonial official in the British Caribbean and Madras. Mindful of the Cathcart debacle, the British monarch also appointed Sir George Staunton as deputy ambassador, "in order to avoid every possibility of interruption in this amicable communication . . . in the case of [Macartney's] death." The embassy was instructed to press for the opening of direct trade at Ningbo, Tianjin, and Zhoushan (an island at the mouth of Hangzhou Bay, Zhejiang); for cession to them of small islands in the vicinities of Canton and Zhoushan to serve as depots; and for the right (which the English believed to have been previously granted to the Russians) to open a commercial warehouse in the capital of Beijing itself.

The British secretary of state, Henry Dundas, cautioned Macartney not to indecorously demand settlement of private commercial debts, and added the following:

It is necessary you should be on your guard against one stipulation which perhaps will be demanded of you, which is that the exclusion of the Trade of Opium from the Chinese Dominions as being prohibited by the Laws of the Empire—If this subject should come into discussion, it must be handled with the greatest circumspection. It is beyond a doubt that no inconsiderable portion of the Opium raised within our Indian Territories actually finds its way to China; but if it should be made a positive requisition, or an article of any proposed

Commercial Treaty that none of that drug should be sent by us to China, you must accede to it rather than risk any essential benefit by *contending for our liberty* in this respect, in which case the sale of our Opium in Bengal must be left to take its chance *in an open market,* or to find a consumption in the dispersed & circuitous traffic of the Eastern Seas.[43]

Again, George III sent a personal letter to Qianlong. This time, in addition to "King of Great Britain, France, and Ireland . . . Defender of the Faith and so forth," he also styled himself "Sovereign of the Seas." He explained British colonial enterprise and the civilizing mission this way:

Not satisfied with promoting the prosperity of Our own subjects in every respect . . . we have taken various opportunities of fitting out Ships and sending in them some of the most wise and learned of Our Own People, for the discovery of distant and unknown regions, not for the purpose of conquest, or of enlarging Our dominions which are already sufficiently extensive for all Our wishes, or for the purpose of acquiring wealth, or even of favoring the commerce of Our Subjects, but for the sake of increasing Our knowledge of the habitable Globe, of finding out the various productions of the Earth, and for communicating the arts and comforts of life to those parts where they were hitherto little known; and We have since sent vessels with the animals and vegetables most useful to Man, to Islands and places where it appeared they had been wanting.

After some respectful words about the grandeur of China and the reputation of Qianlong himself, and repeated subtle hints about British military might, George expounded, as he had in the Cathcart letter, about the mutual advantages of international trade. He closed: "May the Almighty have you in his holy protection!"[44]

In his letter of reply to George III, Qianlong argued at some length that acquiescing to the English requests would unleash a flood of similar demands from China's many other Western trade partners. "The English," he pointed out, "are not the only people who trade at Canton." He went on: "The productions of our Empire are manifold, and in great Abundance; nor do we stand in the least need of the Produce of other Countries. China in particular affords Tea, and fine earthen Ware, Silk and other Materials. All these are in great request, both in your own and the other Kingdoms of Europe. From a Propensity to oblige you, I have directed that public Warehouses of these diverse Commodities, should be opened at Canton."[45] Turning to the issue that may well have troubled him far more than the English understood, the emperor wrote:

> For Ages past you have followed what you esteemed the true Religion. In the Chinese Empire, from its earliest Period to this Day, through Wisdom of its Emperors a Doctrine had been established, and transmitted to Posterity, in which the four Parts of the Empire have been brought to concur for several Centuries. It is not right therefore to disturb them in the Exercise of their Ancient Religion . . . Now your Ambassador seems to have it in Contemplation to propagate your English Religion; which is a Thing I will by no means permit.[46]

Between August 21 and October 7, 1793—first at Beijing, then at the summer capital outside the Great Wall at Chengde (Jehol), then again at Beijing—Qianlong and Macartney performed an elaborate *pas de deux*. The emperor tried to choreograph their encounter in accordance with the "guest ritual" prescribed by the *Comprehensive Rites of the Great Qing* (*Da Qing tongli*), which he had ordered compiled some forty years earlier, and thus force Macartney symbolically to accept his claim to universal rulership. Macartney sought to position himself so as to gain implicit acknowledgment that he was emissary of a "sovereign of the seas" fully coequal to Qianlong. Macartney presented clocks and other products of Western technological ingenuity, designed to awe the Son of Heaven with the capacities of his science. The emperor insisted (with apparent reason) that he was underwhelmed, being already in possession of equal or superior devices presented decades ago by the Jesuits.

Most famously, Macartney fretted about whether or not to perform the *ketou,* the ritual bowing and tapping the head on the ground that was the customary etiquette for anyone granted an audience before the emperor. Already by the time Macartney was en route home, empty-handed, the propaganda machinery had been cranked up to the effect that it was his principled defiance of demands that he so prostrate himself and dishonor his king and country that had doomed his mission. "Kowtow" almost immediately entered the English language as an emblem of everything that was pitiable about the Chinese: their obstinate reliance on archaic ritual, as opposed to Western rationalism and pragmatism, and their abject obeisance to despotic authority, in contrast with Western premises of equality, human dignity, and popular sovereignty. It was a handy metaphor in service of the adventurous projects the Westerners had in mind.[47]

6

CRISES

IN A WIDELY cited and controversial book published in 2000, Kenneth Pomeranz argued that the average standard of living in the Qing empire during the "prosperous age" of the eighteenth century was likely higher than that in Western Europe. Desirable but nonessential commodities such as sugar were consumed in greater quantities by the average Qing subject than by the average European. This changed, however, following the "great divergence" around the turn of the nineteenth century, when, at least for two centuries or so, the West left China far behind. Significantly, Pomeranz saw this divergence as resulting primarily from what happened in the West, rather than what failed to happen in the Qing empire. The difference in the West that facilitated the industrial revolution, he argued, was not accumulated past "progress" nor a more innovative mindset but rather a series of historically specific "contingencies," above all Europe's exploitation of the New World through the use of African slave labor.[1]

Overall, Pomeranz's arguments were in sympathy with the new history of the Qing which over the previous quarter century had looked much more positively at the empire's achievements and capacities, had rejected the conventional "narrative of failure," and had seen the historical experience of the eastern half of the Eurasian continent during the early modern era as more closely mirroring that of the continent's western perimeter than offering its inverse case. Nevertheless, it is undeniable that systemic failures within the Qing empire itself became manifest around the turn of the nineteenth century (Qing rulers and subjects themselves noticed these developments with alarm) which made the nineteenth-century divergence not merely a matter of being left behind by Europe in relative terms but also of an intrinsic and absolute loss of capacity.

The crisis of the Qing empire at the turn of the nineteenth century was, in other words, a perfect storm of three simultaneous problems: the external shock of the expanding West, a secular crisis caused by an accumulation of socioeconomic difficulties over the long term, and more acute political dysfunctions associated with the familiar pattern of the dynastic cycle. We will put the first of these on the back burner for the moment, while tending to the second and third, both of which happened earlier and were more critical in the eyes of most contemporaries.[2]

Secular Change

The most basic cumulative change faced by the Qing in the nineteenth century was population growth. A conservative estimate of China's population in 1400 would be about 100 million persons. After the Qing consolidation of power around 1680 and the *pax sinica* that followed—combined with the dissemination of New World crops, improved agricultural technology, territorial expansion, and the reclamation of new farmland— the population tripled in the next two centuries to 450 million. It grew most rapidly not in cities nor in the already heavily populated regions such as Jiangnan but in peripheral areas of relatively new settlement where the agricultural labor of large families proved more productive.[3]

But gradually, the enormous amount of new farmland that had been brought under cultivation during the Qing's first century and a half began to run out. Between 1753 and 1812, per capita acreage declined a remarkable 43 percent, to less than half an acre per person.[4] Throughout most periods of imperial history prior to the nineteenth century, increased population density per unit of land had led to higher rather than lower food yields, since labor, not land, was almost always in relatively short supply. Having more laborers allowed more intensive farming, expansion and maintenance of irrigation systems, and better fertilization with increased amounts of human excrement. By around the turn of the nineteenth century, however, the cost-benefit ratio reversed and further growth of population relative to agrarian land led to a reduction in the general standard of living.[5] One key index might be the nineteenth century's growing bachelor population—the rising percentage of males who, despite powerful cultural imperatives to marry and reproduce, never succeeded in attracting a wife and establishing themselves as independent households.[6]

For much of the preceding centuries, newly created jobs in commerce, artisanal manufacture, mining, and especially transport had absorbed this surplus labor. But the early nineteenth century was a time of commercial contraction in much of the empire. The British at Canton had been exporting large amounts of manufactured goods, especially cotton cloth (nankeens), yet as the nineteenth century progressed, ever smaller quantities of these were available for purchase and export—an indication that the industry had contracted.[7] There were several reasons for this slowdown, but one factor was the state's increasingly outmoded industrial policies.

For example, in copper mining, the Qing state had a policy of demanding a certain percentage of each mine's output for state purchase, at set prices, to be used for minting coins, and it allowed any additional output to be sold on the private market at the going price. But as the market price of copper rose steadily over the course of the late eighteenth and early nineteenth centuries, along with the capital costs of extracting less accessible ore, the state, despite the pleas of its own officials in the region, failed to raise the procurement price it paid for monetary copper. These diminishing profits, rather than any exhaustion of copper deposits, led many mines to close.[8] In other words, not only did the Qing state fail to promote or facilitate new kinds of industrial enterprises, but its outmoded policies contributed to the constriction of enterprises already in existence.

A corollary of the population problem was what might be called a talent glut—a predicament familiar to many developing nations today, in which the educational system produces talented individuals faster than the economy or political system can find satisfactory employment for them. This was a true crisis of prosperity. Because of prolonged peace, comfortable standards of living, and an expanding school system over the eighteenth century, the number of literate—even classically educated—members of the population grew faster than the population as a whole. An imperfect index of this is provided by the number of lower degree holders, which increased from around 40,000 in 1400 to around 600,000 in 1700, and to well over 1,000,000 a century later. The index is imperfect because the state imposed a quota on the number of examination degrees awarded, and in the second half of the eighteenth century the court made a conscientious effort to slow the expansion of these quotas. But during a period of continuing prosperity, this action on the part of the state did not slow growth in the numbers of students *studying* to achieve these degrees, and so in effect it merely compounded the problem.

The explicit goal of classical education was to produce a pool of talented officials for the state bureaucracy, and at that it succeeded. Yet the expected reward for a life of diligent study—a well-paying post and the associated social status—was severely constricted because of the Qing's ideology of "benevolent [small] governance." Fearing a popular uprising if it increased the tax rate to expand state services, the court kept taxes—and the number of jobs they could underwrite—relatively low, which meant that the number of salaried official posts lagged well behind the general population growth and also behind the number of legally qualified candidates. In 1800 there were only around 20,000 official posts in the empire, drawing on a talent pool of over 1,400,000 upper and lower degree holders—that is, just one post for every seventy degree holders.

The problem was exacerbated by the state's practice of awarding degrees and even official posts in exchange for contributions of money or other goods to state projects. On the one hand, the sale of degrees and ranks met the upward mobility demands of some of the most talented individuals in Qing society—frequently those whose families had made large amounts of money in the commercial economy—and so it was a welcome trend. On the other hand, men who had labored so hard to actually pass the examinations found this intensified competition for the scarce resource of honor and rank a galling frustration. In one spectacular though unrepresentative case, a disappointed examination candidate named Hong Xiuquan organized the rebellion that became known as the Taiping Heavenly Kingdom. But more commonly, at the local level, lower degree holders and other literate men turned to nonofficial gentry employment, especially the sort of litigation huckstering that raised tensions over land, water, women, and other scarce resources in an increasingly strained society and economy.

At the national level, the increased lag time between achieving high examination success and being posted to substantive office led to disgruntlement, especially on the part of young scholars who had performed spectacularly on the metropolitan examination and had been sent to the glorified holding pool for "the best and the brightest" known as the Hanlin Academy. The Hanlin had traditionally been a locus of loyal opposition on the part of men who did not yet have any real responsibility but instinctively felt morally and intellectually superior to those who did. This sense of their own exceptionalism only increased in the first half of the nineteenth century, as career and political frustrations mounted.

Lacking gainful employment, these talented young men developed a flamboyant and provocative political style and a tendency to form factions outside normal bureaucratic channels. They centered their activities in such "front" organizations as a "poetry club" that convened in the Liulichang book district outside Beijing's Xuannan Gate and a "shrine association" dedicated to the (now virtually deified) early Qing political critic Gu Yanwu. Relentless criticism from these bitter and well-organized members of the literati helped provoke the Qing government into the saber-rattling that led to the disastrous first Anglo-Chinese War.[9]

Cyclical Decline

To the long-term concerns of population pressure and underemployment were added specific and familiar problems associated with dynastic decline—failures of imperial will and oversight, of bureaucratic morale and initiative, and of corruption and maladministration. Neither the Jiaqing emperor (r. 1796–1819) nor his son and successor the Daoguang emperor (r. 1820–1850) were neglectful of their duties or lacking in ability, but both men could be indecisive at key moments, and both were overwhelmed by the magnitude of the crises they faced.[10]

Emblematic of the administrative deterioration confronted by Jiaqing was the career of Heshen (1750–1799), a bannerman of no great pedigree who during his twenties served as a humble palace guard. In 1775 he was noticed by the aging Qianlong emperor, who, it was said, saw in him a resemblance to a palace lady he had courted unsuccessfully in his youth. Within two years the infatuated emperor had heaped upon Heshen some twenty-odd bureaucratic appointments, including membership in the Grand Council and presidencies of the Board of Revenue and Board of Civil Office. Intelligent, ambitious, and unmatched in his personal avarice—perhaps no figure in all of Chinese history has been so unanimously vilified by historians—Heshen systematically turned the emperor's favor into his own fortune. By his death, his personal estate was said to have amounted to some 800 million silver taels, or more than half of total imperial revenues collected during his twenty-year ascendancy.

Through elaborate patronage networks whose protection was guaranteed by his personal hold over the emperor, Heshen orchestrated systematic embezzlement at all levels of the Qing administration. Virtually no official appointment was made without a "contribution" to one of Heshen's henchmen, and approvals for even the most glaringly necessary official projects were issued only after payment of personal gifts to superiors up the chain of command. Unsurprisingly, fewer and fewer of the critical tasks of government actually got done. From his assumption of rule upon his father's abdication in 1795, the 35-year-old Jiaqing emperor understood the cancer that Heshen represented, but was unable to remove him until the retired emperor's death four years later—indeed, during these years the corruption spread to even higher levels of government. But immediately upon Qianlong's death in 1799 Jiaqing arrested Heshen and his immediate circle and ordered him to commit suicide.

As was customary upon assuming the throne, the new emperor threw open the "pathways of words" (*yanlu*) for a controlled period to hear criticisms and suggestions on how his reign should proceed—specifically, in this case, how the evils of the Heshen era might be corrected. Not unlike Mao Zedong during his "Hundred Flowers" moment of the mid-1950s, Jiaqing heard more than he wanted or imagined—it quickly became clear that the entire bureaucracy had been contaminated beyond repair by Heshen's machinations. The emperor was faced with a dilemma: either clean house entirely or settle for a few highly visible scapegoats and let rank-and-file officials off with a reprimand. He chose the latter course. Historians have tended to see Jiaqing's failure of nerve in purging the bureaucracy of all tainted officials as something of an original sin whose commission predetermined the dynasty's steady decline. But given the need for at least some continuity in routine administration, it is not at all clear that he could have acted otherwise.

Whatever the real possibilities for total reform might have been, Jiaqing's timidity energized literati opposition in the capital. The lead was taken by a senior and respected Hanlin academician named Hong Liangji (1746–1809), the same man who would subsequently be known to historians as "China's Malthus" because of his dire analyses of the empire's population growth. Though not entitled by his rank to write memorials to the throne, Hong composed a strong personal criticism of the emperor's failure of nerve during his house-cleaning efforts, which he sent in a letter to another capital official in the autumn of 1799. Then, in the style of the new intimidationist politics practiced by literati reformers, he leaked his letter widely throughout Beijing. Hong wrote in part:

As long as representatives of the government do not command respect, so long will the people lack a dependable means of making a living. As long as people cannot make a living, so long will it be impossible to bring order to the country . . . Officials must serve as the models for conduct. Only think how consistently these very officials have committed crimes and defiled the administration of government in recent years!

It is fortunate that since the present emperor began his reign, [a few of the guilty have been punished]. But apart from these . . . the others who used to hold office in large provinces or who were in charge of the defense of certain territories, are still in power. If you go traveling in any official capacity, you have to pay "customary fees" at the courier posts, and tip the gatekeepers. There are always presents for festivals, gifts to be sent for birthdays, and also the annual patronage expenses . . . All of this money is extracted from county officials, who in turn get it from the people . . .

It is my opinion that at present the Emperor ought to first emulate the decisive severity of the Yongzheng Emperor, to ensure the respectability of the administration and the happiness of the people. Only thereafter he can turn to the liberal humanitarianism of the Kangxi Emperor, in order to transform popular mores . . .

With head bowed, I await your judgement.[11]

The incensed Jiaqing emperor had Hong arrested and sentenced to death, but here he faced yet another dilemma. He knew Hong was right on principle, even though what he had done could not be condoned. Consequently he commuted the death sentence into banishment to the northwest—in effect, conceding the truth of Hong's criticisms. Hong became a hero and model for a younger generation of oppositionist literati in the capital.[12]

Internal Rebellion

The concrete effects of decades of corruption and maladministration were increasingly visible and severe, especially in the White Lotus sect uprising in north China between 1796 and 1804. It originated in the upper reaches of the Han River highlands in northeastern Hubei and southeastern Shaanxi. This area had been brought under cultivation largely during the Qing by a particularly complex system of entrepreneurship: a "mountain lord" would gain title to a large swath of hillside, usually through political connections of some sort, and then lease sectors of his estate to developers. They would in turn recruit immigrant families to perform the actual reclamation of household-scale plots of land, often enlisting even later arrivals to do the actual farming. Eventually a multilayered hierarchy of proprietorships over each plot emerged, with all the earlier and larger-scale proprietors retaining some claim of rent.

This worked as long as the land was productive enough to support so many claimants. But over the course of the late eighteenth century, as population density in the northeast continued to climb, the productivity of many farms declined due to the exhaustion of the topsoil and erosion from denuded hillsides. This economic strain compounded the built-in social tensions between multiple landlords and their tenants, between older natives and new arrivals, and between highland and lowland cultural groups. The spark that ignited this volatile mixture was sectarianism.[13]

Part of the White Lotus rebellion's proximate cause was exploitative taxes levied on the local population by functionaries in the elaborate bureaucratic extortion racket headed by Heshen. And the initial failure to contain the rebellion was largely the result of corruption among Qing commanders, notably Heshen's brother Helin. Instead of putting down the rebellion, the military establishment kept the war going long after it could have ended in order to profit from funds allocated to employ local militia units. By the last years of so-called rebellion in the early nineteenth century, most of the genuine sectarians had been dispersed, and the militia units on either side that continued to fight each another were both financed by the Qing state. The Jiaqing emperor was aware of what was going on, and on two occasions he issued public declarations of victory that were intended to shut down hostilities. But he still needed nearly half a decade to rein in his own renegade military.[14]

The White Lotus rebellion was a multifaceted disaster from which the Qing never fully recovered. The sectarians themselves were brought under control, but the sect was not expunged. In 1813 an offshoot styled the Eight Trigrams broke into the Forbidden City and threatened to assassinate the Jiaqing emperor himself (an event that sparked the formation of the literati's Xuannan Poetry Club).[15] More dramatic still was the impact on government finances. The accumulated reserves in the Board of Revenue treasuries, which probably peaked at over 80 million silver taels in the late 1770s and were still around 60 million at the end of the Qianlong reign, were more than wiped out by the cost of suppressing the rebellion, which was estimated at 120 million taels.[16] This had a devastating and permanent effect on the capacities of the Qing administration, at all levels, for the remaining century of imperial rule.

Economic Depression

By the 1820s, the empire's monetary problems had reached a point of crisis. Whereas a string of one thousand copper cash carried a par value of one silver tael, the disastrous experiences of the late Ming had convinced the Qing that administrative mandates to enforce a 1000:1 exchange rate, or any other rate, were counterproductive. Instead, the government settled for the goal of maintaining stability in the money market over time and space. In this effort it enjoyed only mixed success. In the late seventeenth century, when silver was relatively scarce, exchange rates of well over 1000:1 were not at all unusual, but in the early eighteenth century, when copper coin became increasingly valuable, rates of 700:1 or 800:1 were the norm. This changed again in the late 1780s, after which rates of over 1000:1 became common again. The value of silver soared during the nineteenth century, so that in the province of Shanxi, for example, exchange rates rose from 730:1 in 1758 to as high as 1800:1 by 1846.

This trend was a function of both the scarcity of silver and a shift in the empire's balance of payments with foreign countries. Contemporaries attributed this chiefly to the Qing's inability to offset its mushrooming imports of foreign opium with exports of domestic commodities, and most modern scholars would agree. But silver was scarce worldwide in the early nineteenth century, due in part to short-term curtailments of production during revolutions in Latin America. In the case of the Qing, a short-term contraction of Western demand for Chinese manufactures such as silk and cotton cloth was probably also a factor. From the sixteenth through the eighteenth century, China with its booming silver-based commercial economy had been the world's greatest recipient of silver inflows, and as late as the first decade of the nineteenth century it still made a net gain of approximately 28 million silver dollars. At that point, however, the flow of silver dramatically reversed. Between 1808 and 1856 the outflow of silver from China was approximately 384 million dollars, an average of 8 million per year. At its most severe, in the late 1840s and early 1850s, the average annual drain exceeded 17 million dollars.[17]

This disruption of the currency system, aggravated by hoarding on the part of investors, was one of the major causes of the so-called "Daoguang-era depression." A crisis of credit caused the collapse of many native banks, while increased costs and deflated prices contributed to declining production by manufacturers, which in turn led to decreased hiring and rising unemployment. Prices paid to rural producers also fell, and farmers experienced the familiar "price scissors" between depreciating income and appreciating essential expenditures. As the tax burden grew heavier on small landholders who paid in devalued copper coins, many lost their farms. The income gap between rich and poor widened, giving rise to a wave of tax and rent resistance movements and other forms of civil unrest.

The Qing state suffered declining tax revenues, to the point where the annual silver outflow to address the imbalance of payments was equivalent to one quarter of each year's land tax assessment. Infrastructure decayed because the cost of maintenance was so high, and relief efforts for hard-hit communities lagged. The real income and morale of state officials at all levels fell, and corruption filled the vacuum. Funding for defense evaporated, causing military efficacy to plummet just at the moment when it would be most needed to combat new domestic and foreign threats. The depression may have played a significant role in the outbreak of the Taiping rebellion itself. There seems to have been a widespread perception, at home and abroad, that by the 1840s economic depression had brought the Qing empire perilously near the point of collapse.

Reformism and the Statecraft Revival

The throne was deeply concerned about the crises it faced. Both the Jiaqing and Daoguang reigns were punctuated by reform efforts emanating from the center. They opened the *yanlu* to invite suggestions on specific problem areas and followed up with attempts at solutions that, invariably, did not go far enough. A stronger chorus of reformism came from outside the administration, especially from the private Confucian academies.

Alert to the dangers posed by these hotbeds of factionalism, the early Qing had closed many local academies after the dynastic transition and had let others go unreconstructed. But in the 1720s and 1730s, the Yongzheng emperor and his corps of activist provincial officials energetically founded new academies and revived or expanded others, mostly at provincial capitals, to serve as quasi-governmental centers for the direction of the emperor's elaborate system of local schools. These academies were not primarily intended as centers of independent learning (though some of them evolved in this direction) but rather as sites to offer higher-level training for the most promising provincial youths in the curriculum of the civil service examinations.

In the early nineteenth century, a new wave of academy founding and reconstruction took a much more autonomous and localist turn. One example was the Sea of Learning Academy founded in Canton during the 1820s by provincial governor Ruan Yuan (1764–1849) and underwritten by the area's booming maritime trade. An experienced provincial official and a leading classical scholar, Ruan imported to the far southeast the sort of critical philological research for which his native Yangzhou and the lower Yangzi region had become famous, in the process putting this intellectual backwater onto the map of the empire's major cultural centers.[18] Celebration of local Cantonese history became a focus of the Sea of Learning Academy. Though classical philology was in its own way vigorously free-thinking, it was not necessarily politically engaged, and by this era its glory days of radicalism had passed.

A very different kind of scholarship, on the surface more traditionalist yet holding the seeds of something new, dominated the academies of Hunan's Xiang River valley, especially the Yuelu Academy outside the provincial capital Changsha. Throughout the mid-Qing heyday of classical philology and Han learning, in which the Four Books that formed the basis of Song Neo-Confucianism (the *Analects, Mencius, Great Learning,* and *Doctrine of the Mean*) had been devalued in favor of the more venerable Five Classics of antiquity (the *Canon of Changes, Canon of History, Canon of Odes, Rites of Zhou,* and *Spring and Autumn Annals*), Hunan scholars—imbued with their province's self-conscious "heartland" mentality—had stayed true to the Song learning of moral self-cultivation, community solidarity, and social hierarchy. But scholars at the Yuelu Academy in particular increasingly married their staunchly conservative moral vision to a hard-headed study of advanced techniques in warfare, political economy, hydraulic engineering, and practical administration—

a combined orientation they labeled *jingshi*—"statecraft" or, more literally, "ordering the world."

Yan Ruyi, a Hunanese official who had served in the northwest during the White Lotus rebellion and was heralded as a chief strategist of the uprising's defeat, was a product of the Yuelu Academy and returned there to inspire students of the next generation. These included such reformist luminaries as Tao Zhu, He Changling, and Wei Yuan, as well as still-younger scholar-activists who would eventually defeat the Taiping and dominate imperial officialdom after midcentury. Like Yan Ruyi, Tang Jian returned to teach at his alma mater, where throughout the 1830s and 1840s he mentored Zeng Guofan, Hu Linyi, and others in his very stern philosophy of life—a philosophy that combined ascetic regimens intended to recognize and overcome one's personal failures with a driving personal mission intended to save the world from the decadence of the times. A Yuelu network of messianic alumni spawned similar academies throughout the remoter regions of central China where they served.[19]

Three individuals stand out as the most visionary of the early nineteenth-century reformist thinkers. None of the three spent appreciable time in an official post of his own. These men lived instead as private scholars or as secretaries in the growing retinues of reform-minded regional administrators. The oldest by a generation was Bao Shichen (1775–1855) from Anhui. The son of a low-ranking military officer, Bao developed a precocious reputation as a strategic and logistic specialist, serving in Sichuan during the White Lotus campaigns and fighting pirates off the Shanghai coast. He later became an acknowledged expert in agronomy and flood control. Bao advocated sweeping institutional reforms: eliminating the Grand Council and the post of provincial governor to improve administrative efficiency, introducing systematic means for the court to consult broad literati opinion, awarding lower gentry degrees to farmers on the basis of their agricultural skill, and significantly strengthening the ancient *baojia* system as a vehicle of economic redistribution and poor relief within the rural community.[20]

Gong Zizhen (1792–1841) hailed from Hangzhou but spent much of his life in Beijing, where he developed empire-wide notoriety for his poetry and his romantic liaisons. A devotee of the New Text school of classical study, Gong read the commentary to the *Spring and Autumn Annals* as a manifesto for continual reform, in order to keep up with the reality of historical change. More pessimistic than most of his contemporaries on the question of dynastic decline, he argued for the systematic replace-

ment of older officials by younger scholars and advocated a radical up-
dating of all government procedures. He accorded great weight to ritual, but demanded that rituals be modified regularly to suit the times.
Specifically, he wanted to eliminate bowing and other gestures of personal deference on the part of government ministers toward the throne,
and also on the part of commoners toward local gentry.

Gong went farther than others in developing a theory of property, arguing, for example, against the customary practice of partible inheritance
because it impoverished those who had accumulated wealth through their
own hard work. In his early writings he condemned agricultural commercialization and rural monetization, at one point recommending decapitation for anyone discovered growing cash crops. But gradually he became a vehement champion of both, as aids to national economic prosperity. In his later years, Gong was said to have been an assiduous reader of
translated Western books, though we do not know which specific books
these were.

Wei Yuan (1794–1856), a Hunanese alumnus of the Yuelu Academy
and occasional member of the Xuannan Poetry Club at Beijing, has received the most attention from Western historians. His importance was
first established on the basis of his 1844 *Illustrated Gazetteer of the Maritime Nations* (*Haiguo tuzhi*), the most intensive study of Europe undertaken in Chinese by that time and an astute warning of the growing danger that Western powers represented for the Qing empire.[21] Important as
this work is, however, it comprised but a small part of Wei's overall scholarship and reformist project. In response to resurgent resistance movements in Qing Inner Asia, for example, Wei wrote a history of past imperial conquests in these regions, enjoining the current occupant of the
throne to live up to the precedent of his forebears and detailing how this
might be accomplished.

Probably most important, while serving in the secretariat of He Changling—a fellow Yuelu alumnus and the Jiangsu provincial treasurer—Wei
was principal editor of the 1826 *Compendium of Writings on Statecraft
from the Present Dynasty* (*Huangchao jingshi wenbian*). This enormous
120-chapter work, topically arranged to cover virtually every aspect of
social organization and government policy, served as the bible of statecraft reformists for decades afterward and spawned many sequels throughout the remainder of the empire. Though on most topics Wei presented a
range of writers espousing alternative policy options, by far the most
heavily represented author among the thousands of texts compiled was

Gu Yanwu, whom Wei and his fellow reformers revered as much for his critique of centralized bureaucracy and defense of local elite activism as for his hardheaded and deeply-informed policy analyses.

Reform Proposals and Policies

Apart from the regular civil administration and the military establishment, the Qing had three functionally specialized bureaucracies, known as the Three Great Administrations, to oversee maintenance of the Yellow River infrastructure, the collection and delivery of grain tribute, and the government's monopoly on the production and sale of salt. Each of these special agencies had suffered greatly from corruption and maladministration during Heshen's dominance at court, and it was here, especially in the last two, that the Daoguang-era reformists concentrated their attention once they found themselves in positions of authority.

The empire's Salt Administration was divided into several large districts, the busiest of which was known as Liang-Huai. Headquartered in Yangzhou, it had a distribution area spanning the middle Yangzi provinces of Hubei, Hunan, Jiangxi, and Anhui. Wholesale shipment of salt from the production area in coastal Jiangsu to consumers throughout the district was in the hands of some two hundred holders of hereditary franchise licenses—men whose status was somewhere between that of an official and a merchant. Each of these monopoly franchise-holders was tasked with annual distribution of a huge quantity of salt, as much as 12,000 *yin* (each *yin* comprising eight bags of salt, at approximately 100 pounds per bag), and in most cases each man was granted exclusive rights of sale to a specific local area. By the early nineteenth century, this system was in massive disarray. Franchisees were failing to fulfill their commitments and were passing along greatly inflated costs to consumers, which priced this essential item beyond the reach of many. A flourishing black market in salt arose to meet the need, and when smuggled salt began to serve a greater percentage of Liang-Huai consumers than did official salt, the government's revenue from its salt monopoly rapidly declined.

In 1832, the Liang-Huai salt commissioner, Yuelu Academy graduate Tao Zhu, acted decisively to abolish the two-century-old franchise system and to throw open the distribution of legal government salt to any merchant of good repute who could purchase a ticket authorizing him to make a single shipment of a much smaller quantity (as little as ten *yin*) to whichever retail market within the district he could find. Tao's goals were to combat smuggling, better serve consumers, and recapture government revenues, and he was quite successful in doing all three. Privatization shifted the salt trade from enfeoffed official-merchants to private investors and commercial agents at all scales of capitalization. Tickets were widely bought and sold on the open market.[22]

Problems in the Grain Tribute Administration were more critical. Whereas the regular land tax had been progressively commuted to silver over the course of the late Ming through mid-Qing eras, the court still felt the need to deliver grain in kind to its various military and civil stipendiaries, mostly in the capital itself and along the northern frontiers. For this purpose it levied an additional grain tribute twice annually on landholders with the largest presumed rice surplus, most heavily in the Yangzi drainage basin. To ship this bulky grain down the river and then north via the Grand Canal required an enormous army of boatmen and other functionaries stationed along the way. By the early nineteenth century this task force had turned into an elaborate network of vested interests, including private brokers and expectant local officials appointed to sinecure posts along the route, where they demanded payoffs to allow the grain to pass through their jurisdictions. The boatmen themselves were by now organized into a quasi-religious mutual interest group known as the Luo Sect, the antecedent of the later mafialike Green Gang.

During the Heshen decades, neglect of scheduled dredging along the Yellow River had aggravated the perennial problem of silt buildup in the Grand Canal, which joined the river just upstream from its mouth. Over the Jiaqing and early Daoguang reigns this deposition had increasingly inhibited passage of grain tribute up the canal. Less and less grain actually arrived in the Beijing area, and whatever did arrive came late and at ever greater cost. The 1824 shipment proved an unprecedented disaster, with only about a quarter of the anticipated grain making it through. The remainder was aboard boats that ran aground in the silted-up canal and was either plundered by local populations or left to rot. The Daoguang emperor opened the *yanlu*, broadly soliciting suggestions as to how grain tribute might be saved, and many respondents noted that the empire now had the capacity to ship Yangzi valley grain north along the coast, from Shanghai to Tianjin and other northern ports, rather than inland along the Grand Canal.

This alternative was actually implemented for the 1826 shipment, under the supervision of Tao Zhu and He Changling, based on plans drawn up by Bao Shichen and their fellow Yuelu Academy alumnus Wei Yuan. Like Tao's subsequent reform of the Liang-Huai Salt Administration, the project involved solicitation of private commercial shippers to perform state functions and represented in effect a privatization of a major sector of the imperial economy. The 1826 experiment was generally judged a success. Ultimately, however, the court's fear of aggravating entrenched interests along the inland route and removing the livelihoods of the already unruly tribute boatmen outweighed its concerns about grain supply, and after this one deviation the grain tribute reverted to the older system of shipment. But after 1840, when almost none of the year's grain tribute reached the capital, the inland route was abandoned once and for all, and the so-called sea route became the standard means of tribute shipment. The millennium-old Grand Canal was condemned to obsolescence.[23]

Another area of reformist attention involved the empire's currency system. The Daoguang depression was sparked by an outflow of silver in payment for foreign opium at Canton. As early as 1819, the Hanlin academician Cai Zhiding had memorialized that the remedy might be for the court to introduce paper currency unbacked by specie; he paid for his boldness with his post. In the worsened economy of the late 1830s, however, another relatively obscure scholar, Wang Liu, published a treatise arguing in detail that not only would paper currency resolve the monetary shortage and bring the empire out of the depression, but it would also establish an unprecedented degree of national monetary sovereignty for the Qing empire, which he pointedly referred to as "Zhongguo" (China). Wang argued that the wide circulation of the Mexican silver dollar in the domestic economy was a gross infringement on China's inherent "rights," while the paper currency already in circulation in the form of privately issued banknotes represented usurpation by private merchants of monetary functions that ought properly to belong to the state. Wang's proposals prompted wide debate, with eminent reformers like Bao Shichen endorsing them in modified form and others like Wei Yuan, with his penchant for privatization, condemning them as overly statist. They were not enacted, however, at least during the Daoguang reign.[24]

But the most intense object of reformist concern was the opium question. Wang Liu had argued for the introduction of a national paper currency in part because making foreigners accept Chinese paper notes, which were useless outside the country, in exchange for opium would "automatically" dissuade them from importing this destructive drug.

With the emperor's encouragement, memorials streamed in to the throne throughout the Daoguang reign proposing all manner of solutions to the perceived crisis. Some advocated legalization and taxation of the drug. This was the position in 1836 of the court official Xu Naiji, a former stalwart of Guangzhou's Sea of Learning Academy, and seems to have represented the opinion of the Cantonese commercial elite who financed the academy and depended on the opium trade for their livelihood. The alternative, hard-line position demanded strict enforcement of the opium ban that had been on the books since the Yongzheng reign, along with punishment of domestic dealers and users and curtailment of foreign imports by whatever means. This position was articulated most forcefully in 1838 by the middle Yangzi governor-general Lin Zexu, a Fujian native, former Hanlin academician, member of Beijing's Xuannan Poetry Club, and friend of Wei Yuan and other reformers. At least initially, Daoguang chose to follow this enforcement policy, with calamitous results.

The Western Shock

Among European nations, England had been a relatively late arrival in China. The engine of the British presence in East Asia was the English East India Company, chartered by the crown in 1600 and granted a legal monopoly over trade with the Qing empire. The company was a product of the dominant European economic logic of the day, mercantilism, which argued, first, that foreign trade was to be conducted primarily in the interests of the state and, second, that its utility was to be measured in terms of its ability to generate a favorable balance of trade, that is, more specie flowing into the country than flowing out. After concentrating its activities in South Asia through most of the seventeenth century, the East India Company had reached the south China coast in the 1680s, coinciding fortuitously with Kangxi's lifting of the sea ban and encouragement of maritime trade. Although the company's activities in China were restricted in the 1760s under the Canton system, at the time this was a source of little or no friction.

British trade with the Qing grew rapidly, and while it probably never eclipsed China's participation in intra-Asian trade, it quickly became the key component of the empire's commercial relations with the West.[25] Like the Qing's other Western trading partners, the English initially purchased luxury goods: silks, porcelains, spices, medicinal herbs, and especially tea, which quickly turned from a luxury good into a staple. Chinese tea caught on like wildfire on the British domestic market, growing from an unknown beverage to one that commanded nearly five percent of the annual income of the average British household in the nineteenth century. The East India Company's imports of Chinese tea grew exponentially, from around 200 pounds per year in the late seventeenth century, to around 400,000 pounds just a few decades later, to over 28,000,000 pounds in the early nineteenth century. The question, for the mercantilist-minded British, was how to pay for this.

The first important item of exchange was cotton. Around the middle of the eighteenth century, the East India Company had in effect begun a military conquest of India, an enormously costly project that necessitated borrowing millions of pounds sterling from the British Crown. It envisioned repaying this debt by means of profits generated from a great triangular trade. Raw cotton cultivated on the company's plantations in India was shipped to the Qing empire, where it fed the empire's booming spinning and weaving handicraft industry. Tea received in exchange for cotton at Canton was then shipped to London, and the proceeds from the sale of the tea was in turn sent to company colonists in India, in the form of salaries, provisions, and British manufactured goods. This scheme seemed at the outset to work splendidly, but by century's end a declining demand for Indian cotton in the Qing (resulting from the substitution of Chinese-grown cotton and a downturn in the Qing domestic economy) forced the British to come up with another commodity to sell to China in exchange for tea.

One possibility was New World silver, for which the Qing economy had long shown a voracious appetite. A second triangular trade emerged, by which British merchants re-exported Chinese tea from London to Britain's North American colonies, along with British manufactures, and there obtained the American silver to exchange at Canton for tea. What frustrated this initiative was the revolutionary inclinations of British colonists—it was Chinese tea, after all, that got dumped in Boston Harbor. Early nineteenth-century independence movements in the Latin American sources of New World silver further disrupted access to this component of Britain's ever-growing China trade. Desperate for a substitute, the British turned to Indian opium.

Opium had been introduced into China by Arabs during the Tang dynasty, but Chinese did not traditionally cultivate or consume it except for medicinal purposes.[26] Opium's use as a recreational drug caught on in the Qing empire in much the same way that tea took hold in England. Cultivated on East India Company plantations in South Asia, it quickly replaced cotton as the company's major import to China. For the most part, the company avoided the embarrassment of shipping opium in its own vessels by contracting with private shippers, both British and American, in what was known as the "country trade." Over the late eighteenth and early nineteenth centuries, the amount of opium imported through Canton increased as much as tenfold. The British knew that the trade was reprehensible. Their missionaries routinely condemned it, and one prominent British merchant, the Scots Presbyterian Alexander Matheson, resigned from his firm Jardine Matheson rather than continue pushing the drug on China. But by the start of the Daoguang reign as much as one-sixth of British Crown revenues derived from the China trade, which would have collapsed without its opium component. To the Crown, there seemed little choice but to continue.

For its part, the Qing had prohibited the sale and use of opium as early as the Yongzheng reign, and this prohibition was repeated throughout the early nineteenth century. The subject was of deep and genuine concern to both the throne and the literati, who understood opium's detrimental effect on the empire. Advocates of legalization were defeated in the debates of the 1830s, but by the middle of the nineteenth century perhaps ten percent of the population was addicted—with heaviest use among the literati and the military, whose declining effectiveness had already been demonstrated during the White Lotus campaigns at the turn of the century. Domestic smuggling of the drug spawned an enormous underworld of clandestine fraternities such as the infamous Triad Society. Most alarming of all to the Qing government was the growing imbalance of trade, the hemorrhaging of silver, and the disruption of the domestic exchange rate between silver and copper. Most contemporaries identified opium as the chief cause of the Daoguang depression.

The opium trade was partly responsible for a dramatic change in the way the Qing empire was depicted in Western writings over the course of the eighteenth and nineteenth centuries. Typical of Western appreciations of China during the High Qing were the words of the Boston writer William Douglass, in his 1749 *Summary of the British Settlements in North America*. Decrying the cultural failures of Native Americans, Douglass summed up their status as that of the "youngest" and "meanest" sibling in the family of man, by contrast with China, which, in terms of moral character, civility, formal government, productive agriculture, religion, and letters, "seems to be the elder brother of all the nations of mankind."[27] Yet less than half a century later another Bostonian, the commercial emissary Samuel Shaw, would write that "the knavery of the Chinese, particularly those of the trading classes, has become proverbial." Of Qing government, Shaw added, "It may perhaps be questioned whether there is a more oppressive one to be found in any civilized nation upon the earth. All offices in the provinces are bestowed upon such as can make most interest for them with great mandarins at court, in consequence the subject undergoes every species of oppression. He is squeezed by the petty mandarins, these again by the higher, [and] they in turn by their superiors, the governors and viceroys."[28]

There were very good objective reasons for Westerners to see the Qing empire after the late Qianlong reign as less admirable than it had been earlier. But the shift in Western perceptions probably derived as well from the changing character of the reporters. Opium pushers of the early nineteenth century, like Shaw, could hardly be expected to share the magnanimous perspective of the refined Jesuit intellectuals of the late Ming and early Qing. But even more importantly, basic attitudes and outlooks in the West itself were radically altered over the intervening years.

The advent of steam-powered manufacturing during the industrial revolution had led to a new vision of foreign trade. No longer were the British interested solely in shipping commodities from one market to another. Now, with the systematic overproduction of textiles in the factories of Manchester and other centers, the task became to aggressively seek new consumers for mass-produced goods, and their chief attention was drawn to what they imagined as a huge "China market." This new trade goal found ideological justification in the gospel of economic liberalism articulated most famously in Adam Smith's *The Wealth of Nations* (1776). Arguing against the mercantilist view that international commerce must be controlled by the state in order to assure a favorable balance of trade, the liberal Smith had argued that a maximum volume of trade, regardless of the direction of bullion flow, was good for all parties and that this maximum volume could best be achieved by leaving trade in the hands of private entrepreneurs.

Armed with this new "free trade" philosophy, the British were justified in pushing the Qing—for that empire's own good—to abandon all its limitations on Western commercial penetration, and most immediately the Canton system that restricted personal movement. A member of Parliament from Liverpool, for example, wrote to his constituency in 1812 that "the trade to India and China ought to be now opened to the unrestrained enterprise and commerce of this country."[29] A resolution delivered to their MP by several London merchants in 1830 argued further that:

> Of all the various countries on the face of the globe, the Empire of China is pre-eminent in those peculiarities which render it desirable to cultivate with it the most intimate relations of trade . . . The Chinese are not merely disposed, but most anxious to enjoy a more extended intercourse with Great Britain, from which they are quite aware that considerable benefits to themselves must ensue . . . [Yet] from this vast and inexhaustible source, both of consumption and supply, British Merchants and British Seamen generally are nevertheless at present entirely excluded, not by any edict of the Chinese, but by the act of our own Legislature, which gives up the whole of our mercantile transactions with China to the East India Company, on various pretenses of danger and difficulty, which are alleged to stand in the way of more general intercourse—all of which pretenses are now proved, however, by incontrovertible evidence to be entirely without foundation.[30]

When in 1834 the British Crown grew so vexed with the ballooning debt of the East Indian Company that it abolished the trade monopoly of this last vestige of mercantilism, it effectively yielded to the growing clamor for unrestricted trade with China and virtually ensured the onset of war.

In addition to economic theories, new political ideas propped up the West's increasingly aggressive policy toward China. The dissolution of the Napoleonic empire by the Congress of Vienna in 1815 gave impetus to a growing nationalist view of political organization: that the governing of each discrete population or "nation" by a powerful, centralized state was not only maximally efficient but also an index of the level of progress and civilization the population had achieved.[31] The congress affirmed that these "nation-states" should relate with one another under the legal principle of mutual and equal sovereignty, regardless of their respective size, wealth, or power—a system that became known as the "comity of nations" or, more tellingly, the "comity of Christian nations."

This newly enshrined international order left no room for the universalist pretensions of the Qing empire; and the West, in this view, was fully justified in forcibly disabusing the Chinese of their retrogressive diplomatic model. The end of the Napoleonic wars freed up European forces

for overseas expansion, while steel-making and other steam-powered industrial technologies ensured the modernization of the military. (The
great German arms-maker Krupp was, not coincidentally, founded in
1830.) The West, in other words, now found itself suddenly in possession
of the motives (a need for foreign markets), the ideological justification
(the comity of nations and free-trade liberalism), and the means (new
military technologies) to force the "opening" of the Great Qing empire.

By the late 1830s, both sides seemed to be increasingly dissatisfied with
the Canton system and were firmly set on a collision course. The British
wanted much greater commercial penetration, while the Qing wanted an
end to the opium traffic. British attempts at a diplomatic solution had
collapsed. Embassies led by Lord Amherst in 1816 after the Congress
of Vienna and by Lord Napier in the aftermath of the East India Company's loss of its monopoly in 1834 both failed when their leaders, like
Macartney before them, balked at compliance with Qing diplomatic protocol. Amherst reached Beijing but never got to see the Jiaqing emperor,
while Napier never made it beyond Guangzhou. For his part, the Daoguang emperor, having opened the *yanlu* on the question of the opium
trade, had decided to suppress that trade at any cost. The result was the
conflict known retrospectively as the Opium War or the First Anglo-
Chinese War.[32]

Briefly, the anti-opium hard-liner Lin Zexu arrived in Guangzhou in
early 1839 bearing the title imperial commissioner. In late spring, he ordered foreign merchants to surrender all opium in their possession, and
he confined them in their factories until they did so. On the advice of the
British superintendent of trade, Charles Elliot, the merchants eventually
gave up their opium, which Lin ceremoniously dumped into the sea on
June 25. Elliot then demanded compensation, which Lin refused on the
grounds that opium, after all, was a contraband substance. This refusal
to compensate provided the British with their excuse for war.

Although landing parties of British marines were occasionally defeated
by local militiamen—most famously at the village of Sanyuanli in the
Canton delta—British naval power and artillery easily overmatched their
Qing adversaries (Fig. 13). In early 1840 they sent their fleet up the coast,
occupying Dinghai in July, and the next month they threatened to move
directly on Beijing. Grand Secretary Qishan, sent by Daoguang to confront the British at Tianjin, met the invaders with extreme courtesy, and
they withdrew. In September, Qishan was sent to Guangzhou to replace
the disgraced Lin Zexu. But Qishan's conciliatory policies failed to mol-

Fig. 13 *H.M.S. Nemesis Destroying Chinese War Junks, January 17, 1841.* Engraving by E. Duncan, 1843. Courtesy of National Maritime Museum, Greenwich, London.

lify Elliot, who in early 1841 ordered the occupation of Hong Kong island and the capture of forts guarding the entrance to Canton harbor. For his evident failures, Qishan was cashiered and dragged back to Beijing in chains. Daoguang again assumed an aggressive posture toward the British, in consequence of which they sailed up the mouth of the Yangzi and occupied Nanjing. There, in August of 1842, a treaty of peace was concluded.[33]

While the Treaty of Nanjing was not the watershed event inaugurating "modern" Chinese history that it is often taken to be, it was significant.[34] First, the Qing agreed to pay Britain a total of $21 million over four years in reparations and in compensation for the destroyed opium. It was not of course unusual in the practice of European warfare for the loser to be held accountable for the victor's costs, but $21 million represented a considerable imposition on the already straitened Qing treasury. Also, it set a precedent for the several wars that the Qing would lose to foreign powers over the remainder of the nineteenth century.

Second, the treaty ceded to Britain the island of Hong Kong, which Elliott had seized a year earlier. This represented a clear violation of Qing territorial sovereignty at the very time when Britain was ostensibly fighting to get the Chinese to accept the Western notion of a comity of sovereign nations. This concept was stressed in Article XI of the Treaty, which demanded that the Qing accept a British "chief high officer" as a quasi-ambassador and recognize the principle of "the Subordinates of both countries [communicating] on a footing of perfect equality." The Cohong and the detested Canton system were abolished, and the five coastal cities of Canton, Amoy, Fuzhou, Ningbo, and Shanghai were opened for the free trade and residence of Her Britannic Majesty's Subjects. This inaugurated the era of the so-called treaty ports, which allowed the British and other foreigners to eventually lease large suburban tracts of land as concessions.

Three other provisions of the Treaty of Nanjing and its immediate successors (the Treaty of the Bogue with Great Britain, signed the next year, and the Treaty of Wangxia, signed with the United States in 1844) were unambiguously "unequal" in that rights ceded to the Western parties were not also ceded reciprocally to the Qing. Article X of the Treaty of Nanjing stipulated that "the regulated Customs and Duties agreeable to the Tariff . . . be hereafter fixed." In other words, the Qing gave away the sovereign right, presumably enjoyed by all nation-states, to determine its own taxes on imported goods; these rates could be adjusted in the future only with the agreement of Britain. For an empire that within a few decades would find itself engaged in catch-up industrialization, the inability to impose protective tariffs to nurture nascent industries would be crippling.

The Qing also granted "extra-territoriality" to Britain and the United States, which meant that nationals of those countries could be tried only under their own national laws and by their own courts for criminal offenses allegedly committed in China. This provision also allowed foreigners to conduct business in China under their own country's usually more lenient civil and commercial laws—a significant advantage in their dealings with Chinese trading partners. And finally, Britain was granted "most favored nation" status, which meant that "should the Emperor hereafter, from any cause whatever, be pleased to grant additional privileges or immunities to any of the Subjects or Citizens of such Foreign Countries, the same privileges and immunities will be extended to and enjoyed by British Subjects." In other words, the Qing had abrogated its presumably sovereign right to favor certain of its foreign trading partners over others. Most subsequent treaties signed by the Qing with foreign powers would include this provision as well, effectively compromising the empire's diplomatic autonomy. Because of the Treaty of Nanjing and its successors, the Qing entered the new era of Western expansion and intense international competition with its hands tied behind its back.

As an additional, crucial fallout, the Opium War brought into the open feelings of anti-Manchuism among the Chinese that had festered under the surface for two centuries. As the British approached Nanjing in July 1842, for instance, the Manchu garrison commander at Zhenjiang placed that city under martial law, out of a seemingly paranoid fear of "Chinese traitors." After he arrested, tortured, or executed scores of local townspeople, ethnic relations turned very ugly, and panicked citizens accused the commander of genocidal intentions. Only the banner troops resisted the successful takeover by the British, and over four hundred of them perished while their Chinese neighbors looked on impassively. If the Manchus had effectively invented themselves as a "race" over the course of the sixteenth through the eighteenth centuries, they had done so successfully enough by this time to invite racial hatred.[35]

But this was not all. Heroic victories by hardy Chinese farm boys in places like Sanyuanli, and the hard line toward opium-dealing foreigners taken by the upright Han official Lin Zexu, was contrasted in the collective memory of Chinese with the traitorous sellout of the nation by the Manchu Qishan and the chief Qing negotiator at Nanjing, Qiying. A new sentiment began to emerge, which we might call "instrumental anti-Manchuism," an attitude based less on racial animosity than patriotic zeal. In this new view, if China was to defend itself effectively against the encroaching West, the alien Qing rulers first had to go.[36]

7

REBELLION

IN CHINA during the Qing era there was an idealized Confucian view of the operation of society, and also a pragmatic world in which these normative prescriptions were put into practice through the agrarian regime, family system, ritual performance, and myriad forms of interpersonal etiquette. Both the ideal world and the real world valued order, stability, precedence, and social harmony, yet both existed alongside another reality in which violent disorder was commonplace. Even during the "prosperous age" of the eighteenth century, Confucian prescriptions served, in essence, as mechanisms for coping with an underworld of willful disorder—a brutal domain teeming with bandits, clandestine fraternal associations, millenarian sects, and rebels.[1]

Individuals, families, and communities routinely flowed into and out of this underworld, for Qing society, despite its rigid appearance, was exceptionally fluid. These deviant groups often had alternative, heterodox ideologies and organizational structures every bit as finely tuned as those of orthodox Confucian society, and—in an era of small government—officials were forced from time to time to rely on them to achieve their goals, in the same way they routinely relied on more traditional groups such as lineages and guilds. Indeed, the Qing were masters at this kind of co-optation. All types of deviance grew more prevalent from the late eighteenth through the early twentieth centuries, as robbers, rebels, and religious sectarians became the chief beneficiaries of the Qing state's decline.

Bandits

Despite considerable overlap among types, we may think of Qing heterodoxy in terms of a rough typology, the first type being bandits or, more
properly, local bandits (*tufei*). Men (and occasionally women) went into
banditry for a variety of reasons: as a survival strategy in a world of
diminishing per capita resources, as a shortcut for upward social mobility, and as a way to right the perceived wrongs of society. Banditry
had existed alongside the official administration and conventional society
throughout imperial history. If we imagine the grid of local administration as a loose network of military camps located in the most hospitable
and populated areas of the terrain, bandits occupied the interstices between these camps—mountains, forests, and swamplands. When administrative scrutiny became too intense in one jurisdiction, they deliberately
crossed borders into another. In what David Robinson has characterized
as an "economy of violence," the forces of order—both official armies
and private militia under local strongmen—existed in easy symbiosis
with these outlaw groups, each opponent using the other to justify its
continued existence and showing considerable willingness to cross over
to the other side under advantageous circumstances.[2]

Local banditry was chronic, but its intensity was inversely propor-
tional to the short-term economic health of the surrounding society. Probably the great majority of bandits expected to discontinue their looting
once a subsistence crisis abated, and for this reason they usually preyed
on communities other than the one into which they expected to reinte-
grate. As the maxim went, "A rabbit doesn't eat the grass around its own
nest." Indeed, one community's bandits might well be another's local militia or crop-watching society. Bandits operated in bands, usually small.
In most cases they had no ability to link up beyond the locality, and no
systematic program that might give them an organizational permanence.
But small bandit groups were capable of growing to impressive numbers
in the hands of a talented leader.

In Qing times a highly developed and persistent set of cultural models
swirled around banditry, and these were by no means exclusively negative. Central to the self-image of most bandits and some rebel groups
(such as the mid-nineteenth-century Nian) was the cultural ideal of the
haohan or "tough guy."[3] As much or more than the ideal of the successful
scholar, this role model served to socialize young boys and construct their
sense of Chinese masculinity. Though it was probably most compelling in

the lower classes, the tough guy model held an attraction for sons of the elite as well. The *haohan* cherished personal honor and male comradeship and deprecated as weakness both sexual indulgence and the pursuit of material wealth. He valued the ability both to inflict and to withstand violence, often simply as entertainment for its own sake.

This model had antecedents in antiquity—for, example in the lives of the "knights errant" celebrated by the Han historian Sima Qian—but by Qing times its most authoritative literary embodiment was the sprawling sixteenth-century novel *The Water Margin* (*Shuihu zhuan*), a standard edition of which had been compiled and partly written by the late-Ming iconoclast Li Zhi. It found an institutional locus in the thousands of martial arts academies and clubs that dotted the Qing landscape. With the growth over the course of the dynasty of an unemployed bachelor population lacking the stabilizing influence of home and family, the *haohan* model's natural constituency expanded as well. Efforts by elites and officials to deprecate or criminalize such men as "bare sticks" or "thugs" did little to diminish their romantic appeal to young men.

If the tough-guy model was ubiquitous among Qing males (and surely some females as well), a trope more narrowly appealing to practicing bandits was that of the "greenwood" (*lulin*).[4] Strikingly resonant with the English model of Sherwood Forest, where Robin Hood and his band of Merry Men hid out, the greenwood in late imperial China was the mythical habitat of "social bandits," men supposedly forced into outlawry by the corruptions of local officials and dedicated to righting the wrongs of society by unconventional, often violent, means. An icon of this behavior was the Southern Song general Yue Fei, martyred for his refusal to follow the court's weak-kneed policy of appeasing the northern barbarians.

Like Yue Fei, late imperial social bandits were often presumed to embody Confucian teachings, albeit in a more muscular and arguably more authentic form. Frequently, the goals of social banditry were stated in deeply orthodox terms: loyalty, filial piety, female chastity (paramilitary groups such as the twentieth-century Red Spears routinely carried out attacks on local adulterers), and love for the people. In theory, social bandits did not despise officials per se but merely corrupt or lax officials who did not live up to their duties of public service. (Think of Robin Hood's attitude toward the Sheriff of Nottingham.) Not infrequently, successful social bandits ended up being recognized by the true ruler (like Robin Hood's Good King Richard) and ended up as officials themselves, as did several of the 108 outlaws of the marsh in the *Water Margin* saga.

In practice, many outlaws no doubt took on the role of social bandit to cloak their nakedly predatory behavior. As with ordinary bandits, their ideological underpinnings were weak, and most such groups melted away upon the death, retirement, or capture of their leader.

"Secret Societies"

Many gangs, particularly those with strong social-bandit ideologies, overlapped with more lasting organizations that historians have often referred to as "secret societies." But whereas social bandits espoused a violent form of Confucianism, these so-called secret societies adhered more or less consciously to heterodox values. Typically, they professed not to worship the gods, ghosts, and ancestors of popular religion, and they organized themselves through linkages other than patrilineal kinship and common native place—the cement of conventional late imperial society. In Chinese, the term for secret society, *mimi shehui,* is a modern usage rarely found in Qing-era discourse, and many Western scholars today are dubious about the usefulness of the concept.[5] "Secrecy" was by no means always a salient characteristic of these groups, and other differences among them appear more pronounced than the qualities they shared. Most significantly, we usually tend today to see fraternal associations and religious sects as fundamentally distinct forms of organization and belief. Still, there were enough commonalities uniting all such groups that mutual borrowing and blurring of the lines between them was increasingly routine over time.

Socially, most "secret" groups explicitly resisted the hierarchical organization of orthodox society, which compelled deference to state officials, lineage and generational elders, and property holders. In some instances, they offered alternative forms of discipline, regimentation, or hierarchy, based on degrees of indoctrination and initiation into cultic lore, on master-disciple ties, or on fictive kinship or brotherhood. In other instances, they replaced hierarchical relationships with more egalitarian ones, such as membership in a community of coequal believers in some deity or other. Much like nativized Islam and Christianity with which these societies coexisted, they were often tightly congregational—a trait much distrusted by imperial authorities and one that contributed in no small part to the groups' felt need for secrecy. Many, but hardly all, such groups denied the prescriptions of orthodox society for gender hierarchy, and in some of them women played active leadership roles.

Spiritually, many "secret" groups adhered to an apocalyptic or messianic belief that they were harbingers of a new and better order, both cosmically and socially. This was especially true for groups reflecting Maitreyan Buddhist, Manichean, or White Lotus ideologies, which conceived of the world as progressing through successive ages of increasing corruption, occasionally renewed through millenarian interventions in which the true believers—often identifiable by their strict regimens of vegetarianism and sexual abstinence—would take the lead. This kind of belief was functionally similar to the millenarian sectarianism that arose within the Judaic, Christian, and Islamic belief systems of the West. But such apocalyptic impulses were not confined to sectarian devotees of Buddhism or other imported religious traditions but had been pervasive in native Chinese popular religion since antiquity. During the Qing, long-held and pervasive beliefs in malevolent spirits spawned radically messianic demon-smashing, world-cleansing paradigms among otherwise seemingly orthodox groups—and under the direction of a charismatic leader, these urges might prompt them into political rebellion, such as that of Ma Chaozhu on the Anhui-Hubei border in 1750–1752.[6]

Politically, many "secret" societies shared a strong Han protonationalism and an antipathy to Manchu rule. This sentiment drew on a collective memory of the role played by popular organizations in the Han-led rebellions that overthrew the Mongol Yuan in the fourteenth century. The importance of this factor before the last years of the dynasty is extremely difficult to assess, however, for two nearly opposite reasons. On the one hand, the self-congratulatory internal histories generated by such groups toward the end of the Qing and afterward stress this as a factor in their early organization far more than most scholars would credit. On the other hand, the taboo on official acknowledgment of anti-Manchuism throughout the dynasty means that our best source of information about these societies—the correspondence generated by administrators charged with their suppression—likely systematically understated that sentiment as a basis for their organization.

What seems clear is that practical reasons for organizing a secret society were usually more important than ideological ones. Probably the most basic rationale was mutual aid, administered through a local chapter or lodge. Members were expected to sacrifice for one another, come to one another's defense, and help one another in need. Leaders performed concrete services for their constituents, such as medicinal healing, providing access to jobs, or teaching martial arts. While local chapters were held together by collective self-interest, they were usually linked into larger networks that seemed to cohere on the basis of shared ideology or eschatology, such as anti-Manchuism or millenarianism. Self-interest versus ideology became more or less compelling depending on the particular moment.

The flexible hold of ideology on secret societies meant that they were vulnerable to co-optation not only by the Qing state but also by other forces such as local property-holders (as with the Red Spears) and highly ideologized twentieth-century political movements. Sun Yat-sen, for example, sought to mobilize the Triads for his republican revolutionary ambitions. His Nationalist Party successor, Jiang Jieshi, very effectively co-opted the Green Gang—which, despite its nationalist claims, was also successfully appropriated by the Japanese in the 1930s as a tool of their occupation of central China.[7] The early Communist Party sought, with erratic success, to win over the Red Spears and the Society of Elder Brothers.

The most significant divergences among "secret" societies have been found between fraternal associations and religious sects. But given their often considerable overlap, it might be better to view the two less as mutual alternatives than as poles of a spectrum, with each individual case varying in its level of secretiveness and heterodoxy. Local associations of farmers or workers calling themselves fraternal organizations date at least to the late Ming. In the Great Divide highlands on the Hubei-Hunan frontier, for example, an organization known as the Village Benevolent Association appeared in the 1630s to provide mutual protection from bandits and marauding anti-dynastic rebels. Eventually falling under the leadership of aggrieved bondservants, the association itself rose up and killed several local landholders.[8] Echoes of this kind of highly localized activity recurred in the Qing, as with the Iron Cudgel Association organized in 1755 by certain tenant-farmers of Fujian to resist rent payments and terrorize their landlords in a local market town. On the urban front, the fraternal organization of Suzhou cloth calenderers killed their labor boss in the 1720s and plotted to burn down the city's major textile warehouses.

All of these seem to have been sporadic and highly localized groups that came together for specific ad hoc purposes. But a more enduring type of fraternal organization emerged in the late seventeenth century and took more definite form by the middle of the eighteenth. This seems to have been something new to the Qing—a product of socioeconomic forces specific to that era. Its context was the intense and systematic settlement and land reclamation in southeast China, Taiwan, and Sichuan. While much of the migration to these areas was sponsored by large lineage organizations able to mobilize the capital and labor necessary to stake out, defend, and develop the best new farmland, significant numbers of less advantaged single males migrated to these regions as well. To protect themselves as best they could from the predations of the large lineages, these bachelors organized associations based on oaths of sworn brotherhood, with the practical purposes of sharing farm tools, guarding their fields, extending mutual credit, and burying the dead. Through the Yongzheng and early Qianlong reigns most of these fraternal organizations remained nameless, but gradually they began to give themselves euphonious titles like Father and Mother Society. The more entrepreneurial of such groups eventually linked up with others at the regional level, combining their muscle not only for self-protection but also for racketeering.

The most expansive of these fraternities became known as the Heaven and Earth Society, or Triads. Founded in 1761 by Zheng Kai in Fujian's Zhangpu county—which was both an epicenter of lineage feuding and a major jumping-off point for emigration to Taiwan—the Triads re-exported to the mainland the smuggling activities, armed quarrels, and propensity for intermittent uprisings they had nurtured on the Taiwan frontier. Less than three decades after its founding, the society mounted a full-scale rebellion in Taiwan under the leadership of Lin Shuangwen, which cost the Qing some ten thousand combat deaths and merited inclusion as one of the Qianlong emperor's self-professed Ten Great Campaigns.[9]

Somewhat analogous to the Triads was a sprawling Mafia-type organization that seems to have developed in the 1740s in Sichuan. Known initially as the Guluhui, the group's long-gowned members were single males who had immigrated as part of the Qing's orchestrated resettlement of the province following the genocidal campaigns of Zhang Xianzhong. The group seems to have been somewhat less agrarian and more urbanized than its counterparts along the southeast coast. From the outset it was also deeply involved in racketeering, especially salt smuggling. When the Guluhui encountered the Triads some decades after its founding, it adopted the notion of sworn fraternity and rechristened itself the Society of Elder Brothers (Gelaohui). Still later it began to absorb various religious beliefs from the region's White Lotus sectarians. During the broad militarization of the mid-nineteenth-century Taiping campaigns, the Elder Brothers made deep inroads into anti-Taiping military forces. It was rumored that some outstanding anti-Taiping generals such as Zeng Guofan and Zuo Zongtang were secret members of the society.[10]

An even more striking case of merger between mutual aid societies and religious sects was the so-called Green Gang. It began as an occupational association of Yangzi River and Grand Canal boatmen involved in the Grain Tribute Administration, which offered retirement assistance to those too old to work or short-term aid to those who fell ill or were injured on the job. At some point in the late seventeenth century it merged with or appropriated a pre-existing Buddhist sect called the Luo jiao, which had been founded by the patriarch Luo Jing in the early sixteenth century and which maintained a network of temples in and around Hangzhou prefecture. Green Gang boatmen began practicing the Luo jiao ritual and appropriated the sect's temples as hostels for its members. Increasingly wary of the subversive teachings of the sect, however, the Qianlong emperor finally moved in 1768 to raze its temples and confiscate their endowments. At this point the Green Gang became more fully a clandestine organization and eventually metamorphosed into an underworld mob in the twentieth century.[11]

The White Lotus Rebellion, 1796–1805

At the other end of the spectrum from bachelor fraternities like the early Triads were the various sectarian groups usually subsumed under the label White Lotus. These were all more or less millenarian or apocalyptic groups that combined elements of folk Buddhism, Manicheism, and devotion to the monotheistic Eternal Mother. Whereas fraternal associations, even those that eventually adopted elements of White Lotus belief, were exclusively male, sects were open to women and very frequently incorporated entire village communities into its structure. Like fraternal associations, many White Lotus groups were orientated toward martial arts, but instead of using swords and other sophisticated weaponry, sectarians—whose local leaders were as likely to be boxing teachers as priests—prided themselves on their skill in manual combat and their invulnerability to weaponry, which they attributed to their devotionalism and regimens of personal hygiene, including vegetarianism and sexual abstinence.

White Lotus sects were essentially diffuse and local, with little in the way of a centralized religious hierarchy or systematic theology. A sprawling cadre of priests traversed provinces throughout the countryside to proselytize and tend to various local congregations. They preached from a proliferation of sacred texts, some of which circulated fairly widely while others were produced by the individual leader himself. At times, White Lotus sects shared temple precincts with fully orthodox Buddhist or Daoist cults. Although the wider population often viewed them with suspicion or contempt, they tended to be openly evangelical. They went underground only in response to official campaigns of repression, which came and went according to the whims of incumbent officials and the court's oscillating fears of social instability. And although their millenarian beliefs had a definite anti-establishment bent, their proclivity to uprising varied greatly according to the individual teacher and the degree of imminence assigned to the coming apocalypse.[12]

Out of this northern sectarian tradition emerged the devastating White Lotus rebellion at the turn of the nineteenth century. As was the case in the Wang Lun rebellion of 1774, official pressure more than any other factor drove the sectarians into rebellion. The mounting wave of bureaucratic investigations, spurred by the Qianlong court, growing out of the emperor's new awareness of just how threatening sectarian activity could be, seems to have played a direct role in fomenting this uprising two decades later. Another factor was rural immiseration in the Han highlands, the result of decades of ecological deterioration. Yet a third determinant was fiscal exploitation by clients of the Heshen faction at court, which had not been a concern two decades earlier when Wang Lun rebelled.

Even so, specific features internal to the local tradition of the Han River highlands made these sectarians, more than their co-believers elsewhere, inclined to active rebellion. There were two distinctive patterns of White Lotus organization in northern and northwestern provinces during the late eighteenth century. The plains were dominated by the Primal Chaos tradition, whose stable priesthood, with its scriptural canon, tended to keep a low profile to protect well-established congregations from prying official eyes. The more diffuse religious practice of the highlands, by contrast, was traceable to the Dragon Flower Association of Shanxi, whose founder, Zhang Jindou, had been arrested and executed during the Yongzheng reign for plotting the massacre of local landlords. By the late eighteenth century, this sect was in the hands of a number of charismatic proselytizers who tended to write their own scriptures, actively compete with one another for followers, and teach a more incendiary doctrine aimed at rebellion. Despite attempts to unify these two traditions, they rarely cooperated with each other, and this proved to be the case once the rebellion broke out in the first year of the Jiaqing reign.[13]

The actual "outbreak" of the rebellion was rather fuzzy. In 1793 Qing forces that had been dispatched to Nepal to protect Tibet from Gurkha-led subversion were redeployed to the Han River highlands, to be joined two years later by other troops that had been suppressing a Miao rebellion in western Hunan. The ostensible goal in amassing these forces was to intensify persecution of sectarians and stamp out smuggling and protection rackets in the hands of local bandits. The intensified official crusade had immediate and counterproductive results for the peace of this deeply militarized region, and in 1796 the first of several linked sectarian risings took place in Jingzhou prefecture of western Hubei. Two corrupt leaders of the Qing military force, including Heshen's brother Helin, were among the early fatalities of the campaign. The suppression of the rebellion fell to local officials under the command of Sichuan's governor-general.

The cornerstone of this counterinsurgency effort was a draconian scorched-earth policy developed by a number of strategic advisors including the Fujianese Gong Jinghan and the Hunanese Yuelu Academy graduate Yan Ruyi. The idea was to withdraw all the highlands' crops and livestock into designated strategic villages, turn these villages into armed forts, organize their separate militia into linked-village leagues, and gradually encircle, starve out, and exterminate the rebels. One can easily see how this strategy might have driven locals into the rebels' camp. But according to Yan's fellow Yuelu alumnus Wei Yuan, after several years of hard fighting, this innovative strategy—and not the tactics of the banner and Green Standard forces—ultimately defeated the White Lotus. Maybe so, but the sectarian rebellion was never as large as the Qing field commanders claimed it was, and most of the rebel leaders were killed or captured fairly quickly. By early 1799, when the retired Qianlong emperor died and Jiaqing assumed his personal rule, fewer than two thousand actual sectarians were still alive and fighting.[14]

Yet, despite several announcements of victory, the new emperor was unable to wind down the campaign. Because so much of the fighting on the government side was undertaken by mercenaries paid through channels controlled by local military officials, and because the Qing's own troops in the region were being paid bonuses for engaging in combat, the entire military establishment had much to gain and little to lose from prolonging the war through every possible deception, and that is what they conspired to do. It took more than five years for the frustrated Jiaqing to end the charade. Not only did the White Lotus rebellion represent a milestone in the Qing's continuing loss of control over its military, but it prevented the court from redeploying its forces to combat the pirate threat along the southeast coast or to resist the looming threat of British aggression and domestic rebellion. Moreover, this needless war crippled, perhaps once and for all, the central administration's financial capacity. The treasury surplus that had accumulated during the Qianlong reign was entirely spent putting down this trumped-up war.[15]

The Taiping Heavenly Kingdom, 1850–1864

Roughly half a century after the White Lotus rebellion wound down, another massive cataclysm, this time originating in the deep south, yet more seriously challenged the survival of the Qing empire. Perhaps no event in Qing history, even the Opium War or the revolution that ultimately toppled the regime in 1911, has attracted more attention—or more politicized treatment—from historians than the Taiping rebellion. From the 1950s through the 1970s, Taiping historiography was a front in the intense ideological conflict known as the Cold War. The Taiping rebels served as a surrogate for Chinese Communists and as such became a touchstone for each individual scholar's attitude toward the People's Republic of China.

In the PRC itself, the rebellion was the focus of an enormous corpus of historical writing in which the Taiping "revolutionary movement" was portrayed not only as a war of Han national liberation against the Qing but more basically as the prototypical "peasant uprising" against the landlord class and the feudal political administration they supported. The fact that the Taiping briefly promulgated a program for collectivization of land made them even more attractive to Chinese Marxist scholars, who explained away the sect's idiosyncratic Christian beliefs as the "superstition" that had doomed all movements prior to the clearheaded revolutionary theory of Marx, Lenin, and Mao.[16] On the Western and Nationalist Chinese side, even the best Cold War scholarship on the Taiping found it necessary to thoroughly condemn a movement that the Communists had appropriated as their own. They dismissed the collectivization schemes as insincere (even at times denouncing the Taiping vision as totalitarian) and insisted that the movement was not really a revolution but simply another anti-dynastic rebellion, albeit one that very nearly succeeded.[17]

The gestation of this movement in the region around Guangzhou was no coincidence, since in many ways it was an outgrowth of the Opium War fought there a decade earlier.[18] Following the British invasion of the late 1830s, the Triads had been the greatest beneficiary of disruptions to local society and to orthodox channels of authority, and recruitment into the fraternal association had been extremely successful during the following decade. But the Triads had been deeply involved in opium smuggling during the years when Canton monopolized importation, and with the shift of the trade to northern ports after 1842, these highly organized racketeers, along with the rest of the southeast, experienced massive unemployment. In addition, local militia units that had been mobilized to combat the British during the war also became idle and began to suffer from the economic downturn. Having kept their arms, these militiamen turned to banditry.

Finally, the Canton region in the 1840s seems to have seen the emergence of an anti-Manchuism of a new kind, based on a theory of betrayal. Local people readily contrasted the success of hearty Cantonese farmboy militias against British landing parties, most famously at Sanyuanli, with the failure of Qing officials to keep the barbarian at bay. It was easy to suppose a conspiracy of traitorous Cohong merchants with the Manchu overlords to sell out the good Han people—it did not escape notice that both the staff of the Imperial Household Department that raked in the profits of the opium trade and the negotiators of the surrender at Nanjing were Manchus, whereas the stout local gentry militia leaders and the heroically defiant Lin Zexu were Chinese, and southern Chinese at that. The heroism of the latter had been fatally undermined by the craven weakness of the former. In order to protect the fatherland from the foreign devils of the West, the Manchus had to be overthrown. This early stirring of Chinese nationalism was a very fruitful tool of early Taiping recruitment.

The originator of the Taiping movement was one Hong Xiuquan (1813–1864), a Hakka village schoolteacher whose family had migrated in recent generations into the highlands around Guangzhou. Hong's initial aspirations were quite orthodox: he passed the local level of the civil service examination and on three separate occasions during the late 1830s he sat for the provincial-level examination at Guangzhou. Like many other candidates who found this path to upward mobility increas-

ingly congested, he failed all three times. Hong's reaction to this disap-
pointment was, however, unique. During his first trip to the city for
the provincial examination, he had been handed a Christian missionary
tract, in Chinese translation, which he kept but did not read with any se-
riousness. As the strain of failure mounted, Hong recalled his book and
turned to it again, interpreting its contents in original ways that came to
him in a series of dream visions. During these supernatural events, Jesus
spoke to Hong and persuaded him that he was Christ's younger brother.
In 1843, with a friend who had also read and been influenced by the
tract, Hong baptized himself.[19]

Over the next decade, he and a group of friends and relatives moved
peripatetically throughout the highlands of Guangdong and neighboring Guangxi, preaching and forming congregations of what they called
the Society of God Worshippers. Many of their converts were fellow
Hakka—highland residents of Han descent who believed that Han populations in the lowlands had ostracized them for being late arrivals in the
long southern migration of the Han people from the north China plain.[20]
Other converts came from marginalized occupational groups such as
charcoal burners and boatmen, from former pirates driven ashore by the
actions of the British navy to clear the waterways for trade, and Triad
smugglers and racketeers. Although the Taiping ideology was basically
different from that of the Triads, the two groups shared the belief that
southerners were the "true" Chinese, since northerners had been contaminated by centuries of mixed blood from Inner Asian conquest dynasties.
Like most Chinese, Hong also believed in flesh-and-bone-devouring demons who must be smashed, and like many Triad leaders, he carried a
demon-slaying sword.[21]

For more than a decade, Hong continued to produce scriptures and re-
veal his visions to his followers, whose numbers steadily grew with the
sect's fervent proselytizing. Although the Taiping occasionally fell afoul
of the conservative local gentry, for the most part they blended in with
surrounding society. Gradually over the course of the 1840s, Hong decided that Confucius was not his ally in the campaign to smash idolatry
but rather his major doctrinal enemy, and that agents of the Manchu
Qing regime were also demons to be destroyed. In mourning for his father's death in 1849, he began to eschew the legally mandated queue and
grow his hair long. In June of the next year, at the height of a regional
famine, Hong raised the flag of rebellion.

The Taiping were not the first to use an eschatology imported from the

West as the basis of their rebellious organization. Sectarian movements during the late Ming and before, as well as the White Lotus rebellion, had built upon imported elements of Buddhism and Manicheism. However, the Taiping belief system included a number of indigenous strands as well. Its vision of a coming era of Great Peace (the Taiping) drew its name from a section of the *Book of Changes* (*Yijing*) and placed the movement in the long tradition of Chinese millenarian rebellions. In Hong's theology, Christianity itself was not a Western import but rather the true original religion of the Chinese people themselves, which had been corrupted and effaced largely by successive waves of idol-worshipping northern barbarian invaders, of which the Manchus were simply the most recent. This sentiment placed the movement squarely within the Han chauvinist tradition of secret societies in the south. When Hong's armies moved north, they were customarily identified by their opponents not as Taiping or God Worshippers, which is the way they styled themselves, but as "long-haired bandits" or "southern rebels."

From their base area in the Guangxi highlands, the initial Taiping force of around ten thousand fighters swooped down on the provincial capital, Guilin, and attempted unsuccessfully to capture it before moving on. At Yong'an, Guangxi, in September 1851, Hong was proclaimed the Heavenly King. The forces moved northward through Hunan and overland to the east of the Xiang River, besieging the provincial capital Changsha unsuccessfully but capturing several other important cities and swelling their ranks with local recruits along the way. After a protracted siege in the first two months of 1853, they captured the Wuhan cities, node of the Qing's domestic commerce, then turned eastward down the Yangzi to take the great port cities of Jiujiang, Anqing, Nanjing, Zhenjiang, and Yangzhou. In March, Nanjing was declared the Heavenly Capital, and Hong remained enthroned there for nearly a decade. Further northward thrusts toward Beijing were thwarted during 1855, and repeated attacks on Shanghai were rebuffed primarily by a hybrid Sino-Western force known as the Ever Victorious Army, commanded first by the American Frederick Townsend Ward and after Ward's death by the Englishman Charles "Chinese" Gordon, later killed at Khartoum. Throughout the late 1850s and early 1860s, meanwhile, Taiping forces repeatedly captured and relinquished various urban centers in the lower and middle Yangzi, with accumulating loss of life among both inhabitants and combatants.

While besieging Wuhan in 1853, the occupying rebels led a bloody manhunt for all Qing soldiers, civil servants, and sympathizers, eventually extending this to "criminals" and other social undesirables. They evicted the surviving urban population from their homes and housed them in twenty-five-person dormitories, keeping women and men in separate parts of the cities. They commandeered as much private wealth as they could lay their hands on, storing it in centralized treasuries for the service of God and his Taiping agents. The trade of the city was shut down, and the population was impressed into Taiping armies or into service as bearers for their troops. During the eastward march that followed, many of these elements were enshrined in a central planning document, *The Land Regulations of the Heavenly Dynasty* (*Tianchao tianmou zhidu*). The expropriation of private farmland and collective labor in agriculture were decreed but only haphazardly and ineffectively implemented.[22]

The great urban center of Nanjing, the newly declared Heavenly Capital, was the site of Hong's greatest social experiment. Nanjing remained largely calm, quiet, and, according to Western visitors, strikingly clean in the midst of the surrounding chaos and genocidal warfare.[23] It was the God Worshippers' great opportunity but also a great challenge, for the urbane local residents who survived the city's capture despised their occupiers. Even setting aside their outlandish beliefs, the Taiping were seen as déclassé, uncouth, and unrefined—befitting their Guangxi and Hakka origins. Their coarse tastes in food, garish clothing, and delight in painting their houses with bright primary colors and adorning them with pictures of elephants and tigers were juvenile and savage, clear demonstrations of their unfitness for rule.

In a strenuous effort to convert the Nanjing population to their faith, the Taiping burned almost all the city's great Buddhist and Daoist temples to the ground, smashed their statuary, and defrocked or killed their priests. Confucianism fared somewhat better—the conquerors allowed that some of the classical canon might still be usefully read, albeit in Taiping redaction, and locals noted that the newly installed Heavenly bureaucracy drew its titles from the *Rites of Zhou*. The population was commanded to attend massive open-air sermons, where brightly colored banners streamed on all sides, to observe the Saturday sabbath and the new solar calendar, and to pause for prayer each morning and evening.

More dedicated still was the Taiping effort to remake Nanjing's economy and society. Buildings were seized and converted into *guan* (institutes). This basic communal unit of residence and production superseded the household, shop, guild, and temples on which Nanjing society had been built. *Guan* were divided by occupation (bakers, weavers, bricklayers) or by specialized function (firefighting, medical provision). Each had its own collective treasury and its own place of Christian worship and was overseen by a lower official known as a corporal. All property was theoretically public, to be distributed as necessary by Taiping authorities, and an ultimately unsuccessful effort was made to demonetize the urban economy. Over the decade of Taiping rule, the problem of provisioning the city grew ever more acute.

The greatest and most sustained popular resistance was occasioned by Taiping efforts to remake the gender and family system. Based on their ideology of gender equality, the occupying forces outlawed footbinding and prostitution (formerly a mainstay of Nanjing's economy), encouraged women to roam freely through open streets, and promoted female officials. But they also mandated strict chastity and gender segregation. Female *guan*, like their male counterparts, were occupationally specialized into traditionally sanctioned women's work such as weaving and tailoring and also hard physical labor such as porterage and construction. Husbands and wives, fathers and mothers, sons and daughters reportedly camped out *en masse* in front of the confines of their loved ones and wailed incessantly. By 1855, faced with the evident failure of this three-year experiment, the Taiping authorities backed down and abolished gender segregation in the Heavenly Capital.

At the height of the Taiping crisis, the Qing court found itself presented with an unwonted distraction—a second wave of European invasion. At first it paid little attention, in order to concentrate on the apocalyptic challenge posed by the Heavenly Kingdom. But before long the foreign invasion mushroomed into a threat unparalleled in the more than two-century history of the Great Qing empire.

The Second Anglo-Chinese War

British merchants and officials in China had become increasingly dissatisfied with the degree of commercial activity allowed under the Treaty of Nanjing and by resistance on the part of local authorities to direct penetration of the interior. Gradually they convinced themselves that the solution to their problems would be a formal exchange of ambassadors and the permanent residence of the British ambassador at the imperial capital of Beijing. This would allow China—finally, belatedly, and forcibly—to take its place among the "family of nations."[24]

The British pretext for pressing their claims militarily while the Qing was conveniently embroiled in civil war came with the *Arrow* incident of October 1856. The *Arrow* was a lorcha, a refitted European commercial hull with Chinese sails, owned by a Chinese merchant from Hong Kong and lying at anchor outside Canton. More than a decade after the Opium War, this city remained a festering sore in relations between the Qing and the British. Local officials and the urban population had staunchly and successfully resisted the actual admission of foreigners into the town—though they had routinely entered the other ports opened by the Treaty of Nanjing. The interests of the two governments at Canton, moreover, were represented at the time by two especially hotheaded individuals, Imperial Commissioner Ye Mingzhen (heir to a middle Yangzi pharmaceutical fortune) and British Canton Consul Harry Parkes.

The outbreak of the war involved a bewildering series of lies, deceptions, and ambiguities. A Cantonese constabulary force had boarded the *Arrow* to arrest the Chinese crew for importing opium. In the process, Parkes claimed, the police had insulted the Crown by hauling down the Union Jack, although subsequent investigations revealed that the flag had not been flying at the time. The British captain claimed to have been on board, though he later admitted he was not. The *Arrow*'s British registry had expired and the ship was no longer entitled to British protection, though Parkes hid this fact from the Chinese and from British Admiral Seymour, who peremptorily opened hostilities by bombarding Canton city.

The uproar at home over the large number of Chinese civilian casualties temporarily dissolved Parliament and brought down the government. And yet the British pursued the fighting, largely because British Prime Minister Palmerston had been planning this war for months. The true *casus belli* was opium, which had become absolutely central to Britain's China trade, its Indian colonies, and its home economy. Despite its victory in the Opium War, Britain had never succeeded in getting the Qing to lift the legal ban on opium imports, and just three months prior to the *Arrow* affair Commissioner Ye had proclaimed a "final and complete rejection" of British requests for legalization. War seemed like the only option.[25]

Eventually, the British government dispatched James Bruce, Lord Elgin, to prosecute the war with the Qing. The French sent a task force and declared themselves co-belligerents, while Russia and the United States sent along representatives as part of a "peaceful demonstration" of their allied interests with Britain. The Second Anglo-Chinese War replicated that of the First: the Qing tried to localize the conflict as much as possible around Guangzhou, while the British sought to expand it and outflank their adversary. Whereas in the Opium War this had meant sailing up the coast and via the Yangzi to Nanjing, in light of the fact that Nanjing was currently the capital of the Taiping Heavenly Kingdom, this tack would no longer do. So Elgin proceeded yet further north, in April 1858 breaching the blockade at the Dagu forts and occupying Tianjin, north China's most important commercial city and barely a hundred miles from Beijing (Fig. 14).

There the Qing and the foreigners met and concluded the Treaty of

Fig. 14   Dagu forts, with corpses of Chinese defenders, 1860. Photograph by Felix Beato. Courtesy of Peabody Essex Museum, Salem, Massachusetts.

Tianjin on June 26, which granted the British as well as their allies the right to station a permanent ambassador in Beijing. It also opened ten new treaty ports (several on the Yangzi as far upriver as Hankou, Newchwang, on Manchuria's Liaodong peninsula, and two on Taiwan), granted freedom of travel throughout the interior for Western missionaries and merchants, and stipulated war reparations of four million silver taels for Britain and two million for France. Implicitly, opium imports were legalized.[26]

Britain had gotten all that it wanted, but its gains proved difficult to enforce on the Qing court and its local officials. More than two years of complicated campaigning in north China followed, with Parkes and others engaging in Kipling-esque exploits of derring-do colorfully described in their memoirs.[27] In the fall of 1860, a furious Elgin occupied Beijing, forcing the Xianfeng emperor and his court to flee outside the Great Wall, to the imperial summer retreat at Chengde. Elgin considered burning down the Imperial Palace but settled for destroying the Summer Palace north of the city, which, he reasoned, would punish the Qing court but not the good people of China (Fig. 15). On October 24 he forced the rump imperial government, in the person of the emperor's 27-year-old younger brother Yixin (Prince Gong), to sign the Beijing Convention. The convention ratified the court's commitment to comply with the Treaty of Tianjin, doubled the reparations due the British, ceded the lease of Kowloon peninsula, and added Tianjin to the list of open treaty ports. Just as his father had done with the Parthenon frieze in Greece, the younger Lord Elgin carted home magnificent loot from his mission for public display in London, including a Qing imperial throne for installation at the Victoria and Albert Museum.[28]

The Great Qing Empire Survives the Taiping

The eventual suppression of the Taiping rebellion was accomplished far less by forces under the direct control of the Qing state than by regional armies led by members of the local gentry. Actions of the Taiping such as desecrating temples, lineage halls, and grave sites, as well as recruiting poor farmers to attack and kill their landlords or richer neighbors, profoundly alienated the literati, especially those of higher rank and status. Nowhere was this more the case than in Hunan's Xiang River valley, which the Taiping trampled during their northward march in 1852 and threatened again periodically.

Fig. 15   Imperial Summer Palace, Beijing, prior to its burning by Lord Elgin, 1860. Photograph by Felix Beato. Courtesy of Peabody Essex Museum, Salem, Massachusetts.

The Xiang valley was dominated by wealthy planters whose rice crop, largely grown by tenants, was shipped downriver to feed urbanites or cultivators of nonfood crops, especially cotton, in the lower Yangzi. The culture of this region was highly nativist; it would become a center of the anti-foreign movements of the late nineteenth century and would subsequently spawn the most nativist of Communist revolutionaries, Mao Zedong. The people of the Xiang valley believed that they constituted the true Chinese, and this mentality was expressed in such identity-affirming rituals as the Dragon Boat races of the eighth lunar month, when outsiders of all types found themselves vulnerable to physical attack.[29]

The elite culture of the region was also deeply conservative, in its partisan adherence to the teachings of strict moral integrity, social hierarchy, and ritual correctness found in Song Neo-Confucianism and the Four Books, but it was also eminently practical, eschewing literary refinement, philological erudition, and metaphysical speculation in favor of "substantive learning" and the techniques of practical statecraft—a tradition embodied in Changsha's Yuelu Academy.[30] From the circle that formed around academy alumnus Tang Jian emerged the group of activist upper gentry who ultimately defeated the Taiping, especially the metropolitan degree-holders Hu Linyi, Zeng Guofan, and Zuo Zongtang. These extraordinarily wealthy, erudite, well-connected, and impassioned men drew upon the new techniques of warfare that had emerged from the White Lotus campaigns—in part at the hands of their Hunanese compatriot Yan Ruyi—and further refined them.[31] First applied to the anti-Taiping wars by Hu but subsequently perfected by Zeng, these techniques stressed two new forms of military organization. In the spirit of the seventeenth-century culture hero Gu Yanwu, they were based on natural rather than administrative social groupings, and they relied on indigenous rather than bureaucratic structures of leadership.

The new thinking about statecraft held that the most effective fighting force would be one acting in defense of its own property and home community. So local gentry mobilizers in central China organized village-level groups of farmboys—part-time farmers, part-time soldiers—to protect their homes. But these were trained by local elites, who often paid, armed, and uniformed them as well. They then linked these militia up with neighboring village militia into larger scale fighting forces, through local systems of commercial exchange centered on a periodic market or market town, or through kingship networks. A hierarchically coordinated, but extra-bureaucratic, command structure gradually formed out of local gentry members. Over time, the power of these local elites increased, as military command and control of a certain percentage of the region's economic surplus was added to their existing financial power as major landholders and to their sociocultural status as members of the literati. Power and influence that had formerly been monopolized by the county magistrate—the agent of the central Qing state—at least for the time being slipped into local elite hands.

In December 1852, the Xianfeng court appointed Zeng Guofan commissioner of militia organization for central China, and Zeng took the opportunity to construct a larger military force under his personal command. A product of the Changsha academy scene, he had passed the metropolitan examination in 1838, spent several years in that hotbed of political debate, the Hanlin Academy, and by midcentury was vice president of the Board of Civil Office at Beijing, where he served as mentor to a group of younger activist literati, especially those from his native Hunan. He had observed with deep concern the military situation back home while on assignment to oversee the provincial examination in neighboring Jiangxi earlier in 1852. He had also been influenced by his compatriot Hu Linyi, who while serving in various prefectural posts in Guizhou had gradually put together a personal army, and by Luo Zenan, who had been tinkering with a similar project in Zeng's native Xiangxiang county itself.

Within a year or so Zeng, Luo, and others had cobbled together a province-wide military force they dubbed the Hunan Army. Posted as governor of neighboring Hubei province in 1855, Hu Linyi subsumed that province's many existing local militia groups into a corresponding Hubei Army. Other local leaders throughout the Yangzi valley followed suit, notably the Hefei native Li Hongzhang. After winning the metropolitan degree in 1847 and studying for several years in the Hanlin Academy under Zeng Guofan, Li returned home and over the late 1850s gradually put together his own Anhui Army.

These provincial armies offered an offensive, mobile counterpart to the essentially defensive role of the local militia, comprised of part-time soldiers protecting their home turf. Soldiers in the provincial armies were known as "local braves" (in effect, mercenaries). The recruit pool comprised not only farmers but also bandits, secret society types, and other marginal elements who were already under arms prior to recruitment. The structure of such armies differed dramatically from the highly bureaucratized and now essentially moribund military forces controlled directly by the central Qing state. Their leadership came from the upper gentry of the province—many of them widely respected *jinshi* scholars who had traditionally been seen as indifferent to the military establishment. As members of the provincial elite, they shared ties from study and examination preparation in their respective provincial capitals and in Beijing, notably in the Hanlin. Their leadership structure was based very much on scholarly teacher-student or classmate ties, not infrequently overlaid with relations among lineages. Within each unit of the army, soldiers owed personal loyalty to their commanding officer, who often recruited, armed, and paid his troops himself. It was a feudal style of organization.

The financing of these armies was likewise personal and extra-bureaucratic. To organize his Hunan Army, Zeng Guofan had initially requested and received permission from the Hunan governor to divert funds from that province's network of collection stations, which imposed tolls on bulk transport of commercial goods. Over time he and his counterparts in other provinces developed highly sophisticated methods to solicit funds from local landholders and merchants. The collection of these "contributions" was managed through a network of bureaus run by members of the nongovernmental local elite.

Though their financial base was firmly in their home region, these armies ranged farther afield. Li Hongzhang, for example, took much of his Anhui Army with him when he was posted as governor-general of Zhili (Hebei) in 1870. As early as the late 1850s these new regional forces began to turn the tide of the Taiping campaigns. In 1856 the Heavenly Kingdom was greatly weakened by internal strife among its leaders. Its most effective military commander, the Eastern King Yang Xiucheng, after declaring himself the incarnation of the Holy Spirit and plotting to usurp power from Hong Xiuquan, was assassinated on the latter's orders. The Heavenly Kingdom's most brilliant field general, Assistant King Shi Dakai, abandoned the Heavenly Capital and took off on campaigns of his own upriver on the Yangzi.

Over the next two years, Hu Linyi's Hubei Army recaptured Wuchang, and Zeng Guofan's Hunan Army retook most of Jiangxi. Despite some military recovery and extremely bloody fighting throughout the lower Yangzi region over the next several years, the Taiping capital fell under ever-tightening siege. In June 1864 Hong Xiuquan died from either suicide or illness, and the following month the Hunan Army, under Zeng Guofan's brother Guoquan, breached the walls of Nanjing and slaughtered its inhabitants. The Heavenly Kingdom was extinguished.

For most localities of central China, the Taiping rebellion left gaping wounds. The physical infrastructure of county seats—magistrates' offices, civil service examination halls, bell and drum towers, the Confucian temple, lineage and guild halls, and city walls and gates, everything that made the place a community and an administrative component of the Great Qing empire—all had to be rebuilt from ruins. So too did the rural infrastructure of irrigation and flood control. Fields that had gone to waste had to be reclaimed. The surviving local population had to be fed, their bodily health tended to, and their loyalties rekindled. The dead required burial, both literally and figuratively. Many localities found themselves with mountains of decaying corpses or piles of bones that demanded identification and proper internment. Martyrs who had fallen in defense of personal chastity, locality, and dynasty—in many places, a significant percentage of the local population—needed to be honored and commemorated on gravestones, in published martyrologies, and in public lectures and recited tales.

In spite of the fact that large numbers of local people had been recruited to the Taiping cause, the loyalty of every locality had to be reaffirmed beyond question. The entire apocalyptic experience of the great rebellion had to be domesticated, its lessons understood and packaged in a historical narrative, usually in the form of a new edition of the county gazetteer compiled by surviving local elites a decade or two following the restoration of order. All of these acts of "reconstruction" cost considerable money, and the process of collectively soliciting funds forged new community solidarities that would remain in place for decades.

The fifteen-year-long Taiping rebellion, along with the Nian and Muslim separatist rebellions that arose in its wake, had a profound impact on the Qing polity, society, and economy.[32] Despite the conventional tendency to divide Qing history into periods before and after the Opium War, this was unquestionably much more of a watershed event for the Qing population. The Taiping wars were extraordinarily bloody, directly causing perhaps thirty million deaths. Some regions of the country—the middle Yangzi and, still more, the lower Yangzi, the empire's economic center—were decimated, as populations died or moved out and only gradually resettled there. The numerical decline of the agrarian workforce in the Yangzi delta meant that labor, for the first time in centuries, became relatively more expensive than land; this was reflected in the increased granting of "permanent tenancy" rights, "surface ownership," and other favorable leasehold arrangements by landowners eager to attract tenants. Well into the twentieth century, despite this region's relatively high tenancy rates, the continued favorable position of tenants worked to the great disadvantage of Communists who sought to organize them to overthrow their landlords.[33]

The economy was similarly disrupted. Agricultural yield was depressed in the most productive areas of the country, and trade along the empire's single most important transport route, the Yangzi river between Wuhan and Jiangnan, was curtailed both by fighting and by the Taiping's occupation of Nanjing. The ability of steamships to run this blockade, more than any more general technological superiority or cost-effectiveness, gave the advantage to British and American shippers and provided them with a foothold into Qing domestic commerce.[34] The changing structure of domestic trade brought about by the Taiping wars permanently reduced the prominence of merchants from Huizhou (Anhui) and to a lesser extent from Shanxi, and put members of the Cantonese and Ningbo diasporas in their place. Perhaps most strikingly of all, the modest Yangzi delta maritime port of Shanghai, which had been opened to foreigners a decade earlier by the Treaty of Nanjing but had not yet experienced any great commercial boom, suddenly received as refugees the empire's greatest merchants, displaced from Suzhou, Ningbo, Shaoxing, Yangzhou, and Nanjing. Suzhou and Nanjing never recovered their commercial position, while Shanghai began a meteoric rise to the very pinnacle of China's urban hierarchy.[35]

The court's imprudent decision to introduce unbacked paper currency to underwrite the rebellion's suppression met with little popular acceptance and aggravated the spiraling wartime price inflation. While this experiment was quickly aborted, other fiscal innovations introduced not by the center but by the masters of the new provincial armies—notably but not exclusively the new commercial transit tax known as *likin*—probably more than anything else decisively shifted the burden of government revenue from agriculture to the more elastic commercial sector. No one was more innovative than Hu Linyi, whose tenure as Hubei provincial governor between 1855 and his death in 1861 placed him in control of the dominating node of the empire's long-distance domestic commerce at Wuhan. Hu energetically set up customs stations throughout the region and extended into most of central China the salt-market reforms that his fellow provincial Tao Zhu had introduced at Yangzhou two decades earlier. He produced and sold licenses to government brokers in order to resuscitate and tax wholesale trade throughout the region. And he commuted tribute grain collections to cash throughout his jurisdiction, effectively shifting the last remaining instrument of the government's grain supply to reliance on the commercial market.

All of these changes had profound social as well as economic implications. Previous Qing policy was based on the goal of "delimiting" the respective spheres of literati and merchant power by keeping the former out of trade and denying the latter the right to sit for the examinations. Based on his "statecraft" faith in the gentry's public-mindedness and moral rectitude and his desire to stimulate regional commerce for fiscal and developmental reasons, Hu Linyi actively recruited local degree-holders into service as commodities brokers, salt distributors, and other mercantile roles. Collectively, these innovations went far toward creating what would become arguably the dominant social class in the

Qing's final half century, the new, hybrid, business-oriented gentry-merchant.

At the other end of the social scale, the Taiping and other midcentury rebellions left in their wake an enormous problem of demobilization. A very large number of young men had been systematically withdrawn from village life to campaign in Hu Linyi's, Zeng Guofan's, and Li Hongzhang's regional armies, fighting at times far away from their homes. What was society to do with them after the rebellions were over? Zeng disbanded the 120,000 members of the Hunan Army under his command almost immediately after the capture and looting of Nanjing in 1864 (Zuo Zongtang, for the moment, kept his own forces intact). Although they were told to go home and provided a financial subsidy for their return trip, very few of these mercenaries were reabsorbed into their local agrarian economy. They either slipped the noose of government control and remained in port cities along the route or they stayed at home only briefly before returning to some more inviting urban area they had passed through along the way.

Urban populations in central China during the post-Taiping era were thus qualitatively different from those of the same cities prior to midcentury, swollen as they were with large numbers of unemployed or underemployed tough guys, showing off their martial arts in the streets and marketplaces and intimidating the rest of populace. Nor were these elements necessarily unorganized: many of them, during their years on military campaigns or after demobilization, had swelled the ranks of martially-oriented and criminally-inclined organizations such as the Society of Elder Brothers. They represented a new kind of threat to Qing officialdom and local elites.

8

RESTORATION

IN LATE 1860 the Great Qing empire was near extinction. The court, headed by the thirty-year-old Xianfeng emperor—far the weakest ruler the Qing had yet endured—was cowering in exile outside the Great Wall. Foreign barbarians occupied the imperial capital and had burned down the Summer Palace. Domestic rebels with a wildly uncivilized worldview held the southern capital of Nanjing, where they had successfully established a rival government. There was little reason for an observer to suspect that the Qing would survive another year. And yet, it did survive; indeed, it entered a new era of prosperity. How was that possible?

Following the signing of the Beijing Convention and the declaration by the Western expeditionary force that the hostilities in north China were over, the Xianfeng court continually procrastinated its return to Beijing. The emperor himself, overwhelmed and deeply depressed, never did so, dying of illness in Chengde in August 1861. On his deathbed he named as successor his five-year-old son, Aisin Gioro Zaichun. A complicated power struggle ensued over who should act as regent, culminating in a palace coup and the execution of three imperial princes from the losing faction in early November. The victors were an ad hoc coalition of power-holders who effectively controlled imperial policymaking.

The coalition's leader was Xianfeng's once low-ranking concubine Yehonala (more commonly known in English language sources by her title the Empress Dowager Cixi), who had the good fortune to be mother of his only male heir, now the new emperor. It included as well the young Prince Gong, who had been left holding the bag in Beijing when his brother and the rest of the imperial family fled. Prince Gong had shown unanticipated competence under the circumstances and gained the respect of the terrifying Westerners with whom he dealt. The coalition also included the most powerful Chinese official in the empire, Zeng Guofan, the de facto representative of Qing control in most of central and south China. Zaichun's reign title was candidly proclaimed as Tongzhi or "Joint Rule."

Four Views of the Tongzhi Restoration

As early as 1869, Qing literati had begun to declare the Tongzhi reign (1862–1874) a "restoration," and this usage quickly was adopted in proud self-reference by the court itself.[1] In imperial political thought, a restoration might occur a century or more into a dynastic cycle, when a constellation of talented ministers and a virtuous monarch righted the foundering ship of state. This happened after the Wang Mang usurpation in the Han dynasty, according to the conventional view, and after the An Lushan rebellion in the Tang. Historians in the West have recognized the Tongzhi restoration as a seminal era in Qing history, but they have assigned it very different—and in some cases nearly antithetical—significances. Here, we will look at four interpretations whose differing emphases capture various elements of this complex, pivotal reign period.

Probably the most widespread depiction of the restoration was, and remains, the one John King Fairbank first enunciated in 1954.[2] For him, a number of factors made the Tongzhi reign the first great age of Western impact on China and thus of Qing "modernization." On the diplomatic front, by virtue of the 1858 Treaty of Tianjin and the subsequent Beijing Convention, the West had fulfilled its mission of bringing China into the comity of nations. Ambassadors of foreign nations—the resident ministers for whom the British had fought the Second Anglo-Chinese War—quickly took up their posts in Beijing, led by Lord Elgin's secretary, Frederick Bruce, representing Britain and Anson Burlingame representing the United States. The Qing court slowly began the process of reciprocally dispatching its own emissaries abroad, most notably Guo Songtao—former classmate of Zeng Guofan at Changsha's Yuelu Academy, *jinshi* of 1847, heroic commander of the Hunan Army's 1853 liberation of Taiping-occupied Nanchang, and in the late 1870s joint ambassador to Britain and France.

On March 11, 1861, the regents established an ad hoc subcommittee of the Grand Council called the Zongli Yamen (Office of General Management). It eventually grew into a sprawling bureaucracy and the Qing's first effective Foreign Office, which was headed, off and on, for twenty-seven years by Prince Gong.[3] Most critically, the Western powers, who had gradually come to favor the Qing over the "Christian" Taiping and now had substantial privileges guaranteed by treaty, recognized their stake in the restoration's success. Led by Bruce and Burlingame, the foreign diplomatic corps gradually evolved what became known as the "cooperative policy," a gentlemen's agreement to subordinate individual national interests to the collective progress of the West's civilizing mission, and a diplomatically brokered holiday from adventurous military expansion that would remain in place through the end of the Tongzhi reign.

Freed from many administrative restrictions, commercial intercourse between the Qing and the West greatly intensified. Although this was hardly a Western-inspired commercial revolution—since the late Ming, China had been one of the most commercialized agrarian economies in the world, and the empire's foreign trade had long been extremely significant—it did lead to considerable socioeconomic restructuring.[4] Western merchants employed scores of Chinese buyers and commercial agents, and many independent Chinese trading firms specialized in the collection of goods for foreign export and the distribution of foreign imports. The resulting "compradores" emerged as often very wealthy cultural intermediaries from whose ranks many of the most important figures in late nineteenth- and early twentieth-century China would be drawn. Lauded by some as a "bridge between East and West," compradores would also become a convenient target for nativist Chinese of all political stripes.[5]

Treaty ports were opened along the north China coast and up the Yangzi into central China, within whose "concessions" a direct foreign presence and something of a hybrid culture emerged. The most notable was Shanghai, which effectively began its rise to the status of a global commercial metropolis in this period. In 1861 Prince Gong established the Imperial Maritime Customs, a new hybrid institution almost entirely directed by Westerners, to formally replace the native-staffed Kangxi-era maritime customs as China's regulatory and taxing authority for Sino-Western trade.

On the cultural front, according to the Fairbank narrative, study of the West and things Western, which had first become serious with the work of Wei Yuan and others in the Daoguang era, greatly intensified in the Tongzhi reign. In 1862 a Translation Bureau was set up to train young Qing subjects in Western languages and to translate important works of

European scientific, social, and political thought. Protestant missionaries contributed to this project as well. In 1874 in Shanghai, the American John Fryer organized a subscription drive to establish a school and reading room, the Chinese Polytechnic Institute, to translate and disseminate scientific and technical knowledge. It produced a coterie of young Chinese who would become important engineers, intellectuals, and publicists of reform in decades to come. Beginning in 1872, several classes of selected young Chinese men were dispatched by the court to the Chinese Educational Mission in Hartford, Connecticut, to be acculturated in aspects of American life, including baseball.

Literati and commoners alike expressed considerable resistance to this movement devoted to the learning and adoption of "foreign things." The better families would never allow their sons to enter training programs in Western languages, no matter how strongly these initiatives were endorsed by the court. And no less patriotic a military hero and Confucian scholar than Guo Songtao was violently attacked by a gentry-led crowd in his native county in Hunan when his intention to accept an ambassadorship to Europe was announced. But a growing number of elites both inside and outside government were beginning to adapt to the critical needs of the time. They came to believe that the empire's very survival demanded systematic "self-strengthening" via a program of selective borrowing from the West, especially in industrialization.

Almost immediately in the wake of Fairbank's exposition of the Tongzhi restoration as the high tide of Westernization, a contrary reading of the era's significance emerged. Mary Clabaugh Wright described the same events as a tragedy, whose failed heroes were largely the heartland scholar-officials who came out of the Hunan Army: Hu Linyi, Zuo Zongtang, Guo Songtao, and above all Zeng Guofan. These patriotic men, though Chinese, were steadfastly loyal to the Manchu Qing (which represented civilized norms, unlike the Chinese Taiping) and relatively selfless. Wright emphasized their deep Neo-Confucian convictions, their heartfelt concern for the moral rectification of their social class, and their postrebellion quest to reestablish incorrupt and vigorous benevolent governance on a rather traditional model. The few Western borrowings they felt they must make were merely grudging compromises in their conservative reformist crusade.[6]

Yet a third interpretation of the restoration saw in the Tongzhi reign the beginnings of a decentralization of political power in favor of provincial or regional governance that would culminate in the disaster of twentieth-century warlordism.[7] The focus of this view was less on the Confucian idealist Zeng Guofan than on the more pragmatic Li Hongzhang, who became the dominant statesman in the Qing empire for the last three decades of the nineteenth century (Fig. 16). The fact that Li was Chinese rather than Manchu was significant, as was his factional partisanship and personal acquisitiveness (Li died in 1901 as one of the empire's wealthiest men). The process of decentralization grew out of regional armies, especially those from Hunan and Anhui, that were personally loyal to their commanders rather than to the throne or the empire as a whole. Although Zeng Guofan formally disbanded his Hunan Army in 1864 immediately after defeating the Taiping, portions of that force remained in the service of Zuo Zongtang and others. Li Hongzhang did not disband the Anhui Army at all. It moved with him when his power base shifted from the lower Yangzi to north China, where it ultimately bore the brunt of the fighting during the Sino-Japanese War of 1895.

These armies were supported by extraordinary revenues, most notably the transit tax on commercial goods. Following the suppression of the Taiping and the Nian, an accord was reached whereby the central government recaptured a share of these provincially imposed collections, but only a small percentage was ever effectively remitted upward to the throne. Within the late Qing empire's expanding commercial economy, taxation of trade was an elastic source of fiscal revenue, while agrarian taxation, upon which the central government depended, remained relatively fixed. The land tax, which comprised approximately 75 percent of total government revenues in 1750, had fallen to around 35 percent by the dynasty's last years. Fiscal resources were thus systematically diverted over time from the center to regional administrations.

A further shift of power came when these irregular private army commanders were appointed by the court to regular administrative positions. Zeng Guofan was appointed to the empire's most important regional post, governor-general of Jiangsu, Anhui, and Jiangxi, in 1860, and six years later his brother Guoquan was made governor of Hubei. Zuo Zongtang became governor of Zhejiang in 1862 and governor-general of Shaanxi and Gansu in 1866. Li Hongzhang was acting governor of Jiangsu in 1861, promoted to acting governor-general of Jiangsu and Jiangxi (succeeding Zeng Guofan) four years later, to governor-general of Hunan and Hubei in 1869, and to governor-general of the metropolitan province of Zhili the following year. His brother Hanzhang governed Hubei from 1870 to 1882 and Guangdong from 1889 to 1895.

Fig. 16   Zhili Governor-general Li Hongzhang, 1870s. Courtesy of Peabody Essex Museum, Salem, Massachusetts.

Segueing into such posts, of course, gave these men control over collection of the one source of revenue that had escaped them in the past, the land tax. And although the law of avoidance was observed in these appointments, the weakened Qing court gradually lost many of the other checks and balances over its most powerful regional officials. Their terms of office, for example, sometimes greatly exceeded the previous Qing norm of roughly three years: Li Hongzhang remained in Zhili for nearly a quarter century, and Zhang Zhidong—a powerful field administrator of the next generation—held the Hunan-Hubei governor-generalship for nearly two decades. Such regional satraps assumed unprecedented discretion over the appointments of provincial treasurers and judges, prefects and county magistrates, who were often nominated from the ranks of their own personal staffs. Moreover, these informal "tent governments" of private secretaries mushroomed into what were effectively personal bureaucracies. Zhang Zhidong employed a staff of well over 600 men, including some 239 foreigners.[8] With the establishment of "self-strengthening" industrial enterprises by these regional administrations, whose managers were also drawn from these officials' personal staffs, even greater autonomous power devolved into their hands.

According to a fourth and final reading of the Tongzhi reign, the militarization that continued throughout the restoration years caused the power of nongovernmental elites in local society to rise at the expense of county magistrates and other centrally appointed agents of the imperial bureaucracy. In contrast with partisans of the decentralization argument, which held that political power migrated away from the throne and into the hands of regional administrators, this subsequent view saw a parallel trend that effectively moved power out of the hands of government officials altogether and into the hands of private local notables.[9] The rising influence of these elites and the nongovernmental organizations they controlled was part of a growing popular mood in favor of local autonomy that would eventually receive official blessing in the early twentieth century.

The process went something like this. The widespread formation of elite-led local militia for community self-defense in the Taiping campaigns—itself building upon their earlier use in the White Lotus rebellion and Opium War—enhanced the power of local gentry degree-holders. In addition to their social status and landholding wealth, they now took over military commands, administration of (military) justice, and dispensation of rewards in the form of soldiers' pay. All of these functions were formally claimed as monopolies of the throne in the constitutional system of the Qing. Most important, these private elites wrested control of local tax collection away from administrators and clerks. The key institution here was the "bureau" (ju), a kind of quasi-governmental public office used in the past on an ad hoc basis to oversee the financial management of civil construction and other projects but now used for the collection of commercial or other levies such as transit tolls or brokerage fees. In certain areas of Jiangnan, these bureaus of gentry-landlords even succeeded at inserting themselves into the collection of the land tax itself, blurring the distinction between rent and taxes. This process, added to the new military powers of local elites, might be interpreted as a form of refeudalization during late Qing China.

Accompanying the rising power of nongovernmental elites was a continuing political discourse on statecraft.[10] The key figure here was Feng Guifen (1809–1874), who came from a family of wealthy Suzhou landowners, passed the metropolitan examination in 1740, and served as a compiler in Beijing's Hanlin Academy during the Opium War years, where he joined other young reform-minded scholars as a member of the Gu Yanwu Shrine Association. When the Taiping rebels ravaged his homeland, Feng returned to organize and command the local militia. During the Tongzhi reign he served as headmaster of academies at Suzhou and Shanghai and as private secretary to the governor-general of Liang-Jiang, Li Hongzhang. In this capacity he argued for self-strengthening industrialization by borrowing from the West, and at the same time articulated his views on local government reform. Feng's political thought about statecraft was a blend of indigenous Neo-Confucian ideas with notions absorbed from the West. He was a key figure in adapting late Qing statecraft to changing conditions, by recognizing an affinity between the tradition of local autonomy inherited from the thought of Gu Yanwu and imported notions of Western representative democracy.

With respect to local administration, Feng took over from Gu the idea of using large gentry landlords (the class to which both Gu and Feng belonged) as more or less permanent county magistrates serving in their own native place—eliminating, in other words, the law of avoidance. But he added to this another feature, the development of a finer political infrastructure below the county level. Drawing on a revived notion of the *baojia* mutual responsibility system, Feng argued that subcounty headmen should be popularly elected by secret ballot and that these headmen should be fully salaried professionals in order to avoid becoming simply lackeys of wealthy or powerful local interests. They were to be responsible to their constituents, not controlled from above.

Thus, Feng proposed a two-level structure of local administration to resolve the problems of absolutism, bureaucratism, and official inertia. Whereas his magistrate would be a local gentry member serving in a permanent or hereditary capacity (and in that sense feudal), he would be matched with a coterie of subordinate headmen who were also local men but were commoners serving elected terms of office. As with the prescriptions of Gu Yanwu some two centuries earlier, those of Feng Guifen were never enacted in his lifetime, but they circulated among sympathetic literati and served as inspiration for later generations of political reformers.

The Revival of Empire

The midcentury Xianfeng reign had witnessed not only the Taiping and Nian rebellions, both mounted by persons self-identified as Han Chinese, but also large-scale separatist movements along the western frontiers. The separatists were ostensibly Qing subjects of varying cultural origins who shared a Muslim faith and were thus lumped together by both the Chinese and the Qing state as Hui. In the southwest, growing ethnic tensions between indigenous and immigrant populations sparked a massacre of at least four thousand Muslims in the Yunnan provincial capital of Kunming in May 1856, following a call for ethnic cleansing by the Manchu provincial judge. The snowballing response led to the creation of a breakaway Muslim state headquartered at the multicultural city of Dali, situated on major trade routes to both Tibet and Burma. This so-called Panthay rebellion was not finally suppressed until 1873, when a campaign of genocide reportedly reduced the population of Yunnan by five million persons.[11]

In the northwestern New Dominion (Xinjiang), so brutally conquered over the course of the eighteenth century by the Kangxi and Qianlong emperors, an autonomous regime led by the charismatic Muslim holy warrior Ya'qub Beg and fueled by decades of Qing misrule established diplomatic relations with both Britain and Russia and survived until Ya'qub's sudden death (probably from a stroke) in 1877. The regime was suppressed by Hunan Army commander Zuo Zongtang at a cost estimated in the late 1870s to be one sixth of the total annual expenditure of the Qing treasury.[12]

What Zuo Zongtang accomplished in Xinjiang in the late 1870s was not simply the pacification of a rebellion but the reconquest of Muslim Central Asia, a vast area that had been slipping away from Qing control for nearly a century and whose political infrastructure had been wiped out by Ya'qub Beg's regime.[13] To deal with the campaign's immense cost, maritime customs revenues and proceeds of the land tax on interior provinces were diverted to the Inner Asian frontier, at a time when the Qing had costly post-Taiping reconstruction projects to finance and coastal defenses to maintain. This reconquest was precisely what the statecraft reformer Wei Yuan had demanded in 1842, but there were loud complaints by Han literati about such a frivolous expenditure. This time the chief critic was none other than Zuo's former anti-Taiping ally Li Hongzhang, now ensconced as Zhili governor-general and covetous of these funds to develop his Northern Seas Navy.

Unlike the campaign of the eighteenth century, the conquest of Xinjiang in the third quarter of the nineteenth was not a crusade to piece together a universal empire, and its victorious soldiers were not multinational bannermen in service of the Great Qing. The conquering general was a Hunanese gentryman and militia leader, and the conquest of the New Dominions was accomplished by the self-consciously Han patriots of Zuo's Hunan Army. After the military reconquest was effectively completed with the Qing occupation of Khotan in January 1878, indigenous Uighur and Mongol leaders were replaced by regular bureaucratic county officials (more than half of them Zuo's fellow Hunanese), land was reclaimed for sedentary farming, thousands of Chinese settlers (again, predominantly Hunanese) were brought in, and a network of Chinese-Confucian primary schools was established.[14] This vast region, although considered part of the Qing empire for more than a century, was sinicized for the first time, and in 1884 (once more under protest by Li Hongzhang and others) it was declared a province of China.

This was part of a more general late Qing provincialization of the frontier that saw Taiwan granted provincial status three years after Xinjiang, and preparations begun for carving up the Manchu homeland into what would become the "three northeastern provinces" in the early twentieth century. Most immediately the goal was to secure Chinese claims to these borderlands in an era of predatory Western and Japanese threats. But it was also indicative of a broader transformation of the very nature of the Qing polity. Under the Ming, the name "China" (Zhongguo or Zhonghua) had been clearly understood to denote the political organization of the Han or Chinese people, and this understanding persisted among Han Chinese well into the succeeding dynasty. Prior to the Qing conquest, the Aisin Gioro rulers shared this view as well. But within decades of conquering the Ming, the Qing came to refer to their more expansive empire not only as the Great Qing but also, nearly interchangeably, as China. This new Qing China was not the old Ming concept of an exclusively Han ethnic state but rather a self-consciously multinational polity. It took Han Chinese literati quite a while to come around to this reconceptualization, but in the early nineteenth century, in the writings of activist Chinese like Wei Yuan, the idea of China as a multinational state with its new, highly expanded boundaries became standard nomenclature. These were the origins of the China we know today.[15]

Early Qing rulers saw themselves as multi-hatted emperors ruling multiple, compartmented national constituencies separately but simultaneously, and not as alien custodians over a "Chinese" empire. But by the Tongzhi reign, the Qing empire had become a player, albeit reluctantly, in a comity of sovereign nations on the European model and had signed a series of treaties with Western nations in which its ruler was invariably referred to as the emperor of "China" and his regime as the government of "China." Though we do not know with certainty, it seems likely that Prince Gong and the regents for the Tongzhi and subsequent Guangxu emperors saw things this way too, and that their reconquest of Xinjiang was the act of rulers of China, not rulers of a universal Qing empire. From this perspective, making Xinjiang "Chinese" was the appropriate way to go.

The same was true of Manchuria. Vastly depopulated by the move of the banners into China proper during the conquest era, migration of Han Chinese northeast of the Willow Palisade was made illegal after the 1660s. Some migration occurred despite the ban, however, and in times of dearth the court relaxed the prohibition; nearly a million refugees arrived in the year 1876, at the outset of the calamitous north China famine. Faced with Russia's eastward expansion in the second half of the nineteenth century, however, the Qing responded by dropping the prohibition altogether—first in 1860 for the northernmost areas near the contested Amur River valley, then in 1887 for the entire region—and actively encouraged Han settlement. So began the massive movement of Chinese that would more than double the population of the northeast in a half century.[16]

But rather than an assimilation of the Manchus that would merge them invisibly into the dominant Han population, precisely the reverse probably took place. Ethnic or national identities, which were somewhat fungible and negotiable in the early and mid-Qing, seem to have hardened over the course of the nineteenth century. For rank-and-file bannermen—those most urbanized and increasingly impoverished of Qing subjects, living in ghettolike garrison enclaves in major Chinese cities—consciousness of difference was routinely driven home by the contempt they endured from the host population. Ethnic tension was further heightened by anxiety over the empire's declining security and fear of "Chinese traitors."[17]

The Taiping's frontal attempt to exterminate the Manchu "other" crystallized the bannermen's self-identity as a distinctive ethnic group. In 1865 an edict of the Tongzhi court eliminated the residential and occupational restrictions on banner personnel but did not bring an end to ethnic strife.[18] Significant acculturation into Chinese ways, including adoption of the Chinese language, had of course been the Manchu experience in China since the conquest, as had the decline of Manchu martial prowess. But in the early twentieth century the political exploitation of Manchu identity among the Qing and of anti-Manchuism among Chinese were both founded on ethnic sentiments that had only grown stronger over the course of the Qing empire.

Early Industrialization

By the middle of the nineteenth century, China was a highly commercialized agrarian society with a high level of handicraft production, at least some of which was organized into capitalist-style workshops where several artisans worked alongside one another under the control of an owner-manager.[19] But China had little or no industrialization, in the sense of an assembly-line division of labor in factories powered by steam or other inanimate means. This kind of industrialization and the technology that underlay it was never developed indigenously; it was imported from the West, beginning in the Tongzhi reign. A number of general socioeconomic developments in the late Qing empire (c. 1860–1911) provide some background for this turn of events.

Rural society during the late Qing seems to have experienced an acceleration of a longer-term shift, beginning in the late Ming, from payment of rent in kind to payment in cash. In part, this was a response to the state's commutation of the last remaining agrarian tax—tribute grain—from kind to cash. The result was a yet fuller monetization of the rural economy, accompanied by rising absentee landlordism among the increasingly urbanized upper elite (a process accelerated in the Yangzi valley by the violence of the Taiping campaigns). Urban investors in rural farmland paid fees to bursaries to solicit and manage tenants and collect taxes, and any paternalist ties that may have pertained earlier between landlord and tenant were replaced by a contractual, cash nexus along the lines of the capitalist model.

In cities, the large reservoir of free mobile labor detached from agriculture that had been growing for several centuries was augmented by soldiers or civilians dislocated by the midcentury rebellions. Another longer-term trend that accelerated in the post-Taiping era was the *"embourgeoisement"* of the population. One reason for this was the merger of literati and merchant social types into a hybrid gentry-merchant class. Another was the growing sophistication of sojourning merchant groups from a common place of residence, who now coordinated their activities in major commercial centers in pursuit of mutual interests.[20] Related to this was the sporadic assumption of quasi-governmental powers by guilds and other organizations in urban areas, owing to either the default or encouragement of the imperial administration. The rapidly growing scale and scope of urban philanthropy in the hands of "benevolent halls" financed and managed by groups of merchants was the most obvious example.

Several striking incidents illustrate the direction of change. In the upper Yangzi river port of Chongqing, a collection of sojourner merchant guilds known as the Eight Provinces mobilized collectively in the early 1860s to defend the city against siege by the Taiping general Shi Dakai, who had fled westward from the collapsing Taiping capital of Nanjing, and then again to ransom the city from French reprisals following a crowd attack on local missionaries. Two decades later, in downriver Hankou, a linked network of merchant militia sponsored by guilds of many different trades and local origins assumed responsibility for maintaining peace and securing property in the wake of an aborted anti-dynastic secret society rebellion. In Shanghai in 1905, local literati and sojourner merchant groups cooperated to establish the empire's first municipal council. They invoked Western vocabulary and took the municipal councils of the city's foreign concessions as their direct model, but they also clearly built on precedents established in commercial cities of the interior.[21] Together, these trends point toward the availability of liquid capital in a growing cash economy, the pervasiveness of capitalist economic relations, a large and mobile labor force, and creative managerial entrepreneurship. In other words, although the specific organizational models and technology of industrialization were imported, the society and economy seem to have been reasonably ripe to accept that importation.

From 1865 to 1895 the face of urban China was changed by the opening of a significant number of mechanized factories, all owned by Chinese (since foreign-owned plants in China were still illegal) but all based on foreign designs and using imported technology. This development, conventionally referred to as the "self-strengthening movement," might be better characterized as catch-up industrialization. Every one of the newly founded enterprises was located in a recently opened treaty port and relied on foreign designers, engineers, managers, and machinery. The initiative for these enterprises came not from the central government but from provincial or regional administrations and from governors and governors-general—specifically, from a certain few provincial officials, above all Li Hongzhang and Zhang Zhidong, who were amenable to selective Western borrowing and became known collectively as the Foreign Affairs Party (*yangwu pai*).

Li was governor-general in Jiangnan during the late 1860s when the Jiangnan Arsenal was founded, and he relocated to Zhili from 1870 to 1895 during the heyday of early industrialization at Tianjin. Zhang Zhidong, as governor-general at Guangzhou after 1883, oversaw the founding of the Canton Textile Mill, and after being transferred to Wuhan in 1889, he set up the Hanyang Ironworks and the various textile mills at Wuchang. His plan for the ironworks had originally been intended for his jurisdiction at Guangzhou, where it would have taken advantage of the established trade and handicraft production of iron at nearby Foshan; it was only the accident of his transfer to Wuhan that allowed that city rather than Guangzhou to become China's predominant steelmaking center in the early twentieth century.

These early industrialization efforts were not the fruit of private entrepreneurial capitalism but rather of bureaucratic capitalism, and consequently their problems are sometimes likened to those of the state-owned enterprises of the Maoist era. In this style of management, planning and oversight were conducted by state officials, while day-to-day management was left in the hands of private merchants. In most cases, investment and risk were shared by both the public and private sectors, but with officials (or more precisely members of the staff of these officials) setting policy. The idea that officials authorize, plan, and oversee projects while local elites provide most of the financing and manage the actual work of construction was not especially novel to the early industrialization effort. Qing administrators had long used the formula in developing hydraulic works and other large-scale construction projects. The notion of inviting in private merchants was likewise a venerable one; in mid-Qing projects such as opening copper mines or providing logistical support for expansionist military campaigns, the government would typically outline the task to be accomplished and set the parameters for operation and profit-making, then "invite" merchants to bid for the right to finance and manage the actual venture.

Self-strengthening industrialization was concerned first and foremost with national defense—an emphasis directly precipitated by the shock of Western armies occupying the imperial capital at Beijing and by Western-armed military forces successfully protecting Shanghai against the Taiping. Thus, industrialization efforts concentrated first on defense and munitions industries such as the Jiangnan Arsenal and Fuzhou Naval Dockyard. These were followed shortly by heavy industries (coal and iron, heavy machinery) that directly supported armaments manufacture. In contrast with the experience of other late-industrializing countries—and of China itself in the post-Mao reform era—the founding of textile mills and other light industries to produce consumer goods came only belatedly. And even these were prompted by the recognition that the protection of domestic consumer markets from foreign penetration was an act of national defense.

As first articulated by Feng Guifen and subsequently elaborated by Zhang Zhidong, the strategy of self-strengthening proposed that, in the face of the unprecedented Western threat and a new world of international competition, militant resistance was for the moment doomed to failure, as had been made clear in the two Opium Wars.[22] Diplomacy was necessary instead, but diplomacy was only a temporary palliative. The real answer was a new view of the imperial state. In contrast with Western notions of the pursuit of private profit as the engine of economic development and national power, and equally in contrast with inherited Confucian notions of minimal state finance and maximal popular livelihoods as the goal of statecraft, the key in this new and different era was the frank pursuit of state "wealth and power" (*fuqiang*). Only this approach could make China less vulnerable to foreign predations in the future.

Feng Guifen believed that the two problems he addressed—the administrative issue of local self-governance and the need for industrial and military self-strengthening—were interrelated. The Qing empire, as he saw it, was in the grip of widespread bureaucratic malaise. Administrative power was in the hands of a group of do-nothing time-sitters. Men of genuine talent surely existed in the empire, but the current system prevented them from coming to the fore. To bring about the necessary reinvigoration of political leadership, he advocated the wholesale training of technical experts—a concept first implemented in the naval academy attached to the Fuzhou dockyard—and putting them in positions of official authority. At the same time, he proposed quasi-feudal reforms in local administration.

Feng's call for the election of local subofficials—in effect a move toward representative government—was not derived from any foundational notion of natural rights, social contract, or popular sovereignty but instead arose from a perceived need to enhance the "wealth and power" of the state.[23] Still, these ideas were radical. Advocating the naked pursuit of state power seemed to contradict the political goal of maintaining harmony and equilibrium above all, a goal endorsed in such canonical documents as the *Great Learning* (*Daxue*) on which all classically trained scholars had cut their teeth. And the idea of promoting technocrats into positions of political power, while it had antecedents in the late imperial discourse on statecraft, contradicted the basic assumption that the right to govern belonged to men of superior personal virtue.

Did Self-Strengthening Fail?

Many of the self-strengthening enterprises enjoyed a period of initial productivity and profitability, but their chief goal was to achieve national strength. The debacle of the Sino-Japanese War of 1895 thus gave rise to a general consensus that the first three decades of China's early industrialization had been an abject failure, especially when contrasted with Japan. This verdict has been nearly universally adopted by historians. Meiji Japan's "success" versus China's "failure" has over the years been a dominating theme of late Qing historiography. The vast majority of scholarship in both China and the West has concentrated on explaining *why* China's early industrialization failed, not whether.

One set of explanations has emphasized the weakness of political resolve, in spite of the manifest sense of crisis. Zhang Zhidong explicitly (and Feng Guifen before him, implicitly) presented the industrializing reformist credo as "Chinese learning as the substance, Western learning as the functional attributes" (*Zhongxue wei ti, yangxue wei yong*). For Fairbank and his followers, this substance/function dichotomy—signaling an unwillingness to sacrifice Confucian principles of morality, ritual correctness, and social organization while at the same time hoping to achieve the material and technological advantages of the West—betrayed a lack of clear commitment and sufficient sense of urgency. For these historians, industrial society had an entirely different set of cultural premises and schemes of value, the adoption of which was a prerequisite to successful industrialization. Japanese policymakers were willing to accept this value shift, whereas Qing scholar-officials were not.

A yet stronger set of "traditional culture" explanations for the so-called Qing failure were advanced by modernization theorists. Marion Levy, Jr., argued that Chinese Confucian culture favored the selection of business partners, suppliers, and subordinates according to "particularist" ties of kinship and native origin, rather than the "universalist" criteria demanded by industrial enterprise. Meiji industrializers, while they paid similar lip service to Confucian ties and obligations, were in fact far more "rational" in their business practice.[24] Such ideas about Chinese "nepotism" and "corruption" underpinned Albert Feuerwerker's magisterial *China's Early Industrialization* (1958), which decried the "bureaucratic capitalist" style of these projects. Feuerwerker stressed the aversion to risk-taking built into the Qing administrative system, and its special dysfunctionality when men acculturated to this approach found themselves in charge of catch-up industrialization.[25]

Other more concrete obstacles identified by historians as confronting self-strengtheners included the regional rivalries among provincial officials sponsoring these projects, their inability to procure from the West the best and most up-to-date machinery and engineers, and the necessity to promise hesitant investors immediate distribution of profits—this in an era of rapid technological advance worldwide, when all industries, especially those trying to catch up, demanded continuous *re*investment in upgrades.[26]

Of course, with the rapid rise of the Four Little Dragons in the late twentieth century—who touted the virtues of Confucian business practice as the key to their success—and then of post-Mao China itself, mere cultural explanations for the failure of Qing self-strengthening seemed increasingly untenable. Economic and demographic formulations of the failure narrative were more convincing. An especially appealing version was the "high-level equilibrium trap" first advanced by Mark Elvin in 1972. Much simplified, the HLET argued that late imperial China's preindustrial economy operated at such a peak of efficiency that all possible surplus had already been squeezed out of the existing technology and expended on population growth. Consequently, there was an active disincentive to move to a higher level of technology (industrialization) because the dislocation cost would be too great. This step could be introduced only from outside the system, in other words from the West, and even then it would be resisted so long as it operated at a lower level of efficiency than had the earlier technology.[27]

More recently, Elvin has added a related argument, "technological lock-in." Using the example of hydraulic infrastructures, he has argued that the cost of maintaining the old technology was so great that investment in new technologies was nearly impossible, and yet the social cost of *not* maintaining the old technology, in order to free up resources for innovative investment, was too great to bear. This technological lock-in had been reached by most regions of the empire in the nineteenth century, and in many as early as the eighteenth century.[28]

An alternative cause of the Qing's failure to industrialize as adeptly as Meiji Japan might be the disproportionate impact of Western "imperialism" in China. Much of nationalist Chinese historiography on the mainland and in Taiwan accorded this factor considerable weight, while most Western historiography implicitly or, in the case of modernization theorists, explicitly dismissed it. Other Western historians, however, argued that the nineteenth-century West was simply far more covetous of the China market than it was of the Japan market, and therefore used its military and legal power to more effectively reduce the Qing to "dependency" or "peripherality" within the world economy. Western nation-states took advantage of the Qing's loss of tariff autonomy to dump their own industrial products in the empire, and by this unfair competition captured for themselves China's market for industrial goods. They invested in China's industrial development and repatriated the profits to their home economies, thus siphoning off capital that otherwise might have been applied to indigenous industrialization projects. To maintain their advantage, Western nations deliberately propped up the antiquated and tottering Qing imperial regime in order to prevent China from reorganizing politically as an effective nation-state.[29]

Regardless of which of these causes they emphasize, historians arguing for China's "retarded" industrial development must take account of not only its rise to economic power in the late twentieth century but also the small-scale industrial revolution took place there in the quarter-century following 1895. The most recent historiography on the self-strengthening movement has cautiously moved away from the failure narrative altogether, challenging older views and emphasizing instead several impressive areas of success during this era. Benjamin Elman has argued that the naval defeat of 1895 was not due to the technological inferiority of Qing warships, and that at least through the 1880s "the Jiangnan Arsenal and the Fuzhou Navy Yard were more advanced technically that their chief competitor in Japan, the Yokosuka Dockyard."[30] Business historians have also begun to argue that the China Merchants Steamship Company operated profitably for some two decades as a primarily merchant-run enterprise, until the Qing court bureaucratized it in the late 1880s. Zhang Zhidong's state-owned Hubei Textile Company, after its bankruptcy in 1909, was leased to private operators, and its successor has continued to operate profitably in one form or another up to the present day. In this new historiography, the dramatic successes of the post-Mao reform era grew ultimately, if indirectly, out of the experiences of early industrialization in the late Qing.[31]

The Deterioration of Qing Foreign Relations

The quarter century between 1870 and 1895 was marked by the gradual collapse of the "cooperative policy" that had subordinated individual national interests to the West's civilizing mission—and with it, some might say, the collapse of the Tongzhi restoration as a whole.[32] The cooperative policy was undone primarily by two events: the British rejection of the Alcock Convention and the "massacre" at Tianjin in 1870. But both of these singular events may be seen as products of longer-term pent-up grievances and popular pressures, and not the result of official policies. In fact, the governments of the Qing and the various Western powers were content to continue the cooperative agreements worked out in the wake of the Beijing Convention of 1860—but their attitudes were increasingly out of step with large elements of their constituencies.

The background to the Alcock debacle was the rapidly mounting dissatisfaction of British merchants—the so-called "old China hands"—with the gains they had won as a result of the Second Anglo-Chinese War. This sentiment was in effect a replay of their rapid dissatisfaction with the advantages gained from the First Anglo-Chinese War in 1842. The rising discontent had as much to do with changing aspirations of the merchants themselves as it did with conditions on the ground in the Qing empire. Following the Treaty of Nanjing, British mercantile goals had quickly shifted from the simple desire to exchange raw products like tea and opium to a new vision of opening up the "China market" to British manufactured goods, especially textiles. The rallying call for this had been "free trade" liberalism, and the result had been Lord Elgin's invasion of 1858. Subsequently, British goals shifted even further, as entrepreneurs began to see the Qing empire not only as a potential market but also as a source of industrial raw materials and as a potential production site. If the Chinese were not effectively exploiting their own mineral resources, Westerners should and would do that for them; if they were not building the railroads that the country so manifestly needed, the West would do that as well. Ultimately, Westerners began to conceive of building factories in China and using cheap Chinese labor to manufacture goods to sell the Chinese— thus eliminating the added cost of shipping these goods from the West.

The 1858 Treaty of Tianjin contained a clause calling for revision after ten years. Impressed by Western nations' seeming custom of adhering to their treaties, Qing authorities looked forward to the opportunity presented by this upcoming treaty revision and diligently prepared themselves for its negotiation. In conference with the British minister to China, Rutherford Alcock, the Zongli Yamen worked out a revised draft that included moderate and mutually beneficial reforms, such as the exemption of foreign merchants from internal transit tolls in exchange for a slightly higher tariff paid on imported goods at entry. The Convention was signed at Beijing on October 23, 1869. However, the presumed formality of ratification by the British Parliament proved difficult. Over the preceding years, Britain's old China hands had been clamoring ever more loudly for opening up the entire Qing empire to foreign trade and for other new privileges. When these were not found in the Convention as drafted, they lobbied their MPs to reject it, which Parliament did in July 1870. Qing policymakers were shocked by this perceived betrayal, and the position of conciliatory Westernizers such as Prince Gong at court and Li Hongzhang in the provinces was severely undermined.

The second event auguring the collapse of the cooperative policy grew out of tensions resulting from Western missionary activity. The early treaties had allowed Christian missionaries to enter the interior of the empire and had mandated the protection of Western proselytizers and Chinese converts by local officials. But legal conflicts and violent incidents between Christians and practitioners of Chinese popular religion proliferated, many of which had little to do with differences of belief per se. For example, Christian converts frequently defied the customary norms of their native community by refusing to contribute to temple maintenance and annual festival funds imposed at the village or township level, claiming these to be "idolatrous." Or, to take another example, when leaders of Christianized lineages (conversion often took place by the lineage, not the individual) engaged in financial disputes with their neighbors, they not infrequently claimed religious persecution and invoked treaty protection when they presented their case to the county magistrate. The privileged access they gained to officials—access that was formerly an unstated monopoly of the degree-holding gentry—could become a seriously destabilizing force in local society.[33]

One of the ways orthodox local elites responded to this challenge was to spread wild rumors of Western missionary barbarism and secret occult activity, as they did in Tianjin in 1870. Tianjin had been a hotspot of anti-foreignism ever since its occupation by Anglo-French forces in 1858. French authorities had subsequently seized an imperial villa there for use as their consulate, and in 1869 the French Roman Catholic order of Notre Dame des Victoires had razed a local Buddhist temple so that an orphanage could be constructed on the site. Payment of a bounty by that institution's directors for delivery of orphans to their care seems to have brought about a wave of child abduction, and rumors began to circulate that these children were being murdered behind the orphanage's walls for ritual purposes or for medicines made out of their body parts. The issue came to a head in June 1870, when local Qing officials forcibly conducted a search of the orphanage. Though they reported discovering nothing suspicious, the local French consul stormed into the office of one of the inspectors and, amidst a heated argument, shot and killed an attendant. The consul and his party were murdered on the spot, and an indignant local population destroyed the orphanage and several other foreign churches, killing and mutilating some seventeen foreigners, including ten French nuns. As foreign gunboats swarmed to the harbor, yet another war seemed inevitable.

The Qing court sent no less a personage than Zeng Guofan, governor-general of Zhili and the most respected official in the empire, to investigate. His careful report calmed the French by reasserting the orphanage's innocence of any wrongdoing and recommending capital punishment for fifteen of those most responsible for the "massacre." For its part, the French government—embarrassed by the hotheaded behavior of its consul and now preoccupied by the Franco-Prussian War—was equally conciliatory. But Zeng's recommendations were rejected at the imperial court, and he was unceremoniously transferred to the Liang-Jiang governor-generalship at Nanjing. Li Hongzhang—who was brought in to replace Zeng in Zhili—conducted his own investigation and recommended slightly fewer executions, the payment of an indemnity, and the dispatch of a Qing apology mission to Paris. A compromise was worked out by the two governments, but the legacy of goodwill had been effectively squandered, and hardline anti-foreignism at court and throughout Qing society was inflamed by the affair. Zeng Guofan, humiliated and despondent, effectively retired from official life and died early the next year.

Beginning in the 1870s, a continuing series of incidents augured a renewed era of escalating Sino-foreign tension, involving most of the so-called Great Powers. First came the Margary affair of 1875. Desirous of opening up a trade link between the upper Yangzi and its presence in India, Britain had dispatched a 28-year-old subconsul, Augustus Margary, up the river and from there southwest to the Burmese border. As local Chinese officials had feared and predicted, he was murdered by local militia forces while camped along the border. An outraged British minister to China demanded reparations for Margary's family, to the tune of 200,000 taels of silver, and the dispatch of an apology mission to the British throne. This mission, headed by Guo Songtao, eventually became the permanent Qing legation in London. The pattern of a foreign nation demanding monetary payment and other privileges in exchange for a perceived affront had become ingrained in the Qing's foreign relations.

Conflict with Russia was more protracted. The Ili River valley in northern Xinjiang was an agriculturally and minerally rich area and also a strategic point of entry into the entire New Dominions. Imperial Russia had progressively been colonizing its Asian borderlands and in the process had developed strong commercial and other ties with Muslim Central Asia. In 1871, at the height of Ya'qub Beg's separatist movement, Russian armies occupied Ili, ostensibly as a temporary and friendly gesture to secure them for the Qing but in fact to prevent the area from falling into British hands (since Russia assumed Ya'qub Beg to be a British client) and with an eye to its own permanent colonization of the region. With the suppression of Ya'qub's regime by Zuo Zongtang, the Qing court dispatched Chonghou—a Manchu member of the Zongli Yamen who had earlier been involved in investigating the Tianjin massacre and who led the subsequent apology mission to France—to negotiate a Russian withdrawal from Ili.

The treaty he signed in 1879 instead granted Russia permanent possession of the majority of the Ili valley and agreed to pay five million rubles to compensate Russia for its military intervention on the Qing empire's behalf. When news of Chonghou's concessions reached Beijing, there was general outrage. Zhang Zhidong—at this point in his career merely a young Hanlin academician—submitted a memorial demanding Chonghou's immediate decapitation and renunciation of his treaty. Zhang became an instant celebrity, and his rise to official prominence was assured. Drawing on behind-the-scenes support of Britain and the other powers, the Zongli Yamen ultimately succeeded in securing a revised treaty in 1881, negotiated by Zeng Guofan's son Zeng Jize. It reduced the territorial cession made to Russia, but only in exchange for an increased payment of reparations.

More serious than these disputes with Britain and Russia was the festering conflict with France over Vietnam. During the middle period of Chinese imperial history Annam had been a directly ruled protectorate, but by Ming and Qing it had evolved into an autonomous tributary state. France had been involved in missionary activities there since the late Ming, and beginning in the late eighteenth century had increased its commercial and military presence and begun to coerce the Vietnamese court into following its will. The Nguyen dynasty, established in 1802, was heavily, though grudgingly, dominated by the expanding French interests. Treaties of 1862 and 1874 ceded the southern part of Vietnam, known as Cochin China, directly to France and allowed further French military buildup in the northern section, known as Tongkin. Even as it signed these treaties, however, the Nguyen court increased its tributary missions to the Qing and invoked its protection against further French colonization. The Qing responded by organizing a force of unofficial and deniable mercenaries known as the Black Flags, which began guerrilla activities in Tongkin in 1882. A year later, the Qing surreptitiously began to send in regular military units to back these up.

At the same time, diplomatic efforts to pacify the French were undertaken by the Qing's de facto foreign minister, Li Hongzhang. But by mid-1884, with the fighting progressively escalating, the Cixi regency took several dramatic steps. It issued a declaration of war against France; it appointed the saber-rattling Hanlin scholar Zhang Zhidong as governor-general of Guangdong and Guangxi, the staging ground for incursions into Vietnam; and it dismissed the conciliatory Prince Gong from his posts as grand councilor and head of the Zongli Yamen, replacing him with the more bellicose and less competent father of the Guangxu emperor, Prince Chun.

Qing ground forces achieved sporadic success on the battlefield against the outnumbered and poorly supplied French army in Tongkin and especially in Taiwan, where the French sought to expand the war and where they instituted a naval blockade. But the naval war was decisive, and it went very badly for the Qing. In an engagement lasting little more than an hour on August 23, 1884, the French destroyed eleven of the Qing's newest and best warships off the coast of Fujian and went on to blast into smithereens the empire's premier naval facility, the Fuzhou Shipyard. Fears of French naval attacks on Shanghai helped precipitate a wave of bankruptcies and collapse of credit and real estate markets as far inland as Hankou, devastating the empire's emergent industrial entrepreneurial class.[34]

When the Qing eventually capitulated, with the peace agreement signed by Li Hongzhang in June 1885, it formally granted France dominion in Vietnam in exchange for its withdrawal from Taiwan. The French demanded no reparations, but the cost of war, both direct and indirect, was still very great. The failures of self-strengthening were exposed, and the industrial progress it had promised was disastrously set back. Two decades of cautious diplomacy and patient nurturance of Qing military power under Prince Gong's stewardship had come to an end, and the successive stripping away of purported Qing "tributary states" would become relentless.

The Japanese Challenge

Eventually, it was not the Western Great Powers but rather Japan that emerged in the Qing's final half-century as the empire's most dangerous foreign antagonist. The Japanese challenge that reached its climax with the Pacific war of 1937–1945 began during the Tongzhi reign, when Japan was undergoing its own restoration prompted in part by a newly expansionist Western presence. In Japan's case, the "black ships" of Commodore Matthew Perry arrived in 1853, bearing the American threat of severe military consequences if the Tokugawa shōgunate did not abandon its policy of *sakoku*—very tightly restricted contact with the outside. Japan's reaction to the Western shock was more rapid and decisive than China's, perhaps because the Qing's humiliation in the two Opium Wars and the Anglo-French occupation of Beijing were well known in Japan. The realistic appraisal of this unprecedented threat to national autonomy was a major factor leading to one of the world's most profound revolutionary events: the overthrow of the centuries-old Tokugawa shōgunate and the (alleged) restoration of direct imperial rule—an event known as the Meiji restoration of 1868.

While the expressed purpose of the activist young samurai who overthrew the Tokugawa was to "restore the old" (*fuko*), in fact the restoration led almost immediately to a ruthless destruction of a 600-year-old system of decentralized feudal rule and its replacement by a Western-style centralized bureaucratic administration and civil service. And while "expel the barbarians" (*jōi*) was a central rallying cry of the restoration, Meiji Japan very quickly instituted the wholesale adoption of Western technology, industrial production, a high-tech conscript military, and even social and aesthetic models, on its way to becoming a modern industrial and military power, to the detriment of the Qing. Meiji Japan also undertook a crash course in the principles of Western-style diplomacy and international law. Japan, for whom mastery of these conventions came perhaps a bit quicker, immediately put its new knowledge to work, not only to negotiate a better deal for itself with the newly arrived Western powers but also to redefine its inherited relationship with imperial China.

For more than a millennium, since Japan's gradual incorporation into the Confucian cultural sphere during the seventh and eighth centuries, Chinese dynastic rulers had conceived of their insular neighbor as a tributary state. The reality varied greatly, depending on the degree of centralization and power of the Chinese empire at any given time but also on the perceived utility of ties to China on the part of power-holders in Japan itself. The Ashikaga shōgun Yoshimitsu (r. 1368–1408), impressed and worried by the vigorously coalescing Ming empire, had sent tribute to Ming Taizu and acknowledged his vassal status, in large part to shore up his shaky legitimacy at home. The founding Tokugawa shōgun, Ieyasu (1603–1616), would have liked to use Chinese ties in a similar way to buttress his own domestic rule, but he balked at acknowledging vassal status to so clearly enfeebled a fount of authority as the late Ming court. The third Tokugawa shōgun, Tokugawa Iemitsu (1623–1651), made a relatively clean break from China; in correspondence with the Ming, Iemitsu styled himself "great prince" (*taikun*, the origin of the English word *tycoon*), in deliberate avoidance of the term "king" customarily applied in the tribute system. Under the succeeding Qing, Japan's vassal status was loosely assumed but never enforced.

In September 1870, just two years after its restoration, the Meiji government dispatched an envoy to the Qing in quest of a treaty of mutual recognition and amity. In November Li Hongzhang, who had just been posted as Zhili governor-general some months earlier, received a concurrent appointment as superintendent of northern ports and was placed in charge of the Qing's relations with Japan. On Li's advice, the Qing and the Japanese signed a treaty in September 1871—China's first Western-style treaty concluded on the basis of equality and reciprocity—in which the Qing for the first time acknowledged Japan's status as a sovereign nation and agreed to a formal exchange of ambassadors. The two signatories pledged not to interfere with each other's "states and territories" and to come to each other's aid in the event of aggression by a third party. Extra-territoriality was granted reciprocally. A mutual bequest of most-favored-nation status was also considered but, on Li's insistence, was ultimately left out of the final treaty.

No sooner had the ink dried than Japan began to assert claims over two states and territories long claimed by the Qing as its tributaries, Liuqiu and Korea, as well as part of the Qing empire itself, the island of Taiwan. Liuqiu, an archipelago south of Japan that included the island of Okinawa, had for centuries been an independent kingdom, sending regular tribute to the Ming and Qing imperial courts. Under the Tokugawa shōgunate, however, it was also developed commercially by the powerful daimyō domain of Satsuma in southwestern Japan.[35] In 1874 Meiji troops forcibly occupied the kingdom and forbade it to send further tribute to the Qing. Preoccupied with the reconquest of Xinjiang and border disputes with Russia, the Qing did not respond militarily. Japan's own difficulties at home (notably the Satsuma rebellion) likewise prevented the Meiji regime from quickly pushing its claims further. In 1879, however, it hauled off the Liuqiu court to Tokyo and declared the island kingdom a part of Japan, under the name "Okinawa prefecture." After heated debate, Qing authorities opted not to resist this seizure of their presumed tributary; Li Hongzhang himself observed that the tribute-state system as a whole was by then no more than an "empty name."[36]

Taiwan, which had been progressively colonized by Chinese since the seventeenth century, was administered in the 1870s as a prefecture of Fujian. Throughout the decade Japan ever more assertively advanced claims that the island was fair game for colonization, capitalizing on several incidents involving Japanese or Liuqiu sailors and Taiwanese aborigines to point out the ineffectiveness of Qing governance there. In the late 1870s and 1880s, however, Japan temporarily backed off, in tacit exchange for Qing acquiescence to its incorporation of Liuqiu. In 1887 the

Qing reinforced its own claim to Taiwan by promoting the island to pro-vincial status.

The real festering sore in Qing-Meiji relations, however, was Korea. Over the last decades of the nineteenth century, the Korean peninsula loomed ever larger in the strategic concerns of both parties, Japan view-ing it as the springboard for a possible invasion by Russia and the Qing seeing it as a critical buffer against Japanese expansion into Manchuria. Korea also came to assume a key position in the complex gamesmanship among the Western powers, most especially in the emerging rivalry be-tween Britain and Russia. On top of this, Korean domestic politics in the waning years of the long-lived Yi dynasty (1392–1910) was in tur-moil. King Kojong had ascended the throne as an eleven-year-old child in 1863, with his father, the grand prince Hŭngsŏn, serving as regent dur-ing the first decade of his reign and pursuing a vigorous domestic re-form agenda, matched by a radically isolationist foreign policy. Follow-ing Kojong's assumption of direct rule in 1873, a bitter behind-the-scenes struggle for power was waged between his wife's Min lineage and his fa-ther. Overlaying these court intrigues but none too neatly was an inten-sifying factional struggle between groups of politicians known as the Sadae party, which favored tributary relations with the Qing, and the Kaehwa party, which favored a closer relationship with Japan.

As early as 1873 the Meiji government engaged in a heated debate over the advisability of invading Korea but decided to put its ambitions on hold in favor of other domestic and foreign agendas. Two years later, however, Japan provoked an incident by sending a warship into the mouth of the Han River (the gateway to Seoul) where, as expected, it was fired upon. Japanese protests led to the eventual signing of the Treaty of Kanghwa in 1876 which awarded Japan various commercial privileges in Korea, including the opening of three treaty ports. Though the Ko-rean negotiators were closely advised by their Qing patrons, the lan-guage of the treaty declared Korea an independent and sovereign state, in effect denying its tributary status to the Qing. Immediately upon Li Hongzhang's formal appointment by the Qing court as its representative for Korean affairs in 1879, Li sought to offset Japanese hegemony by brokering a series of treaties between Korea and various Western nations, including the United States, Britain, and Germany in 1882, in the classic imperial strategy of "using barbarians to offset other barbarians."

Korean military antagonism against the Japanese culminated in the

Imo riots of July 1882, in which many Japanese were killed and the conservative grand prince was briefly restored to power. Rather than capitalizing on this, however, Li Hongzhang opted to appease the Japanese by having the grand prince abducted and held under house arrest in Tianjin. However, in December 1884 when the pro-Japanese Kaehwa party led another coup, assassinating much of the Korean cabinet and issuing a spate of reform decrees, Li aggressively sent in troops to crush the movement. The Meiji government dispatched Itō Hirobumi to Tianjin, where he negotiated with Li for the gradual withdrawal of both Qing and Japanese armies; ongoing personal diplomacy between Li and Itō proved essential for delaying outright warfare in the decade to follow.

Qing diplomacy in late nineteenth-century Korea is customarily viewed as a rear-guard action to maintain suzerainty over a wayward vassal state in the antiquated "Chinese world order," by contrast with the "modernizing" thrust of expansionist Japan. This view also tends to portray Qing partisans within the Korean elite as Confucian conservatives and their pro-Japanese opponents as progressives. To a considerable extent, however, this view was a deliberate creation of Japanese expansionist propaganda rather than a simple description of fact. One might just as accurately envision the Qing in Yi Korea as engaging in a fully modern, remarkably Western-style imperialism of its own.[37] China's actions in late nineteenth-century Korea were virtually unprecedented in the empire's long history of relations with that country, having much more in common with the practices of expansionist Western powers in the East Asian region. They were also more akin to the frontier provincialization initiatives in Xinjiang, Taiwan, and Manchuria that began in the 1880s as part of the Qing's revival of empire.

Overseen by Li Hongzhang's personal representative in Korea, Yuan Shikai, China pushed hard for a sort of multinational imperialism in Korea, as an antidote to Japan's monopolistic imperialism. Li's orchestration of treaties between Korea and the United States, Germany, and China itself in 1882 was in the interests of furthering not only China's national security but also its extractive commercial interests on the peninsula. Collectively, these nations set up a group of treaty ports and a foreign-staffed Maritime Customs Service modeled after what the Western powers had done in China itself. Neither the Qing nor its predecessor imperial regimes had ever so directly used the agency of government to push China's commercial interests abroad. The Qing also employed other instruments of late-nineteenth-century Western expansionist penetration in

Korea: diplomatic representation, government advisors, and what might with some justification be seen as a kind of colonial army in the country, dispatched initially in response to the Imo mutiny of 1882 but remaining for decades thereafter.

War in Korea was ultimately precipitated by a domestic rebellion. Like the Taiping movement in China, the Tonghak (Eastern Learning) was a new religion founded in the mid-nineteenth century by a disaffected Confucian scholar. Christianity was the target of the sect, which claimed to combine the best elements of Confucianism, Daoism, and Buddhism. Forced to go underground when its founder was executed by the court, the Tonghak nevertheless grew rapidly, organizing periodic rallies to press for its legalization and to protest onerous and corrupt taxation. In spring 1894 the sect's followers emerged in overt rebellion. King Kojong, backed by his Min relatives and seconded by his Chinese advisor Yuan Shikai, invited Qing military intervention to suppress the movement, and in early June these forces arrived. The Japanese Diet had previously decided that should the Qing send in troops, Japan would respond with troops of its own, and in late June the two forces confronted one another on Korean soil. Japanese troops brutally suppressed the Tonghak rebellion and in July occupied the Korean court, apprehended King Kojong, reinstalled the grand prince as titular head of state, and declared a systematic program of Meiji-style government reform. The cautious Li Hongzhang sought Western aid—first from Russia and then from Britain—in brokering a truce but received little support. On August 1, Japan declared war on the Qing, and the Guangxu court responded in kind.

The Sino-Japanese war was a disaster of inconceivable proportions for the Qing empire. Li Hongzhang's Anhui Army and his Beiyang Navy—which he had tried systematically to build up since the 1870s, competing unsuccessfully for funding against the Inner Asian campaigns of Zuo Zongtang and the luxury spending of the empress dowager—received little support from other regional Qing forces in central and south China. Though they had better rifles and larger battleships, they were technologically inferior to their Japanese adversaries in many key areas. But most critically, the Qing ground forces performed very badly, proving strategically inept, disorganized, and quick to flee the battlefield. Li's army was routed at Pyongyang in September 1894, and his navy was nearly totally destroyed at the mouth of the Yalu River later that month. Having dislodged Qing forces from Korea altogether, Japanese troops pushed the fighting into Manchuria's Liaodong peninsula, capturing the major cities of Dairen and Port Arthur (Lushun) in November and seizing the port of Weihaiwei in Shandong in February 1895. The Qing suffered hundreds of thousands of casualties, and the bloody fighting was marked by gruesome atrocities on both sides, all breathlessly reported in the Western press. Throughout the early months of 1895, Qing authorities—notably the venerable and now suddenly rehabilitated Prince Gong—increasingly sought peace with Japan, which they achieved with the Treaty of Shimonoseki signed on April 17.

Overall, the Sino-Japanese War was a major watershed in Chinese imperial history—far more so than the Opium War of 1839–1842, which is so often assigned this significance. As S. C. M. Paine has argued, "Ever since the war, the focus of Chinese foreign policy has been to undo its results whereas the focus of Japanese foreign policy has been to confirm them."[38] Yet more broadly, the war showed the world for the first time how astonishingly weak the Great Qing empire—which had been aggressively flexing its muscles around its peripheries for several decades—really was. The power vacuum created by China's demonstrated vulnerability caused a flood of imperialism across East Asia, far more destructive than anything seen before. The war was equally a shock to Qing subjects themselves, for most of whom defeat at the hands of the Japanese had been inconceivable. To lose such a war so decisively, to such a puny and previously despised neighbor, demonstrated to many the absolute necessity of Japanese-style Westernization, at nearly any cultural cost. One result was a greatly intensified program of sending students abroad to study, in Japan as well as in the West.

A crucial element of this reconception of priorities by young reform-minded Chinese intellectuals like Liang Qichao (1873–1929) was an appreciation of the virtues of constitutionalism. The fact that Meiji Japan had adopted a constitution in 1889 that mobilized the national identity of its citizens and granted them a new stake in the fate of their country could not be unrelated to Japan's startling victory over Qing forces just five years later. Thus began the "constitutional movement" that would soon play such an important role in bringing about the end of the Chinese imperial system. Finally, and not least, were the specific conditions imposed by the Treaty of Shimonoseki itself, to which we now turn.

9

IMPERIALISM

HISTORIANS of the Qing empire use the word "imperialism" in at least two very different senses. Those on the political left, whether Chinese, Japanese, or Western, tend to employ the term in the sense defined by Lenin as "the highest stage of capitalism." In this essentially economic definition, capitalism—as the most efficient mode of production, exploitation, and surplus accumulation developed to that time—presented a critical problem for metropolitan countries such as Great Britain in which capitalist production was most advanced: find an external outlet for investment of this surplus capital or else face strangulation and collapse of the domestic economy itself. In societies such as China that became the targets of this surplus capital investment, the profits it generated were repatriated to the metropolitan economy. The result was a drain of the target society's own capital and a consequent inability to finance catch-up industrialization of its own. In the Nationalist and Communist revolutions of the 1920s and 1930s, the degree to which imperialism, understood in this way, had been realized in China would prove to be a point of vigorous dispute and a key determinant of revolutionary strategy. But imperialism in this Leninist sense also had a very broad time frame: it was applicable to the analysis of China's history at any moment following its contact with the capitalist West, and, for some scholars, remains applicable even today.[1]

A very different definition of "imperialism" has been employed by non-Marxist diplomatic historians. This definition is more political and military than economic and focuses on the worldwide competitive scramble for territorial colonization by the Western Great Powers (and eventually Japan). Scholars using this notion of imperialism see it as a system of diplomatic communication, informed by its participants' continual search for a balance of power among themselves. "Imperialism" in this definition is also much more historicist: it is usually seen as beginning in the late nineteenth century and coming to an end in the suicidal conflagration of nationalism that was the First World War.[2]

In a classic study of the imperialist era (so-defined) in East Asia, Akira Iriye observed that it was characterized in the West by a new and pervasive sense of cultural malaise, of sudden insecurity. Witnessing with shock Japan's easy victory over the Qing empire drove home among Western opinion-makers in and out of government a sense of great opportunity. The newly revealed "sick man of Asia" (analogous to the tottering Ottoman empire, characterized at the time as the "sick man of Europe") was the place where Western nations had to make their mark. Arguing in 1900 that the United States ought not to be left out of this competition, the historian Brooks Adams wrote that "Eastern Asia is the prize for which all the energetic nations of the globe are grasping . . . Our geographical position, our wealth, and our energy preeminently fit us to enter upon the development of Eastern Asia and to reduce it to part of our own economic system."[3]

But there was also a new sense of fear and anxiety, epitomized in the trope of the "Yellow Peril" that rapidly gained currency in the Western press. Japan's rising strength was challenging, but, ironically, the lesson of the Sino-Japanese War seemed to be that China was potentially even more menacing. If Meiji Japan, with its relatively meager resource base, could become so powerful so quickly after adopting a program of forced-draft Westernization, how terrifying would the infinitely wealthier and more populous China be once it got its house in order as Japan had done? Under these conditions it was incumbent on Western nations to act aggressively toward the Qing empire while the opportunity still existed, not only for their own advantage but also as a defensive strategy to forestall China's rise.

Another new element in Western expansionism of this era, as noted by Iriye, was its strikingly particularist nature. The social Darwinist worldview that now pitted the white "race" against the yellow also rendered obsolete the confident view of European nations that they were acting cooperatively, as collective agents of a triumphant Western civilization. With this ideal itself in some doubt, the goal of national policies became instead to advance national interests competitively, in a struggle for existence with other Western nations. Ironically and somewhat counter-intu-itively, then, the unprecedentedly ferocious onslaught of Western preda-tion toward the Qing in the final half decade of the nineteenth century and the first decades of the twentieth was the result not of Western self-confidence but rather of its opposite.

At the very moment of its unleashing, critics of this new aggression arose within the West itself. One of the most skeptical, the maverick Brit-ish scholar J. A. Hobson, wrote in 1902 in proto-Leninist terms that

> the controlling and directing agent of the whole process . . . is the pressure of financial and industrial motives, operated for the di-rect, short-range, material interests of small, able, and well-organized groups in a nation. These groups secure the active co-operation of statesmen and of political cliques who wield the power of "parties" . . . by appealing to the conservative instincts of mem-bers of the possessing classes, whose vested interest and class domi-nance are best preserved by diverting the currents of political energy from domestic on to foreign politics. The acquiescence, even the ac-tive and enthusiastic support, of the body of a nation in a course of policy fatal to its own true interests is secured . . . chiefly by playing upon the primitive instincts of the race.[4]

Imperialism in *Fin de Siècle* China

Assuming the historicist definition advanced by Iriye, we can date the age of imperialism in East Asia rather precisely from April 1895, with the signing of the Treaty of Shimonoseki that formally ended the Sino-Japanese War. As one might expect, the agreement was very tough on the Qing—though it certainly would have been tougher had not Japan's chief negotiator, Itō Hirobumi, been embarrassed by an assassination attempt on his respected Qing counterpart, Li Hongzhang, by a radical Japanese nationalist. By declaring Korea an independent nation, no longer a tribu-tary of the Qing, the treaty in effect rendered Korea a Japanese protector-ate, and it was formally annexed some fifteen years later. The agreement also ceded to Japan the long-coveted island of Taiwan. A coalition of Qing officials and local elites on the island promptly declared a Taiwan Republic, only to be suppressed by Japanese troops within a few months. Taiwan would remain a Japanese possession until the end of the Second World War. The treaty also granted Japan an indemnity from the Qing of

200,000,000 silver taels. But ultimately more significant than any of this were two further provisions responsible for upsetting the delicate balance of power which, in retrospect, was all that had preserved the Qing's integrity since the collapse of the "cooperative policy" a quarter-century earlier.

First, the Treaty of Shimonoseki explicitly granted Japan the right to set up industrial factories within the Qing domain. Foreign factories had been illegal in China up to this point, and few had been built. But this concession to Japan opened the floodgates to foreign industrial investment and economic imperialism. Western nations, already enjoying most-favored-nation status, immediately received the same right to open factories in China that Japan received, and most did so almost immediately. The foreign population in treaty ports beyond Shanghai mushroomed; in Hankou, for example, it rose from about a hundred during the early 1890s to nearly three thousand (1,495 Europeans and 1,502 Japanese) some twenty-five years later.[5] As native entrepreneurs adroitly followed foreign models and established their own factories in the treaty ports and beyond, this quarter century saw what can only be described as an industrial revolution. Prior to the Treaty of Shimonoseki, China was by no means an industrialized country, but by the close of the First World War it most certainly was.

Second, the treaty ceded to Japan the Liaodong peninsula of southern Manchuria, including the ports of Dairen and Port Arthur, where much of the fighting in the war's last phase had taken place. Korea, of course, had never been a Qing possession; and Japan could plausibly argue that the Qing claim even to Taiwan was less than indisputable. But Manchuria was the very homeland of the Qing ruling house. Thus, the cession of Liaodong totally upset the unspoken principle of balance-of-power diplomacy that the Qing empire itself was off limits to colonization and that the Qing's basic territorial sovereignty was to be respected. This provision of the 1895 treaty fundamentally undermined the equal-opportunity principle of Great Power expansionism in East Asia and in effect spelled the need for an entirely new international system.

The Qing empire's dismemberment began with the so-called Triple Intervention on April 23, immediately after the terms of Shimonoseki were announced. Russia greatly feared the advantage that the cession of Liaodong would offer Japan, should it decide to make inroads into Siberia. Joined by France and Germany, Russia threatened military action if the cession was not revoked. After a few weeks of negotiations, Japan opted to withdraw its troops from Dairen and Port Arthur and retrocede the peninsula in exchange for as additional 50,000,000 taels of indemnity. Russia had claimed to be acting in the Qing's interests, and many Chinese saw it that way, at least for a short while.

As thanks for its good agencies against Japan, Germany immediately demanded the cession of the bay of Kiaochow (Jiaozhou) on the southern shore of China's Shandong peninsula, which Germany had coveted as a naval base since its first arrival in the region in 1860. For a time the Qing was able to resist this demand, but in early November 1897, when two German missionaries were hacked to death by an anti-foreign crowd in western Shandong, Kaiser Wilhelm II used this incident as pretext to seize Jiaozhou by force. Shortly thereafter a ninety-nine-year lease of the bay to Germany was negotiated. German colonists quickly built up the adjacent territory into the modern city of Qingdao and in 1903 founded the famous Tsingtao Brewery (arguably the most unambiguously positive product of Western imperialism in China!). The "scramble for concessions" was on.

In early 1898 Russia demanded and received a similar lease of Port Arthur and Dairen—which it had so recently "saved" for the Qing—in order to counter the possible advance of its putative ally, Germany. From this base Russia began the effective colonization of the entire Liaodong peninsula. To counter Russia, Great Britain obtained the lease of Weihai (Weihaiwei), the naval port at the eastern tip of the Shandong peninsula, once the base of the Beiyang Navy and a site of its defeat during the Sino-Japanese War. The term of the lease was for the same length of time that the Russians occupied Port Arthur, which it directly confronted across the Yellow Sea. While they were at it, Britain forced the lease of the New Territories, a peninsular area of the Canton delta that abutted Kowloon, which was just across Victoria Bay from Hong Kong Island. The immanent expiration of this ninety-nine-year lease is what prompted the British retrocession of Kowloon and Hong Kong to China in 1997. Not to be outdone, the French leased Kwangchow Bay (Guangzhouwan), a small inlet on the Leizhou peninsula facing the island of Hainan.

The United States was too preoccupied with a revolutionary movement in its newly acquired colony of the Philippines to stake a claim on the Chinese mainland. Instead, Secretary of State John Hay issued the Open Door notes in 1899 and 1900, which rather lamely pledged to protect the Qing empire's territorial sovereignty. More concretely, however, the notes also proclaimed that within the "spheres of influence" of the foreign powers, nationals of other foreign powers would not be financially discriminated against and "vested interests" of other powers would be protected. The American declaration was not signed on to by any of the other powers, but neither was it openly contested.[6]

Thus, by the turn of the twentieth century, an elaborate round of secret diplomacy and gentlemen's agreements had established that—well beyond the rather small bits of coastal territory explicitly ceded or leased to foreign nations—large sectors of the Qing empire were divided among the powers as their respective zones of economic hegemony. Manchuria was tacitly Russian, Shandong and parts of adjacent north China were German, the Yangzi valley was British, Fujian (across the strait from Japanese Taiwan) was Japanese, and southeast China (near to Indochina) was French. Within these spheres, the appropriate power was understood to have first priority at mineral exploitation, railroad construction, and other economic development activities, and the Qing was pledged not to "alienate" or cede parts of that jurisdiction to any other foreign power. Qing territorial sovereignty, despite the claims of the Open Door notes, was transparently a myth.

Chinese Responses to Imperialism, 1895–1900

The manifest threat posed by imperialism had the effect of greatly catalyzing several trends already under way among the Qing population. Words such as "imperialism" (diguozhuyi) itself, and the more graphic "carving the melon" (guafen)—reflecting the growing fear of the actual physical partition of the empire or, worse, the final extinction of China as a political entity—became common parlance. The fin de siècle saw the rise of mass politicization—the widespread belief that the individual could substantially affect the quality of his or her life by some form of direct personal involvement in the political process. If it had been true that for most Qing subjects the best practice was (to paraphrase Confucius) "respect the officials, but keep them at a distance," this was no longer widely believed.[7]

This era also saw the first stirrings of a genuine Chinese nationalism.[8] This spirit was in the air as early as the end of the first Opium War, with the celebration of the heroic militiamen of Sanyuanli and the emergence of political anti-Manchuism—the sentiment that Manchu rule was undesirable not merely because of Manchu cultural inferiority but because it prevented the Chinese from effectively defending themselves against the

West. If this was not precisely nationalism, neither was it mere cultural-ism or anti-foreignism. It is not too great a stretch to label this Chinese "patriotism"—self-sacrificing defense of the *patria*. What would trans-form patriotism into true nationalism would be the emergence of the idea of the "nation" in the Western sense—an object of personal identification and loyalty that was competitive with loyalties to family, kin group, and locality. This understanding and sentiment was beginning to emerge in the last years of the nineteenth century and would become widespread in the decade to follow.

Qing subjects—now more justly conceivable as "Chinese"—were newly stirred to radical political action in this half-decade following the Treaty of Shimonoseki, action that may be seen as of three types. The first was a top-down modernist reformism. The second was a bottom-up nativist, popular reaction. And third was revolution.

Let us begin with revolution. This era saw the first stirrings of a violent movement to do away with the entire system of imperial rule, which had been the prevailing mode of governance in the two millennia since the Qin empire was proclaimed in 221 B.C. Something called a "republic" (*gongheguo*) was suggested to take its place, though even among its parti-sans there was little clarity about what this entailed. In March of 1895 the Society to Revive China (*Xingzhong hui*), led by the Western-trained physician Sun Yat-sen (Sun Wen), launched a quixotic and easily crushed republican revolution at Guangzhou. In 1900 a more potentially threat-ening plot on the part of the Independence Army (*Zili jun*), a somewhat broader coalition of radical students and sectarians led by the Hunanese Tang Caichang, was discovered and aborted before it could launch its revolution in Hankou. Though they, of course, would be the wave of the future, in these years republican revolutionary sentiments affected only a minute segment of the Qing population. The more significant forms of political action during this period were radical reformism and nativist re-action.

The movement for radical reform in the last years of the nineteenth century coalesced around a firebrand Cantonese scholar by the name of Kang Youwei (1858–1927). Born in a well-to-do landlord-literati family in the Guangdong commercial town of Foshan and grandson of a fa-mous scholar and academy headmaster of the conservative Cheng-Zhu (Songxue) school, Kang received an impeccable classical education and progressed steadily through the orthodox examination route to win his *jinshi* degree in 1895. But he was also extremely sensitive to the Qing's political crises and, having visited British Hong Kong in his youth, was also deeply impressed with what he saw as Western orderliness and efficiency. His thought and his many publications thus blended Neo-Confucian and radical imported ideas. Kang was clearly a self-promoter of no little arrogance, but he was also a man of indisputable brilliance and originality.[9] As early as the mid-1880s he began to publish his vision of a utopian world community. He wrote as well on classical philology, on practical administrative reform, and on the need to liberate Chinese women to strengthen the national cause. In his later years he also sought to establish Confucianism as a true religion of personal salvation, offering an image of himself as China's Martin Luther.

One key element in Kang's thought, set forth in his early publication *An Exposé of the Forged Classics* (*Xinxue weijing kao*, 1891), was his acceptance of the "new text" (*jinwen*) rather than the more commonly accepted "old text" (*guwen*) version of the classical canon, and his preference for the *Gongyang Commentary* on the *Spring and Autumn Annals* (*Chunqiu*) over the conventionally accepted *Zuo Commentary*. These choices led Kang to see Confucius as the actual author rather than a redactor and transmitter of the classics and as a flexible and practical-minded political thinker responsive to the changing conditions of his day. In his *Confucius as a Reformer* (*Kongzi gaizhi kao*, 1897), Kang insisted that the slavish preservation of ancestral precedent long associated with Confucian statecraft was actually a gross perversion of the sage's true intent. He thus discovered a classical and thoroughly indigenous legitimation for the most radical Westernizing reform.

Somewhat later in his career, Kang Youwei also developed ideas on local administration that show, despite his appearance as a radical Westernizer, how comfortably he could fit into the long-term development of Qing discourse on statecraft. Kang adopted the notion, from the *fengjian* tradition of Gu Yanwu, that governance of the county by indigenous local elites, based on faith in their pursuit of enlightened self-interest, was preferable to governance imposed by bureaucratic outsiders. He accepted as well Feng Guifen's modification of this idea, advanced in the 1860s, that elected subofficials one step below the inherited magistrates could serve as a check on the magistrates' potential for self-aggrandizement. To the statecraft ideal of local autonomy, however, Kang added the specific ideal of "self-government," which he got from Western political theory via Japan. Thus, Kang's model of county governance included, along with Gu's inherited magistrates and Feng's elected subofficials, elected representative assemblies to mobilize and give voice to a new type of local individual, the "citizen" (*gongmin* or *guomin*).

Behind this subtle modification of received ideas about statecraft lay a more dramatic transformation of political goals: from social control and social harmony to social mobilization. As Kang envisioned it, self-governance by local communities was the most effective way to release the energies of the entire population and make China strong enough to compete in a predatory international environment. Local government would now be dedicated not merely to keeping the peace and collecting taxes but to rallying the citizenry for economic development, educational advancement, and national defense. It was the key, Kang thought, to a thoroughly revitalized Chinese nation.[10]

Kang was no less innovative in the styles of political action he introduced. While he was in Beijing to sit for the metropolitan examination in April 1895, word broke of the humiliating provisions of the Treaty of Shimonoseki. Kang responded by organizing more than 1,200 of his fellow candidates, from eighteen different provinces, to sign an unprecedented (and illegal) collective message of protest to the throne, the so-called Ten Thousand Word Memorial. Shortly thereafter he founded the Study Society for [National] Strengthening (*Qiang xuehui*)—the model for many other such study societies in the late Qing—which echoed scholarly associations of the late Ming but added new, Western-derived content.[11] Kang's society had branches in Beijing and Shanghai, and its chief secretary was Kang's pupil, the brilliant young Cantonese publicist Liang Qichao (1873–1929). Liang himself would become the pioneering political journalist of the late Qing and early republican era, his many short-lived newspapers designed above all to transform late imperial subjects into what one of these papers referred to in its title as the *New Citizen* (*Xin gongmin*).[12]

But the place where the radical reform movement really took off was neither Beijing, Shanghai, nor Guangzhou but the provincial backwater of Hunan.[13] The Yuelu Academy and similar private institutions in Changsha—which had produced several generations of militant, activist, yet culturally conservative scholar-gentry, including Zeng Guofan and the other anti-Taiping heroes of the Hunan Army—still simmered by century's end and still yielded conflicting radicalisms. This environment produced both rabidly nativist rioters in the early 1890s and equally impassioned reformers sympathetic to Western-influenced change, epitomized by two close friends from northeast Hunan's Liuyang county. One was

Tang Caichang, leader of the doomed Independence Army uprising at Hankou in 1900, and the other was Tan Sitong (1865–1898), a brilliant young Confucian scholar who gradually merged his classical learning with elements of Buddhism, Christianity, and Western scientism to produce a new philosophy that he called Benevolence (*Renxue*). During the late 1880s and early 1890s Tan had seen service throughout central China as a military advisor, systematically paying his respects at the graves of assorted heroes of the past. By 1896 he, along with Tang, was back in Changsha, part of a group of young reformers clustered around the Academy for Critical Examination of the Classics (Jiaojing Shuyuan).

A fortuitous constellation of reform-minded regional officials helped turn Hunan province into an experimental laboratory for many Western-inspired innovations. The self-strengthener Zhang Zhidong was ensconced as governor-general of Hubei and Hunan. Chen Baozhen (1831–1900) came in as Hunan governor in 1895, spearheading such reformist projects as new mining enterprises, a new police system, and paved streets and street lighting in Changsha. (Tan Sitong's own father, notably less sympathetic to reform, was currently serving as governor of Hubei.) But the really radical element in Hunan's provincial administration lay at the next level down, with a group of young men Chen brought in as his subordinates. Chief among these was the Cantonese Huang Zunxian (1848–1905), a somewhat older associate of Kang Youwei who had served in diplomatic posts in Europe and Japan and had published a laudatory account of the Meiji Westernization projects.[14] Huang came to Hunan initially as provincial salt intendant and was promoted in July 1897 to provincial judge. Among his first acts in this post was to found the School of Current Events (Shiwu xuetang) at Changsha and to bring in his 24-year-old fellow-Cantonese Liang Qichao as its chief lecturer.

Using the school as their institutional base, Liang, Tan, and Tang began a frenetic campaign of reformist propaganda in Changsha. They founded and edited the province's first newspaper, the *Hunan Studies News* (*Xiangxue xinbao*), to propagandize their reformist vision among the province's elite. They overhauled the local civil service examination curriculum, requiring study of translated Western works such as Robert MacKenzie's *The Nineteenth Century: A History*. Spurred on by the humiliating German seizure of Jiaozhou in November and the Qing's timid response, and following the model of Kang Youwei's Study Society for National Strengthening, Tan Sitong founded the Southern Study Society

(Nan xuehui), an activist lobby that eventually claimed as members over 1,200 literati from Hunan and throughout south China.

The content of the young reformers' agenda turned progressively more radical. Tan Sitong argued that the core element of Chinese society, the patrilineal family system, demanded immediate overhaul if the country was to survive. The Southern Study Society bylaws stipulated that all members, regardless of age or degree-holding status, be treated as equals. The *Hunan Studies News* called for "people's rights" and parliamentary government. Tan argued, indeed, that the idea of popular sovereignty was actually of Chinese, not foreign, origin and was an integral part of the Confucian legacy, stemming from the *Spring and Autumn Annals* and the *Gongyang Commentary*, which only his Hunanese fellow-provincials had correctly understood.

And, between the lines, anti-Manchu sentiments were increasingly discernable. Liang Qichao arranged the republication at Changsha of the incendiary eyewitness account of atrocities attending the Qing conquest, Wang Xiuchu's *Record of Ten Days at Yangzhou*. Writings of the overtly racist seventeenth-century Hunanese philosopher Wang Fuzhi, whose rehabilitation had been cautiously pioneered by fellow-provincial Zeng Guofan in the 1860s, appeared in an expanded edition in Tan and Tang's native Liuyang county in 1897. Whereas Guo Songtao (who had died in 1891 and whom Tan and Tang honored as their inspiration) had emphasized Wang Fuzhi's reformist ideas and downplayed his nativist ones, the younger men gave equal weight to both. Merging Wang's racial ideas with those of social Darwinism (the struggle for survival via natural selection among racial-national groups), Tan emerged with a powerful "scientific" anti-Manchu ideology. Gradually, the reformers called for Hunan's "complete local self-governance" and secession from the Qing domain. Liang Qichao equated the province with the progressive Tokugawa domains of Satsuma and Chōshu, whose autonomous actions, he argued, had precipitated the nationwide Meiji restoration, but Tan seems more closely to have envisioned an independent Hunanese nation that would emerge from the ashes of the empire.

Conservative elements within the provincial elite greeted these developments with growing horror, the more so since Western ideas in the hands of suspect Cantonese like Huang and Liang brought to mind the devastations visited on Hunan by the Taiping less than fifty years earlier. Even the head of Changsha's venerable Yuelu Academy, an early champion of the reforms, urged provincial authorities to intervene. In early summer, Governor-general Zhang Zhidong ordered the new Hunan newspapers muzzled and the School of Current Events renamed and reorganized as a technical school. Governor Chen Baozhen was dismissed and replaced by his more conservative lieutenant governor. And, one by one, the young reformers themselves left Hunan, heading for the new target of opportunity: Beijing.

Beginning in January 1898, expressly permitted by order of the Guangxu emperor (an increasingly independent-minded young adult by this time), Kang Youwei had been peppering the court with memorials offering his proposals for reform. On June 16 the emperor for the first time received Kang in person and on the same day appointed him secretary of the Zongli Yamen, with wide authority to initiate reforms in all aspects of government. Over the next few months he was joined at Beijing by Liang Qichao, Tan Sitong, and other young zealots, and together they drafted a series of far-reaching reform decrees issued in the emperor's name. These included establishing an imperial university at Beijing and Western-curriculum schools at the local level throughout the empire and shifting the contents of the civil service examinations from classical study to current events.

The central and field administrations were streamlined, with several sinecure posts and three governorships (Hubei, Guangdong, and Yunnan) abolished. Processes were begun to replace the Six Boards with Western-style cabinet ministries and to revise the judicial system and establish an independent judiciary. The *yanlu* (pathways of words) were opened to encourage reform suggestions from private citizens, which would be immediately forwarded to the court. The central government would take charge of railroad and industrial projects begun by regional administrations and greatly expand them. In the future, anyone aspiring to high office would be required to first undertake a tour of foreign countries to observe their state of development.

Over the summer of 1898 many in the court, and even moderate reformers such as Li Hongzhang and his protégé Yuan Shikai, became increasingly alarmed at what Kang and his followers were up to and rallied around the Empress Dowager Cixi. On September 21 the grand dame suddenly returned to Beijing from her retreat at the Summer Palace, declared herself once again regent, and effectively placed her 28-year-old son, the emperor, under house arrest on an island in the Imperial Park west of the Imperial Palace. Over the next several days the leading reformers were successively purged. Kang Youwei fled to Hong Kong and Liang Qichao to Japan, but Tan Sitong and five others were publicly executed.

The Hundred Days Reforms of 1898 were over, and on September 26 Cixi revoked nearly all their provisions. Reform-minded literati throughout the empire, however, even many who had doubts about Kang Youwei himself, were demoralized by the conservative coup. It seemed that reform from above might no longer be possible after all, and, with the evident failure of the Guangxu emperor to hold the reform program together, sentiments that Manchu rule itself was the major problem spread more widely. Tan Sitong's friend Tang Caichang organized his ill-fated Wuhan putsch of 1900, and even Sun Yat-sen's republican revolutionary propaganda began to look less incomprehensible than before.

Nativism

Revolution and radical reform were for the most part responses of elites to foreign imperialism in the final years of the nineteenth century. A third response, more populist in its origins, was a violent anti-foreignism that culminated in the 1900 movement of the Righteous and Harmonious Fists (*Yihe quan*), known to Westerners more simply as the Boxers. The spawning ground of these nativists was in northwestern Shandong, in the hinterland of the Grand Canal city of Linqing, also the birthplace of earlier rebellions in the northern White Lotus tradition, including those of Wang Lun in the 1870s and the Eight Trigrams in 1813. This was an ecologically fragile region of small cultivators with little concentration of landownership. Its poverty had been exacerbated by the administration's abandonment of the use of the Grand Canal for grain tribute transport in the second quarter of the nineteenth century. Though cotton cultivation had helped slow the region's decline for a while, foreign competition in cotton goods had diminished this resource by the 1880s and 1890s. Major flooding of the Yellow River in 1898 and drought in 1900 added acute short-term immiseration to a baseline of poverty and discontent.

But more incendiary than the smoldering economic crisis in rural areas was the proselytizing of foreign missionaries, especially German Catholics of the Society of the Divine Word. Active in Shandong since the early 1880s, the society rapidly became more aggressive in the years following the German seizure of Jiaozhou in 1897 during the "scramble for concessions." Nearly a thousand small, localized "incidents" of conflict with foreigners were reported in Shandong in the years that followed, and gradually a loosely organized movement of Spirit Boxers emerged out of this, eventually spilling beyond Shandong into other parts of north China. These groups targeted foreign artifacts such as railroad and telegraph lines, and they violently attacked both foreigners and Chinese Christian converts. By the time the Boxer movement had been suppressed, some 231 foreigners and several thousand Chinese converts had been killed.

The Boxer uprising was extremely localized and complex, and its subsequent political use has been powerful and conflicted.[15] Scholars differ over the relationship of the Boxer movement with the White Lotus sectarian tradition, and over whether at the outset it had been Ming-restorationist and anti-Manchu, as well as anti-foreign.[16] What is incontestable is that the Boxer movement represented a remarkable instance of the Qing court doing what it had done best for nearly three centuries: co-opting existing popular movements, organizations, and leadership for its own purposes. Following her coup of September 1898, Empress Dowager Cixi had not only rescinded most of the reformers' legislation but had moved the court much more to an aggressively anti-foreign stance, placing saber-rattling conservatives such as princes Duan and Zhuang, Grand Councilor Ronglu, and Grand Secretary Gangyi in positions of the highest authority. Her ire at foreigners was further stoked by the threatening response of the Western diplomatic community in Beijing to rumors that Cixi intended to depose the Guangxu emperor in favor of Prince Duan's more tractable son. As the Boxer movement became increasingly violent during the early months of 1900, she issued repeated decrees that regional officials tolerate rather than suppress them. Zhili Governor-General Yulu complied, but Shandong Governor Yuan Shikai emphatically did not. The center of Boxer activities thus migrated from Shandong to Zhili.

Beijing became increasingly anarchic. Foreign diplomats in the legation quarter, southeast of the Forbidden City near the Front Gate, called in military support from naval vessels at Tianjin. Telegraph lines connecting the city with the rest of the empire were cut. Boxers and their Qing military supporters burned the British summer legation in the Western Hills on June 10, murdered the Japanese mission's chancellor the next day, and on June 20 killed the German ambassador. Throughout the summer the legation quarter was under siege, with some Qing troops defending it and others attacking it. The Zongli Yamen twice sent in emergency food supplies.

The court itself was in chaos. Five high officials who counseled a crackdown on the Boxers, including the presidents of the boards of War and Revenue, were arrested and executed. On June 21, when more foreign troops landed near Tianjin to relieve the siege, the Cixi court declared war on all foreign nations, ordering all provincial officials to support the Boxers and expel the foreigners. Leading governors and governors-general, however, including the rehabilitated Li Hongzhang at Guangzhou, his protégé Yuan Shikai in Shandong, Liu Kunyi at Nanjing, and Zhang Zhidong at Wuhan, announced their collective refusal to comply. In effect, much of China had seceded from the Qing court's authority.

In midsummer a cobbled-together Allied Expeditionary Force took Tianjin and marched toward Beijing. The army of over 18,000 included British soldiers, Russians, French, Americans, Austrians, Italians, and— by far the largest contingent—some 8,000 Japanese. The expeditionary force took the capital with ease (Fig. 17). The court fled, as it had done in 1860, but this time to Xi'an, near the ancient site where the Qin founded China's first empire. In exile, Cixi begged Li Hongzhang to come north to lead the peace negotiations, in cooperation with Ronglu, who had earlier foreseen the folly of the court's action and worked surreptitiously to protect the besieged foreign diplomats. On September 11, 1901, after prolonged deliberations, the Boxer Protocol was signed between "China" and eleven "Great Powers."[17] It required the execution or suicide of Prince Zhuang and several lesser officials and the posthumous rehabilitation of those officials who had been executed in the past for opposing the Boxers. Monuments were to be erected in honor of the murdered foreign diplomats, and missions of apology dispatched to their home countries.

The Boxer Protocol was a disaster not only for the Qing empire but for its various twentieth-century successor regimes. Particularly devastating was the combined indemnity of 450 million silver taels awarded to the various foreign signatories. Since the Qing treasuries contained nothing like this amount, the sum was ordered to be payable over forty years at 4 percent annual interest. The total payment came to over 668 million taels. As security for this huge debt, virtually the entire revenue structure of the empire other than the land tax—the salt administration, the domestic customs administration, and the Imperial Maritime Customs—

Fig. 17   Boxer fighters in captivity at Tianjin, 1900. Photograph by James
Ricalton. Courtesy of Christopher Lucas.

was placed in receivership under foreign control. The enduring financial
burden of this indemnity would prove a debilitating legacy for a country
embarking on catch-up industrialization and infrastructural development
in the decades leading up to the Second World War.[18]

   In addition to this, the protocol stipulated that troops of foreign nations would remain stationed throughout north China for the future protection of their nationals there. In practice, most foreign powers fairly
rapidly withdrew all but a token force, but Japan did not; these troops
would still be on the ground in north China, legally, when Imperial Japan
began its wholesale invasion of the country in 1937. Following the Boxer
Protocol, the national sovereignty of the Great Qing empire was a myth
that almost no one any longer believed.

Personal Politics

Much historiography on late nineteenth-century China divides Qing political actors into Westernizing progressives and chauvinist reactionaries. While ideologies frequently informed the political behavior of the time, we should keep in mind, however, that in the late Qing empire, as in other times and places, personal self-interest and careerism—along with politics on a local level that was largely impervious to broader ideological conflicts—played an important role in determining the direction of historical change.

From the 1860s on, a force of growing importance was a political style known self-consciously as "pure discussion" (*qingyi*).[19] Echoing a neo-Daoist practice of the early imperial era known as "pure conversation" (*qingtan*), in which like-minded elites—ostensibly "purified" of material attachments and concerns—sat around and speculated about the nature of the cosmos, practitioners of late Qing pure discussion claimed to be able to distance themselves from mundane politics and articulate an unencumbered policy of the transcendent "public" interest. Literati identifying with this movement communicated opinions among themselves in letters, poetry, and other discrete forms, occasionally "leaking" to the population at large a memorial whose policy recommendations they favored. Growing ultimately out of the conspiracy theory of the Opium War, these activists adhered to a generally fundamentalist Confucian opposition to any institutional change, including industrialization, and to a hard-line militancy on relations with the West and Japan. Most of the pure-discussion men were in fact outsiders to actual policymaking processes and had little understanding of the real strength of their foreign adversaries. They invoked or manipulated idealist positions in an effort to become insiders with real decisionmaking power.

The center of this movement, as with similar ones earlier in the century, was in the Hanlin Academy, the holding pool for the most brilliant *jinshi* scholars awaiting official appointments. The Hanlin became home to the so-called Pure Stream Party (*Qingliu pai*), a literati faction functionally similar to those of the late Ming such as the Donglin and the Fushe. Though outsiders, Pure Stream affiliates became expert at politically intimidating their chosen targets. Among their first successful campaigns were hounding the anti-Taiping hero Zeng Guofan out of political life for his conciliatory handling of negotiations following the Tianjin "massacre" of 1870 and publicly humiliating Zeng's Hunan Army colleague

Guo Songtao for accepting an ambassadorial post to England in the 1860s.[20] As reactionary as their political positions may seem, however, the political style of the Pure Stream Party was remarkably progressive in its claim to articulate a new kind of public opinion. No less reformist a figure than Liang Qichao seemed to recognize this when he appropriated their motto for the title of one of his many short-lived political newspapers, the *Qingyi bao*, following the 1898 debacle.[21]

The routine target of the Pure Stream was a faction that became known as the Foreign Affairs Party (*Yangwu pai*). These men were the consummate insiders—high-ranking officials in the provinces, in most cases old anti-Taiping leaders and their protégés, men like Zeng, Guo, Zuo Zongtang, Li Hongzhang, Sheng Xuanhuai, and Yuan Shikai. These leaders were accustomed to dealing with the West on a daily basis, as well as with domestic socioeconomic problems, and they very likely had a more secure idea of the magnitude of the crisis the empire was facing. They tended to advocate diplomacy in foreign relations and imitation of the West in developing domestic military and industrial technology. They cannot be seen simply as visionary progressives, devoid of personal or factional self-interest, however. As with later nationalist elites elsewhere in the colonial world, they promoted their supposed mastery of vital foreign techniques as essential qualifications for the powerful offices they held. And they were hardly averse to financial profit from industrial patronage. Li Hongzhang died a multimillionaire. Moreover, these so-called progressives were also rivals of one another. Personal animosities and regional-factional interests led them to undercut the reformist projects of their competitors as often as they supported them.

In the middle of all this factionalism was the Qing court. Comprising princes of the imperial clan, Chinese official advisors, the Grand Council, and other interests, the late-nineteenth-century court was itself deeply divided into what may be described as the emperor's party and the empress dowager's party. Most of the time Cixi, a consummate political infighter, managed to stay on top by balancing and astutely playing off against one another not just the Pure Stream and Foreign Affairs factions but the factions within each of these factions—the classic imperial strategy of divide and rule.

The fluidity of the late Qing political scene, as well as its personal and careerist elements, helps explain the otherwise anomalous ideological shifts of key participants. There is perhaps no better example than the strange odyssey of Zhang Zhidong. Born in the hinterland of Beijing to a hereditary family of lesser officials, Zhang received an impeccable classical education and passed the *jinshi* examination at the age of twenty-six. For the next fifteen years he held various lower-level commissions from the court, in the performance of which he refined his personal scholarship while frequently blowing the whistle on abuses of the examination's integrity in various provinces. An affiliate of the Pure Stream Party, Zhang gained admission to the Hanlin Academy in 1880. Typical of his self-promotion during this period was a memorial he submitted in 1879 regarding a dispute over a waterworks project in central Hubei. The powerful local interests on either side had over the years brought onto their camp an ever more exalted range of official patrons lobbying for the particular outcome they sought. In his censorial capacity, Zhang Zhidong intervened, self-righteously denouncing the factional interests of both parties and trumpeting his own proposed solution to the conflict as uniquely nonpartisan and objective.[22]

A year later, Zhang again stepped uninvited into a political debate when he demanded the immediate execution of Board of War vice-president Chonghou for negotiating a treaty with Russia that was, in Zhang's view, demeaning to Qing honor. This last piece of saber-rattling gained Zhang his long-sought attention from the throne and helped secure his appointment in 1884 as governor-general of Guangdong and Guangxi. One of his first acts in this post was to send government troops into Vietnam, precipitating the ultimately disastrous Sino-French War of 1884–1885. At this point, Zhang rescued his career by reversing course, suddenly becoming a patron of self-strengthening industrialization. The reactionary and chauvinist pure-discussion monger had become a progressive Westernizer. But his approach to reformism remained deeply proprietary: when Zhang was transferred to a new post at Wuhan in 1889, he put the ironworks project he first drew up for Guangdong in his back pocket and took it along with him.

At Wuhan, Zhang presented himself as a pioneer of educational reform, founding a number of new-style academies and Westernized schools to produce a generation of cosmopolitan young technocrats. After the debacle of the Sino-Japanese War, he at first patronized the reform activities of Tan Sitong, Tang Caichang, and Liang Qichao in Hunan, before recoiling from their manifest radicalism (which incidentally undermined his own vanguard status in the reform movement) and moving to assert tighter ideological control over the renegade province. In 1898, at the very peak of Kang Youwei's aborted Hundred Days Reforms, he published his own manifesto, *Exhortation to Study* (*Quanxue pian*), which calculatedly played to the interests of both the emperor's party and the empress dowager's party at court and shored up his own position as reformist guru. In 1900 he arrested and executed the reformer-turned-revolutionary Tang but at the same time courted Western approval by publicly distancing himself from the pro-Boxer position of the Cixi court. In the first years of the twentieth century, Zhang would vigorously suppress nationalist activism for "rights recovery" in Hunan (in a sense the direct heir of the pure-discussion activism of his youth) on the grounds that it undermined rightful government authority—his own.[23] The one-time outsider was now the consummate government insider.

While the genuine patriotism of each of Zhang's rapidly evolving political stances is undeniable, in each case his vision of the Qing's (or China's) best interests was directly in line with promotion of his own political career. Ideology was surely important, but it was hardly everything. Men such as Zhang Zhidong must be seen in the context of their world. Measuring them against the simple yardstick of "China's response to the West" goes only so far in helping us understand their motives, accomplishments, and shortcomings.

Local Politics

Another particularly revealing way to understand the politics of the Qing empire's final half century is to concentrate on the localities, and on the struggle for power at the county level between appointed agents of the central bureaucracy (the magistrate) and indigenous local magnates—the problem we have already seen discussed theoretically by Gu Yanwu, Feng Guifen, and Kang Youwei. In at least one key region of the empire—the lower Yangzi—activist local elites increasingly, over the Qing's final half century, won the struggle in practice, through a multistage process.[24]

The first stage was reconstruction following the Taiping rebellion. Like many other parts of the empire, but more severely than most, the province of Zhejiang had been laid waste by the Taiping campaigns. Hydraulic works, city walls, government offices, and other infrastructural elements had been destroyed; fields had gone fallow and the population was dislocated; the values and moral fabric of local society had unraveled. As elites of the region reassembled at the county level in the 1860s, they found themselves in possession of a gentry-led apparatus of bureaus designed originally to raise subscriptions for financing local militia defense, and saddled with an enfeebled local officialdom that nevertheless encouraged gentry initiative in confronting the tasks of reconstruction. The elites determined to act collegially in what they identified as the communal or "public" interest—a sector distinguished from both the governmental and the private sectors—to finance and manage relief efforts, the repair of irrigation systems, land reclamation, construction of defense works and schools, and so on. In areas near Shanghai and other treaty ports, the reconstruction agenda came gradually to include public sewer systems, street lighting, medical facilities, and other foreign innovations.

After reconstruction, the second stage of the process was translocal networking. The key moment here was the founding of the first lasting Chinese-language newspaper, *Shenbao*, at Shanghai in 1872. Though established and owned by an Englishman, Ernest Major, *Shenbao* was staffed and read almost exclusively by Chinese, mostly by activist elites of Jiangnan, the Yangzi valley, and the coast. Though professedly apolitical on issues of national policy—at least at the outset—*Shenbao* was in fact deeply political in representing the interests of the reformist class who comprised its readership and in urging them to undertake projects in the public sphere. Much of its coverage was focused on reconstruction and other initiatives undertaken in various localities. By reading the newspaper on a regular basis, elite collectivities within particular counties learned who was doing the same sorts of things in other localities, and this led to mutual emulation and experimentation. Though they continued to act locally, these reformists began to think globally.[25]

A third stage was reached when activist local elites began for the first time to target projects outside their own community. The critical turning point was probably the great drought-induced north China famine of 1876–1878, in which likely more than ten million people died and millions more were driven from their farms. Systematically exhorted by local officials and *Shenbao* to realize that Qing subjects were all in this together, elites from throughout central and southern China, working through their local subscription bureaus, mobilized financial resources for a massive relief project far from home. For the first time, local elites began to act on the belief that the problems of north China were the problems of all Chinese.[26]

The final nineteenth-century phase of this process came when elite activism began to take on an overtly politicized dimension, spurred by interest in foreign relations and growing nationalist sentiments. In both the Sino-French War of 1884–1885 and the Sino-Japanese War of 1895, local elites throughout China, encouraged by editorials and war reportage in *Shenbao,* found themselves shocked by the Qing empire's humiliating losses in wars they had imagined as easy victories. Collectively, these Chinese gentry, who had so impressively demonstrated their ability to get things done locally and nationally, began to wonder whether they couldn't do a better job of conducting international affairs than the pitiful (alien) court that ruled their country. Events in the first decade of the twentieth century would finally turn these local elites into a constituency for republican revolution, but by the end of the nineteenth century the die was already cast. For activist local elites throughout much of the empire, the imperial regime was not so much a hated tyrant as an impediment to getting things done right.

10

REVOLUTION

ONE DOMINANT theme of China's history during the early years of the twentieth century was the attempt to form a nation-state out of the remains of the Qing empire. "State" here refers not to a place but to a deliberately created *organization* that claims ultimate control over a particular territory, while "nation" denotes a group of *people* defined variously depending on the different circumstances. Members of a nation may be identified as persons sharing a common "race" or gene pool, a common language, a common delimited territory, or a common history. Perhaps the most inclusive criterion for nationhood is the subjective one proposed by Benedict Anderson: an "imagined community" agreed upon by negotiation among its members and, in most but certainly not all cases, accepted by its neighbors.[1] The "nation-state" comes about when a sovereign political organization is grafted onto this imagined community. Nationalism—the force that progressively consumed many late Qing subjects—arises when members of a nation or nation-state assign a high degree of personal loyalty to the national group, relative to self, family, locality, class, or any other entity that might compete for that loyalty.

It is worth remembering that in the early twentieth century the rise of nationalism and of nation-states was not terribly old even in the West. A self-conscious notion of the state probably first took shape with the state-making monarchs of the seventeenth century—the Hohenzollerns in Brandenburg-Prussia, the Bourbons in France, Gustavus Adolphus in Sweden—whose ideology of statism reinforced their vigorous attempts to set up administrations staffed by government officials, a bureaucratized military, and centralized fiscal control within their realms.[2] Feelings of nationalism among the populace probably did not begin much earlier than the French Revolution, took hold more broadly during the European revolutions of 1848, and did not reach their full stride until the turn of the twentieth century.[3] So China was not very far behind the other end of the Eurasian continent in getting swept up in the frenzy to turn itself into a nation-state in the decades leading up to the First World War.

Nationalism in these years was by no means unequivocally a progressive force. Whereas early nineteenth-century nationalist movements such as the Greek independence movement in the 1810s and uprisings in Hungary and elsewhere in 1848 were explicitly liberal-democratic, by the time of the Italian radical nationalists of the 1870s, and certainly during the Bismarckian expansionism of the 1880s and 1890s, nationalism had been harnessed in service of a highly illiberal statism.[4] The influence of social Darwinism immeasurably heightened this anti-democratic, repressive, and militarist reading of nationalist concerns. When nationalist appeals really took hold in the Qing empire around the turn of the century, then, they may in some cases have sounded radically democratic, but they already held within them (for example, in the "national essence" rhetoric of Zhang Binglin and Liu Shipei) the seeds of the illiberalism that after 1911 would manifest itself in eugenics movements to "purify the race" and in the successive dictatorial ambitions of such leaders as Yuan Shikai, Jiang Jieshi, Mao Zedong, and Deng Xiaoping—good "nationalists" all.[5]

A final note of caution regarding the rise of Chinese nationalism in the late Qing comes from the perspective known as postcolonialism. This critique states that just because the nation-state as eventually worked out in Western Europe proved to be a highly effective form of political organization, there is no reason to view it as the necessary end of history, even in the West. Still less is there any reason to impose it on populations outside the unique historical experience of Europe, or to judge those populations on their relative failure to organize themselves in this way. There were other conceivable political forms (the Heavenly Kingdom of the Taipings, for example) to which the Qing empire might have given way. But a particular political elite in early twentieth-century China, as elsewhere in the non-Western world, saw itself as uniquely visionary in recognizing the need to reconstruct its society as a European-style nation-state—a mission that was, not coincidentally, empowering to itself—and this contingency of history certainly lay in part behind the drive toward nationalism in China.[6]

While the postcolonial critique seems to me both plausible and compelling, it is important to remember that Chinese elites of the late Qing did not have the luxury of such hindsight. For growing numbers of them, the need to reconstruct their polity as a powerful, Western-style nation-state in order to survive in the war of all against all going on around them was a matter of immediate urgency.

Court-Centered Reform

Late in 1900 the Qing dynasty, having occupied the throne of China more than two and a half centuries, was manifestly on the verge of collapse. The situation was reminiscent of 1860: in both years the imperial court was in exile, having fled for its life as an army of Western barbarians occupied the sacred imperial capital. But in 1900 matters were even worse than before: the Manchu ancestral homeland, where the court had taken refuge in 1860, was occupied by Japanese and Russians, and the court was forced to flee to Xi'an in northwestern China. Thankfully, the southern capital of Nanjing was not also occupied by a domestic rebel regime, as it had been in 1860. This time around, the rebels (the Boxers) had been successfully co-opted by the court. But the rebellion had been put down by foreign invaders, and the Qing court had been forced to give up important chunks of its territory (concessions) to foreigners in order to keep the barbarians at bay. Consequently, the situation was arguably worse that it had been before. The central treasury was broke and had mortgaged most of its foreseeable future revenue to foreign nations for the crime of having lost a succession of wars. And domestic subversive movements were breaking out with gathering frequency. For the moment, these could still be crushed with relative ease, but they were alarming in that they threatened not merely the incumbent dynasty but also the entire 2,000-year-old imperial system itself.

Astoundingly, however, just as it had done in 1860, the Qing dynasty in 1900 not only managed to survive but displayed a new spurt of vigor—a revival of relatively strong central leadership and competent administration. This was announced by the court as the era of New Policies (*xinzheng*) and has been known most often in English as the "late Qing reforms." The Manchu ruling house took over a number of projects that had been going forward at the provincial level since the 1860s under the name of self-strengthening, but it went far beyond the self-strengthening principle, which left basic social, political, and ideational structures undisturbed. If the New Policies were more sober in tone and pace than the abortive Hundred Days Reforms of 1898, they were more far-reaching and fundamental.

In January 1901 at Xi'an the Empress Dowager Cixi, in the name of the Guangxu emperor, issued a Penitential Edict and a basic Reform Edict to acknowledge the court's awareness of the need for profound change and its commitment to lead that process. The Reform Edict stated in part that

> certain principles of morality are immutable, whereas methods of governance have always been subject to alteration. The *Book of Changes* states that "When a measure has lost effective force, the time has come to change it" . . . Throughout the ages, successive generations have introduced new ways and abolished the obsolete. Our own august ancestors set up new systems to meet the requirements of the day. Times differ, such as when our dynasty ruled at Shenyang and after it had breeched the Great Wall. Since the Jiaqing and Daoguang periods, as well, rulers have changed many old practices of the Yongzheng and Qianlong eras . . .
>
> It is well known that the new laws promulgated by the Kang rebels were less reform laws than lawlessness. These rebels took advantage of the court's weakened condition to plot sedition. It was only by an appeal for guidance from the Empress Dowager that the court was saved from immediate peril, and the evil rooted out in a single day . . .
>
> We have now received Her Majesty's decree to devote ourselves fully to China's revitalization, to . . . blend together the best of what is Chinese and what is foreign . . . To sum up, administrative methods and regulations must be revised, and abuses eradicated. If regeneration is truly desired, there must be quiet and reasoned deliberation . . . The Empress Dowager and We have long pondered these matters. Now things are at a crisis point where change must occur, to transform weakness into strength. Everything depends upon how the change is effected.[7]

The *yanlu*—the pathways of words—were opened to an extent they had never been before, as all Qing subjects were invited to submit recommendations for reform. A Bureau of Governmental Affairs was established to systematically sort through these proposals and implement those that were approved. Thereafter, until Cixi's death in 1908, a continual series of edicts ordered major changes at all levels of government and society.

The process accelerated midway, spurred on by Japan's shocking defeat of Russia in the war of 1904–1905. Fought almost entirely on Qing soil, Meiji Japan's dramatic defeat of one of the awesome Great Powers opened new prospects of a revived Qing power, if it could only get its house together. Epitomizing this new wave of "Yellow Peril" in the West was a fable by the American adventure writer Jack London, penned in 1907 but set in an imagined future seventy years later:

> The Japanese-Russian War took place in 1904, and the historians of the time gravely noted it down that that event marked the entrance of Japan into the comity of nations. What it really did mark was the awakening of China . . .
>
> China's swift and remarkable rise was due, perhaps more than to anything else, to the superlative quality of her labor. The Chinese was the perfect type of industry. He had always been that. For sheer ability to work, no worker in the world could compare with him. Work was the breath of his nostrils. It was to him what wandering and fighting in far lands and spiritual adventure had been to other peoples. Liberty, to him, epitomized itself in access to the means of toil. To till the soil and labor interminably was all he asked of life and the powers that be. And the awakening of China had given its vast population not merely free and unlimited access to the means of toil, but access to the highest and scientific machine-means of toil.
>
> China rejuvenescent! It was but a step to China rampant.

As London imagined it, world domination by this "awakened" unstoppable China could only be countered by a genocidal extermination of the entire Chinese people, via an American-led campaign of germ warfare.[8]

Ultimately, the New Policies did not offer China world domination nor solve its manifold problems—in fact, in many ways they exacerbated social tensions and political restiveness. But the intent of the reforms was indisputably genuine, their impact real, and their long-term significance enormous. They represented a dramatic and sudden reversal of the centuries-long process—observable perhaps (with some oscillations) since the middle period of imperial history—of government shrinkage relative to the size of the society and economy the state claimed to oversee, and a decisive move toward the steady construction of a more intrusive and powerful modern state, a process that would continue to grow at least into the Maoist era of the late twentieth century.

The New Policies aimed, first of all, to streamline the Qing administrative system and more clearly define the duties and responsibilities of individual posts. Several sinecure positions were simply abolished, as were some provincial governorships (including that of Sichuan) where the overlap of responsibility with a governor-general was now seen as redundant. Within the metropolitan administration, the venerable Six Boards were gradually replaced by cabinet ministries, akin to those operating in Japan and other parliamentary governments. The Board of Revenue was replaced by a Ministry of Finance, the Zongli Yamen was succeeded by a more formalized Foreign Ministry, and the Board of Punishments was transformed into a Ministry of Justice, with a Supreme Court established as the cornerstone of a new judiciary independent of the omnicompetent field administration. Other new ministries included a Ministry of Trade (a major departure for an imperial system that, for two millennia, had nominally held private commerce to be unworthy of systematic government support and regulation), a Ministry of Education, a Ministry of Police (later renamed Ministry of the Interior), and a Ministry of Posts and Communications, set up to assert centralized control over the ongoing and uncoordinated process of railroad building.

More far-reaching still was a proposed change in the Qing's basic governmental structure designed to foster citizenship and popular participation in governance—a comprehensive program directed, to be sure, by the monarchy for its own and the state's interests. In 1907 a Commission to Study Constitutional Government was established, with the long-time constitutionalist champion Liang Qichao himself invited back from exile in Japan and enlisted as an advisor. High-level delegations were dispatched in 1905 and 1906 to study the political systems of Japan, the United States, and various European states. The establishment of representative assemblies was preliminarily scheduled on the local, provincial, and national levels.

To cultivate industrialization and commercial development, the fledgling Ministry of Commerce sought to establish and coordinate chambers of commerce in the various provinces and in important commercial cities. Some of these institutions had been operating on local initiative since at least the turn of the century, but an edict of 1904 formally sanctioned and sought to standardize and regulate them. In classic Qing style, existing and effectively functioning social institutions were co-opted and their imitation in other localities was promoted. By 1909 about 180 chambers of commerce throughout the empire brought together local merchants and industrial entrepreneurs from disparate trades and native origins for the purpose of studying and promoting local economic activity. These institutions also served as officially authorized vehicles for communication between local actors and the administration. Like many other innovations of the time, the new chambers of commerce proved to be important in forging a new professional interest group recognized by the state: businessmen.

Militarily, the New Policies expressed the court's commitment to creating a powerful, centralized modern army that would supplant the dilapidated banner forces and Green Standard Army and at the same time finally bring under central control the remnants of the Taiping-era regional military forces. To this end, a Commission on Military Reorganization was set up in 1903, headed jointly by the Manchu prince Tieliang and the most powerful Chinese field official of the day, Yuan Shikai (1859–1916). A protégé of Li Hongzhang, Yuan had inherited control of much of Li's former Anhui Army, and in 1901 upon Li's death became governor-general of Zhili. In that capacity Yuan instituted numerous Westernizing reforms in education, industry, and public security and also cobbled together what would become the most efficient and well-equipped military force in early twentieth-century China, the Beiyang Army.[9] Out of his senior officer corps emerged many of the most important warlords of the early Republican era.

Outside the capital area, the Military Reorganization Commission set up Provincial Military Boards to supervise the founding of new military academies (which frequently employed Japanese instructors) and regional-level, technologically sophisticated New Armies. The officers and men of these armies were primarily drawn from the respective province itself, the officers were graduates of the new military academies, and a high percentage of the enlisted men possessed at least a modicum of literacy. In the face of China's manifest need for national defense, military service had acquired a new prestige among the educated elite, and the personnel of the New Armies was thus not altogether different in social background from civilian students in the new Western-curriculum schools. Moreover, in this security-conscious age, the military offered new kinds of advancement opportunities and served as an avenue for upward social mobility. As with businessmen, modern military men emerged as a new professional elite.

The most tradition-shattering aspect of the New Policies came in the area of educational reform. In 1905, just after Japan's eye-opening defeat of imperial Russia, the Qing court suddenly abolished the civil service examination, which had served as the orthodox path to official service and social advancement for over a millennium. In its place, the court decreed the establishment of Western-curriculum schools in all localities. From about 4,000 such schools in the empire in 1904, with an estimated student body of 92,000, the number of schools grew to 52,000 five years later and the total number of students to 1.5 million. The facilities that housed these thousands of new schools were often local temples commandeered for this purpose—the latest manifestation of the elite's ongoing battle against "superstition." Formerly fought in the name of Confucian civilization, this war was now waged in the name of Westernizing progress, science, and national defense.[10]

Almost overnight, the modern school diploma replaced the examination degree as the most basic credential for entering government service and achieving social status. Many members of the traditional gentry fought hard against it, and the hapless classically educated scholar, cast adrift after a lifetime of intense study, with his career aspirations suddenly snatched away from him, became a stock character in both reformist and popular fiction.[11] Yet a surprising number of long-established elite families adapted rather quickly to this revolutionary event, having even already taken the precaution of sending at least one promising son to a Western school before the axe fell on the examination system. Menfolk in this class retrained themselves to become Western school instructors or to enter other new and promising careers. With these kinds of adaptations, the "gentry"—originally a product of the examination system—managed to survive the abolition of that system by a generation or two at the very least.[12]

New armies, schools, police forces, and railroads, along with expanded administrative staffs, industrial and communications development, and all the rest of the New Policy reforms, cost a great deal of money. The Qing government's revenues around 1900—including those of the Imperial Maritime Customs, which had been attached to service the Boxer indemnity debt—equaled only about 6 percent of the gross domestic product, a remarkably low percentage. In the United States in

2008, by comparison, the revenues of the federal government were close to 11 percent of the GDP, and those of the combined federal, state, and local governments exceeded 30 percent. Where did the Qing government expect to find the resources to finance its ambitious new programs? The most obvious sources were loans from foreign governments and banks. Consequently, on top of the enormous loans that had already been contracted to pay off indemnities and to meet routine administrative costs such as payroll,[13] the New Policies brought with them oppressive new obligations that sank the government ever deeper in debt.

But a second source of funding presented itself in the form of fiscal restructuring. There had been a long-term trend, at least since the mid-century rebellions, for provinces to become fiscally independent of the center. The transit tax and other expanding commercial levies were generally assessed and collected directly by regional administrations and were poorly reported, still less remitted, to the throne. The Boxer indemnity changed that, and in this sense it was a blessing in disguise. Suddenly saddled with this enormous debt, the central government had no choice but to require provinces to make "contributions" toward debt repayment. The province of Hubei, for example, committed 1,200,000 silver taels per year to service the Boxer debt.[14]

The reinvigorated central government continued and extended the restructuring process that the Boxer debt had started. It imposed a series of new annual contributions on the provinces, nationalized a number of profitable self-strengthening industries, mines, and shipping lines, and in 1909 launched intensive audits of provincial "fiscal realities"—three-year studies with final reports to be presented to the throne in 1911. The result was a redistribution of fiscal resources throughout the empire and a sudden reversal of the long-term trend of decentralization. Just as political authority was being dramatically reconcentrated in the hands of the central administration, so too was the center's monopoly over fiscal resources being reclaimed. This was state-making at its most basic.

Ultimately, the burden of financing the reforms was borne by the local population in the form of increased taxes. Revenues at all levels of government probably doubled in the final decades of the Qing empire, with the greatest share coming in the few years after 1905. A wide variety of new regulations were imposed either by the central government itself or by provincial and local administrations to ensure upward remission of revenues. In some provinces surtaxes of up to 20 percent were added to the land tax. New urban real estate taxes also represented a ready source of revenue. Existing networks of government-licensed brokers, who in the past had paid modest annual fees for their licenses, were now mobilized as government tax agents to collect direct taxes on wholesale transactions. Retail sales of some consumer goods were subjected to excise taxes for the first time. In cities, the treasuries of merchant guilds were confiscated to meet the costs of chambers of commerce, while in villages the temple endowments formally used to underwrite annual festivals and operatic performances were confiscated to finance rural schools. Most burdensome of all was indirect taxation in the form of seignorage—the minting of new copper coins with face values well above the value of their metallic content—and the issuance of paper currency not backed up by precious metals. This debasement of the money supply benefited the government but represented a cost to the population in the form of inflated commodity prices.

In short, there was something in the financing of the New Policies to offend everyone in Qing society, though the burden undoubtedly fell most heavily on the poor, who directly benefited least from the reforms. However, if one accepts the logic that a more powerful, centralized, and penetrating state was a useful thing for twentieth-century China to possess in the face of its manifold threats, the questions then become: How many of the reforms were really necessary and worth the cost? And were they equitably and efficiently carried out? The answers given to these questions, it seems, reflect the philosophical stance of the individual observer.

The Western View of the 1911 Revolution

Western—especially American—historians' views of China's Republican Revolution of 1911 have been reactions to the two master narratives put forth by the political parties that dominated Chinese politics for most of the twentieth century. The orthodox interpretation of the Chinese Nationalist Party (Guomindang) has been paramount and even today forms the core of popular understanding of this event in the West.[15] This narrative stressed the nationalist aims of the revolution—against the West, certainly, but more importantly against the alien occupying dynasty, the Manchus. It emphasized the revolution's leadership: the conspiratorial, enlightened, progressive, self-consciously revolutionary, and coordinated men whose political alliance was seen as the direct predecessor of the Guomindang Party itself. Above all, it stressed Sun Yat-sen, who, like

George Washington, was the "father of his country" and of the Nationalist Party.

China, the story goes, had chafed for nearly three centuries under the Manchu yoke. Sun was a visionary who, before nearly anyone else, perceived this as tyranny. Accordingly, he led a heroic series of uprisings in the first years of the twentieth century and by 1911 had finally put together a workable coalition that succeeded in establishing a republic. In the process Sun laid down the Three Principles of the People—popular rights, democracy, and popular livelihoods—invoking, perhaps deliberately, Lincoln's "of the people, by the people, and for the people." After his success, Sun graciously withdrew, leaving governance in the hands of others, who betrayed the revolution.[16] He returned to the political stage in order to lead a movement to throw the rascals out and put the country back on the proper track—a task that was finally achieved by Sun's rightful heir, Jiang Jieshi (Chiang Kai-shek). Helped along by sympathetic interpreters, this flattering narrative was designed to appeal to patriotic Americans, and it did.[17]

In the revolutionary narrative of the Chinese Communist Party, by contrast, the events of 1911 were never accorded the status of a foundation myth, as they were for the Guomindang. For decades, the revolution of 1911 was downplayed as being of lesser significance than those of the genuine Communist revolution of 1949. But in the immediate post-Mao era an enormous spurt of interest and new scholarship appeared—including international conferences and translations of Western studies—in an effort by the Chinese Communist Party to claim the events of 1911 as their own. Essentially, these studies in the People's Republic—some of them extremely good—took an economic determinist approach that stressed the revolution's class character.[18] The "bourgeois democratic" uprising of 1911 was akin to the French Revolution of 1789—a revolt by a "national bourgeoisie," as opposed to the "compradore bourgeoisie" that had been a client of the West. It was progressive, insofar as it was anti-feudal and anti-imperialist, but it did not centrally involve the peasant and proletariat masses, nor did it express their interests. That task would fall to the revolution of liberation led by the Communist Party. For all its depersonalization, the Communist narrative found an important place for Sun Yat-sen, whom the Communists claimed as their "nationalist bourgeois" forebear.

Both of these narratives suffer from being somewhat "Sun Yat-sentric." Sun was actually in Denver, Colorado, when the revolution broke out, and a great many complex forces at work in the revolution were at least as important as Sun's personal contribution, if not more so. While the earliest Western studies of the revolution placed Sun firmly at the center,[19] the second wave shifted the focus a bit to acknowledge the contributions of his closest associates, Huang Xing and Song Jiaoren.[20] Then came studies of revolutionary activities among elements less clearly linked with Sun himself, such as students and intellectuals.[21] Around the same time, the revolutionary contributions of individuals and forces not avowedly revolutionary at all, or even opposing revolution, were acknowledged.[22] Finally, and perhaps most revealingly, came case studies of the actual social history of the revolution in specific localities.[23]

In the process of widening the circle of investigation, Western historians have come closer to the Chinese Communist narrative of 1911 than they were at the start. That said, however, they have also come to perceive a revolution that was not consistent from place to place, that was not exactly "bourgeois" in its social basis, and that was at times not entirely "progressive." What current Western historiography emphasizes is the interplay of particular private and local interests in influencing how revolutionary events would work themselves out.

Students

As in the late nineteenth century, some activist Chinese in the early twentieth century played roles as reformers, while some others took the part of overt revolutionaries. The revolutionaries were far fewer, and their republican movement peaked and spent itself first. To a very large extent it originated in Japan, which was China's most threatening foreign antagonist but also its most important model, having sparked two frenetic waves of Qing reform in direct response to Japan's major victories on Chinese soil.

Cultivation of young Chinese radicals became a pet project of many Japanese activists, self-conscious heirs to the "men of spirit" (shishi) of the Meiji restoration era, who carved out lives as "knights-errant" (Shina rōnin) in the field of Chinese commerce, politics, and revolution. The new ideology firing such adventurers was Pan-Asianism, the call for all people of the yellow race to unite in the struggle against the white race. The journalist and educator Naitō Konan (1866–1944), who established the holistic discipline of East Asian history at Kyoto University, argued emphatically that Japanese culture was born of Chinese culture, and that it was now time for the vigorous offspring to lend a hand to its increasingly senescent parent. Out of this sense of common heritage as well as common economic interests, the East Asian Common Culture Association (Tōa Dōbunkai) was established in Tokyo in 1898. A combination of study society, business lobby, and intelligence operation, it set up bookstores throughout China and proselytized its members' faith much as Western missionaries had done. Pan-Asianism was a mood shared, to a considerable extent, by the Japanese government itself, which offered political asylum to Qing radical reformers such as Kang Youwei and Liang Qichao and revolutionaries such as Tang Caichang and Sun Yat-sen.[24]

Of greatest significance, however, were the growing numbers of Chinese students who made their way to Japan in the Qing's final decade. The migration of Chinese students overseas began in earnest after 1895 and picked up considerably in 1905, after Japan's defeat of Russia and China's abolition of the civil service examination. Some went to Europe, some to the United States, but most of them went to Japan, due to considerations of cost, distance, and linguistic closeness. They comprised not only the largest mass movement of students overseas in world history up to that point but also most of the first-generation leaders of the Chinese Republic. The vast majority were men, but some women studied abroad as well. The numbers of students, male and female, grew from a dozen or so in the late 1890s to a few hundred in the first years of the twentieth century to more than 8,000 in 1905.[25] If they had not already done so before leaving home, these young queue-wearing Chinese, taunted by a self-consciously modernized Japanese public, quickly converted to Chinese nationalism. In the preface to his short story collection *Call to Arms*, the writer Lu Xun told of his experience as a young medical student in Japan in 1905, when he was forced to watch a slide show of the beheading of a Chinese "spy" by Japanese troops, with local Chinese crowded around to observe the spectacle. It was for Lu a life-changing experience.[26]

The rapid politicization of these overseas students in Japan was catalyzed by the lectures of exiled political figures, by newspapers published in Japanese and also in Chinese by the sojourning community itself, and by Japanese translations of Western social and political thought. These translations bequeathed to twentieth-century China a new political vocabulary: in order to render unfamiliar Western concepts into Japanese, scores of neologisms were coined by employing traditional Chinese characters in new combinations and with new meanings, and these Japanese inventions were then reimported into Chinese discourse itself. Included among these terms were such potent mobilizing concepts as *minzu* (nation or race), *minquan* (people's rights), *minzhu zhuyi* (democracy), *xianfa* (constitution), *ziyou zhuyi* (liberalism), *shehui zhuyi* (socialism), *gongheguo* (republic), and, not least, *geming* (revolution).

The students also organized. Like examination candidates within the empire itself or sojourning merchants in the commercial diaspora overseas, they formed clubs based on their place of origin. Some of these organizations published their own newspapers, such as *Tides of Zhejiang* (*Zhejiang chao*) or militant tracts such as Yang Yulin's *New Hunan* (*Xin Hunan*), to promote a new, radicalized provincial patriotism.[27] They also formed revolutionary cells. Not unaware of this, the Qing court used spies to infiltrate these organizations and urged Japan to extradite troublemakers for trial at home. For its part, the Meiji government, with its own Pan-Asianist sentiments, tended for a time to practice benign neglect toward radical Chinese students, as it did to Qing political exiles of various persuasions.

Problems for Qing authority really began when these radicalized students returned home and interacted with the much more numerous graduates of the new Western-style schools and military academies. The radicalization of this entire generation might be seen as an unanticipated fallout of the New Policies reforms (and further testimony to those policies' genuineness). Returned students hung out in or near foreign enclaves such as Shanghai or Hankou, where they continued to absorb Western influences but in a radically nationalist way. Their activities involved a fair amount of romantic idealism and adolescent "acting out." An exemplar of this was the charismatic young Qiu Jin (1875–1907), who immersed herself in traditional martial romances like the *Water Margin* (*Shuihu zhuan*) and envisioned herself as a heroic knight-errant. She was fond of being photographed in Western men's clothing or in the attire of famous female sectarian leaders from China's past. She also organized a student army, taking particular care in the design of their uniforms.[28]

Many in this generation were attracted to the Japanese cult of body-building, competitive sports, and martial arts—practices that are still part of Chinese culture today. Imbibing the Japanese *shishi* ideal of the selfless young samurai who would enthusiastically give up his (or her) life for the fatherland, young Chinese students deliberately courted martyrdom and pledged mutual bonds in "dare-to-die" corps. A not uncommon dramatic gesture was suicide, as when the young Hunanese pamphleteer

Chen Tianhua (1875–1905) drowned himself in Tokyo Bay in 1905, partly to protest the Japanese clampdown on Chinese student mobilization. That same year, 25-year-old Feng Xiawei (1880–1905) poisoned himself on the steps of the American embassy in Shanghai to protest the U.S. Exclusion Acts.[29] Another gesture was anarchist-inspired assassination attempts, as when the Cantonese returned student Wang Jingwei (1883–1944) tried to murder the imperial regent in 1909.

Some students forged links with secret societies to lead local uprisings, the most celebrated of which came in the highlands along the border area known as Ping-Liu-Li between Hunan and Jiangxi provinces. Here, in the native place of Tan Sitong and Tang Caichang (who had pioneered the idea of uniting with secret societies in his Independence Army of 1900), a group of returned Hunanese students led a revolutionary strike among local coal miners in 1906, which ended in bloody failure. More than anything else, the specter of students from elite backgrounds mobilizing such declassé groups as secret societies and miners prompted the Qing government to redouble its efforts to suppress student activism at home and abroad.

An increasingly strident anti-Manchu rhetoric fired the young revolutionaries. To the historic memory of Qing conquest "atrocities" and the Manchu "sellout" during the Opium War was added a newer belief that racial solidarity was a prerequisite for nation-building. The soon-to-be martyr Chen Tianhua, echoing the nativist Boxer rhetoric of just three years earlier, wrote in his incendiary 1903 pamphlet *Alarm Bell* (*Jingshi zhong*): "Kill! Kill! Kill! . . . Advance *en masse*: kill the foreign devils, kill the Christian converts who surrender to the foreign devils! If the Manchus help the foreigners kill us, then first kill all the Manchus . . . Advance, kill! Advance, kill! Advance, kill! Kill! Kill!"[30]

A more intellectualized but nonetheless devastating brand of anti-Manchuism was developed by the Yangzhou native Liu Shipei (1884–1919). His grandfather had been on Zeng Guofan's staff when Zeng supervised the first republication of Wang Fuzhi's works in 1862, and Liu Shipei invested his own reading of Wang with newer social Darwinist theories of race war. Like other young patriots from the lower Yangzi, Hunan, and Guangdong, he picked up on Wang's theme that, following successive waves of northern barbarian invasion, the authentic Chinese race and culture had migrated to the south. A competent classical scholar, Liu reread the *Spring and Autumn Annals* as encoding a secret theme of *rangyi* (expel the barbarians), which was echoed in the rallying cry of the

young samurai at the time of the Meiji restoration. Borrowing the Ger-
manic notion of *volksgeist* (national spirit) as mediated through the Meiji
Japanese *kokusai* (national essence), Liu and his colleague, the classicist-
racist Zhang Binglin, posited a similar "national essence" of the Han
Chinese that had been systematically suppressed for centuries under
Manchu rule. At Shanghai in 1903, at age nineteen, he founded the *National Essence Journal* and published a series of volumes aiming to re-
cover these hidden transcripts—essays, poems, paintings, calligraphy—
that embodied the true Han "national soul" and would inspire his people
in their racial struggle against the Manchus.[31]

Probably the single most influential tract produced by radical students
in these years was *The Revolutionary Army* (*Geming jun*), published in
1903 by Zou Rong (1885–1907), an eighteen-year-old Sichuanese newly
returned from Japan. Zou's piece is deeply informed by social Darwinist
racial thought: "The world has white and yellow races. This is a state of
nature which enables men of ability and intelligence to compete with
each other in the process of evolution . . . so that the fittest may survive.
The love of people for their own race is due to the need for consolidation
against outside forces."[32] Reasoning in this vein, Zou produced a "scientific" taxonomy of the races of Asia and concluded that "the Han race is
the most outstanding race in East Asian history—that is the race of my
fellow countrymen." This led him to attack the hegemony of "the Tun-
gusic race," the Manchus: "Ah! Our Han race, isn't that the race which
can make our motherland strong? . . . Is it not the great race of a great
people? Alas! The Han race, although made up of so many, have become
merely the slaves of another race . . . The Han race are nothing but the
loyal and submissive slaves of the Manchus."

Echoing John Stuart Mill, Zou argued that the Chinese are a people
without history: "The so-called Chinese history of twenty-four dynasties
is nothing but a history of slaves." He fit this into an anti-imperialist position and, invoking Confucian logic, found this predicament shaming
and unfilial: "Those who were formerly the loyal subjects of the Jin,
Yuan, and Qing dynasties have gone; now there are those who have become the loyal subjects of Britain, France, Russia, and America. The reason for this is that the people have no ethnocentric or national ideas; thus
they can do things humiliating to our ancestors, the men becoming robbers and the women prostitutes." In a bold gesture of historical revision-
ism, the heroes of the anti-Taiping campaign became for Zou "running
dogs," traitors to the race:

Zeng Guofan, Zuo Zongtang, and Li Hongzhang were the loyal officers of the Qing emperors . . . These three persons . . . considered
themselves educated compared with former sages, and yet they were
willing to butcher their fellow countrymen, contrary to justice and
righteousness, to be loyal slaves to the Manchus . . . They butchered
their compatriots and asked the Manchus to rule China so that they
might obtain honor and position for their children and wives. Them
I cannot forgive.[33]

For all his ethnocentrism, Zou demonstrated a striking global cosmopolitanism. The Indians and the Vietnamese, like the Chinese, had become slaves to foreign powers. But there were also inspiring foreign models for revolution:

The British Parliament disobeyed King Charles I because the King
extended great privileges to the nobility [and] endangered the business life of the people . . . The French Revolution was a result of titles given without merit. People were not well protected and taxes
were levied arbitrarily . . . The Americans struggled for independence because a heavy tea tax and a stamp tax were levied and garrison forces were stationed in America without the consent of the leg-
islature. Consequently, the Americans rose in protest against the
British, with the American flag waving at Bunker Hill.

Zou's vision of a new postrevolutionary polity was grounded in social
contract and natural rights theories that would have been wholly un-
imaginable for a Qing subject only a few years earlier. (Rousseau's *Du
Contrat Social* first appeared in Chinese translation in 1901; and in the
same year that Zou published his tract, Liu Shipei published a study systematically tracing hints of an indigenous social contract theory in the
Chinese classics.)[34] Zou wrote: "The people possess inalienable rights.
Life, liberty, and all the other benefits are natural rights. No one shall in-
fringe upon freedom of speech, freedom of thought, or freedom of the
press . . . If the government insists on corrupt ways, then it is not only the
right but the obligation of the people to overthrow it, and set up a new
government to protect their rights . . . Take revolution as every man's
duty," Zou concludes, "consider it as necessary as your daily food." Kill
the emperor, the Manchus, and all the foreign oppressors. In this orgy of
bloodshed "the shame of the nation will be washed clean."

By late 1907, the romantic student-led phase of the revolution had largely burned out. After a period of patronizing the follies of their talented youth, the Qing authorities cracked down, with support from the Japanese government. Qiu Jin was arrested and executed. Zou Rong died in prison at age twenty-three. Chen Tianhua had taken his own life two years earlier. Liu Shipei had a very public change of heart, announcing that he now saw the best path to safeguarding the Han "national essence" in the preservation of the Qing empire, not its eradication. The student movement had accomplished its mission to raise the consciousness of the Qing general public and put the idea of republican revolution very much on the table, but it had not brought about the revolution itself. When that revolution came, it would be led by others.

The Professional

Sun Yat-sen was born in 1866 in Xiangshan, a county in Guangdong's Pearl River delta adjacent to British Hong Kong. Though a fellow provincial of his political rival Kang Youwei, born just eight years earlier in nearby Foshan city, Sun was a different sort of person. Whereas Kang enjoyed an impeccable classical education and achieved the *jinshi* degree, Sun had few literati credentials and was more socially marginalized. He visited Hong Kong during his childhood, and by the age of thirteen was packed off to live with his elder brother in Hawaii, where he attended Christian missionary school. Speaking and writing English more comfortably than classical Chinese, he became a Western-style professional by attending medical school in Hong Kong. Sun was also at home in Japan, where he learned to speak the language comfortably, Japanized his alternate name Zhongshan (central mountain) into the surname Nakayama, and sported a well-groomed Meiji-style moustache. At the same time, far more than Kang, Sun self-consciously identified himself as a southerner, stressing his links with the southern anti-Manchuism of both the Taipings and the underground fraternal tradition of the Triads.

Sun's personal contributions to the republican revolutionary movement have been much debated—unrealistically magnified by his disciples and categorically dismissed by his detractors.[35] A balanced assessment might identify among Sun's personal assets his oft-attested personal good looks and charisma, his skills as a public speaker (a political art form relatively new to his day), and his flair for the dramatic.[36] In 1896, for example, he was raising money for his revolutionary activities in London when he was detained by the Qing legation in that city. His release was secured after Sun managed to communicate his captivity to a British doctor friend. Sun's characteristic response was immediately to publish a self-promoting account of his adventure, in English, entitled *Kidnapped in London!*[37]

As a revolutionary organizer, Sun's strengths were his doggedness, his popularity among overseas Chinese (he was fundraising among this group in Denver just as the revolution was breaking out), the recognition and respect he developed among foreign governments and elites, and, less clearly, his ties among domestic secret societies such as the Triads. His liabilities included his *déclassé* status among progressive elites at home (which frustrated Sun's periodic efforts to initiate cooperation with his fellow Cantonese Liang Qichao) and at times a romantic naiveté about his revolutionary project. He was best suited to serve as a propagandist, a broker among other revolutionary elements, and above all a symbol.

It was Sun, however, who in 1894 formed indisputably the first organization dedicated to anti-Qing revolution, the Revive China Society. Fittingly, the site of this founding was far from China itself, in Hawaii. The following year Sun opened a second chapter in Hong Kong. Members of the society at the start were nearly all Cantonese, most were émigrés, and a large percentage were Christians. During the uproar over the signing of the Treaty of Shimonoseki, Sun and his supporters seized the chance to organize their first uprising attempt, planned for Guangzhou city in mid-1895, but it was discovered and aborted by Qing authorities before ever getting off the ground. Sun fled to Japan, where he founded another branch of the Revive China Society in Yokohama and later yet another in Hanoi; he was rarely back on Chinese soil from then until after the revolution had actually succeeded. In 1900, under cover of the Boxer mayhem in north China, Sun launched a second uprising in the Guangzhou suburb of Huizhou (Waichow), but this too was crushed with ease by imperial forces. Other quixotic efforts followed in succession, including one on the Guangxi-Vietnam border in 1907. By this time Sun had become something of a laughingstock among a younger generation with revolutionary ambitions of their own.

Sun had many competitors. There were various provincially-based revolutionary cells, especially among students and the New Army troops. Moreover, he needed to compete for funding with professedly nonrevolutionary groups, especially the Society to Protect the Emperor, which was established in exile by Kang Youwei in 1899 after his aborted reform movement of the previous year. With the house arrest of Guangxu, who embodied the constitutional monarchy aspirations that still fired many reformist elites at home and abroad, Kang could easily make the case that constant public vigilance was required to ensure that conservatives at court did not conveniently do away with Guangxu. It was not an uncommon sight in early twentieth-century overseas Chinese communities like those in Honolulu or San Francisco to see representatives of Kang's society making soapbox appeals at one intersection and Sun Yat-sen's partisans campaigning for support just a block away.[38] Sun tried, without success, to bring the two camps together.

It was Sun's eventual alliance with students that gave his revolutionary vision a new lease on life. The Hunanese student radicals had begun to think of a new level of organization that would unite their own provincials with similarly inclined students from Hubei, Guangdong, Zhejiang, Sichuan, and other provinces. The Hunanese Revive China Society, founded at Changsha in 1903 and distinct from Sun's similarly named group, began under Huang Xing's leadership to systematically cultivate ties with other provincial student groups.[39] In Tokyo in 1905, brokered by their Japanese Pan-Asianist sympathizers and further inspired by Japan's victory over Russia, representatives of Huang's group and others met with Sun Yat-sen and organized the most inclusive and significant anti-Qing front yet put together, the Revolutionary Alliance, with Sun as their leader. For the next few years this umbrella organization took the clear lead in spreading the gospel of republican revolution in China. But internal disagreements began to fracture its unity almost from the start—competition over leadership positions, disputes over revolutionary strategy (the timing and location of uprisings), debates over the advisability of continuing links with Japanese and other sympathetic foreigners. By 1908 it was generally acknowledged that the Revolutionary Alliance, for all its several thousand members, was effectively moribund.

So what was the real role of Sun Yat-sen in the revolution of 1911? His Revolutionary Alliance had collapsed several years earlier. After orchestrating one last putsch at Guangzhou in April 1911, he fled to the United States in search of yet more funding from overseas Chinese. He still enjoyed some strength at home among the most Westernized Qing subjects, but only a few. When the revolution began at Wuchang in October of that year, neither Sun nor any of his close colleagues had been part of its planning, nor were they even informed of it beforehand. They were only somewhat more involved in the wave of sympathetic uprisings that followed in other localities. However, Sun and his collaborators—most energetically the Hunanese Huang Xing—were often either called in, or invited themselves in, to pick up the pieces and offer advice and strategy after the fact.

Once the revolution was largely a *fait accompli,* many people recognized that Sun Yat-sen, and nearly he alone, had the legitimacy accorded by a revolutionary pedigree of matchless longevity, a relatively worked-out vision of the postrevolutionary future, and, not least, sufficient respect in the foreign community to deter outside forces from opportunistic aggression once the Qing regime had collapsed. In retrospect, he seemed to be the revolution's iconic leader.

The Reformist Elite

Both radical students and professional revolutionaries had played important roles in creating a climate favorable to republican revolution. But the influence of both groups had faded after 1908, and neither group was the direct agent of the revolution. The key role fell to a class of persons who had never been overtly revolutionary but who in practice might have been the most revolutionary of all: the reformist elite. Virtually to a man, they were urbanites with very weak ties to the agrarian regime of the countryside. To this extent they looked like the bourgeoisie in the Marxist model, but if one adheres to a strict Marxist definition of the bourgeoisie—that is, capitalists in a system of industrial production—then such persons, while not altogether absent in early twentieth-century China, were far too insignificant numerically to be of much political influence. But by broadening this category into a more generalized "urban reformist elite," we can bring into focus the group who lay behind, and principally profited from, the events of 1911.[40]

This expanded category would include a variety of disparate but overlapping types. The first would be traditional merchants of substantial scale—wholesalers and brokers, some but not all involved in production operations, and including both those concentrating on domestic commerce (the so-called national bourgeoisie) and foreign trade (the compradorial bourgeoisie). A related type, increasingly visible since the late nineteenth century, was the hybrid gentry-merchant.[41] Such men practiced business for their livelihood but typically held civil service degrees, often by purchase, or at least embodied a familiar Confucian literati lifestyle. The appearance of this group in the late Qing was the outcome of several social trends. One was the increasing involvement of degree-holding literati in commerce, an activity formally prohibited by a Qing legal principle that segregated literati and merchant roles but then actively encouraged during the Taiping and post-Taiping reconstruction era by officials eager to bolster the empire's commercial economy and at the same time grant control of that economy to presumably upright Confucian gentlemen.[42] A subset of this type was the gentry-manager who, especially in the reconstruction decades, worked hand in hand with merchants in local charity, water conservancy, and other areas and in the process became more personally involved in commercial activities himself.

The gradual fusion of two traditionally distinct roles into gentry-merchants (in other words, into modern businessmen) over the course of the late nineteenth century was accelerated by key initiatives of the New Policies era: the abolition of the civil service examination system—the formal badge of gentry exclusiveness—and the establishment of local and provincial chambers of commerce that gave nongentry merchants an unprecedented voice in policymaking.

Yet a third sector of the new urban reformist elite was drawn from the older literati class itself. After about 1895 the examination gentry had more or less bifurcated into two groups: one that continued to stress the primacy of classical education and long-established gentry roles in society, and another (sometimes dubbed the "new-style gentry") that embraced more cosmopolitan educational and social agendas. This latter group, including those with civil service examination degrees, provided modern schoolteachers, bankers and investors in industrial, mining, and transportation enterprises, white-collar professionals in law, medicine, and journalism, and a new Chinese intelligentsia. Such men made up the core of the local and provincial representative assemblies of the New Policies era.[43]

Altogether, these merchants, gentry-merchants, and new-style gentry coalesced into a development-minded, business-oriented class that was becoming increasingly impatient with the constraints placed on their activities by the old political system. Over the course of the first decade of the twentieth century, this reformist elite was decisively converted to nationalism by the venerable treaty-port newspaper *Shenbao* but also by a host of new journals such as *The Eastern Miscellany (Dongfang zazhi)*, founded in 1904 and a persistent proselytizer of "local self-governance," and *Shibao,* established the same year as a mouthpiece for Liang Qichao and other progressives.[44] In 1905 a widespread boycott of American goods to protest the United States' exclusion of Chinese immigration brought together many of these elements: the defense of national dignity abroad, orchestration by the new politicized press, the concept of commercial warfare, and encouragement by nationalist-minded businessmen who sought to derive a competitive advantage for domestic manufactures.[45] In the process, the boycott helped develop a repertoire of popular mobilization techniques—speechmaking, public rallies, participation by professional and voluntary associations—that would be turned to many other purposes in the years to follow.

A telling shift in the rhetoric of the final Qing decade was from the defensive goal of "saving the country" from partitioning or extinction to the much more aggressive declaration of "sovereign rights"—the newly popularized concept of sovereignty serving as a rallying call for militant nationalist action. What kinds of rights were at stake? The most immediately visible were territorial rights, and this era saw the rise of a compelling irredentist urge to recapture lost national territory—a theme that underlies so much of twentieth-century Chinese politics and is still observable today in the ongoing crusade of the People's Republic to repatriate Taiwan.

In Tibet, the British, who had long sought to expand their foothold and consolidate control, occupied Lhasa in 1904. The Dalai Llama, meanwhile, maneuvered to assert greater Tibetan autonomy under his personal power, while rumors of a Russian invasion circulated in the Chinese press. Spurred on by reformist agitation, Qing officials aggressively countered these threats after 1908 by sending in several waves of expeditionary troops and converting as much as they could of this venerable Qing possession from indirect headman rule to regularized prefectural and county administration. On February 12, 1910, amidst internal bickering on the part of Qing officials, a rifle-toting New Army force under the Mongol bannerman Lianyu seized Llasa, dissolved the Tibetan government, and sent the Dalai Lama into exile in India.[46]

Even more compelling than territorial rights, however, was the articulation of economic rights, in a widespread movement to repatriate concessions granted to foreigners for mining and communications development, most especially railroads. One of the lessons the central government had drawn from the Sino-Japanese War was the need for a more encompassing network of railroads for military as well as commercial transport. Agreements with several foreign companies to finance or construct rail lines were hastily signed in 1898, and a major trunk line from Beijing to Hankou was completed by French and Belgian firms in 1905. The southern extension of this line from Hankou to Guangzhou was to be built by an American firm, but it met with concerted local elite opposition, especially in Hunan. Various Hunanese investor groups proposed to build the railroad themselves, and in 1905, after mobilizing a significant but peaceful protest movement, they succeeded in getting Huguang's governor-general, Zhang Zhidong, to broker a settlement with the American contractor and turn over development rights to them. Internal disputes and financing difficulties delayed the completion of the line until after the Qing had fallen.

The railway rights recovery movement was more contentious in Zhejiang and Sichuan. In 1898 a British company had been granted the right to build a railroad linking Shanghai, Hangzhou, and Ningbo, but seven years later two literati-led local companies lobbied regional officials to cancel the British agreement and award railroad construction rights to them. When the Ministry of Foreign Affairs nevertheless signed a loan agreement with the British in 1907 for this purpose, gentry, merchants, and students in Shanghai and Zhejiang, stirred up by the political press, mobilized in protest. Scores of local branches of the protest organization sprang up overnight. The two Chinese companies went ahead and built the rail lines themselves in 1909, effectively ending the controversy in Jiangnan.

In the Sichuan case, however, the Manchu governor-general Xiliang set up his own quasi-governmental Sichuan Railway Company in 1904 to build lines around Chengdu, and when little private investment was forthcoming he imposed a property surtax to finance it. Facing gentry-led protests, Xiliang more fully privatized the company in 1907. Because of Sichuan Railway's rampant corruption and poor results, however, the Ministry of Posts in spring 1911 nationalized all Sichuan railroad operations. Over the next several months, a Sichuan Association of Comrades to Protect the Railway mobilized thousands of persons from all elements in the province—literati, students, soldiers of the provincial New Army, local militia, laborers, and Society of Elder Brother gangsters—into a protest movement that rapidly turned violent. In several counties, government tax offices and police stations were attacked. Scores of protesters were killed or wounded in Chengdu in early fall, and the entire province appeared on the verge of anti-dynastic rebellion. The railroad rights recovery movement in these provinces, which was ostensibly directed at eliminating the foreign presence, in most instances turned instead against the Qing government, as local populations devised new styles of mobilizational politics to demonstrate their loss of faith in the regime's ability to protect their interests.[47]

Beyond nationalism, the reformist elite came to champion the notions of constitutionalism and representative government. The idea of a Qing constitution, understood as a formal statement specifying and delimiting the scope of government action, had first been raised during the 1898 reforms. Here again Japan provided the model. The fact that the Meiji constitution had been issued in 1889 and just five years later Japan proved capable of humiliating the Qing empire in a foreign war seemed to imply a necessary correlation: a population endowed with a constitution would be more invested in the fate of the nation and hence much more mobilizable for national purposes. In the early twentieth century, constitutionalism became the guiding ideology of the urban reformist elite, and after 1905 constitutionalist societies sprang up at the provincial level throughout the empire to lobby the Qing court to promulgate such a document without delay. In 1908 the court announced its intention to issue a constitution, setting 1917 as the target year, but the constitutionalists urged quicker action. The tenor of their movement was liberal and moderate, and its vocal leader was Liang Qichao, who persistently argued that an empowering constitution, not a revolution, was China's most pressing need. For the moment his goal was a constitutional monarchy, but he proved capable of shifting his rhetoric to a constitutional democracy after the revolution succeeded.

As part of its New Policies, the Qing court pledged to set up self-governing representative assemblies at various levels of administration, on the supposition that this was the means to forge a modern citizenry still loyal to the throne. However, once established, these assemblies quickly became the mouthpieces for the reformist elite and for their ideology of constitutionalism. Assemblies at the county, township, and municipality levels were established beginning in 1908. The next year, provincial assemblies were elected and convened, and in 1910 they began to select representatives to a National Assembly. According to the court's schedule, the National Assembly would not become permanent until the constitution was promulgated in 1917, but a Provisional National Assembly was established in the meantime and actually convened at Beijing in October 1910. Unsurprisingly, the major voice in this institution was that of Liang Qichao.

The key representative bodies were clearly the provincial assemblies. The election of 1909 that gave birth to them was an unprecedented event in the history of imperial China: despite stringent educational and property-holding requirements that narrowed the (all-male) electorate to less than 0.5 percent of the empire's population, an estimated two million Qing subjects went to the polls and got a taste of political participation undreamt of up to that time. The composition of these provincial assemblies was what one might have expected. Perhaps 90 percent of their members empire-wide were gentry—formal degree-holders from the recently abolished examination system. Of the assemblies for the twenty-one provinces, fourteen were headed by a holder of the *jinshi* degree, while another six were led by a recipient of the provincial degree. But this was no necessary indication of the conservative nature of the assemblies, since most of their gentry members, including many of the *jinshi*-holders, were firmly in the reformist new-style gentry camp.[48]

In their range of activities and styles of action, the late Qing provincial assemblies effectively transformed an administrative reform program into a political movement.[49] They vied with the centrally appointed outsider governor for control over policy within the province itself. They took over the rights-recovery movements against both foreigners and the new Qing ministries. And they aggressively pressured the court to speedily adopt a constitution, convene a permanent National Assembly, and immediately establish a "responsible cabinet," that is, a cabinet-style government whose ministers would wield genuine political decision-making power and would be selected by the National Assembly rather than the throne.

The late Qing provincial assemblies played a very important but complicated role in the evolution of twentieth-century Chinese politics. On the one hand, they added considerably to the decentralizing regionalist trend that had been under way since the rebellions of the 1850s and 1860s, culminating in the late 1910s and 1920s in the regional autonomy of warlord regimes. On the other hand, they at least partly represented popular interests within the province and thus were a stage in the growth at the local level of popular Chinese nationalism. In other words, they were the embodiment of what might be called provincial nationalism. Through these institutions, provincial elites really first emerged as solidary self-conscious forces. The provincial assemblies and their variously renamed successors survived the 1911 transition and remained for decades one of the most potent political institutions in republican China.[50]

The greater crisis for the Qing regime came when this reformist elite, already fired by a nationalist spirit, embraced the desirability, or at least the inevitability, of anti-imperial revolution. The conversion for many came over the course of a mere two days, on November 14 and 15, 1908. On the fourteenth the Guangxu emperor died at age thirty-seven, and when the Empress Dowager Cixi died the following day at age seventy-three, suspicions of foul play immediately arose and remain to this day. The death of the Guangxu emperor left the most temperate of the reformist parties, Kang Youwei's Society to Protect the Emperor, without a focus of personal loyalty, and, for many, loyalty to the dynasty died along with Guangxu's demise. Despite his nondescript personality, Guangxu had emerged as the symbol of China at home and in the diaspora: his death prompted mass memorials and the construction of altars in Chinatowns throughout the world. The death of Cixi after a three-month illness was not similarly mourned, but it removed the person who had in fact ruled and stabilized the Qing empire for nearly half a century and replaced her with a far less politically astute group of regents for the new Xuantong emperor, Aisin Gioro Puyi. He was three years old.

The actions of these marginally competent and highly defensive Qing princes signaled an acceleration of two basic trends that had marked the New Policies period as a whole. Just as the reforms had been designed to reassert the power of the central government over the provinces and localities, they had also been designed to concentrate power in the hands of Manchu officials rather than Chinese—a disruption of the principle of balanced "dyarchy" that had governed the administration since the Kangxi reign—and in the hands of the imperial clan rather than less well-born Manchus. This power grab was bitterly resented and fanned an already incendiary anti-Manchuism and Han racial nationalism, both of which rapidly swept up the social ladder and into the Chinese literati elite. Probably the last straw was the naming of the "responsible cabinet" long demanded by the reformists. When a thirteen-member cabinet was announced in April 1911, it contained four Han officials, one Mongol, and eight Manchu princes of royal blood.

To this insult was added dissatisfaction over the court's foot-dragging in promulgating the constitution, and the discovery that the provisional National Assembly, when convened in 1911, had been granted only advisory rather than legislative powers. Perhaps even more important was the regency's announcement in spring 1911 of the court's plan to national-ize railroads, after provincial merchant-gentry groups had expended so much financial and political capital to repatriate them. Popular riots broke out in Sichuan, but elite resistance to nationalization was nation-wide. Turning against the throne, the reformist elite emerged as the en-gine of revolution.

Empire's End

A revolution needs three things: ideology, organization, and opportunity. In the final days of the Qing empire, there certainly was ideology, but it was weak and mostly ill-defined. A vision of representative government had been articulated by some radical intellectuals, and a less well-defined republicanism motivated the followers of Sun Yat-sen. Far more perva-sive than these was the negative ideology of anti-Manchuism. Organiza-tion was not absent but it too was extremely diffused, in small cells of professionals, students, and New Army soldiers; the broader based orga-nization offered by the Revolutionary Alliance was effectively defunct. But the third component, opportunity, was there in spades. China in mid-1911 presented a "revolutionary moment" *par excellence.*[51] A Chinese analog to the French Great Fear on the eve of the revolution of 1789 gripped society—the sudden, widespread, and anxious recognition that the Qing dynasty had lost the Heavenly mandate.

Several factors contributed to this fear. One was acute fiscal crisis. When the commissioners in charge of the three-year audits of "provincial fiscal realities" reported their findings in 1911, it became clear that nearly all provinces were running huge, chronic deficits. On top of this, the em-pire's first annual budget revealed massive insolvency at the central level as well. The problem was not new, but admission and general aware-ness of it was. Where were the funds going to come from? Second were natural disasters—repeated floods and poor harvests led to critical grain shortages in 1910 and 1911, and the Qing regime failed to respond. Third was the proliferation of small, localized outbreaks of violence: popular tax revolts (such as one at Laiyang county, Shandong, in which the county magistrate was killed by a crowd of protesters); food riots (in-cluding the major incident in Changsha in 1910 that forced the flight and eventual removal of the Hunan provincial governor); and railway riots (notably in the Chengdu area in the summer and fall of 1911).[52] Few of these incidents were directly connected to any overt revolutionary movement, their goals being more circumscribed and immediate, but collectively they were symptomatic of the Qing's inability to govern the empire.

When the actual events of the revolution finally came, they were almost anticlimactic. The principal agents, ironically, were all institutions created by the New Policies reforms themselves: the New Armies, the chambers of commerce, and the provincial assemblies. On October 10, 1911, a mutiny broke out in the barracks of a New Army unit in Wuchang, the capital city of Hubei province. The Hubei New Army was the among the largest and most literate of these provincial-level forces, and the particular unit involved consisted of army engineers who were well-educated and in many cases belonged to a local revolutionary cell. The rebellion spread quickly, as unit after unit sent to quell it went over to the insurgents' cause. Qing officials fled the city.

Within days the chambers of commerce of Wuchang and Hankou (the major river port facing Wuchang across the Yangzi) declared their support and donated funds. Meanwhile, they mobilized their private militia into Peace Preservation societies to support the political revolution as a *fait accompli* without allowing it to threaten property and business interests. By the afternoon of October 11 the Hubei Provincial Assembly had declared the province's secession from the Qing empire, the formation of a Provisional Military Government under Li Yuanhong (commander-in-chief of the Hubei New Army who, according to most accounts, had been persuaded only at gunpoint to join the revolution), and its intent to create a Han national state, the Republic of China (*Zhonghua minguo*). Beiyang Army forces loyal to the court led a counter-attack in November that razed most of Hankou, but this was the last gasp of organized Qing resistance.[53]

The spread of the revolution from Wuchang into other provinces was almost entirely an urban phenomenon. The provincial capitals Changsha, Xi'an, and Taiyuan declared for the revolution in October; Hangzhou, Fuzhou, Guangzhou, and Chengdu in November; and Nanjing on December 2. In most provinces of the south and northwest the revolution took the form of independent secessions proclaimed by the new provincial assemblies. Many Qing officials, especially those of Han origin at the prefectural and county levels simply went over to the revolutionary side. In coastal cities such as Shanghai, popular response was remarkably passive, conditioned for over a decade by the unregulated tabloid press's dismissive contempt and ridicule of the imperial administration.[54]

Although the Han majority suffered little bloodshed, considerable violence of a deliberately genocidal nature was directed against bannermen and others identified by speech, costume, or ethnic markers as Manchu. In some garrison cities, this violence was prompted by active loyalist resistance on the part of banner populations, but in others it was gratuitous. The worst instance was in Xi'an, where, according to a local British observer, no fewer than ten thousand Manchu men, women, and children—about half of the total garrison population—were summarily murdered in late October. Lesser massacres occurred in Zhenjiang, Fuzhou, and elsewhere. Contrary to conventional nationalist historiography, to these Chinese missionaries of "national revenge" the Manchus had hardly assimilated to the point of invisibility.[55]

In practice, the shifts in power and control varied considerably from province to province, locality to locality, with specific interests dictating the outcome. At the provincial level, something of a power struggle developed among committed revolutionaries, New Army leaders, and the provincial assemblies (the organs of the civilian reformist elite), with the latter two usually banding together in the interests of "preserving the peace"—that is, preventing social revolution and safeguarding the developmental projects already under way. In this they were generally successful, and the progress of industrial, mining, communications, educational, and other infrastructural development did not miss a beat as a result of revolution. Neither was the foreign establishment in China much a target of the disturbances, or much affected by the change of regime.

Sun Yat-sen, the revolutionary organizer with the broadest recognition, was still on his North American tour, but his associates in the dormant Revolutionary Alliance sought with mixed success to appropriate the revolution as their own and impose on it some national coherence. Most notable among them was the Hunanese Huang Xing, who in Hong Kong exile had been alerted to the Hubei New Army's uprising plans beforehand and counseled against them. Huang nevertheless returned to Wuchang on October 28 to offer guidance to the fledgling regime. Yuan Shikai, the empire's senior reformist bureaucrat and leader of its most powerful military force, the Beiyang Army—at the moment in a politically calculated temporary "retirement" from official service—was invited in November to intervene and broker the Qing court's peaceful abdication. In December, representatives of the various autonomous provinces met in Nanjing to draw up a provisional union and bestow the title of provisional president on Sun Yat-sen (who returned to China on Christmas day). January 1, 1912, of the Western solar calendar was proclaimed the founding date of the new Republic of China. When the Xuantong emperor formally abdicated on February 12, not merely the Qing dynasty but also the two-thousand-year-old Chinese empire was gone.

CONCLUSION

FOR MOST ordinary Chinese, the end of the Great Qing probably changed very little about their lives in the short term. One woman who experienced the revolution as a factory laborer in Shandong later recalled that the reality of the transition for her was simply the unit of currency: after the revolution the money was denominated in silver dollars and cents rather than Qing copper cash, but the buying power of her wages remained unaffected.[1] For others, however—elite males, in particular—this was a cultural event of profound and disturbing significance. An occasional scholar committed suicide as a quixotic act of loyalism to the departed dynasty, and well into the 1920s pockets of men throughout the new nation refused to cut their queues and adopt modern hairstyles, out of a mix of deference to the Qing and filiality to fathers and grandfathers who had proudly worn their hair this way. More broadly, the end of the Qing brought with it a crisis of masculinity that manifested itself in a mannered nostalgia for such mundane, morbidly erotic, and now politically incorrect vestiges of the old culture as the female bound foot.[2]

The Great Qing empire was something qualitatively different from the successive Chinese or alien conquest dynasties that had preceded it. As a multinational, universal empire of a distinctively early modern Eurasian type, it had with astonishing success expanded the geographic scope of "China" and incorporated non-Han peoples such as Mongols, Jurchens, Tibetans, Inner Asian Muslims, and others into a new kind of transcendent political entity. Gradually, Han Chinese literati came to accept this new definition of China and to identify it as their fatherland.[3] But when a new kind of social Darwinist nationalism appeared on the scene in the late nineteenth century, arguing that the proper basis of a nation-state was a racial or ethnic homeland, this seemed to imply that the fledgling Republic of China was the proprietary domain of the Han Chinese alone.

What, then, would be the fate of the various non-Han peoples who had come to accept their identity as subjects of the Qing? Almost immediately, certain communities of Mongols announced their intention not to be a part of the Chinese republic.[4] As early as 1913 efforts were made to establish a sovereign homeland in the northeast for the "Manchu" people, and various "Manchukuos" were intermittently declared, up to and including that grand failed imagined community established as a client state by Japan in 1932 and headed by imperial China's "last emperor," Aisin Gioro Puyi.[5] As evidenced by the problems of Tibetan, Muslim, and other separatist movements still confronted by the government of the People's Republic in the early twenty-first century, this is one legacy of Qing history that was never satisfactorily resolved during the entire century following the empire's demise.

The passing of imperial China brought one further change of subtle but very real significance. The emperor as the Son of Heaven—the universally acknowledged legitimating center of political and social action throughout the breadth and duration of the empire—had been removed. In place of his expressed will, the far more manipulable and contestable interests of "the people" (min) would now be invoked.[6] Anxiety over this issue, as much as personal ambition, no doubt prompted some Chinese to support the periodic imperial restoration attempts that punctuated the early Republican era. The problem of how to stabilize and legitimate political action would remain a nagging worry in the new order yet to be constructed.

Viewing the Qing as a fairly typical example of an early modern land-based Eurasian empire, we could argue that its final expiration in 1911 arrived just about on time.[7] The Romanov empire collapsed only a few years later, in 1917, and the Ottoman empire was progressively dismembered during the decade or more before its official demise in 1922. In the technologically transformed world of the twentieth century, these early modern models of political organization appeared to suffer from, among other failures, a drastic diseconomy of scale.

If, on the other hand, we view the Qing empire in the context of imperial China's long-standing dynastic cycle of prosperity and decline, where periods of political breakdown often set one aspiring "empire" against another (for example, the era of Northern and Southern Dynasties between the Han and the Tang, and that of the Five Dynasties between the Tang and the Song), then perhaps 1911 is less of a marker than it might appear. The chaos and violence of that year was not very profound, at least in comparison with the decades that would follow, and no centralizing political entity of any real effectiveness immediately emerged to take control. Thus, the end of the Qing "cycle" may not have truly come until the Nationalist Revolution of 1927, or the Japanese occupation of 1937, or even the Communist "liberation" of 1949.

One of the persistent political features of the Qing empire was the relative smallness of the formal state apparatus compared with the size of the society and economy. In this system of government-on-the-cheap, many quasi-governmental tasks were farmed out to indigenous elites (gentry, local headmen and militia leaders, commercial brokers) or groups (lineages, villages, guilds). The Yongzheng reign of the late 1720s and early 1730s represented an effort to reverse the shrinking density of state personnel on the ground and "regovernmentalize" policy implementation, but this initiative was reversed or at least neglected under subsequent reigns. This low but efficient governmental presence might have actually been a sound way to do things, so long as the Qing could maintain the image and conditions of universal empire, with relatively little in the way of outside threats. But by the mid-nineteenth century the empire had become merely one of many antagonists in a predatory international war of all against all, and under these competitive circumstances a larger, more powerful, more interventionist state apparatus came to appear necessary for political survival.

The reforms of 1898 were an abortive initial attempt to grow a modern state, but the New Policies of the first decade of the twentieth century represented a truly new beginning. From that moment down through at least the Great Leap Forward of the 1950s (and perhaps until the post-Mao era, when second thoughts about having *too* big a state took over), China experimented ever more ambitiously with big government, radically and wrenchingly reversing the shrinkage of the state that had begun as early as the Southern Song dynasty in the thirteenth century. Seen in the context of this dramatic decades-long state-building project of the first half of the twentieth century, China's political reordering during and after the 1911 revolution was actually a fairly orderly affair that built on the New Policies state and sustained its growth.

A related way of viewing the achievements of the late Qing empire would employ the concept of "public" (gong), increasingly articulated in

Qing and republican discourse as a middle ground between governmental (*guan*) and private (*si*). At least from the middle decades of the nineteenth century, if not slightly before, the range of undertakings—in philanthropy, defense, infrastructure, and economic development—that were created and legitimated in the name of communal interests seems to have dramatically and progressively expanded. The agents of change were nongovernmental elites, initially at the local level but progressively acting in concert on an ever-expanding geographic scale. This process may be seen as a disguised form of state expansion, one that far outran the capacity of the enfeebled imperial administration to respond to the ever-greater managerial demands of the society and economy. And here again, 1911 did little to alter the trajectory of change. State expansion at the local level, including the development of representative political institutions as well as managerial bureaus in all areas of public activism, went on apace throughout the early republican era, despite the continued progressive disintegration of the central administrative apparatus.[8] From this perspective, both the Nationalist and the Communist revolutions may be seen in part as increasingly successful attempts to reassert formal governmental control over a *de facto* state expansion that had been going on for a century or more, transcending (and largely ignoring) the 1911 watershed.[9]

Between the mid-seventeenth and early twentieth centuries a remarkable entity known as the Great Qing Empire occupied an expansive and expanding space on the Eurasian continent. This was by no means the inward-looking and hermetic "Celestial Empire" that Westerners once believed it to be. On the contrary, its history was intimately intertwined with global historical processes in diverse ways that we are just beginning to comprehend. And, to a greater degree than we once assumed, it was qualitatively different from the dynastic empires that preceded it and from the states that were still to come on this piece of territory. Yet its history profoundly and inescapably set the conditions for the polity and society we know today as "China."

EMPERORS AND DYNASTIES

EMPERORS OF THE GREAT QING

Years of Reign	Personal Name	Reign Title
1636–1643	Hong Taiji	Chongde
1644–1661	Fulin	Shunzhi
1662–1722	Xuanye	Kangxi
1723–1735	Yinzhen	Yongzheng
1736–1795	Hongli	Qianlong
1796–1820	Yongyan	Jiaqing
1821–1850	Minning	Daoguang
1851–1861	Yizhu	Xianfeng
1862–1874	Zaichun	Tongzhi
1875–1908	Zaitian	Guangxu
1909–1912	Puyi	Xuantong

CHINESE DYNASTIES

Shang	CA. 1600–1027 B.C.
Zhou	1027–256 B.C.
Western Zhou	1027–771 B.C.
Eastern Zhou	771–256 B.C.
Spring and Autumn Period	722–481 B.C.
Warring States Period	476–221 B.C.
Qin	221–206 B.C.
Western (Former) Han	206 B.C.–A.D. 8
Xin	8–23

Eastern (Later) Han	23–220
Three Kingdoms (Wei, Sui, Wu)	220–280
Western Jin	265–317
Northern and Southern Dynasties	317–589
Sui	589–618
Tang	618–907
Five Dynasties	907–960
Song	960–1279
Northern Song	960–1126
Southern Song	1126–1279
Yuan	1279–1368
Ming	1368–1644
Qing	1644–1912

PRONUNCIATION GUIDE

Pronunciation is as in English unless noted below.

c	as *ts* in *nets*
ch	as in *chat*
g	as in *girl*
j	as in *jingle*
q	as *ch* in *cheese*
x	as *sh* in *sheer*
y	as in *year*
z	as *dz* in *adze*
zh	as *j* in *John*
a	as *e* in *pen* for yan, jian, qian, xian; otherwise as *a* in *father*
ai	as in *aye*
ang	as *ong* in *wrong*
ao	as *ow* in *now*
e	as *e* in *yet* in the combinations ye, -ie, -ue; otherwise as *e* in *the*
ei	as in *neigh*
en	as *un* in *fun*
eng	as *ung* in *rung*
er	pronounced as *are*
i	as in the *i* of *sir* after c, s, z; as in the *ir* of *sir* after ch, sh, zh, r
ie	as *ye* in *yet*
iu	as *yo* in *yoyo*
ong	as *ung* in German *Achtung*
ou	as in *oh*
u	after j, q, x, and y as *ui* in *suit*; otherwise as *u* in *rule*
ua	after j, q, x, and y as *ue* in *duet*; otherwise as *wa* in *water*
uai	as in *why*
ue	as *ue* in *duet*
ui	as in *way*
uo	similar to *o* in *once*

NOTES

Introduction

1. The Mongol empire of the thirteenth and fourteenth centuries, of course, was yet vaster than the Qing, but its Chinese component—known locally as the Yuan dynasty—was not its center.

2. For but one example, see Wong, "Qing Granaries and World History."

3. Zhao, *Qingshi gao*. The mammoth and lavishly funded project, still under way at this writing, to compile a definitive "Qing History" under Chinese government auspices, headed by the distinguished historian Dai Yi, is in part a throwback to this old historiography. For an introduction to this endeavor, with reflections on its relationship to the dynastic history model, see Ma, "Writing History during a Prosperous Age."

4. Xiao, *Qingdai tongshi*.

5. This division is enshrined, for example, in the twin textbooks by Fairbank and his Harvard colleagues Reischauer and Craig, *East Asia: The Great Tradition* and *East Asia: The Modern Transformation*. The Opium War as the starting point of modern Chinese history is an organizing device of the crucially influential sourcebook *China's Response to the West*, eds. Teng and Fairbank.

6. Fairbank did, however, convey at least the image of stagnancy in such works as his important edited volume *The Chinese World Order* (see further discussion in Chapters 5 and 6, below) and in his unfortunate frequent reference to contemporary China as "the People's Middle Kingdom"; see Fairbank, *China: The People's Middle Kingdom and the United States.*

7. The most notable of such textbooks was Hsu's *The Rise of Modern China*, first edition 1970, with many revisions to follow.

8. The Qing History Institute itself was established only in 1978.

9. For a concise statement of the *Annaliste* method, see Braudel, "History and the Social Sciences."

10. Cohen, *Discovering History in China.*

11. The phrase is that of Philip A. Kuhn, Fairbank's student and Harvard successor.

12. Arrighi, *Adam Smith in Beijing;* Frank, *Re-Orient;* Pomeranz, *The Great Divergence;* Wong, *China Transformed.* For representative arguments by Chinese scholars, see Li, "Kongzhi zengchang yibao fuyu"; Fang, "Lun Qingdai Jiangnan nongmin de xiaofei."

13. Wakeman, "Introduction" to Wakeman and Grant, eds., *Conflict and Control,* 2.

14. Whereas the view of a coherent "late imperial" or "post-Mongol" China has usually been based on the assumption that the Mongol Yuan dynasty was the key divisive aberration, several historians have recently argued that it was not the Yuan itself (which saw essentially a continuation of the economic and social developments of the Tang and Song) but rather the culturally reactionary and economically commandist policies of the first Ming emperor, Zhu Yuanzhang, that represented the real hiatus in China's historical development. See Smith and von Glahn, eds., *The Song-Yuan-Ming Transition in Chinese History.*

15. In my experience, the first self-conscious appropriation of the "early modern" rubric in the title of an American work of Chinese history was in Ropp, *Dissent in Early Modern China* (1981). I myself invested heavily in this periodization in Rowe, *Hankow* (1989), esp. "Introduction: An Early Modern Chinese City."

16. No less a pioneer of the revisionist Qing history than Frederic Wakeman angrily denounced my enthusiastic embrace of the "early modern" rubric and some implications I drew from it; see his "The Public Sphere and Civil Society Debate"; a more sympathetic critic, Philip Huang, termed my invocation of a European-style early modernity in China "poignant" in Huang, "The Paradigmatic Crisis in Chinese Studies," 321.

17. The pioneer of this line of thinking, Pamela Kyle Crossley, elaborated her ideas in a long series of publications, bringing them together most fully in *A Translucent Mirror.*

18. Waley-Cohen, "The New Qing History," 195.

19. On the Qing emperors' many hats, see especially Crossley, "Review Article." The multinationalism of the Qing polity was symbolically encapsulated in the construction of an imperial "theme park," with pavilions devoted to each national grouping, just outside the Great Wall at Rehe; see Millward et al., eds., *New Qing Imperial History.* For a conference volume surveying the negotiation of ethnic identities under Qing, see Crossley, Siu, and Sutton, eds., *Empire at the Margins.*

20. The most sustained argument along these lines is Duara, *Rescuing History from the Nation.* The South Asian inspiration for this line of argument is well expressed in Chatterjee, *The Nation and Its Fragments.*

21. For examples of works self-consciously designed as "world history" which

include attention to late imperial China, see McNeill, *Plagues and Peoples;* Curtin, *Cross-Cultural Trade in World History;* and Adas, *Machines as the Measure of Men.* For pioneering local and regional studies of ecological history in late imperial China, see Schoppa, *Xiang Lake,* and Marks, *Tigers, Rice, Silk, and Silt.* For a bolder attempt to chart the ecological history of the empire as a whole, see Elvin, *The Retreat of the Elephants.* A still more ambitious attempt to fit the Qing experience into a global ecological history is Richards, *The Unending Frontier.*

22. For differing perspectives on this phenomenon, see Adshead, "The Seventeenth-Century General Crisis in China"; Atwell, "Some Observations on the Seventeenth-Century Crisis in China and Japan"; Wakeman, "China and the Seventeenth-Century Crisis." For a recent overview of the debate, see Marmé, "Locating Linkages or Painting Bull's-Eyes around Bullet Holes?"

23. See especially Lieberman, ed., *Beyond Binary Histories.* A conference volume that reflects the influence of such ideas on Qing historiography is Struve, ed., *The Qing Formation in World-Historical Time,* especially contributions by Perdue, Millward, di Cosmo, Rawski, and Goldstone.

24. The major work here is Perdue, *China Marches West.*

25. Rawski, "The Qing Formation and the Early Modern Period."

1. Conquest

1. Crossley, "The Tong in Two Worlds."

2. For a summary view, see Crossley, *A Translucent Mirror.*

3. Elliott, *The Manchu Way.*

4. The standard study of the Ming-Qing transition in English is Wakeman, *The Great Enterprise.*

5. Di Cosmo, "Before the Conquest," cited by permission. See also the discussion of "Manchu mercantilism" in Zhao, "Shaping the Asian Trade Network."

6. One of Nurhaci's first acts after inventing a written form of his people's spoken language was to have the Chinese dynastic history of the Jin (1115–1234) translated into "Manchu." Di Cosmo speculates that, in fact, it was primarily through the vehicle of such translated Chinese texts that the seventeenth-century Aisin Gioro and their neighbors learned about—or imagined—their past and their collective identity.

7. Elliott, *The Manchu Way,* 77, 177–181.

8. Crossley, "Review Article."

9. Wakeman, *The Great Enterprise,* 164–224.

10. Translation from Wang Fuzhi's *Yellow Book* (*Huangshu*) by de Bary in de Bary et al., eds., *Sources of Chinese Tradition,* vol. 1, 544–546.

11. On the cult of Wang Fuzhi in the late Qing, see Platt, *Provincial Patriots;* Zeng Guofan's republication project is discussed on pp. 23–28.

12. I Songyŭ, "Shantung in the Shun-chih Reign."

13. Cheng and Listz, eds., *The Search for Modern China*, 33.

14. Rowe, *Crimson Rain*, chap. 6.

15. Dennerline, *The Chia-ting Loyalists;* Wakeman, "Localism and Loyalism during the Ch'ing Conquest of Kiangnan," in Wakeman and Grant, eds., *Conflict and Control.*

16. Translated by Struve in Struve, ed., *Voices from the Ming-Qing Cataclysm,* 36.

17. There is some scholarly debate about just how strongly the Ebai regency represented a (temporary) return to preconquest modes of governance and rejection of sinicized rule on the part of the Qing court. For classic (though quite different) expositions of the anti-sinicization thesis, see Oxnam, *Ruling from Horseback,* and Miller, "Factional Conflict and the Integration of Ch'ing Politics." For a more recent rebuttal, suggesting a smoother process of transition, see Struve, "Ruling from Sedan Chair."

18. No full-length study of the Three Feudatories rebellion has yet appeared in English. The best existing history is Liu, *Qingdai sanfan yanjiu.*

19. Beyond the commonly accepted account of the Zheng regime, I am influenced here by an unpublished paper by Hung, "The Ming-Qing Transition in Maritime Perspective."

20. Dennerline, "Fiscal Reform and Local Control," in Wakeman and Grant, eds., *Conflict and Control.*

21. Meyer-Fong, *Building Culture in Early Qing Yangzhou.*

2. Governance

1. Elvin, *The Pattern of the Chinese Past.*

2. The best analysis I have seen of this system and its implications is in Fujii, "Shin'an shōnin no kenkyū."

3. Hucker, *A Dictionary of Official Titles in Imperial China,* 92.

4. For analysis of one aspect of this indirect governance, the Qing state's systematic use of merchants to perform quasi-governmental tasks, see Mann, *Local Merchants and the Chinese Bureaucracy.*

5. There is no detailed study in English of the Censorate in Qing times. For a study of its operation under the Ming, see Hucker, *The Censorial System of Ming China.*

6. Lui, *The Hanlin Academy.*

7. Hucker, *Dictionary,* 88, 255, 534. This process of regularizing regional field administration is the subject of a major work in progress by R. Kent Guy, who refers to it as "the Qing invention of the province."

8. Spence, *The Death of Woman Wang.*

9. Chia, "The Li-fan Yuan in the Early Ch'ing Dynasty."

10. Torbert, *The Ch'ing Imperial Household Department*. On the silk factories, see Spence *Ts'ao Yin and the K'ang-hsi Emperor*; on the north China estates, see Huang, *The Peasant Economy and Social Change in North China*.

11. Bartlett, *Monarchs and Ministers*.

12. Wu, *Communication and Imperial Control in China*.

13. Kuhn, *Soulstealers*, 213.

14. Guo Songyi, "Lun tanding rudi."

15. Wang, *Land Taxation in Imperial China*.

16. It may not be coincidental that spurts of population growth occurred in the wake of Kangxi's freezing of the land tax in 1712, and of Qianlong's land and corvée tax cuts of the 1740s. Rowe, *Saving the World*, 159.

17. Xu, *Qingdai juanna zhidu*.

18. Two important studies, not restricted to the Qing but dealing extensively with that era, are Miyazaki, *China's Examination Hell*, and Elman, *A Cultural History of Civil Examinations in Late Imperial China*.

19. Nivison, "Protest against Convention and Conventions of Protest." In his *Cultural History of Civil Examinations*, Elman suggests that policy questions were at least *somewhat* more significant in the overall grading of the examinations than the usual stereotype presumes.

20. Guy, "Fang Pao and the *Ch'in-ting Ssu-shu wen*."

21. The classic study in English is Ho, *The Ladder of Success in Imperial China*. For an important qualification of Ho's estimates, see Wou, "The Extended Kin Unit and the Family Origins of Ch'ing Local Officials."

22. Ch'u, *Local Government in China under the Ch'ing*; Hsiao, *Rural China*.

23. A classic study is Watt, *The District Magistrate in Late Imperial China*.

24. Zelin, *The Magistrate's Tael*.

25. Park, "Corruption and Its Recompense."

26. Thompson, "Statecraft and Self-Government."

27. Cole, *Shaohsing*.

28. Reed, "Money and Justice."

29. A now somewhat dated but still informative study of this institution is Folsom, *Friends, Guests, and Colleagues*.

30. Hsiao, *Rural China*; Rowe, "Urban Control in Late Imperial China."

31. Morse, *The Trade and Administration of China*.

32. Among many English-language studies of Qing provisioning, see Chuan and Kraus, *Mid-Ch'ing Rice Markets and Trade*; Will, *Bureaucracy and Famine in Eighteenth-Century China*; Will and Wong, eds., *Nourish the People*; Wong and Perdue, "Famine's Foes in Ch'ing China"; Rowe, *Saving the World*, chap. 5; and Li, *Fighting Famine in North China*.

33. The literature on this subject in Chinese and Japanese is large. In English, see Vogel, "Chinese Central Monetary Policy," and Rowe, "Provincial Monetary Practice in Eighteenth-Century China."

34. See especially Huang, *Civil Justice in China*.

35. On the Song-era "statecraft" movement, see Hymes and Shirokauer, eds., *Ordering the World*.

36. On "substantive learning" in the Qing, see de Bary and Bloom, eds., *Principle and Practicality*, and Rowe, *Saving the World*, chap. 4.

37. On the *fengjian-junxian* distinction in the late imperial era, see Yang, "Ming Local Administration"; Min, *National Polity and Local Power*.

38. This and the following translations from "Junxian lun" are my own, adapted from those in de Bary et al., eds., *Sources of Chinese Tradition*.

39. Peterson, "The Life of Ku Yen-wu"; the affair of the murdered servant is discussed on pp. 154–156.

40. First edition, 1670; second, much expanded edition published posthumously in 1695.

41. Delury, "Despotism Above and Below," cited by permission.

42. The pioneering study in English of the subsequent legacy of Gu's proposals is Kuhn, "Local Self-Government under the Republic."

3. High Qing

1. For a consensus Chinese-language assessment of the "prosperous age," see Dai, "Shiba shiji Zhongguo de chengjiu, quxian, yu shidai tezheng." For a pioneering English-language attempt to characterize this era, see Wakeman, "High Ch'ing, 1683–1839."

2. The "long eighteenth century" spanned from Kangxi's final consolidation of Qing rule, around 1680, to the death of the Qianlong emperor in 1799. See Mann, *Precious Records*.

3. On Kangxi's early administrative policies, see Kessler, *K'ang-hsi and the Consolidation of Ch'ing Rule*.

4. Jami, "Imperial Control and Western Learning."

5. Hanson, "Jesuits and Medicine in the Kangxi Court."

6. Spence, *Emperor of China*, 105–106.

7. For a detailed account of the Yongzheng succession, see Wu, *Passage to Power*.

8. Paderni, "The Problem of *Kuan-hua* in Eighteenth-Century China."

9. The only comprehensive work in English is the now somewhat dated *Autocracy at Work* by Huang. An excellent biography in Chinese is Feng, *Yongzheng zhuan*.

10. There are two solid biographies of the Qianlong emperor in Chinese: Dai, *Qianlong di ji qi shidai*, and Bai, *Qianlong zhuan*. The former is more conceptual, the latter more detailed. A recent and concise English-language biography is Elliott, *Emperor Qianlong*. Some aspects of the Qianlong emperor's style of rule are discussed in Kahn, *Monarchy in the Emperor's Eyes*.

11. Gao, "Yige weiwanjie de changshi."

12. Rowe, "Education and Empire in Southwest China."

13. Crossley, "The Rulerships of China."

14. For a lively account of this case, see Spence, *Treason by the Book.*

15. Crossley, *A Translucent Mirror.* See also Farquhar, "Emperor as Bodhisattva in the Governance of the Ch'ing Empire."

16. Zhuang, *Qing Gaozong shiquan wugong yanjiu.*

17. See Millward et al., eds., *New Qing Imperial History.*

18. Chang, *A Court on Horseback;* Meyer-Fong, *Building Culture in Early Qing Yangzhou.*

19. For two recent arguments along this line, see Perdue, "Comparing Empires," and Rawski, "The Qing Formation and the Early Modern Period."

20. My account of the Zunghar campaigns follows Perdue, *China Marches West;* quotations are from pp. 161, 285.

21. Millward, *Beyond the Pass;* Perdue, *China Marches West,* chap. 9; Waley-Cohen, *Exile in Mid-Qing China;* Hsu, *The Ili Crisis.*

22. Waley-Cohen, *Exile in Mid-Qing China.*

23. The following paragraphs draw on Dabringhaus, "Chinese Emperors and Tibetan Monks," which summarizes the author's much more detailed work in German.

24. Qing caution in incorporating Taiwan is stressed in Shepherd, *Statecraft and Political Economy on the Taiwan Frontier.*

25. Woodside, "The Ch'ien-lung Reign," in *Cambridge History of China,* vol. 9, 269.

26. See, among others, Lee, "Food Supply and Population Growth in Southwest China"; Rowe, "Education and Empire"; Herman, "Empire in the Southwest"; Herman, "The Cant of Conquest."

27. Sutton, "Ethnicity and the Miao Frontier in the Eighteenth Century."

28. Herman, *Amid the Clouds and Mist,* chap. 6.

29. Translation from Herman, "Empire in the Southwest," 47. See also Smith, "Ch'ing Policy and the Development of Southwest China."

30. The following paragraphs draw on Giersch, *Asian Borderlands.*

31. Chan, "The *Hsing-li ching-i* and the Ch'eng-Chu School of the Seventeenth Century"; Rowe, *Saving the World,* chap. 3.

32. Ropp, *Dissent in Early Modern China,* esp. chap. 1. Ropp characterizes this trend as "bourgeoisification," which might be a bit strong.

33. Waley, *Yuan Mei;* Wakeman, *The Fall of Imperial China,* 52–53; Ropp, *Dissent in Early Modern China,* 49–50.

34. Rawski, *Education and Popular Literacy in Ch'ing China;* Johnson, "Communication, Class, and Consciousness in Late Imperial China."

35. Adapted from the translation in Ropp, *Dissent in Early Modern China,* 53.

36. Mair, "Language and Ideology in the Written Popularizations of the Sacred Edict."

37. See Zeitlin, *Historian of the Strange,* and also the revealing use made of Pu's stories as a source for Qing social history in Spence, *The Death of Woman Wang.*

38. Hanan, *The Invention of Li Yu.*

39. Johnson, *Spectacle and Sacrifice.*

40. Wang, *Street Culture in Chengdu,* 42–44.

41. Mackerras, *The Rise of the Peking Opera.* For the subsequent use of this tradition in late Qing and Republican-era nation-building, see Goldstein, *Drama Kings.*

42. Hay, *Shitao.*

43. Vainker, *Chinese Pottery and Porcelain,* chaps. 5 and 7.

44. Finnane, "Yangzhou's 'Mondernity.'"

45. A key work was Gu's *Yinxue wushu* (*Five Studies in Phonetics*), first published in 1667. Note that the polymath Gu served simultaneously as icon for the philological scholars of the eighteenth century and for the "statecraft" (*jingshi*) scholars who eventually repudiated them in the nineteenth.

46. Elman, *From Philosophy to Philology.* My entire discussion of the *kaozheng* movement is informed by this landmark study.

47. Man-Cheong, *The Class of 1761.*

48. Chow, *The Rise of Confucian Ritualism in Late Imperial China,* esp. chaps. 6 and 7; Brokaw, "Tai Chen and Learning in the Confucian Tradition."

49. Hummel, ed., *Eminent Chinese of the Ch'ing Period,* 120–123. A wonderfully word-searchable CD-ROM edition of the entire library has been created by the Chinese University of Hong Kong: *Wenyuange sikuquanshu dianzibian* (*Electronic Edition of the Siku quanshu*) (Hong Kong: CUHK Press, 1999).

50. Goodrich, *The Literary Inquisition of Ch'ien-lung;* Guy, *The Emperor's Four Treasuries.*

51. Naquin, *Shantung Rebellion.*

52. Will and Wong, *Nourish the People,* 226–232.

4. Society

1. Portions of this chapter draw on my article "Social Stability and Social Change," in *Cambridge History of China,* vol. 9, 475–562.

2. There are many competing estimates of Qing population. Still perhaps the most reliable are those presented in Ho, *Studies on the Population of China.*

3. Lee and Wang, *One Quarter of Humanity.*

4. Li, "Kongzhi zengchang, yibao fuyu."

5. Entenmann, "Szechwan and Ch'ing Migration Policy."

6. Lee, "The Legacy of Immigration in Southwest China"; Herman, "Empire in the Southwest."

7. Shepherd, *Statecraft and Political Economy on the Taiwan Frontier;* Meskill, *A Chinese Pioneer Family.*

8. Millward, *Beyond the Pass,* 50–51.

9. Lee, *The Manchurian Frontier in Ch'ing History;* Gottschang and Lary, *Swallows and Settlers.*

10. Averill, "The Shed People and the Opening of the Yangzi Highlands"; Osborne, "The Local Politics of Land Reclamation in the Lower Yangzi Highlands"; Leong, *Migration and Ethnicity in Chinese History.*

11. Suzuki, *Shinchō chūki shi kenkyū;* Rawski, "Agricultural Development in the Han River Highlands." A general survey is Peng, *Qingdai tudi kaiken shi.*

12. Rowe, *Saving the World,* 56–68.

13. Liu, "Dike Construction in Ching-chou"; Perdue, *Exhausting the Earth.* While conceding the reality of this deforestation in eighteenth-century central China, Nicholas Menzies cautions against a more generalized view of the long-term destruction of "primeval forests" by an ecologically unmindful imperial state and society; Menzies, *Forest and Land Management in Imperial China.*

14. Lojewski, "The Soochow Bursaries," 43–65.

15. Bernhardt, *Rents, Taxes, and Peasant Resistance.*

16. Wei, *Qingdai nubi zhidu;* Jing, *Qingdai shehui de jianmin dengji.* For studies of agrarian servitude in particular localities, see Ye, *Ming-Qing Huizhou nongcun shehui yu dianpu zhi;* Rowe, *Crimson Rain.*

17. Huang, *The Peasant Economy and Social Change,* 1985.

18. Liu, "Lun Qingdai qianqi nongye guyong laodong de xingzhi."

19. On the Yongzheng "emancipations," the classic work is Terada, "Yōseitei no senmin kaihōrei ni tsuite"; for a brief treatment in English, see Huang, *Autocracy at Work.*

20. For an example see *The Art of Ethnography.* The genre is analyzed in Hostetler, *Qing Colonial Enterprise.*

21. Teng, *Taiwan's Imagined Geography,* 194–203.

22. Siu and Liu, "Lineage, Market, Pirate, and *Dan*"; Szonyi, *Practicing Kinship.*

23. Leong, *Migration and Ethnicity.*

24. Perdue, "Insiders and Outsiders"; Honig, *Creating Chinese Ethnicity.*

25. Rowe, *Saving the World,* chap. 12.

26. Shen, *Six Records of a Floating Life,* 28, 40.

27. Indeed, Helen Dunstan has argued that the lesbianism of Shen Fu's wife, and his acceptance of this, was an important part of their relationship; Dunstan, "If Chen Yun Had Written about Her Lesbianism."

28. For a compelling and thoroughly negative view of the life experiences of women in the early Qing, see Spence, *The Death of Woman Wang.*

29. Ng, "Ideology and Sexuality." For a more nuanced view of Qing attempts to enforce gender norms via local courts and the social realities inhibiting such attempts, see Sommer, *Sex, Law, and Society in Late Imperial China.*

30. Meyer-Fong, *Building Culture in Early Qing Yangzhou;* Hershatter, *Dangerous Pleasures;* Yeh, *Shanghai Love.*

31. Among the many studies of the virtuous widow cult in the Qing, see Elvin, "Female Virtue and the State in China"; Holmgren, "The Economic Foundations of Virtue"; and especially Theiss, *Disgraceful Matters.*

32. A landmark study of this trend is Yuasa, "Shindai ni okeru fujin kaihōron reikyōto ningenteki shizen." In English, see Ropp, "The Seeds of Change."

33. Mann, *Precious Records.*

34. For studies of pilgrimage societies see Naquin and Yü, eds., *Pilgrims and Sacred Sites in China.*

35. See Chen's tract "On Women's Education," selections translated by myself in de Bary et al., *Sources of Chinese Tradition,* vol. 2.

36. Mann, *The Talented Women of the Zhang Family;* Widmer, *The Beauty and the Book.*

37. For a challenging treatment of the late Qing and early Republican debate over footbinding, see Ko, *Cinderella's Sisters.*

38. Fei, "Peasantry and Gentry."

39. Hartwell, "Demographic, Political, and Social Transformations of China"; Hymes, *Statesmen and Gentlemen.*

40. Shigeta, "The Origins and Structure of Gentry Rule."

41. For a thoughtful discussion of the issues of labeling this group, see the "Introduction" to Esherick and Rankin, eds., *Chinese Local Elites and Patterns of Dominance.*

42. Naquin, "Funerals in North China"; Brook, "Funerary Ritual and the Building of Lineages in Late Imperial China"; Chow, *The Rise of Confucian Ritualism in Late Imperial China.*

43. Meskill, *A Chinese Pioneer Family.*

44. A classic study of this in Chang, *The Income of the Chinese Gentry.*

45. Barr, "Four Schoolmasters."

46. Chow, *Publishing, Culture, and Power.*

47. Folsom, *Friends, Guests, and Colleagues;* Elvin, "Market Towns and Waterways"; Rankin, *Elite Activism and Political Transformation in China.*

48. Macauley, *Social Power and Legal Culture;* Huang, *Civil Justice in China.*

49. Ho, *The Ladder of Success in Imperial China.*

50. Chang, *The Chinese Gentry,* 102–111. On the nineteenth-century acceleration, see Xu, *Qingdai juanna zhidu.*

51. Adapted from translation in Rowe, *Crimson Rain*, 74–75.

52. For detailed studies of Qing lineages see Beattie, *Land and Lineage in China*; Rowe, "Success Stories"; and various contributions in Ebrey and Watson, eds., *Kinship Organization in Late Imperial China*.

53. Szonyi, *Practicing Kinship*.

54. Dennerline, "The New Hua Charitable Estate and Local Level Leadership."

55. Faure, "The Lineage as Business Company"; Palmer, "The Surface-Subsoil Form of Divided Ownership"; Zelin, *The Merchants of Zigong*.

56. Watson, "Hereditary Tenancy and Corporate Landlordism in Traditional China"; Lamley, "Lineage and Surname Feuds"; Ts'ui-jung Liu, "Dike Construction in Ching-chou."

57. There are two masterful overviews of late imperial philanthropy in East Asian languages: Fuma, *Chūgoku zentai zentō shi kenkyū*, and Liang, *Shishan yu jiaohua*. For the most detailed study in English of the nineteenth-century phase of this process in a particular locality, see Rowe, *Hankow: Conflict and Community*. I do not discuss here two late (primarily post-Taiping) manifestations of the zeal for organization-building with heavy Confucian moral-revival thrusts: the virtuous widow hall and the scrap-paper collection society.

5. Commerce

1. See for example Cooper, *Travels of a Pioneer of Commerce*.

2. For convenient summaries of this medieval "commercial revolution," see Shiba, *Commerce and Society in Sung China*, and Elvin, *The Pattern of the Chinese Past*, part two.

3. Several revisionist studies, arguing that the Yuan impact on long-term economic development was minimal, are collected in Smith and von Glahn, eds., *The Song-Yuan-Ming Transition in Chinese History*.

4. Deng, *Lun Zhongguo lishi jige wenti*.

5. Wu, "Lun Qingdai woguo guonei shichang."

6. Chuan and Kraus, *Mid-Ch'ing Rice Markets and Trade*, 77.

7. Rowe, *Hankow*.

8. The classic study of "managerial landlordism" is Jing and Luo, *Landlord and Labor in Late Imperial China*.

9. Huang, *The Peasant Economy and Social Change in North China*.

10. Liu, "Shilun Qingdai Suzhou shougongye hanghui."

11. Deng, *Lun Zhongguo lishi jige wenti*; Zelin, *The Merchants of Zigong*.

12. Skinner, "Marketing and Social Structure in Rural China," part two.

13. Rawski, *Agricultural Change*, 112. See also Liu, *Ming Qing shidai Jiangnan shizhen yanjiu*.

14. Yang, *Ruxue diyuhua de jindai xingtai*, 162.

15. This and the following section are adapted from Rowe, "Domestic Interregional Trade in Eighteenth-century China."

16. Skinner, "Cities and the Hierarchy of Local Systems."

17. Cochran, *Encountering Chinese Networks*.

18. Perdue, "Insiders and Outsiders."

19. Twitchett, "The T'ang Market System."

20. Rowe, *Hankow*; Rowe, "Ming-Qing Guilds."

21. "Newchwang," in *Decennial Reports, 1882–91*, Shanghai: Inspectorate General of Customs, 1892, 34–37.

22. See for example Wright, *The Last Stand of Chinese Conservatism*, 170; Ch'u, *Local Government in China*, 169.

23. See Rowe, *Saving the World*, part two.

24. Cited in Dunstan, *Conflicting Counsels to Confuse the Age*, 325.

25. Fairbank, ed., *The Chinese World Order*. Many of the ideas in this book had actually been enunciated by Fairbank and Teng some quarter-century earlier, in their lengthy article "On the Ch'ing Tributary System."

26. See for example Hamashita, "The Tribute Trade System and Modern Asia."

27. For example, Fairbank, *China: The People's Middle Kingdom and the U.S.A.*

28. Edwards, "Imperial China's Border Control Law"; Wills, *Pepper, Guns, and Parleys*; Wills, *Embassies and Illusions*.

29. The above paragraphs draw on Zhao, "Shaping the Asian Trade Network."

30. Chia, "The Li-fan Yuan in the Early Ch'ing Dynasty."

31. Zhao, "Shaping the Asian Trade Networks," chap. 6.

32. Kuhn, *Chinese among Others*, esp. chaps. 1 and 2.

33. Blussé, *Strange Company*; Blussé and Chen, eds., *The Archives of the Kong Koan of Batavia*.

34. Zhuang, *Zhongguo fengjian zhengfu de Huaqiao zhengce*.

35. The following paragraphs draw on Mungello, *The Great Encounter of China and the West*, as well as other sources.

36. McDermott, "Friendship and Its Friends in the Late Ming."

37. Feng, *Yongzheng zhuan*, 402–406.

38. Entenmann, "Catholics and Society in Eighteenth-Century Sichuan"; Ma, "Imperial Autocracy and Bureaucratic Interests in the Anti-Christian Campaign of 1784–85 in China."

39. My entire treatment of this system is indebted to conversations on the subject with my former graduate student, Professor Gang Zhao.

40. Fairbank, *Trade and Diplomacy on the China Coast*, 23–53.

41. Cao, "Qingdai Guangdong tizhi zai yanjiu."

42. Morse, *The Chronicles of the East India Company Trading to China*, vol. 2, 167–168.

43. Ibid., vol. 2, 239.

44. Ibid., vol. 2, 244–247. George III's letter is analyzed also in Hevia, *Cherishing Men from Afar*, 60–62.

45. The letter appears, in the official translation received by George III, in Morse, *Chronicles*, vol. 2, 247–252.

46. *China's Response to the West,* ed. Teng and Fairbank, 19–21.

47. For a stimulating revisionist account of the Macartney mission, influenced by "postcolonial" theory, see Hevia, *Cherishing Men from Afar.*

6. Crises

1. Pomeranz, *The Great Divergence.*

2. More than other chapters in this book, this one is informed by the corresponding chapter in the *Cambridge History of China*: Jones and Kuhn, "Dynastic Decline and the Roots of Rebellion," vol. 10, 107–162. That pioneering essay remains, in my view, the standard authority in English on the Jiaqing and Daoguang reigns.

3. Lee and Wang, *One Quarter of Humanity.* See also Li, "Kongzhi zengchang yibao fuyu."

4. Kuhn, *Chinese among Others,* 14.

5. Ho, *Studies in the Population of China.*

6. Telford, "Family and State in Qing China."

7. Peng, "Qingdai qianqi shougongye de fazhan."

8. Wei and Lu, *Qingdai qianqi de shangban kuangye he zibenzhuyi mengya.*

9. Polachek, *The Inner Opium War.*

10. The Jiaqing emperor has not received a great deal of study in English. For a Chinese-language biography, see Guan, *Jiaqing di.*

11. Translation adapted from Jones, "Hung Liang-chi," used by permission.

12. Nivison, "Ho-shen and His Accusers," 209–243.

13. The classic, detailed analysis of this process is Suzuki, *Shinchō chūki shi kenkyū.* In English, see Rawski, "Agricultural Development in the Han River Highlands."

14. Yingcong Dai, "The White Lotus War."

15. Naquin, *Millenarian Rebellion in China,* 39–47.

16. This estimate is that of Dunstan, *State or Merchant,* 446.

17. Lin, *China Upside Down,* 79, 133. Lin points out that in the later nineteenth century Qing opium imports grew yet further, while the silver outflow was reversed.

18. Miles, *The Sea of Learning.*

19. McMahon, "The Yuelu Academy"; Wilhelm, "Chinese Confucianism on the Eve of the Great Encounter," 283–310. On one local offshoot, see Rowe, *Crimson Rain,* chap. 8.

20. Liu, "Shijiu shiji chuye Zhongguo zhishifenzi Bao Shichen yu Wei Yuan."

21. For a study of this aspect of Wei's work, see Leonard, *Wei Yuan and China's Rediscovery of the Maritime World.*

22. Metzger, "T'ao Chu's Reform of the Huai-pei Salt Monopoly."

23. Jones and Kuhn, "Dynastic Decline and the Roots of Rebellion," 119–128; Leonard, *Controlling from Afar*. Leonard has a more charitable view of Daoguang's capacity for governance than do many other scholars.

24. Lin, *China Upside Down*. My own research on the Wang Liu affair, reflected here, differs slightly in its conclusions from those of Lin, though supporting her principal findings. The Xianfeng court briefly and disastrously experimented with paper currency as a means of financing its anti-Taiping campaigns.

25. The following paragraphs draw in part on Wakeman, "The Canton Trade and the Opium War." See also Chaudhuri, *The Trading World of Asia and the English East India Company*.

26. See Spence, "Opium Smoking in Ch'ing China."

27. Douglass, *A Summary, Historical and Political*, vol. 1, 152–153.

28. Shaw, *The Journals of Major Samuel Shaw*, 183–184.

29. *Free Trade to India.*

30. *Speech of Eneas Macdonnell, Esq., on the East India Question.*

31. For a detailed analysis of how this teleology was applied to China, see Duara, *Rescuing History from the Nation*.

32. For a lively account based solely on Western sources, see Fay, *The Opium War*; for a standard treatment more grounded in Qing documents, see Chang, *Commissioner Lin and the Opium War*.

33. Recent Chinese historiography is very harsh on the role of the Daoguang emperor in this affair, castigating him for rushing blindly into a war that he should have known he could not win, alternating unsteadily between policies of "extermination" (*jiao*) and appeasement (*fu*), and scapegoating his two competent ministers, Lin Zexu and Qishan, whom his own vacillations had undermined. See for example Mao, *Tianchao de pengkui*.

34. The English versions of key articles of the treaty may be found in Gentzler, ed., *Changing China*, 29–32.

35. Elliott, "Bannerman and Townsman." For Crossley's restatement of her position in response to Elliott's findings, see her "Thinking about Ethnicity in Early Modern China."

36. This argument was first developed in Wakeman, *Strangers at the Gate*.

7. Rebellion

1. See ter Haar, "Rethinking 'Violence' in Chinese Culture."

2. Robinson, *Bandits, Eunuchs, and the Son of Heaven*. Robinson's specific reference is to the Ming period, but his descriptions are apt for the Qing as well.

3. For an elaboration of this cultural model, see Jenner, "Tough Guys, Mateship, and Honour."

4. On the greenwood ethic see Alitto, "Rural Elites in Transition."

5. For example, Chesneaux, ed., *Popular Movements and Secret Societies in China*. For a more recent and largely authoritative use of this classifier by a Chinese scholar, see Cai, *Zhongguo mimi shehui*.

6. ter Haar, *Ritual and Mythology of the Chinese Triads*, chap. 6.

7. Rowe, "The Qingbang and Collaboration under the Japanese."

8. Rowe, *Crimson Rain*, chap. 5.

9. Two good English-language studies, which summarize and critique the large corpus of Chinese scholarship on this organization, are Murray, *The Origins of the Tiandihui*, and Ownby, *Brotherhoods and Secret Societies*.

10. Cai, *Zhongguo mimi shehui*.

11. The occupational self-help character of the early Green Gang is stressed in the work of Morita, including "Shindai suishu kessha no seikaku ni tsuite"; the religious dimension is highlighted in Kelley, "Temples and Tribute Fleets."

12. Naquin, "Connections between Rebellions"; Naquin, "The Transmission of White Lotus Sectarianism in Late Imperial China."

13. Gaustad, "Religious Sectarianism and the State in Mid-Qing China."

14. Dai, "The White Lotus War," cited by permission.

15. Jones and Kuhn, "Dynastic Decline and the Roots of Rebellion," 144.

16. For but one example, see Mou, *Taiping Tianguo*. An English-language work that conveys some of the flavor of this Chinese scholarship is Jen, *The Taiping Revolutionary Movement*.

17. A work that is both the best English-language history of the Taiping produced during the Cold War era and a deeply anti-Communist tract is Michael, *The Taiping Rebellion*. For a vigorous refutation of Communist historiography of the Taiping, especially the conception of it as a "revolution," see Shih, *The Taiping Ideology*.

18. Wakeman, *Strangers at the Gate*.

19. Hong Xiuquan's religious beliefs are treated seriously in the marvelously readable narrative of the Taiping movement by Spence, *God's Chinese Son*. See also Kuhn, "Origins of the Taiping Vision."

20. For a convincing revisionist account of Hakka origins and history, see Leong, *Migration and Ethnicity in Chinese History*.

21. Spence, *God's Chinese Son*, 48.

22. Pi and Kong, "Taiping jun shouke Wuchang hou de zhanlue juece." On the *Land Regulations*, see Kuhn, "The Taiping Rebellion," in *Cambridge History of China*, vol. 10, part 1, 278–279.

23. The following paragraphs are based on a marvelous doctoral dissertation by Withers, "The Heavenly Capital."

24. Hsu, *China's Entry into the Family of Nations*.

25. Wong, *Deadly Dreams*, 28.

26. Ibid., 415.

27. Parkes, *Narrative of the Late Sir H. Parkes' Captivity in Pekin.*

28. For a fascinating trackdown of the trophies snatched by Elgin's expedition, see Hevia, "Loot's Fate."

29. See Perdue, "Insiders and Outsiders." For the background of these sentiments, see Schneider, *A Madman of Ch'u.* For Hunanese anti-foreignism in the post-Taiping era, see Cohen, *China and Christianity.*

30. Wilhelm, "Chinese Confucianism on the Eve of the Great Encounter."

31. The watershed study of anti-Taiping militarization in Hunan is Kuhn, *Rebellion and Its Enemies in Late Imperial China.*

32. The "Nian," a loose confederation of bandits, fraternal associations, and local militia, were in rebellion in Henan and adjacent provinces between 1853 and 1868. See Teng, *The Nien Army and Their Guerrilla Warfare.*

33. Bernhardt, *Rents, Taxes, and Peasant Resistance.*

34. Liu, *Anglo-American Steamship Rivalry in China.*

35. On Shanghai's displacement of Suzhou, see Johnson, *Shanghai.* This work also usefully demolishes the conventional (and highly Eurocentric) notion that Shanghai was nothing but a "sleepy fishing village" prior to its establishment as a European treaty port; in fact, Shanghai had been for centuries an important staging point for the Ming and Qing maritime trade with Southeast Asia.

8. Restoration

1. Wright, *The Last Stand of Chinese Conservatism*, 48–50.

2. Teng and Fairbank, *China's Response to the West.*

3. For a nice study of this institution's beginnings, see Banno, *China and the West.*

4. Hao, *The Commercial Revolution in Nineteenth-Century China.*

5. Hao, *The Compradore in Nineteenth-Century China.*

6. For example, Wright, *The Last Stand of Chinese Conservatism*, 149.

7. Luo, *Xiangjun xinzhi*; Spector, *Li Hung-chang and the Huai Army.*

8. Li, *Zhang Zhidong mufu.*

9. This line of scholarship was initiated by Philip Kuhn's 1970 book *Rebellion and Its Enemies in Late Imperial China.* Perhaps the strongest argument for the privatization of power during the Tongzhi reign is Polachek, "Gentry Hegemony." This privatization and its long-term consequences is most fully articulated in Rankin, *Elite Activism and Political Transformation in China.*

10. The following discussion is based on Kuhn, "Local Self-Government under the Republic."

11. Atwill, *The Chinese Sultanate.* The population figures are from p. 185.

12. Millward, *Eurasian Crossroads*, 120–128. Much of the material in the following paragraphs follows Millward's arguments.

13. Ibid., 124.

14. Ibid., 139.

15. Zhao, "Reinventing *China*."

16. Gottschang and Lary, *Swallows and Settlers*.

17. Elliott, "Bannerman and Townsman."

18. Wright, *The Last Stand of Chinese Conservatism*, 53–54. See also Crossley, *Orphan Warriors*, 224–228; Rhoads, *Manchus and Han*, 10.

19. There is a very large literature in Chinese on the development of handi-craft workshops in the late imperial era. For a monumental documentary over-view, concentrating on the post-Opium War era, see Peng, *Zhongguo jindai shougongye shiliao*.

20. This is a central argument of my *Hankow*. It is also made in He, *Zhongguo huiguan shilun*. This argument has been challenged by Bryna Goodman, who conclusively demonstrates the continuing power of native-place solidarity among sojourning merchants well into the twentieth century. I would argue, however, that while ties of common local origin remained useful and were actively main-tained, they were at the same time more easily transcended, when necessary, in the post-rebellion era. See Goodman, *Native Place, City, and Nation*.

21. Dou, *Tongxiang zuzhi zhi yanjiu*; Rowe, *Hankow: Conflict and Commu-nity*, chap. 9; Elvin, "The Gentry Democracy in Chinese Shanghai."

22. For English translations of several of Feng's and Zhang's essays on "self-strengthening," see Teng and Fairbank, *China's Response to the West*, 50–55, 166–174.

23. On this ideology, see Schwartz, *In Search of Wealth and Power*.

24. Levy, "Contrasting Factors in the Modernization of China and Japan"; Levy and Shih, *The Rise of the Modern Chinese Business Class*.

25. Feuerwerker, *China's Early Industrialization*.

26. This argument is now somewhat questioned by Elman, *On Their Own Terms*.

27. Elvin, "The High Level Equilibrium Trap."

28. Elvin, *The Retreat of the Elephants*, xviii, 123–124.

29. For an example, see Moulder, *Japan, China, and the Modern World Econ-omy*. For the general theory underlying this argument, see Wallerstein, *The Mod-ern World-System*.

30. Elman, *On Their Own Terms*, chap. 10; the quote is from p. 376.

31. Chi-kong Lai, "Li Hung-chang and Modern Enterprise"; Peng, "Yudahua: The History of an Industrial Enterprise in Modern China."

32. A useful place to start would be the summary article "Late Ch'ing Foreign Relations, 1860–1905," by one of this subject's most experienced students, Im-manuel C. Y. Hsu, in *Cambridge History of China*, vol. 11, 70–141. Although this article, in my view, is marred by what now seems an outdated "China's Re-sponse to the West" perspective, it is factually authoritative and admirably con-cise.

33. Such local conflicts are well explored in Cohen's classic *China and Christianity*, and more recently in Sweeten, *Christianity in Rural China*.

34. Chuan, "The Economic Crisis of 1883." For a study of the domestic politics related to the war, see Eastman, *Throne and Mandarins*.

35. Sakai, "The Ryūkyū (Liu-ch'iu) Islands as a Fief of Satsuma."

36. Leung, "Li Hung-chang and the Liu-ch'iu (Ryūkyū) Controversy, 1871–1881," 169.

37. This and the following paragraph are based on Larsen, *Tradition, Treaties, and Trade*.

38. Paine, *The Sino-Japanese War of 1894–95*, 3. This book offers an engrossing military history of the war, emphasizing in particular its coverage by Western journalists.

9. Imperialism

1. Lenin, *Imperialism, the Highest Stage of Capitalism*. For the revolutionary strategy debates of the 1920s, see Schwartz, "A Marxist Controversy on China."

2. This is the argument of the influential article by Iriye, "Imperialism in East Asia." For Iriye's view of World War I as the end of imperialism, see his *After Imperialism*. For a general study of imperialism in this historicist usage, see Langer, *The Diplomacy of Imperialism*.

3. Adams, *America's Economic Supremacy*, 221, cited in Iriye, "Imperialism," 131.

4. Hobson, *Imperialism*. The quotation is on p. 212 of the third edition, 1988.

5. *Present Day Impressions of the Far East and Prominent and Progressive Chinese at Home and Abroad*.

6. The Open Door notes were a seminal event in the history of American foreign policy, and their significance has been vigorously contested. For a classic analysis largely sympathetic to the Open Door's motivations (though skeptical of its impact), see Griswold, *The Far Eastern Policy of the United States*. For an influential critical reading, informed by the sensibilities of the Vietnam War era, see Williams, *The Tragedy of American Diplomacy*, 43–55. Williams described the Open Door policy as "imperial anticolonialism."

7. The *Analects* quotes Confucius as saying "Respect the *spirits*, but keep them at a distance."

8. For example, Levenson, *Confucian China and Its Modern Fate*, esp. 98–104. Compare Fairbank, *Trade and Diplomacy*, 24, which argues that while Europe had "nationalism" late imperial China had only "ethnocentrism." Levenson received his Ph.D. under Fairbank at Harvard in 1949.

9. See esp. Kwong, *A Mosaic of the Hundred Days*.

10. Kuhn, "Local Self-Government under the Republic," 272–275. Kang's pro-

posals on this subject are contained in a series of three articles he published in the newspaper *Xinmin congbao* during the spring of 1902, under the title "Gongmin zizhi" ("Citizen Self-Governance").

11. A thoughtful reflection on the relationship of late Ming and late Qing "study societies" is Wakeman, "The Price of Autonomy."

12. For Liang Qichao's early journalistic career, see Judge, *Print and Politics.*

13. Among other sources, my account of the Hunan reform movement draws on Platt, *Provincial Patriots,* chap. 3; Esherick, *Reform and Revolution in China,* 13–19; and Chang, "Intellectual Change and the Reform Movement, 1890–1898," in *Cambridge History of China,* vol. 11, 300–318.

14. On Huang's career see Kamachi, *Reform in China.*

15. Cohen, *History in Three Keys.*

16. The best study of the Boxer movement in English—Esherick, *The Origins of the Boxer Uprising*—argues against either White Lotus or anti-Manchu origins. Older scholarship, such as Tan's classic *The Boxer Catastrophe* and Hsu's treatment in his 1980 *Cambridge History of China* article, "Late Ch'ing Foreign Relations," 115–130, see the Boxers as initially anti-Qing. The most sustained study of the Boxers in English since Esherick—Cohen's *History in Three Keys,* 32, 38–39—emphasizes this diffuseness about Boxer goals. On balance, it accepts Esherick's argument against early Ming loyalism but is more skeptical of his denial of significant White Lotus influence.

17. The negotiation process for the Protocol is treated in considerable detail in Tan, *Boxer Catastrophe.*

18. In a rare act of visionary foreign policy, both the United States and Britain dedicated a portion of their shares of the indemnity to a fund for education of Chinese students in their countries, and to found Qinghua University in Beijing. This created a very useful legacy of goodwill toward these countries on the part of influential former "Boxer Indemnity Scholars," observable for many decades thereafter.

19. The pioneering study in English is Eastman, "Ch'ing-i and Chinese Policy Formation during the Nineteenth Century."

20. Platt, *Provincial Patriots,* chap. 2.

21. Rankin, "Public Opinion and Political Power."

22. Rowe, "Water Control and the Qing Political Process."

23. Bays, *China Enters the Twentieth Century,* chap. 8.

24. The following paragraphs follow Rankin, *Elite Activism and Political Transformation in China.* My own book, *Hankow: Conflict and Community,* extends study of the processes identified by Rankin to an intensely urban area in the adjacent middle Yangzi region, likewise devastated by the Taiping wars.

25. Among several recent studies of *Shenbao* and other early Chinese journalistic efforts, see Wagner, *Joining the Global Public.*

26. For a detailed study of the way Jiangnan elites were persuaded to contribute to famine relief in North China, as well as a comparison with how the famine was perceived by other contemporary observers, see Edgerton-Tarpley, *Tears from Iron.*

10. Revolution

1. Anderson, *Imagined Communities.*

2. A classic comparative study of the state-making process in early modern Europe is Rosenberg, *Bureaucracy, Aristocracy, and Autocracy.*

3. See for example Weber, *Peasants into Frenchmen.*

4. Stern, *Gold and Iron,* 468.

5. Dikötter, *The Discourse of Race in Modern China,* and *Imperfect Conceptions.*

6. Duara, *Rescuing History from the Nation.* Duara's ideas are drawn in part from the critique of Westernizing nation-building in South Asia, as articulated for example in Chatterjee, *The Nation and Its Fragments.*

7. Adapted from the translation of the edict *(shangyu)* of January 29, 1901, in Reynolds, *China, 1898–1912,* 201–204.

8. London, "The Unparalleled Invasion." I thank Professor Meredith Woo for bringing this story to my attention.

9. On Yuan's civil reforms, see MacKinnon, *Power and Politics in Late Imperial China.*

10. Among several studies of this elite war against popular culture, see Duara, "Knowledge and Power in the Discourse of Modernity."

11. The most famous of such portrayals is Lu Xun's short story "Kong Yiji." See *The Complete Stories of Lu Xun,* 13–18.

12. See for example my own study of elites in one central Chinese county, "Success Stories."

13. Rowe, *Hankow,* 197.

14. Esherick, *Reform and Revolution,* 114.

15. Establishment histories based on this narrative would include Wen, *Zhonghua minguo geming quanshi.* I am indebted for this paragraph to similar comments in Wakeman, *Fall of Imperial China,* 225–227.

16. For one such betrayal narrative in English, see Chen, *Yuan Shih-k'ai, 1859–1916.*

17. See for example Linebarger, *The Political Doctrines of Sun Yat-sen.*

18. For a prominent example, see Zhang, Lin, et al., *Xinhai geming shi.*

19. For example, Linebarger, *Sun Yat Sen and the Chinese Republic.*

20. Hsüeh, *Huang Hsing and the Chinese Revolution;* Liew, *Struggle for Democracy.*

21. Gasster, *Chinese Intellectuals and the Revolution of 1911;* Rankin, *Early Chinese Revolutionaries;* Furth, "The Sage as Rebel."

22. Chang, "The Constitutionalists"; Chang, *Liang Ch'i-ch'ao and Intellectual Transition in China.*

23. Hsieh, "Triads, Salt Smugglers, and Local Uprisings"; Hsieh, "Peasant Insurrection and the Marketing Hierarchy in the Canton Delta, 1911"; Rhoads, *China's Republican Revolution;* Esherick, *Reform and Revolution in China.*

24. On Naitō, see Fogel, *Politics and Sinology.* On the Tōa Dōbunkai, see Reynolds, *China, 1898–1912.* Liang's Japanese experience is emphasized in Huang, *Liang Ch'i-ch'ao and Modern Chinese Liberalism.* The classic study of Sun's Japanese ties is Jansen, *The Japanese and Sun Yat-sen.* On the students, see Reynolds and also Harrell, *Sowing the Seeds of Change.*

25. Reynolds, *China, 1898–1912,* 48.

26. *Complete Stories of Lu Xun,* vi–vii.

27. Platt, *Provincial Patriots,* 117–21.

28. Rankin, *Early Chinese Revolutionaries,* and especially "The Tenacity of Tradition."

29. Wong, "Die for the Boycott and Nation."

30. Translated in Esherick, *Reform and Revolution,* 48.

31. Bernal, "Liu Shih-p'ei and National Essence"; Chang, *Chinese Intellectuals in Crisis,* chap. 5.

32. All of my citations of Zou are adapted from the translation by Hsüeh in *Revolutionary Leaders of Modern China,* 194–209.

33. On the debates among late Qing radicals on the assessment of Zeng and other anti-Taiping heroes, see Platt, *Provincial Patriots,* 88–90, 104–105.

34. Bernal, "Liu Shih-p'ei and National Essence," 92–93.

35. For an unapologetic hagiography, see Linebarger. An equally incautious debunking is Sharman, *Sun Yat-sen, His Life and Its Meaning.* For a more plausible middle ground, see Schiffrin, *Sun Yat-sen and the Origins of the 1911 Revolution,* and Bergère, *Sun Yat-sen.* As Michael Gasster has concluded, in our understanding today of the Revolution of 1911, "The importance of the [professional] revolutionaries is far less than what it was in older interpretations. This was a revolution bigger than all its leaders." Gasster, "The Republican Revolutionary Movement," in *Cambridge History of China,* vol. 11, 463.

36. On Sun's speechifying prowess, see Strand, "Calling the Chinese People to Order."

37. Sun Yat-sen, *Kidnapped in London!*

38. For a lively depiction of this activity, see Ma, *Revolutionaries, Monarchists, and Chinatowns.* For a general discussion of the politicization of the Chinese diaspora, see Kuhn, *Chinese among Others,* chap. 6.

39. On this process see Platt, *Provincial Patriots,* chap. 5.

40. Esherick, *Reform and Revolution,* chap. 3.

41. On the emergence of this term in common discourse, see Bastid-Bruguiere, "Currents of Social Change," *Cambridge History of China*, vol. 11, 557–558.

42. One of the earliest and boldest officials in cultivating the merger of literati and merchant roles was Hu Linyi, Hubei governor in the late 1850s; see Rowe, *Hankow: Conflict and Community*, chap. 6.

43. Ichiko, "The Role of the Gentry."

44. Judge, *Print and Politics*.

45. Kuhn, *Chinese among Others*, 229–232.

46. Lee, "Frontier Politics in the Southwestern Sino-Tibetan Borderlands during the Ch'ing Dynasty"; Ho, "The Men Who Would Not Be Amban and the One Who Would."

47. See Rankin's excellent article, "Nationalistic Contestation and Mobilizational Politics."

48. Chang, "The Constitutionalists."

49. See especially Fincher, "Political Provincialism and the National Revolution."

50. See Fincher, "Political Provincialism"; Platt, *Provincial Patriots;* and Buck, "The Provincial Elite in Shantung during the Republican Period."

51. On the notion of a "revolutionary situation," see Tilly, *From Mobilization to Revolution*, chap. 7.

52. Prazniak, "Tax Protest at Laiyang, Shandong, 1910"; Rosenbaum, "Gentry Power and the Changsha Rice Riot of 1910."

53. For detailed accounts, see Esherick, *Reform and Revolution*, chap. 6, and Dutt, "The First Week of Revolution."

54. Wang, "Officialdom Unmasked."

55. Rhoads, *Manchus and Han,* chap. 4; the mission of "national revenge" is discussed on p. 203.

Conclusion

1. Pruitt, *A Daughter of Han*, 197.

2. Lin, "The Suicide of Liang Chi"; Cheng, "Politics of the Queue"; Ko, *Cinderella's Sisters.*

3. Zhao, "Reinventing *China*."

4. Nakami, "The Mongols and the 1911 Revolution."

5. A sophisticated reading of the discourses underpinning these efforts is Duara, *Sovereignty and Authenticity.*

6. For thoughtful reflections on this issue see Alitto, "Rural Elites in Transition."

7. See McNeill, *The Age of Gunpowder Empires*—a work of acknowledged influence on several contributors to Struve, ed., *The Qing Formation in World-Historical Time.*

8. An early and persuasive documentation of this process is Schoppa, *Chinese Elites and Political Change*. While Schoppa is ambivalent about the social benefit of this process, unambiguously condemnatory of it (yet still clearly affirming its existence) is Duara, *Culture, Power, and the State.*

9. This has been a central theme of recent work by William C. Kirby. See for example Kirby, "Engineering China."

BIBLIOGRAPHY

Adas, Michael. *Machines as the Measure of Men: Science, Technology, and Ideologies of Western Dominance.* Ithaca: Cornell University Press, 1989.

Adshead, S. A. M. "The Seventeenth-Century General Crisis in China." *Asian Profiles* 27 (1973): 1–80.

Alitto, Guy S. "Rural Elites in Transition: China's Cultural Crisis and the Problem of Legitimacy." *Select Papers from the Center for Far Eastern Studies* 3 (1978–79): 218–277.

Anderson, Benedict. *Imagined Communities: Reflections on the Origin and Spread of Nationalism.* London: Verso, 1983.

Arrighi, Giovanni. *Adam Smith in Beijing: Lineages of the Twenty-First Century.* London: Verso, 2007.

Art of Ethnography: A Chinese "Miao" Album, The. Trans. David M. Deal and Laura Hostetler. Seattle: University of Washington Press, 2006.

Atwell, William. "International Bullion Flows and the Chinese Economy, *circa* 1530–1650." *Past and Present* 95 (1982): 68–90.

———. "Some Observations on the Seventeenth-Century Crisis in China and Japan." *Journal of Asian Studies* 45:2 (1986): 223–244.

Atwill, David G. *The Chinese Sultanate: Islam, Ethnicity, and the Panthey Rebellion in Southwest China, 1856–1873.* Stanford: Stanford University Press, 2005.

Averill, Steven. "The Shed People and the Opening of the Yangzi Highlands." *Modern China* 9:1 (January 1983): 84–126.

Bai Xinliang. *Qianlong zhuan* [Biography of Qianlong]. Shenyang: Liaoning jiaoyu chubanshe, 1990.

Banno, Masataka. *China and the West: The Origins of the Tsungli Yamen, 1858–1861.* Cambridge: Harvard University Press, 1964.

Barr, Allen. "Four Schoolmasters: Educational Issues in Li Hai-kuan's *Lamp at* the Crossroads." In Elman and Woodside, eds., *Education and Society in Late Imperial China, 1600–1900*, 50–75.

Bartlett, Beatrice S. *Monarchs and Ministers: The Grand Council in Mid-Ch'ing China, 1723–1820*. Berkeley: University of California Press, 1991.

Bastid-Bruguiere, Marianne. "Currents of Social Change." In Fairbank and Liu, eds., *Cambridge History of China*, vol. 11.

Bays, Daniel. *China Enters the Twentieth Century: Chang Chih-tung and the Issues of a New Age*. Ann Arbor: University of Michigan Press, 1978.

———, ed. *Christianity in China: From the Eighteenth Century to the Present*. Stanford: Stanford University Press, 1996.

Beattie, Hilary. *Land and Lineage in China: A Study of T'ung-ch'eng County, Anhwei, in the Ming and Ch'ing Dynasties*. Cambridge: Cambridge University Press, 1979.

Bergère, Marie-Claire. *Sun Yat-sen*. Stanford: Stanford University Press, 1998.

Bernal, Martin. "Liu Shih-p'ei and National Essence." In Furth, ed., *Limits of Change*, 90–112.

Bernhardt, Kathryn. *Rents, Taxes, and Peasant Resistance: The Lower Yangzi Region, 1840–1950*. Stanford: Stanford University Press, 1992.

Blussé, Leonard. *Strange Company: Chinese Settlers, Mestizo Women, and the Dutch in VOC Batavia*. Dordrecht: Foris, 1988.

Blussé, Leonard, and Chen Menghong, eds. *The Archives of the Kong Koan of Batavia*. Leiden: Brill, 2003.

Braudel, Fernand. "History and the Social Sciences: The *Longue Durée*." In Braudel, *On History*, trans. Sarah Matthews. Chicago: University of Chicago Press, 1980.

Brokaw, Cynthia. *Commerce in Culture: The Sibao Book Trade in the Qing and Republican Periods*. Cambridge: Harvard University Asia Center, 2007.

———. *The Ledgers of Merit and Demerit: Social Change and Moral Order in Late Imperial China*. Princeton: Princeton University Press, 1991.

———. "Tai Chen and Learning in the Confucian Tradition." In Elman and Woodside, eds., *Education and Society in Late Imperial China, 1600–1900*.

Brook, Timothy. *The Confusions of Pleasure: Commerce and Culture in Ming China*. Berkeley: University of California Press, 1998.

———. "Funerary Ritual and the Building of Lineages in Late Imperial China." *Harvard Journal of Asiatic Studies* 49:2 (December 1989): 465–499.

Buck, David D. "The Provincial Elite in Shantung during the Republican Period: Their Successes and Failures." *Modern China* 1:4 (1975): 417–446.

Cai Shaoqing. "On the Origins of the Gelaohui." *Modern China* 10:4 (1984): 481–508.

———. *Zhongguo mimi shehui* [Chinese Secret Societies]. Hangzhou: Zhejiang renmin chubanshe, 1989.

Cao Wen. "Qingdai Guangdong tizhi zai yanjiu" [A Reexamination of the Canton System]. *Qingshi yanjiu* 2006.2: 82–96.

Carlitz, Katherine. "The Social Uses of Female Virtue in Late Ming Editions of Lienü Zhuan." *Late Imperial China* 12:2 (December 1991): 117–148.

Chan, Wing-tsit. "The *Hsing-li ching-i* and the Ch'eng-Chu School of the Seventeenth Century." In *The Unfolding of Neo-Confucianism,* ed. Wm. Theodore de Bary, 543–579. New York: Columbia University Press, 1975.

Chang, Chung-li. *The Chinese Gentry: Studies on Their Role in Nineteenth-Century Chinese Society.* Seattle: University of Washington Press, 1955.

———. *The Income of the Chinese Gentry.* Seattle: University of Washington Press, 1962.

Chang, Hao. *Chinese Intellectuals in Crisis: Search for Order and Meaning, 1890–1911.* Berkeley: University of California Press, 1987.

———. "Intellectual Change and the Reform Movement, 1890–1898." In Fairbank and Liu, eds., *Cambridge History of China,* vol. 11, 300–318.

———. *Liang Ch'i-ch'ao and Intellectual Transition in China.* Cambridge: Harvard University Press, 1971.

Chang, Hsin-pao. *Commissioner Lin and the Opium War.* Cambridge: Harvard University Press, 1964.

Chang, Michael. *A Court on Horseback: Imperial Touring and the Construction of Qing Rule, 1680–1785.* Cambridge: Harvard University Asia Center, 2007.

Chang P'eng-yuan. "The Constitutionalists." In *China in Revolution: The First Phase, 1900–1913,* ed. Mary C. Wright, 143–183. New Haven: Yale University Press, 1968.

Chartier, Roger. *The Cultural Uses of Print in Early Modern France.* Princeton: Princeton University Press, 1997.

Chatterjee, Partha. *The Nation and Its Fragments: Colonial and Postcolonial Histories.* Princeton: Princeton University Press, 1993.

Chaudhuri, K. N. *The Trading World of Asia and the English East India Company, 1660–1760.* Cambridge: Cambridge University Press, 1978.

Chen, Jerome. *Yuan Shih-k'ai, 1859–1916: Brutus Assumes the Purple.* Stanford: Stanford University Press, 1961.

Cheng, Pei-kai, and Michael Listz, with Jonathan D. Spence, eds. *The Search for Modern China: A Documentary Collection.* New York: Norton, 1999.

Cheng, Weikun. "Politics of the Queue: Agitation and Resistance in the Beginning and End of Qing China." In *Hair: Its Power and Meaning in Asian Cultures,* ed. Alf Hiltebeitel and Barbara Miller, 123–142. Albany: State University of New York Press, 1998.

Chesneaux, Jean, ed. *Popular Movements and Secret Societies in China, 1840–1950.* Stanford: Stanford University Press, 1972.

Chia, Ning. "The Li-Fan Yuan in the Early Ch'ing Dynasty." Ph.D. diss., Johns Hopkins University, 1991.

Chinese University of Hong Kong. *Wenyuange sikuquanshu dianzibian* [Electronic edition of the *Siku quanshu*]. Hong Kong: CUHK Press, 1999.

Chow, Kai-wing. *Publishing, Culture, and Power in Early Modern China*. Stanford: Stanford University Press, 2004.

———. *The Rise of Confucian Ritualism in Late Imperial China: Ethics, Classics, and Lineage Discourse*. Stanford: Stanford University Press, 1994.

Ch'u, T'ung-tsu. *Local Government in China under the Ch'ing*. Cambridge: Harvard University Press, 1962.

Chuan Han-sheng. "The Economic Crisis of 1883 as Seen in the Failure of Hsü Jun's Real Estate Business in Shanghai." In *Modern Chinese Economic History*, ed. Chi-ming Hou and Tzung-shian Yu, 493–498. Taipei: Academia Sinica, 1979.

Chuan Han-sheng and Richard Kraus. *Mid-Ch'ing Rice Markets and Trade: An Essay in Price History*. Cambridge: Harvard University Council on East Asian Studies, 1975.

Clunas, Craig. *Superfluous Things: Material Culture and Social Status in Early Modern China*. Honolulu: University of Hawai'i Press, 2004.

Cochran, Sherman. *Encountering Chinese Networks: Western, Japanese, and Chinese Corporations in China, 1880–1937*. Berkeley: University of California Press, 2000.

Cohen, Paul A. *China and Christianity: The Missionary Movement and the Growth of Chinese Anti-Foreignism, 1860–1870*. Cambridge: Harvard University Press, 1963.

———. *Discovering History in China: American Historical Writing on the Recent Chinese Past*. New York: Columbia University Press, 1984.

———. *History in Three Keys: The Boxers as Event, Experience, and Myth*. New York: Columbia University Press, 1997.

Cole, James. *Shaohsing: Cooperation and Competition in Nineteenth-Century China*. Tucson: Association for Asian Studies Monographs, 1986.

Cooper, T. T. *Travels of a Pioneer of Commerce in Pigtails and Petticoats*. London: J. Murray, 1871.

Crossley, Pamela Kyle. *Orphan Warriors: Three Manchu Generations and the End of the Qing World*. Princeton: Princeton University Press, 1990.

———. "Review Article: The Rulerships of China." *American Historical Review* 97:5 (1992): 1468–83.

———. "Thinking about Ethnicity in Early Modern China." *Late Imperial China* 11:1 (June 1990): 1–35.

———. "The Tong in Two Worlds: Cultural Identities in Liaoning and Nurgan during the 13th–17th Centuries." *Ch'ing-shih wen-t'i* 4–9 (June 1983): 21–46.

———. *A Translucent Mirror: History and Identity in Qing Imperial Ideology.* Berkeley: University of California Press, 1999.

Crossley, Pamela Kyle, Helen F. Siu, and Donald S. Sutton, eds. *Empire at the Margins: Culture, Ethnicity, and Frontier in Early Modern China.* Berkeley: University of California Press, 2006.

Curtin, Philip D. *Cross-Cultural Trade in World History.* New York: Cambridge University Press, 1984.

Dabringhaus, Sabine. "Chinese Emperors and Tibetan Monks: Religion as an Instrument of Rule." In *China and Her Neighbors: Borders, Visions of the Other, Foreign Policy, 10th to 19th Century,* ed. Sabine Dabringhaus and Roderich Ptak, 119–134. Wiesbaden: Harrassowitz Verlag, 1997.

Dai Yi. *Qianlong di ji qi shidai* [Qianlong and His Times]. Beijing: Chinese People's University Press, 1992.

———. "Shiba shiji Zhongguo de chengjiu, quxian, yu shidai tezheng" [The Achievements, Limitations, and Significance of China's Eighteenth Century]. *Qingshi yanjiu* 1 (1993): 1–6.

Dai, Yingcong. "The White Lotus War: A War Fought on the Terms of the Qing Military." Unpublished paper.

de Bary, Wm. Theodore. "Individualism and Humanism in Late Ming Thought." In *Self and Society in Ming Thought,* ed. W. T. de Bary, 145–248. New York: Columbia University Press, 1970.

———, ed. *The Unfolding of Neo-Confucianism.* New York: Columbia University Press, 1975.

de Bary, Wm. Theodore, and Irene Bloom, eds. *Principle and Practicality: Essays in Neo-Confucianism and Practical Learning.* New York: Columbia University Press, 1979.

de Bary, Wm. Theodore, et al., eds. *Sources of Chinese Tradition.* New York: Columbia University Press, 1960.

———, eds. *Sources of Chinese Tradition.* 2nd ed. 2 vols. New York: Columbia University Press, 1999–2000.

Decennial Reports, 1882–91. Shanghai: Inspectorate General of Customs, 1892.

Delurey, John. "Despotism Above and Below: Gu Yanwu on Power, Money, and Mores." Ph.D. diss., Yale University, 2007.

Deng Tuo. *Lun Zhongguo lishi jige wenti* [On Several Problems in Chinese History]. Beijing: Sanlian shudian, 1979.

Dennerline, Jerry. *The Chia-ting Loyalists: Confucian Leadership in Seventeenth-Century China.* New Haven: Yale University Press, 1971.

———. "Fiscal Reform and Local Control." In Wakeman and Grant, eds., *Conflict and Control in Late Imperial China.*

———. "The New Hua Charitable Estate and Local Level Leadership in Wuxi County at the End of the Qing." *Select Papers from the Center for Far Eastern Studies* 4 (1979–80): 19–70.

Di Cosmo, Nicola. "Before the Conquest: Opportunity and Choice in the Construction of Manchu Power." Unpublished paper.

Dikötter, Frank. *The Discourse of Race in Modern China*. Stanford: Stanford University Press, 1992.

———. *Imperfect Conceptions: Medical Knowledge, Birth Defects, and Eugenics in China*. New York: Columbia University Press, 1998.

Dou Jiliang. *Tongxiang zuzhi zhi yanjiu* [A Study of Local Origin Associations]. Chongqing: Zhengzhong shuju, 1946.

Douglass, William. *A Summary, Historical and Political, of the First Planting, Progressive Improvements, and Present State of the British Settlements in North America*. Rev. ed. London: 1755.

Duara, Prasenjit. *Culture, Power, and the State: Rural North China, 1900–1942*. Stanford: Stanford University Press, 1988.

———. "Knowledge and Power in the Discourse of Modernity: The Campaigns against Popular Religion in Early Twentieth-Century China." *Journal of Asian Studies* 50 (1991): 67–83.

———. *Rescuing History from the Nation: Questioning Narratives of Modern China*. Chicago: University of Chicago Press, 1995.

———. *Sovereignty and Authenticity: Manchukuo and the East Asian Modern*. Lanham, MD: Rowman and Littlefield, 2003.

Dunstan, Helen. *Conflicting Counsels to Confuse the Age: A Documentary Study of Political Economy in Qing China, 1644–1840*. Ann Arbor: University of Michigan Center for Chinese Studies, 1996.

———. "If Chen Yun Had Written about Her Lesbianism." *Asia Major* 3rd Series, 20:2 (2007): 103–122.

———. *State or Merchant: Political Economy and Political Process in 1740s China*. Cambridge: Harvard University Asia Center, 2006.

Dutt, Vidya Prakash. "The First Week of Revolution: The Wuchang Uprising." In Wright, *China in Revolution*, 383–416.

Eastman, Lloyd E. "Ch'ing-i and Chinese Policy Formation During the Nineteenth Century." *Journal of Asian Studies* 24:4 (1965): 595–611.

———. *Throne and Mandarins: China's Search for a Policy during the Sino-French Controversy, 1880–1885*. Cambridge: Harvard University Press, 1967.

Ebrey, Patricia Buckley, and James L. Watson, eds. *Kinship Organization in Late Imperial China, 1000–1940*. Berkeley: University of California Press, 1986.

Edgerton-Tarpley, Kathryn. *Tears from Iron: Cultural Responses to Famine in Nineteenth-Century China*. Berkeley: University of California Press, 2008.

Edwards, R. Randle. "Imperial China's Border Control Law." *Journal of Chinese Law* 1:1 (1987): 33–62.

Elliott, Mark C. "Bannerman and Townsman: Ethnic Tension in Nineteenth-Century Jiangnan." *Late Imperial China* 11:1 (June 1990): 36–74.

———. *The Manchu Way: The Eight Banners and Ethnic Identity in Late Imperial China*. Stanford: Stanford University Press, 2001.

———. *Emperor Qianlong: Son of Heaven, Man of the World*. Upper Saddle River, NJ: Pearson Longman, 2009.

Elman, Benjamin A. *A Cultural History of Civil Examinations in Late Imperial China*. Berkeley: University of California Press, 2000.

———. *From Philosophy to Philology: Intellectual and Social Aspects of Change in Late Imperial China*. Cambridge: Harvard University Council on East Asian Studies, 1984.

———. *On Their Own Terms: Science in China 1550–1900*. Cambridge: Harvard University Press, 2005.

Elman, Benjamin A., and Alexander Woodside, eds. *Education and Society in Late Imperial China, 1600–1900*. Berkeley: University of California Press, 1994.

Elvin, Mark. "Female Virtue and the State in China." *Past and Present* 104 (1984): 111–152.

———. "The Gentry Democracy in Chinese Shanghai, 1905–1914." In *Modern China's Search for a Political Form*, ed. Jack Gray, 41–65. London: Oxford University Press, 1969.

———. "The High Level Equilibrium Trap." In *Economic Organization in Chinese Society*, ed. W. E. Willmott. Stanford: Stanford University Press, 1972.

———. "Market Towns and Waterways: The County of Shanghai from 1480 to 1910." In *The City in Late Imperial China*, ed. G. William Skinner, 441–474. Stanford: Stanford University Press, 1977.

———. *The Pattern of the Chinese Past*. Stanford: Stanford University Press, 1973.

———. *The Retreat of the Elephants: An Environmental History of China*. New Haven: Yale University Press, 2004.

Entenmann, Robert. "Catholics and Society in Eighteenth-Century Sichuan." In Bays, ed., *Christianity in China: From the Eighteenth Century to the Present*, 8–23.

———. "Szechwan and Ch'ing Migration Policy." *Ch'ing-shih wen-t'i* 4:4 (December 1980): 35–54.

Esherick, Joseph W. "Harvard on China: The Apologetics of Imperialism." *Bulletin of Concerned Asian Scholars* (1973): 9–16.

———. *The Origins of the Boxer Uprising*. Berkeley: University of California Press, 1987.

———. *Reform and Revolution in China: The 1911 Revolution in Hunan and Hubei*. Berkeley: University of California Press, 1976.

Esherick, Joseph W., and Mary Backus Rankin, eds. *Chinese Local Elites and Patterns of Dominance*. Berkeley: University of California Press, 1990.

Fairbank, John K., ed. *The Cambridge History of China*. Vol. 10. Cambridge: Cambridge University Press, 1978.

———. *China: The People's Middle Kingdom and the U.S.A.* Cambridge: Belknap Press of Harvard University Press, 1967.

———. *Chinabound: A Fifty Year Memoir*. New York: Harper and Row, 1982.

———, ed. *The Chinese World Order: Traditional China's Foreign Relations*. Cambridge: Harvard University Press, 1968.

———. *Trade and Diplomacy on the China Coast: The Opening of the Treaty Ports, 1842–1854*. Stanford: Stanford University Press, 1969. First published Cambridge: Harvard University Press, 1953.

Fairbank, John K., and Kwang-Ching Liu, eds. *The Cambridge History of China*, Vol. 11. Cambridge: Cambridge University Press, 1980.

Fairbank, John K., and Edwin Reischauer. *East Asia: The Great Tradition*. Boston: Houghton Mifflin, 1960.

Fairbank, John K., Edwin Reischauer, and Albert Craig. *East Asia: The Modern Transformation*. Boston: Houghton Mifflin, 1965.

Fairbank, John K., and Ssu-yu Teng. "On the Ch'ing Tributary System." *Harvard Journal of Asiatic Studies* 6 (1941): 135–246.

Fang Xing. "Lun Qingdai Jiangnan nongmin de xiaofei" [Peasant Consumption in Qing Jiangnan]. *Zhongguo jingjishi yanjiu* 3 (1996): 91–98.

Farquhar, David M. "Emperor as Bodhisattva in the Governance of the Ch'ing Empire." *Harvard Journal of Asiatic Studies* 38:1 (June 1978): 5–34.

Faure, David. "The Lineage as Business Company: Patronage vs. Law in the Development of Chinese Business." In *China's Market Economy in Transition*, ed. Yung-san Lee and Ts'ui-jung Liu. Nankang: Academia Sinica, 1990.

Fay, Peter Ward. *The Opium War, 1840–1842: Barbarians in the Celestial Empire in the Early Part of the Nineteenth Century and the War by Which They Forced Her Doors Ajar*. New York: Norton, 1976.

Fei, Hsiao-tung. "Peasantry and Gentry: An Interpretation of Chinese Social Structure and its Changes." *American Journal of Sociology* 52:1 (July 1946): 1–17.

Feng Erkang. *Yongzheng zhuan* [Biography of Yongzheng]. Beijing: Renmin chubanshe, 1985.

Feuerwerker, Albert. *China's Early Industrialization: Sheng Hsuan-huai (1844–1916) and Mandarin Enterprise*. Cambridge: Harvard University Press, 1958.

Fincher, John. "Political Provincialism and the National Revolution." In Wright, *China in Revolution*, 185–226.

Finnane, Antonia. "Yangzhou's 'Mondernity': Fashion and Consumption in the Early Nineteenth Century." *positions* 11:2 (Fall 2003): 395–425.

Fogel, Joshua. *Politics and Sinology: The Case of Naitō Konan (1866–1934).* Cambridge: Harvard University Council on East Asian Studies, 1984.

Folsom, Kenneth E. *Friends, Guests, and Colleagues: The Mu-fu System in the Late Ch'ing Period.* Berkeley: University of California Press, 1968.

Frank, Andre Gunder. *Re-Orient: The Global Economy in the Asian Age.* Berkeley: University of California Press, 1998.

Free Trade to India: letters addressed to the merchants and inhabitants of the town of Liverpool, concerning a free trade to the East Indies, by a member of Parliament. Liverpool: E. Smith, 1812.

Fujii Hiroshi. "Shin'an shōnin no kenkyū" [A Study of the Huizhou Merchants]. Part 1, *Tōyō gakuhō* 36:1 (1953): 1–44.

Fuma Susumu. *Chūgoku zentai zentō shi kenkyū* [Charity Associations and Charity Halls in China]. Kyoto: Dohosha shuppan, 1997.

Furth, Charlotte, ed. *The Limits of Change: Essays on Conservative Alternatives in Republican China.* Cambridge: Harvard University Press, 1976.

———. "The Sage as Rebel: The Inner World of Chang Ping-lin." In Furth, ed., *The Limits of Change: Essays on Conservative Alternatives in Republican China,* 113–150.

Gao Wangling. "Yige weiwanjie de changshi: Qingdai Qianlong shiqi liangzheng he liaoshi wenti" [An Unfinished Experiment: Food Supply Problems in the Qing Qianlong Reign]. *Jiuzhou xuekan* 2:3 (April 1988): 13–40.

Gasster, Michael. *Chinese Intellectuals and the Revolution of 1911.* Seattle: University of Washington Press, 1969.

———. "The Republican Revolutionary Movement." In Fairbank and Liu, eds., *Cambridge History of China,* vol. 11.

Gaustad, Blaine Campbell. "Religious Sectarianism and the State in Mid-Qing China: Background to the White Lotus Uprising of 1796–1804." Ph.D. diss., University of California–Berkeley, 1994.

Gentzler, J. Mason, ed. *Changing China: Readings in the History of China from the Opium War to the Present.* New York: Praeger, 1977.

Giersch, C. Patterson. *Asian Borderlands: The Transformation of Qing China's Yunnan Frontier.* Cambridge: Harvard University Press, 2006.

Goldstein, Joshua S. *Drama Kings: Players and Publics in the Re-creation of Peking Opera, 1870–1937.* Berkeley: University of California Press, 2007.

Goodman, Bryna. *Native Place, City, and Nation: Regional Identities in Shanghai, 1853–1937.* Berkeley: University of California Press, 1995.

Goodrich, L. Carrington. *The Literary Inquisition of Ch'ien-lung.* Baltimore: American Council of Learned Societies, 1935.

Gottschang, Thomas, and Diana Lary. *Swallows and Settlers: The Great Chinese*

Migration from North China to Manchuria. Ann Arbor: University of Michigan Center for Chinese Studies, 2000.

Griswold, A. Whitney. *The Far Eastern Policy of the United States*. New Haven: Yale University Press, 1934.

Guan Wenfa. *Jiaqing di* [The Jiaqing Emperor]. Changchun: Jilin wenshi chubanshe, 1993.

Guo Songyi. "Lun tanding rudi" [On the Merger of the Head Tax and Land Tax]. *Qingshi luncong* 3 (1982): 1–62.

Guy, R. Kent. *The Emperor's Four Treasuries: Scholars and the State in the Late Ch'ien-lung Era*. Cambridge: Harvard University Council on East Asian Studies, 1987.

———. "Fang Pao and the *Ch'in-ting Ssu-shu wen*." In Elman and Woodside, eds., *Education and Society in Late Imperial China, 1600–1900*.

Hamashita Takeshi. "The Tribute Trade System and Modern Asia." In *Japanese Industrialization and the Asian Economy*, ed. A. J. Latham and Kawakatsu Heita. London: Routledge, 1994.

Hanan, Patrick. *The Invention of Li Yu*. Cambridge: Harvard University Press, 1988.

Hanson, Marta. "Jesuits and Medicine in the Kangxi Court (1662–1722)." *Pacific Rim Report* 43 (July 2007): 1–10.

Hao, Yen-p'ing. *The Commercial Revolution in Nineteenth-Century China: The Rise of Sino-Western Mercantile Capitalism*. Berkeley: University of California Press, 1986.

———. *The Compradore in Nineteenth-Century China: Bridge between East and West*. Cambridge: Harvard University Press, 1970.

Harrell, Paula. *Sowing the Seeds of Change: Chinese Students, Japanese Teachers, 1895–1905*. Stanford: Stanford University Press, 1992.

Hartwell, Robert M. "Demographic, Political, and Social Transformations of China, 750–1550." *Harvard Journal of Asiatic Studies* 42:2 (December 1982): 365–442.

Hay, Jonathan. *Shitao: Painting and Modernity in Early Qing China*. Cambridge: Cambridge University Press, 2001.

He Bingdi (Ping-ti Ho). *Zhongguo huiguan shilun* [The History of Chinese Native Place Associations]. Taipei, 1966.

Herman, John E. *Amid the Clouds and Mist: China's Colonization of Guizhou, 1200–1700*. Cambridge: Harvard University Asia Center, 2007.

———. "The Cant of Conquest: *Tusi* Offices and China's Political Incorporation of the Southwest Frontier." In Crossley, Siu, and Sutton, eds., *Empire at the Margins: Culture, Ethnicity, and Frontier in Early Modern China*.

———. "Empire in the Southwest: Early Qing Reforms to the Native Chieftain System." *Journal of Asian Studies* 56:1 (February 1997): 47–74.

Hershatter, Gail. *Dangerous Pleasures: Prostitution and Modernity in Twentieth-Century Shanghai.* Berkeley: University of California Press, 1997.

Hevia, James L. *Cherishing Men from Afar: Qing Guest Ritual and the Macartney Mission of 1793.* Durham: Duke University Press, 1995.

———. "Loot's Fate: The Economy of Plunder and the Moral Life of Objects 'From the Summer Palace of the Emperor of China.'" *History and Anthropology* 6:4 (1994): 319–345.

Ho, Dahpon David. "The Men Who Would Not Be Amban and the One Who Would: Four Frontline Officials and Qing Tibet Policy, 1905–1911." *Modern China* 34:2 (April 2008): 210–246.

Ho, Ping-ti. *The Ladder of Success in Imperial China: Aspects of Social Mobility, 1368–1911.* New York: Wiley, 1964.

———. "The Significance of the Ch'ing Period in Chinese History." *Journal of Asian Studies* 26:2 (February 1967): 189–195.

———. *Studies on the Population of China, 1368–1957.* Cambridge: Harvard University Press, 1959.

Hobson, J. A. *Imperialism: A Study.* 3rd ed. London: Unwin Hyman, 1988. First published 1902.

Holmgren, Jennifer. "The Economic Foundations of Virtue: Widow-Remarriage in Early and Modern China." *Australian Journal of Chinese Studies* 13 (January 1985): 1–27.

Honig, Emily. *Creating Chinese Ethnicity: Subei People in Shanghai, 1850–1980.* New Haven: Yale University Press, 1992.

Hostetler, Laura. *Qing Colonial Enterprise: Ethnography and Cartography in Early Modern China.* Chicago: University of Chicago Press, 2001.

Hsiao, Kung-chuan. *Rural China: Imperial Control in the Nineteenth Century.* Seattle: University of Washington Press, 1960.

Hsieh, Winston. "Peasant Insurrection and the Marketing Hierarchy in the Canton Delta, 1911." In *The Chinese City between Two Worlds,* ed. Mark Elvin and G. William Skinner, 119–141. Stanford: Stanford University Press, 1974.

———. "Triads, Salt Smugglers, and Local Uprisings." In Jean Chesneaux, ed., *Popular Movements and Secret Societies in China, 1840–1950,* 145–164. Stanford: Stanford University Press, 1972.

Hsu, Immanuel. *China's Entry into the Family of Nations: The Diplomatic Phase, 1858–1880.* Cambridge: Harvard University Press, 1960.

———. *The Ili Crisis: A Study of Sino-Russian Diplomacy 1871–1881.* Oxford: Clarendon Press, 1965.

———. "Late Ch'ing Foreign Relations, 1860–1905." In Fairbank and Liu, eds., *Cambridge History of China,* vol. 11, 70–141.

———. *The Rise of Modern China.* New York: Oxford University Press, 1970.

Hsüeh, Chün-tu. *Huang Hsing and the Chinese Revolution.* Stanford: Stanford University Press, 1961.

———. *Revolutionary Leaders of Modern China.* New York: Oxford University Press, 1971.

Huang, Pei. *Autocracy at Work: A Study of the Yung-cheng Reign, 1723–1735.* Bloomington: Indiana University Press, 1974.

Huang, Philip C. C. *Civil Justice in China: Representation and Practice in the Qing.* Stanford: Stanford University Press, 1996.

———. *Liang Ch'i-ch'ao and Modern Chinese Liberalism.* Seattle: University of Washington Press, 1972.

———. "The Paradigmatic Crisis in Chinese Studies: Paradoxes in Social and Economic History." *Modern China* 17:3 (July 1991): 299–341.

———. *The Peasant Economy and Social Change in North China.* Stanford: Stanford University Press, 1985.

Hucker, Charles O. *The Censorial System of Ming China.* Stanford: Stanford University Press, 1966.

Hucker, Charles O. *A Dictionary of Official Titles in Imperial China.* Stanford: Stanford University Press, 1985.

Hummel, Arthur W., ed. *Eminent Chinese of the Ch'ing Period.* Washington, DC: U.S. Government Printing Office, 1943.

Hung, Ho-fung. "The Ming-Qing Transition in Maritime Perspective: A Reappraisal." Unpublished paper.

Hymes, Robert P. *Statesmen and Gentlemen: The Elite of Fu-chou, Chiang-hsi, in Northern and Southern Sung.* Cambridge: Cambridge University Press, 1986.

Hymes, Robert P., and Conrad Shirokauer, eds. *Ordering the World: Approaches to State and Society in Sung Dynasty China.* Berkeley: University of California Press, 1993.

I Songyŭ. "Shantung in the Shun-chih Reign: The Establishment of Local Control and the Gentry Response." Trans. Joshua Fogel. *Ch'ing-shih wen-t'i* 4:4 (December 1980): 1–34, and 4:5 (June 1981): 1–32.

Ichiko, Chūzō. "The Role of the Gentry: An Hypothesis." In *China in Revolution: The First Phase, 1900–1913,* ed. Mary Clabaugh Wright, 297–318. New Haven: Yale University Press, 1968.

Iriye, Akira. *After Imperialism: The Search for a New Order in the Far East, 1921–1931.* Cambridge: Harvard University Press, 1965.

———. "Imperialism in East Asia." In *Modern East Asia: Essays in Interpretation,* ed. James B. Crowley, 122–150. New York: Harcourt Brace and World, 1970.

Jami, Catherine. "Imperial Control and Western Learning: The Kangxi Emperor's Performance." *Late Imperial China* 23:1 (June 2002): 28–49.

Jansen, Marius. *The Japanese and Sun Yat-sen*. Cambridge: Harvard University Press, 1954.

Jen Yu-wen. *The Taiping Revolutionary Movement*. New Haven: Yale University Press, 1973.

Jenks, Robert. *Insurgency and Social Disorder in Guizhou: The "Miao" Rebellion, 1854–1873*. Honolulu: University of Hawai'i Press, 1994.

Jenner, W. J. F. "Tough Guys, Mateship, and Honour: Another Chinese Tradition." *East Asian History* 12 (1996): 1–33.

Jing Junjian. *Qingdai shehui de jianmin dengji* [Debased Status in Qing Society]. Hangzhou: Zhejiang People's Press, 1993.

Jing Su and Luo Lun. *Landlord and Labor in Late Imperial China: Case Studies from Shandong*. Trans. Endymion Wilkinson. Cambridge: Harvard University Council on East Asian Studies, 1978.

Johnson, David. "Communication, Class, and Consciousness in Late Imperial China." In Johnson, Nathan, and Rawski, eds., *Popular Culture in Late Imperial China*.

———. *Spectacle and Sacrifice: The Ritual Foundations of Village Life in North China*. Cambridge: Harvard University Asia Center, 2009.

Johnson, David, Andrew J. Nathan, and Evelyn S. Rawski, eds. *Popular Culture in Late Imperial China*. Berkeley: University of California Press, 1985.

Johnson, Linda Cooke. *Shanghai: From Market Town to Treaty Port, 1074–1858*. Stanford: Stanford University Press, 1995.

Jones, Susan Mann. "Hung Liang-chi (1746–1809): The Perception and Articulation of Political Problems in Late Eighteenth Century China." Ph.D. diss., Stanford University, 1971.

Jones, Susan Mann, and Philip A. Kuhn. "Dynastic Decline and the Roots of Rebellion." In Fairbank, ed., *Cambridge History of China*, vol. 10, pt. 1, 107–162.

Judge, Joan. *Print and Politics: "Shibao" and the Culture of Reform in Late Qing China*. Stanford: Stanford University Press, 1996.

Kahn, Harold L. *Monarchy in the Emperor's Eyes: Image and Reality in the Ch'ien-lung Reign*. Cambridge: Harvard University Press, 1971.

Kamachi, Noriko. *Reform in China: Huang Tsun-hsien and the Japanese Model*. Cambridge: Harvard University Council on East Asian Studies, 1981.

Kelley, David E. "Temples and Tribute Fleets: The Luo Sect and Boatmen's Associations in the Eighteenth Century." *Modern China* 8:3 (July 1982): 361–391.

Kessler, Lawrence. *K'ang-hsi and the Consolidation of Ch'ing Rule, 1661–1684*. Chicago: University of Chicago Press, 1976.

Kirby, William C. "Engineering China: The Origins of the Chinese Developmental State." In *Becoming Chinese*, ed. Wen-hsin Yeh, 137–160. Berkeley: University of California Press, 2000.

Ko, Dorothy. *Cinderella's Sisters: A Revisionist History of Footbinding.* Berkeley: University of California Press, 2005.

———. *Teachers of the Inner Chambers: Women and Culture in Seventeenth-Century China.* Stanford: Stanford University Press, 1994.

Kuhn, Philip A. *Chinese among Others: Emigration in Modern Times.* Lanham, MD: Rowman and Littlefield, 2008.

———. "Local Self-Government under the Republic: Problems of Control, Automony, and Mobilization." In Wakeman and Grant, eds., *Conflict and Control in Late Imperial China,* 257–298.

———. "Origins of the Taiping Vision: Cross-Cultural Dimensions of a Chinese Rebellion." *Comparative Studies of Society and History* 19 (1977): 350–366.

———. *Rebellion and Its Enemies in Late Imperial China: Militarization and Social Structure, 1796–1864.* Cambridge: Harvard University Press, 1970.

———. *Soulstealers: The Chinese Sorcery Scare of 1768.* Cambridge: Harvard University Press, 1990.

———. "The Taiping Rebellion." In Fairbank, ed., *Cambridge History of China,* vol. 10, pt. 1.

Kwong, Luke S. K. *A Mosaic of the Hundred Days: Personalities, Politics, and Ideas of 1898.* Cambridge: Harvard University Council on East Asian Studies, 1984.

Lai, Chi-kong. "Li Hung-chang and Modern Enterprise: The China Merchants' Company, 1872–1885." In *Li Hung-chang and China's Early Modernization,* ed. Samuel Chu and Kwang-Ching Liu, 216–247. Armonk: M. E. Sharpe, 1994.

Lamley, Harry J. "Lineage and Surname Feuds in Southern Fukien and Eastern Kwangtung under the Ch'ing." In *Orthodoxy in Late Imperial China,* ed. Kwang-ching Liu, 255–280. Berkeley: University of California Press, 1990.

Langer, William L. *The Diplomacy of Imperialism, 1890–1902.* New York: Knopf, 1956.

Larsen, Kirk W. *Tradition, Treaties, and Trade: Qing Imperialism in Chosŏn Korea, 1850–1910.* Cambridge: Harvard University Asia Center, 2008.

Lee, James Z. "Food Supply and Population Growth in Southwest China, 1250–1850." *Journal of Asian Studies* 41:4 (August 1982): 711–746.

———. "The Legacy of Immigration in Southwest China, 1250–1850." *Annales de demographie historique* (1982): 279–304.

Lee, James Z., and Wang Feng. *One Quarter of Humanity: Malthusian Myths and Chinese Realities, 1700–2000.* Cambridge: Harvard University Press, 1999.

Lee, Robert H. G. "Frontier Politics in the Southwestern Sino-Tibetan Borderlands during the Ch'ing Dynasty." In *Perspectives on a Changing China,* ed. Joshua A. Fogel and William T. Rowe. Boulder: Westview Press, 1979.

———. *The Manchurian Frontier in Ch'ing History.* Cambridge: Harvard University Press, 1970.

Lenin, V. I. *Imperialism, the Highest Stage of Capitalism: A Popular Outline.* Moscow: Foreign Languages Publishing House, 1920.

Leonard, Jane Kate. *Controlling from Afar: The Daoguang Emperor's Handling of the Grand Canal Crisis, 1824–1826.* Ann Arbor: University of Michigan Center for Chinese Studies, 1996.

———. *Wei Yuan and China's Rediscovery of the Maritime World.* Cambridge: Harvard University Council on East Asian Studies, 1984.

Leong, Sow-Theng. *Migration and Ethnicity in Chinese History: Hakka, Pengmin, and Their Neighbors.* Stanford: Stanford University Press, 1997.

Leung, Edwin Pak-wah. "Li Hung-chang and the Liu-ch'iu (Ryūkyū) Controversy, 1871–1881." In *Li Hung-chang and China's Early Modernization,* ed. Samuel Chu and Kwang-Ching Liu. Armonk: M. E. Sharpe, 1994.

Levenson, Joseph R. *Confucian China and Its Modern Fate: A Trilogy.* Berkeley: University of California Press, 1958.

Levy, Marion, Jr. "Contrasting Factors in the Modernization of China and Japan." *Economic Development and Cultural Change* 2 (1953): 161–197.

Levy, Marion, Jr., and Shih Kuo-heng. *The Rise of the Modern Chinese Business Class.* New York: Institute of Pacific Relations, 1949.

Li Bozhong. "Kongzhi zengchang yibao fuyu: Qingdai qianqi Jiangnan de renkou xingwei" [Restricting Population Growth to Protect Wealth: Population Behavior in Early Qing Jiangnan]. *Xin shixue* 5:3 (1994): 25–71.

Li, Lillian M. *Fighting Famine in North China: State, Market, and Environmental Decline, 1690s–1990s.* Stanford: Stanford University Press, 2007.

Li Renkai. *Zhang Zhidong mufu* [Zhang Zhidong's secretariat]. Beijing: Zhongguo guangbo dianshi chubanshe, 2005.

Liang Qizi (Angela Leung). *Shishan yu jiaohua: Ming-Qing de cishan zuzhi* [Charity and Moral Indoctrination: Philanthropic Organization in the Ming and Qing]. Taipei: Lianjing chubanshe, 1997.

Lieberman, Victor, ed. *Beyond Binary Histories: Re-imagining Eurasia to c. 1830.* Ann Arbor: University of Michigan Press, 1997.

Liew, K. S. *Struggle for Democracy: Sung Chiao-jen and the 1911 Chinese Revolution.* Berkeley: University of California Press, 1971.

Lin, Manhong. *China Upside Down: Currency, Society, and Ideologies, 1808–1856.* Cambridge: Harvard University Asia Center, 2006.

Lin Yü-sheng. "The Suicide of Liang Chi: An Ambiguous Case of Moral Conservatism." In Furth, ed., *The Limits of Change,* 151–170.

Linebarger, Paul Myron Anthony. *The Political Doctrines of Sun Yat-sen: An Exposition of the San min chu i.* Baltimore: Johns Hopkins University Press, 1937.

Linebarger, Paul Myron Wentworth. *Sun Yat Sen and the Chinese Republic.* New York: AMS Press, 1969. First published New York: Century, 1925.

Liu Fengyun. *Qingdai sanfan yanjiu* [A Study of the Qing Three Feudatories]. Beijing: Chinese People's University Press, 1994.

Liu Guangjing (Kwang-Ching Liu). "Shijiu shiji chuye Zhongguo zhishifenzi
    Bao Shichen yu Wei Yuan" [The Early Nineteenth-Century Chinese Intellec-
    tuals Bao Shichen and Wei Yuan]. In *Zhongyang yanjiuyuan guoji Hanxue
    huiyi lunwenji* [Proceedings of the Conference on Chinese Studies at the Ac-
    ademia Sinica], 995–1030. Taipei: Academia Sinica, 1980.

Liu, Kwang-Ching. *Anglo-American Steamship Rivalry in China, 1862–1874.*
    Cambridge: Harvard University Press, 1962.

Liu Shiji. *Ming Qing shidai Jiangnan shizhen yanjiu* [Market Towns in Jiangnan
    during the Ming and Qing]. Beijing: Zhongguo shehui kexue yanjiusuo
    chubanshe, 1987.

Liu, Ts'ui-jung. "Dike Construction in Ching-chou." *Papers on China* 23
    (1970): 1–28.

Liu Yongcheng. "Lun Qingdai qianqi nongye guyong laodong de xingzhi" [The
    Nature of Agrarian Hired Labor in the Early Qing]. *Qingshi yanjiuji* 1
    (1980): 91–112.

———. "Shilun Qingdai Suzhou shougongye hanghui" [Handicraft Guilds in
    Qing Suzhou]. *Lishi yanjiu* 1959.11, 21–46.

Lojewski, Frank. "The Soochow Bursaries: Rent Management during the Late
    Ch'ing." *Ch'ing-shih wen-t'i* 4:3 (June 1980): 43–65.

London, Jack. "The Unparallelled Invasion" (1907). In *The Complete Short
    Stories of Jack London,* ed. Earle Labor, Robert C. Leitz III, and I. Milo
    Shepard, vol. 2, 1234–46. Stanford: Stanford University Press, 1993.

Lu Xun. *The Complete Stories of Lu Xun.* Trans. Yang Xianyi and Gladys Yang.
    Bloomington: Indiana University Press, 1981.

Lufrano, Richard John. *Honorable Merchants: Commerce and Self-Cultivation
    in Late Imperial China.* Honolulu: University of Hawai'i Press, 1997.

Lui, Adam Y. C. *The Hanlin Academy: Training Ground for the Ambitious,
    1644–1850.* Hamden, CT: Archon, 1981.

Luo Ergang. *Xiangjun xinzhi* [New History of the Hunan Army]. Changsha,
    1939.

Ma, L. Eve Armentrout. *Revolutionaries, Monarchists, and Chinatowns: Chi-
    nese Politics in the Americas and the 1911 Revolution.* Honolulu: Univer-
    sity of Hawai'i Press, 1990.

Ma, Zhao. "Imperial Autocracy and Bureaucratic Interests in the Anti-Christian
    Campaign of 1784–85 in China." Unpublished paper.

———. "'Writing History during a Prosperous Age': The New Qing History
    Project." *Late Imperial China* 29:1 (June 2008): 120–145.

Macauley, Melissa. *Social Power and Legal Culture: Litigation Masters in Late
    Imperial China.* Stanford: Stanford University Press, 1998.

Mackerras, Colin. *The Rise of the Peking Opera: Social Aspects of the Theatre
    in Manchu China, 1770–1870.* Oxford: Clarendon, 1972.

MacKinnon, Stephen R. *Power and Politics in Late Imperial China: Yuan Shi-kai in Beijing and Tianjin, 1901–1908*. Berkeley: University of California Press, 1980.

Mair, Victor. "Language and Ideology in the Written Popularizations of the Sacred Edict." In Johnson, Nathan, and Rawski, eds., *Popular Culture in Late Imperial China*, 325–359.

Man-Cheong, Iona. *The Class of 1761: Examinations, State, and Elites in Eighteenth-Century China*. Stanford: Stanford University Press, 2004.

Mann, Susan. *Local Merchants and the Chinese Bureaucracy, 1750–1950*. Stanford: Stanford University Press, 1987.

———. *Precious Records: Women in China's Long Eighteenth Century*. Stanford: Stanford University Press, 1997.

———. *The Talented Women of the Zhang Family*. Berkeley: University of California Press, 2007.

Mao Haijin. *Tianchao de pengkui: Yapian zhanzheng zaiyanjiu* [Imperial Collapse: A Revisionist Study of the Opium War]. Beijing: Sanlian shudian, 2005.

Marks, Robert. *Tigers, Rice, Silk, and Silt: Environment and Economy in Late Imperial South China*. Cambridge: Cambridge University Press, 1998.

Marmé, Michael. "Locating Linkages or Painting Bull's-Eyes around Bullet Holes? An East Asian Perspective on the Seventeenth-Century Crisis." *American Historical Review* 113:4 (October 2008): 1080–89.

McDermott, Joseph P. "Friendship and Its Friends in the Late Ming." In *Family Process and Political Process in Modern Chinese History*, vol. 1, 67–96. Taipei: Institute of Modern History, 1992.

McMahon, Daniel. "The Yuelu Academy and Hunan's Nineteenth-Century Turn toward Statecraft." *Late Imperial China* 26:1 (June 2005): 72–109.

McNeill, William H. *The Age of Gunpowder Empires, 1450–1800*. Washington, DC: American Historical Association, 1989.

———. *Plagues and Peoples*. Garden City: Anchor Press, 1976.

Menzies, Nicholas K. *Forest and Land Management in Imperial China*. New York: St. Martin's Press, 1994.

Meskill, Johanna M. *A Chinese Pioneer Family: The Lins of Wu-feng, Taiwan, 1729–1895*. Princeton: Princeton University Press, 1979.

Metzger, Thomas. "T'ao Chu's Reform of the Huai-pei Salt Monopoly." *Papers on China* 16 (1962): 1–39.

Meyer-Fong, Tobie. *Building Culture in Early Qing Yangzhou*. Stanford: Stanford University Press, 2003.

Michael, Franz. *The Taiping Rebellion: History and Documents*. Vol. 1, *History*. Seattle: University of Washington Press, 1966.

Miles, Steven B. *The Sea of Learning: Mobility and Identity in Nineteenth-Century Guangzhou*. Cambridge: Harvard University Asia Center, 2006.

Miller, Harold Lyman. "Factional Conflict and the Integration of Ch'ing Politics, 1661–1690." Ph.D. diss., George Washington University, 1974.

Millward, James A. *Beyond the Pass: Economy, Ethnicity, and Empire in Qing Xinjiang, 1759–1864.* Stanford: Stanford University Press, 1998.

———. *Eurasian Crossroads: A History of Xinjiang.* New York: Columbia University Press, 2007.

Millward, James A., Ruth W. Dunnell, Mark C. Elliott, and Philippe Forêt, eds. *New Qing Imperial History: The Making of Inner Asian Empire at Qing Chengde.* London: Routledge, 2004.

Min Tu-ki. *National Polity and Local Power: The Transformation of Late Imperial China.* Ed. Philip A. Kuhn and Timothy Brook. Cambridge: Harvard University Council on East Asian Studies, 1989.

Miyazaki, Ichisada. *China's Examination Hell: The Civil Service Examinations of Imperial China.* Trans. Conrad Schirokauer. New Haven: Yale University Press, 1981.

Morita Akira. "Shindai suishu kessha no seikaku ni tsuite" [Boatmen's Associations in the Qing]. *Tōyōshi kenkyū* 13:5 (January 1955): 364–376.

Morse, Hosea Ballou, ed. *The Chronicles of the East India Company Trading to China, 1635–1834.* Oxford: Oxford University Press, 1926.

———. *The Trade and Administration of China.* London: Longmans, Green, 1913.

Mou Anshi. *Taiping Tianguo* [The Taiping Heavenly Kingdom]. Shanghai: Shanghai renmin chubanshe, 1959.

Moulder, Frances V. *Japan, China, and the Modern World Economy: Towards a Reinterpretation of East Asian Economic Development, ca. 1600–ca. 1918.* Cambridge: Cambridge University Press, 1977.

Mungello, D. E. *The Great Encounter of China and the West, 1500–1800.* Lanham, MD: Rowman and Littlefield, 1999.

Murray, Diane H. *The Origins of the Tiandihui: The Chinese Triads in Legend and History.* Stanford: Stanford University Press, 1994.

Nakami Tatsuo. "The Mongols and the 1911 Revolution." In *The 1911 Revolution in China: Interpretive Essays,* ed. Etō Shinkichi and Harold Z. Schiffrin, 129–149. Tokyo: University of Tokyo Press, 1984.

Naquin, Susan. "Connections between Rebellions: Sect Family Networks in Qing China." *Modern China* 8:3 (July 1982): 337–360.

———. "Funerals in North China: Uniformity and Variation." In *Death Ritual in Late Imperial and Modern China,* ed. James L. Watson and Evelyn S. Rawski, 37–70. Berkeley: University of California Press, 1988.

———. *Millenarian Rebellion in China: The Eight Trigrams Rebellion of 1813.* New Haven: Yale University Press, 1976.

———. *Shantung Rebellion: The Wang Lun Rebellion of 1774.* New Haven: Yale University Press, 1981.

———. "The Transmission of White Lotus Sectarianism in Late Imperial China." In Johnson, Nathan, and Rawski, eds., *Popular Culture in Late Imperial China,* 255–291.

Naquin, Susan, and Chün-fang Yü, eds. *Piligrims and Sacred Sites in China.* Berkeley: University of California Press, 1992.

"Newchang." In *Decennial Reports, 1882–91,* 34–37.

Ng, Vivian W. "Ideology and Sexuality: Rape Laws in Qing China." *Journal of Asian Studies* 46:1 (February 1987): 57–70.

Nivison, David S. "Ho-shen and His Accusers: Ideology and Political Behavior in the Eighteenth Century." In *Confucianism in Action,* ed. David S. Nivison and Arthur S. Wright, 209–243. Stanford: Stanford University Press, 1959.

———. "Protest against Convention and Conventions of Protest." In *The Confucian Persuasion,* ed. Arthur F. Wright. Stanford: Stanford University Press, 1960.

Osborne, Anne. "The Local Politics of Land Reclamation in the Lower Yangzi Highlands." *Late Imperial China* 15:1 (June 1994): 1–46.

Overmyer, Daniel. *Precious Volumes: An Introduction to Sectarian Scriptures from the Sixteenth and Seventeenth Centuries.* Cambridge: Harvard University Asia Center, 1999.

Ownby, David. *Brotherhoods and Secret Societies in Early and Mid-Qing China.* Stanford: Stanford University Press, 1996.

Oxnam, Robert. *Ruling from Horseback: Manchu Politics in the Oboi Regency, 1661–1669.* Chicago: University of Chicago Press, 1975.

Paderni, Paola. "The Problem of *Kuan-hua* in Eighteenth-Century China: The Yung-cheng Decree for Fukien and Kwangtung." *Annali* 48:4 (1988): 257–265.

Paine, S. C. M. *The Sino-Japanese War of 1894–95: Perceptions, Power, and Primacy.* Cambridge: Cambridge University Press, 2003.

Palmer, Michael J. E. "The Surface-Subsoil Form of Divided Ownership in Late Imperial China: Some Examples from the New Territories of Hong Kong." *Modern Asian Studies* 21:1 (1987): 1–119.

Park, Nancy Elizabeth. "Corruption and Its Recompense: Bribes, Bureaucracy, and the Law in Late Imperial China." Ph.D. diss., Harvard University, 1993.

Parkes, Harry. *Narrative of the Late Sir H. Parkes' Captivity in Pekin, 1860.* London: Pall Mall Gazette, 1885.

Peng, Juanjuan. "Yudahua: The History of an Industrial Enterprise in Modern China, 1890–1957." Ph.D. diss., Johns Hopkins University, 2007.

Peng Yuxin. *Qingdai tudi kaiken shi* [A History of Land Reclamation in the Qing Period]. Beijing: Nongye chubanshe, 1990.

Peng Zeyi. "Qingdai qianqi shougongye de fazhan" [The Development of Handicrafts in the Early Qing]. *Zhongguo shi yanjiu* 1981.1: 43–60.

———. *Zhongguo jindai shougongye shiliao, 1840–1949* [Historical Materials on China's Modern Handicraft Industry]. Beijing: Zhonghua shuju, 1962.

Perdue, Peter C. *China Marches West: The Qing Conquest of Central Eurasia.*
     Cambridge: Harvard University Press, 2005.

———. "Comparing Empires: Manchu Colonialism." *International History Re-
     view* 20:2 (June 1998): 255–261.

———. *Exhausting the Earth: State and Peasant in Hunan, 1500–1850.* Cam-
     bridge: Harvard University Council on East Asian Studies, 1987.

———. "Insiders and Outsiders: The Xiangtan Riot of 1819 and Collective Ac-
     tion in Hunan." *Modern China* 12:2 (April 1986): 166–201.

Peterson, Willard J., ed. *The Cambridge History of China.* Vol. 9, pt. 1, *The
     Ch'ing Dynasty to 1800.* Cambridge: Cambridge University Press, 2002.

———. "The Life of Ku Yen-wu (1613–1682)." *Harvard Journal of Asiatic
     Studies* 28 (1968): 114–156 and 29 (1969): 201–247.

Pi Mingxiu and Kong Xiankai. "Taiping jun shouke Wuchang hou de zhanlue
     juece" [Policies of the Taiping Army after Its Initial Capture of Wuchang].
     Jianghan luntan 1981.2: 68–72.

Platt, Stephen R. *Provincial Patriots: The Hunanese and Modern China.* Cam-
     bridge: Harvard University Press, 2007.

Polachek, James. "Gentry Hegemony: Soochow in the T'ung-chih Restoration."
     In Wakeman and Grant, eds., *Conflict and Control in Late Imperial China,*
     211–256.

———. *The Inner Opium War.* Cambridge: Harvard University Council on East
     Asian Studies, 1992.

Pomeranz, Kenneth. *The Great Divergence: China, Europe, and the Making of
     the Modern World Economy.* Princeton: Princeton University Press, 2000.

Prazniak, Roxann. "Tax Protest at Laiyang, Shandong, 1910: Commoner Orga-
     nization versus the County Political Elite." *Modern China* 6:1 (1980): 41–
     71.

*Present Day Impressions of the Far East and Prominent and Progressive Chinese
     at Home and Abroad.* London, 1917.

Pruitt, Ida. *A Daughter of Han: The Autobiography of a Chinese Working
     Woman.* Stanford: Stanford University Press, 1967.

Rankin, Mary Backus. *Early Chinese Revolutionaries: Radical Intellectuals in
     Shanghai and Chekiang.* Cambridge: Harvard University Press, 1971.

———. *Elite Activism and Political Transformation in China: Zhejiang Prov-
     ince, 1865–1911.* Stanford: Stanford University Press, 1986.

———. "Nationalistic Contestation and Mobilizational Politics: Practice and
     Rhetoric of Railway-Rights Recovery at the End of the Qing." *Modern
     China* 28:3 (July 2002): 315–361.

———. "Public Opinion and Political Power: *Qingyi* in Late Nineteenth-
     Century China." *Journal of Asian Studies* 41:3 (May 1982): 453–484.

———. "The Tenacity of Tradition." In Wright, ed., *China in Revolution: The
     First Phase,* 319–361.

Rawski, Evelyn S. *Agricultural Change and the Peasant Economy of South China.* Cambridge: Harvard University Press, 1972.

———. "Agricultural Development in the Han River Highlands." *Late Imperial China* 3:4 (December 1975): 63–81.

———. *Education and Popular Literacy in Ch'ing China.* Ann Arbor: University of Michigan Press, 1979.

———. "The Qing Formation and the Early Modern Period." In Struve, ed., *The Qing Formation in World-Historical Time.*

———. "Re-envisioning the Qing: The Significance of the Qing Period in Chinese History." *Journal of Asian Studies* 55:4 (November 1996): 829–850.

Reed, Bradly W. "Money and Justice: Clerks, Runners, and the Magistrate's Court in Late Imperial Sichuan." *Modern China* 21:3 (July 1995): 345–382.

Reynolds, Douglas R. *China, 1898–1912: The Xinheng Revolution and Japan.* Cambridge: Harvard University Council on East Asian Studies, 1993.

Rhoads, Edward J. M. *China's Republican Revolution: The 1911 Revolution in Kwangtung, 1895–1913.* Cambridge: Harvard University Press, 1975.

———. *Manchus and Han: Ethnic Relations in Political Power in Late Qing and Early Republican China, 1861–1928.* Seattle: University of Washington Press, 2000.

Richards, John F. *The Unending Frontier: An Environmental History of the Early Modern World.* Berkeley: University of California Press, 2003.

Robinson, David. *Bandits, Eunuchs, and the Son of Heaven: Rebellion and Economy of Violence in Mid-Ming China.* Honolulu: University of Hawai'i Press, 2001.

Ropp, Paul S. *Dissent in Early Modern China: Ju-lin wai-shih and Ch'ing Social Criticism.* Ann Arbor: University of Michigan Press, 1981.

———. "The Seeds of Change: Reflections on the Condition of Women in the Early and Mid Ch'ing." *Signs: Journal of Women in Culture and Society* 2:1 (1976): 5–23.

Rosenbaum, Arthur L. "Gentry Power and the Changsha Rice Riot of 1910." *Journal of Asian Studies* 34:3 (May 1975): 689–715.

Rosenberg, Hans. *Bureaucracy, Aristocracy, and Autocracy: The Prussian Experience, 1660–1815.* Cambridge: Harvard University Press, 1958.

Rossabi, Morris, ed. *China Among Equals: The Middle Kingdom and Its Neighbors, 10th–14th Centuries.* Berkeley: University of California Press, 1983.

Rowe, William T. *Crimson Rain: Seven Centuries of Violence in a Chinese County.* Stanford: Stanford University Press, 2007.

———. "Domestic Interregional Trade in Eighteenth-Century China." In *On the Eighteenth Century as a Category of Asian History,* ed. Leonard Blussé and Femme Gaastra, 173–192. Aldershot: Ashgate, 1998.

———. "Education and Empire in Southwest China: Chen Hongmou in

Yunnan, 1733–38." In Elman and Woodside, *Education and Society in Late Imperial China, 1600–1900*, 417–457.

———. *Hankow: Commerce and Society in a Chinese City, 1796–1889*. Stanford: Stanford University Press, 1984.

———. *Hankow: Conflict and Community in a Chinese City, 1796–1895*. Stanford: Stanford University Press, 1989.

———. "Ming-Qing Guilds." *Ming Qing Yanjiu* (September 1992): 47–60.

———. "Provincial Monetary Practice in Eighteenth-Century China." In *Chinese Handicraft Regulations of the Qing Dynasty*, ed. Christine Moll-Murata, Song Jianze, and Hans Ulrich Vogel. Munich: Iudicium, 2005.

———. "The Qingbang and Collaboration under the Japanese, 1939–45: Materials in the Wuhan Municipal Archives." *Modern China* 8:4 (October 1982): 491–499.

———. *Saving the World: Chen Hongmou and Elite Consciousness in Eighteenth-Century China*. Stanford: Stanford University Press, 2001.

———. "Social Stability and Social Change." In Peterson, ed., *Cambridge History of China*, vol. 9, 475–562.

———. "Success Stories: Lineage and Elite Status in Hanyang County, Hubei, 1368–1949." In Esherick and Rankin, eds., *Chinese Local Elites*, 51–81.

———. "Urban Control in Late Imperial China: The *Pao-chia* System in Hankow." In *Perspectives on a Changing China*, ed. Joshua A. Fogel and William T. Rowe. Boulder: Westview, 1979.

———. "Water Control and the Qing Political Process: The Fankou Dam Controversy, 1876–1883." *Modern China* 14:4 (October 1988): 353–387.

Sakai, Robert. "The Ryūkyū (Liu-ch'iu) Islands as a Fief of Satsuma." In Fairbank, ed., *The Chinese World Order*, 112–134.

Schiffrin, Harold Z. *Sun Yat-sen and the Origins of the 1911 Revolution*. Berkeley: University of California Press, 1968.

Schneider, Laurence A. *A Madman of Ch'u: The Chinese Myth of Loyalty and Dissent*. Berkeley: University of California Press, 1980.

Schoppa, R. Keith. *Chinese Elites and Political Change: Zhenjiang Province in the Early Twentieth Century*. Cambridge: Harvard University Press, 1982.

———. *Xiang Lake: Nine Centuries of Chinese Life*. New Haven: Yale University Press, 1989.

Schwartz, Benjamin. *In Search of Wealth and Power: Yen Fu and the West*. Cambridge: Belknap Press of Harvard University Press, 1964.

———. "A Marxist Controversy on China." *Far Eastern Quarterly* 13 (February 1954): 143–153.

Sharman, Lyon. *Sun Yat-sen, His Life and Its Meaning: A Critical Biography*. New York: John Day, 1934.

Shaw, Samuel. *The Journals of Major Samuel Shaw, the First American Consul at Canton*. Boston: Wm. Crosby and H. P. Nichols, 1847.

Shen Fu. *Six Records of a Floating Life*. Trans. Leonard Pratt and Chiang Su-
  hui. Harmondsworth: Penguin, 1983.

Shepherd, John Robert. *Statecraft and Political Economy on the Taiwan Frontier, 1600–1800*. Stanford: Stanford University Press, 1993.

Shiba, Yoshinobu. *Commerce and Society in Sung China*. Ann Arbor: University
  of Michigan Center for Chinese Studies, 1970.

Shigeta Atsushi. "The Origins and Structure of Gentry Rule." In *State and Society in China: Japanese Perspectives on Ming-Qing Social and Economic
  History*, ed. Linda Grove and Christian Daniels, 335–385. Tokyo: University of Tokyo Press, 1984.

Shih, Vincent Y. C. *The Taiping Ideology*. Seattle: University of Washington
  Press, 1967.

Skinner, G. William. "Cities and the Hierarchy of Local Systems." In Skinner,
  ed., *The City in Late Imperial China*.

———, ed. *The City in Late Imperial China*. Stanford: Stanford University
  Press, 1977.

———. "Marketing and Social Structure in Rural China," pt. 2. *Journal of
  Asian Studies* 24:2 (1965): 195–228.

———. "Presidential Address: The Structure of Chinese History." *Journal of
  Asian Studies* 44.2 (February 1985): 271–292.

Siu, Helen F., and Liu Zhiwei. "Lineage, Market, Pirate, and *Dan*: Ethnicity in
  the Pearl River Delta of South China." In Crossley, Siu, and Sutton, eds.,
  *Empire at the Margins: Culture, Ethnicity, and Frontier in Early Modern
  China*, 285–310.

Smith, Kent C. "Ch'ing Policy and the Development of Southwest China: Aspects of Ortai's Governor-Generalship, 1726–1731." Ph.D. diss., Yale University, 1970.

Smith, Paul Jakov, and Richard von Glahn, eds. *The Song-Yuan-Ming Transition
  in Chinese History*. Cambridge: Harvard University Asia Center, 2003.

Sommer, Matthew. *Sex, Law, and Society in Late Imperial China*. Stanford:
  Stanford University Press, 2000.

Spector, Stanley. *Li Hung-chang and the Huai Army: A Study in Nineteenth-
  Century Regionalism*. Seattle: University of Washington Press, 1964.

*Speech of Eneas Macdonnell, Esq., on the East India Question: delivered at a
  public meeting of the inhabitants of London and Westminster, at the Crown
  and Anchor Tavern, in the Strand, on Saturday, May 8th, 1830, in reply to
  several statements and resolutions submitted to that meeting*. London:
  James Ridgeway, 1830.

Spence, Jonathan D. *The Death of Woman Wang*. New York: Viking, 1978.

———. *Emperor of China: Self Portrait of K'ang Hsi*. New York: Vintage, 1974.

———. *God's Chinese Son: The Taiping Heavenly Kingdom of Hong Xiuquan*.
  New York: Norton, 1996.

————. *The Memory Palace of Matteo Ricci.* New York: Viking, 1984.

————. "Opium Smoking in Ch'ing China." In Wakeman and Grant, eds., *Conflict and Control in Late Imperial China,* 143–173.

————. *Treason by the Book.* New York: Viking, 2001.

————. *Ts'ao Yin and the K'ang-hsi Emperor: Master and Bondservant.* New Haven: Yale University Press, 1966.

Stern, Fritz. *Gold and Iron: Bismarck, Bleichröder, and the Building of the German Empire.* New York: Knopf, 1977.

Strand, David. "Calling the Chinese People to Order: Sun Yat-sen's Rhetoric of Development." In *Reconstructing Twentieth-Century China: State Control and National Identity,* ed. Kjeld Erik Brødsgaard and David Strand. Oxford: Clarendon, 1998.

Struve, Lynn A., ed. *The Qing Formation in World-Historical Time.* Cambridge: Harvard University Asia Center, 2004.

————. "Ruling from Sedan Chair: Wei Yijie (1616–1686) and the Examination Reform of the 'Oboi' Regency." *Late Imperial China* 25:2 (December 2004): 1–32.

————. *The Southern Ming, 1644–1662.* New Haven: Yale University Press, 1984.

————, ed. *Voices from the Ming-Qing Cataclysm: China in Tigers' Jaws.* New Haven: Yale University Press, 1993.

Sun Yat-sen. *Kidnapped in London! Being the Story of My Capture by, Detention at, and Release from the Chinese Legation, London.* Bristol: J. W. Arrowsmith, 1897.

Sutton, Donald S. "Ethnicity and the Miao Frontier in the Eighteenth Century." In Crossley, Siu, and Sutton, eds., *Empire at the Margins: Culture, Ethnicity, and Frontier in Early Modern China.*

Suzuki Chūsei. *Shinchō chūki shi kenkyū* [A Study of Mid-Qing History]. Toyohashi: Aichi daigaku kokusai mondai kenkyūjo, 1952.

Sweeten, Alan Richard. *Christianity in Rural China: Conflict and Accommodation in Jiangxi Province, 1860–1900.* Ann Arbor: University of Michigan Center for Chinese Studies, 2001.

Szonyi, Michael. *Practicing Kinship: Lineage and Descent in Late Imperial China.* Stanford: Stanford University Press, 2002.

Tan, Chester C. *The Boxer Catastrophe.* New York: Columbia University Press, 1967.

Telford, Ted A. "Family and State in Qing China: Marriage in the Tongcheng Lineages, 1650–1880." In *Family Process and Political Process in Modern Chinese History,* vol. 2, 921–942. Taipei: Institute of Modern History, 1992.

Teng, Emma J. *Taiwan's Imagined Geography: Chinese Colonial Travel Writing and Pictures, 1683–1895.* Cambridge: Harvard University Asia Center, 2004.

Teng, Ssu-yu. *The Nien Army and Their Guerrilla Warfare, 1851–1868.* Paris: Mouton, 1961.

Teng, Ssu-yu, and John K. Fairbank, eds. *China's Response to the West: A Documentary Survey, 1839–1923*. Cambridge: Harvard University Press, 1954.

Terada Takanobu. "Yōseitei no senmin kaihōrei ni tsuite" [The Yongzheng Emperor's Emancipation of Debased People]. *Tōyōshi kenkyū* 18:3 (1959): 124–141.

ter Haar, Barend J. "Rethinking 'Violence' in Chinese Culture." In *Meanings of Violence: A Cross-Cultural Perspective*, ed. Göran Aijmer and Jon Abbink. Oxford: Berg, 2000.

———. *Ritual and Mythology of the Chinese Triads: Creating an Identity*. Leiden: Brill, 1998.

Theiss, Janet. *Disgraceful Matters: The Politics of Chastity in Eighteenth-Century China*. Berkeley: University of California Press, 2004.

Thompson, Roger. "Statecraft and Self-Government: Competing Views of Community and State in Late Imperial China." *Modern China* 14:2 (April 1988): 188–221.

Tilly, Charles. *From Mobilization to Revolution*. New York: McGraw Hill, 1978.

Torbert, Preston. *The Ch'ing Imperial Household Department: A Study of Its Organization and Principal Functions, 1662–1796*. Cambridge: Harvard University Council on East Asian Studies, 1977.

Twitchett, Denis. "The T'ang Market System." *Asia Major* 12:2 (1966): 202–248.

Vainker, Shelagh. *Chinese Pottery and Porcelain*. London: British Museum Press, 2005.

Vogel, Hans Ulrich. "Chinese Central Monetary Policy, 1644–1800." *Late Imperial China* 8:2 (December 1987): 1–52.

von Glahn, Richard. "The Enchantment of Wealth: The God *Wutong* in the Social History of Jiangnan." *Harvard Journal of Asiatic Studies* 51:2 (1991): 651–714.

———. *Fountain of Fortune: Money and Monetary Policy in China, 1000–1700*. Berkeley: University of California Press, 1996.

Wagner, Rudolf G., ed. *Joining the Global Public: Word, Image, and City in Early Chinese Newspapers, 1870–1910*. Albany: State University of New York Press, 2007.

Wakeman, Frederic, Jr. "The Canton Trade and the Opium War." In Fairbank, ed., *Cambridge History of China*, vol. 10, pt. 1, 163–212.

———. "China and the Seventeenth-Century Crisis." *Late Imperial China* 7:1 (1986): 1–26.

———. *The Fall of Imperial China*. New York: Free Press, 1975.

———. *The Great Enterprise: The Manchu Reconstruction of Imperial Order in Seventeenth-Century China*. Berkeley: University of California Press, 1985.

———. "High Ch'ing, 1683–1839." In *Modern East Asia: Essays in Interpretation*, ed. James B. Crowley, 1–28. New York: Harcourt, Brace and World, 1970.

———. "The Price of Autonomy: Intellectuals in Ming and Ch'ing Politics."
    Daedalus 101:2 (Spring 1972): 35–70.

———. "The Public Sphere and Civil Society Debate: Western Reflections on
    Chinese Political Culture." *Modern China* 19:2 (April 1993): 108–138.

———. *Strangers at the Gate: Social Disorder in South China, 1839–1861.*
    Berkeley: University of California Press, 1966.

Wakeman, Frederic, Jr., and Carolyn Grant, eds. *Conflict and Control in Late
    Imperial China.* Berkeley: University of California Press, 1975.

Waley, Arthur. *Yuan Mei: Eighteenth-Century Chinese Poet.* Stanford: Stanford
    University Press, 1956.

Waley-Cohen, Joanna. *Exile in Mid-Qing China: Banishment to Xinjiang,
    1758–1820.* New Haven: Yale University Press, 1991.

———. "The New Qing History." *Radical History Review* 88 (Winter 2004):
    193–206.

Wallerstein, Immanuel. *The Modern World-System: Capitalist Agriculture and
    the Origins of the European World-Economy in the Sixteenth Century.* New
    York: Academic Press, 1976.

Wang, David Der-wei. *Fin-de-Siècle Splendor: Repressed Modernities of Late
    Qing Fiction, 1849–1911.* Stanford: Stanford University Press, 1997.

Wang, Di. *Street Culture in Chengdu: Public Space, Urban Commoners, and Lo-
    cal Politics, 1870–1930.* Stanford: Stanford University Press, 2003.

Wang, Juan. "Officialdom Unmasked: The Shanghai Tabloid Press, 1897–
    1911." *Late Imperial China* 28:2 (Dec 2007): 81–128.

Wang, Yeh-chien. *Land Taxation in Imperial China, 1750–1911.* Cambridge:
    Harvard University Press, 1973.

Watson, James L. "Hereditary Tenancy and Corporate Landlordism in Tradi-
    tional China: A Case Study." *Modern Asian Studies* 11:2 (1977): 161–
    182.

Watson, James L., and Evelyn S. Rawski, eds. *Death Ritual in Late Imperial and
    Modern China.* Berkeley: University of California Press, 1988.

Watt, John R. *The District Magistrate in Late Imperial China.* New York: Co-
    lumbia University Press, 1972.

Weber, Eugen. *Peasants into Frenchmen: The Modernization of Rural France,
    1979–1914.* Stanford: Stanford University Press, 1976.

Wei Qingyuan. *Qingdai nubi zhidu* [The Qing Bondservice System]. Beijing:
    Chinese People's University Press, 1982.

Wei Qingyuan and Lu Su. *Qingdai qianqi de shangban kuangye he zibenzhuyi
    mengya* [Early Qing Commercial Mining and the Sprouts of Capitalism].
    Beijing: Chinese People's University Occasional Paper, 1981.

Wen Gongzhi. *Zhonghua minguo geming quanshi* [Complete History of the Chi-
    nese Republican Revolution]. Shanghai, 1929.

Widmer, Ellen. *The Beauty and the Book: Women and Fiction in Nineteenth-
    Century China.* Cambridge: Harvard University Press, 2006.

Wilhelm, Helmut. "Chinese Confucianism on the Eve of the Great Encounter." In *Changing Japanese Attitudes Toward Modernization*, ed. Marius B. Jansen, 283–310. Princeton: Princeton University Press, 1965.

Will, Pierre-Étienne. *Bureaucracy and Famine in Eighteenth-Century China*. Stanford: Stanford University Press, 1990.

Will, Pierre-Étienne, and R. Bin Wong. *Nourish the People: The State Civilian Granary System in China, 1650–1850*. Ann Arbor: University of Michigan Center for Chinese Studies, 1991.

Williams, William Appleman. *The Tragedy of American Diplomacy*. 2nd ed. New York: Dell, 1972.

Wills, John E., Jr. *Embassies and Illusions: Dutch and Portuguese Envoys to K'ang-hsi, 1666–1687*. Cambridge: Council on East Asian Studies, 1984.

———. *Pepper, Guns, and Parleys: The Dutch East India Company and China, 1662–1681*. Cambridge: Harvard University Press, 1974.

Witek, John. *Dangerous Ideas in China and in Europe: A Biography of Jean-François Foucquet, S.J., 1665–1741*. Rome: Institum Historicum S.I., 1982.

Withers, John L., II. "The Heavenly Capital: Nanjing under the Taiping, 1853–1864." Ph.D. diss., Yale University, 1983.

Wong, J. Y. *Deadly Dreams: Opium, Imperialism, and the* Arrow *War (1856–1860) in China*. Cambridge: Cambridge University Press, 1998.

Wong, R. Bin. *China Transformed: Historical Change and the Limits of European Experience*. Ithaca: Cornell University Press, 1997.

———. "Qing Granaries and World History." In Will and Wong, eds., *Nourish the People: The State Civilian Granary System in China, 1650–1850*.

Wong, R. Bin, and Peter C. Perdue. "Famine's Foes in Ch'ing China." *Harvard Journal of Asiatic Studies* 43:1 (June 1983): 291–332.

Wong, Sin-Kiong. "Die for the Boycott and Nation: Martyrdom and the 1905 Anti-American Movement in China." *Modern Asian Studies* 35:3 (2001): 565–588.

Woodside, Alexander. "The Ch'ien-lung Reign." In Peterson, ed., *Cambridge History of China*, vol. 9.

Wou, Odoric. "The Extended Kin Unit and the Family Origins of Ch'ing Local Officials." In *Perspectives on a Changing China*, ed. Joshua A. Fogel and William T. Rowe. Boulder: Westview Press, 1979.

Wright, Mary Clabaugh, ed. *China in Revolution: The First Phase, 1900–1913*. New Haven: Yale University Press, 1968.

———. *The Last Stand of Chinese Conservatism: The T'ung-chih Restoration, 1862–1874*. Stanford: Stanford University Press, 1957.

Wu Chengming. "Lun Qingdai woguo guonei shichang" [On the Domestic Market in the Early Qing]. *Lishi yanjiu* 1983.1.

Wu, Silas H. L. *Communication and Imperial Control in China: The Evolution of the Palace Memorial System, 1693–1735*. Cambridge: Harvard University Press, 1970.

———. *Passage to Power: K'ang-hsi and His Heir Apparent, 1661–1722*. Cambridge: Harvard University Press, 1979.

Xiao Yishan. *Qingdai tongshi* [General History of the Qing Dynasty]. Shanghai: Commercial Press, 1932.

Xu Daling. *Qingdai juanna zhidu* [The System of Purchase of Gentry Degrees in the Qing]. Beijing: Harvard-Yenching Institute, 1950.

Yang, Lien-shen. "Ming Local Administration." In *Chinese Government in Ming Times: Seven Studies,* ed. Charles O. Hucker. New York: Columbia University Press, 1969.

Yang Nianqun. *Ruxue diyuhua de jindai xingtai* [The Modern Formation of Regional Schools of Confucianism]. Beijing: Sanlian shudian, 1997.

Ye Xianen. *Ming-Qing Huizhou nongcon shehui yu dianpu zhi* [Rural Society and the Bondservant System in Ming-Qing Huizhou]. Hefei: Anhui People's Press, 1983.

Yeh, Catherine Vance. *Shanghai Love: Courtesans, Intellectuals and Entertainment Culture, 1850–1910*. Seattle: University of Washington Press, 2006.

Yuasa Yukihiko. "Shindai ni okeru fujin kaihōron reikyōto ningenteki shizen" [Debates over Women's Liberation in the Qing: Ritual Teachings vs. Spontaneous Humanity]. *Nihon Chūgoku gakkaihō* 4 (1953): 111–125.

Zeitlin, Judith. *Historian of the Strange: Pu Songling and the Classical Chinese Tale*. Stanford: Stanford University Press, 1993.

Zelin, Madeleine. *The Magistrate's Tael: Rationalizing Fiscal Reform in 18th Century China*. Berkeley: University of California Press, 1985.

———. *The Merchants of Zigong: Industrial Entrepreneurship in Early Modern China*. New York: Columbia University Press, 2005.

Zelin, Madeleine, Robert Gardella, and Jonathan Ocko, eds. *Contract and Property in Late Imperial China*. Stanford: Stanford University Press, 2004.

Zhang Kaiyuan, Lin Zengping, et al. *Xinhai geming shi* [History of the 1911 Revolution], 3 vols. Beijing: Renmin chubanshe, 1980.

Zhao Erxun. *Qingshi gao* [Draft History of the Qing Period]. Beijing: Zhonghua shuju, 1977.

Zhao, Gang. "Reinventing *China:* Imperial Qing Ideology and the Rise of Modern Chinese National Identity in the Early Twentieth Century." *Modern China* 32:1 (January 2006): 3–30.

———. "Shaping the Asian Trade Network: The Conception and Implementation of the Chinese Open Trade Policy, 1684–1840." Ph.D. diss., Johns Hopkins University, 2006.

Zhuang Guotu. *Zhongguo fengjian zhengfu de Huaqiao zhengce* [Policies of China's Feudal Government toward Overseas Chinese]. Xiamen: Xiamen University Press, 1989.

Zhuang Jifa. *Qing Gaozong shiquan wugong yanjiu* [A Study of Qianlong's "Ten Great Victories"]. Taibei: National Palace Museum, 1982.

ACKNOWLEDGMENTS

In 1975 Frederic Wakeman Jr. published a slender volume entitled *The Fall of Imperial China*. For those of us who were graduate students at the time, just a few years into our professional study of China, this book hit like a revelation. *The Fall* was an interpretive essay on Qing history, and its thrust was a structural analysis of the problems and concerns that Wakeman had come to see as most salient in China's history between the mid-seventeenth and the early twentieth centuries. These were systematically different from what we had been learning elsewhere. After the publication of this book, Qing history in the United States would never be taught quite the same way again. Far more than earlier Americans in Qing studies, Wakeman was influenced by the social history revolution that had recently taken over in the fields of United States and especially European history. Diplomatic and institutional history, the central stuff of the historiography of modern China in the 1950s and 1960s, though of course not ignored altogether, was now definitely pushed to the side.

For years during my early teaching career I used Wakeman's book as a stepping-off point in my own courses on modern China. But as time went on it became increasingly clear that *The Fall,* refreshing as it had appeared in the 1970s, was—like every work of history—a product of its own day. It was harder and harder to reconcile many of its arguments with newer investigations and interpretations of the Qing. My hope in writing this book has been to provide a current counterpart to Wakeman's inspiring volume.

Although a career of reading Chinese-language primary sources and the enormous volume of Chinese and Japanese scholarship on Qing history underlies my descriptions and arguments in this book, I have chosen largely to limit references in the notes to secondary works in English, for those who may wish to read further on material presented here. References to scholarly works in Chinese and Japanese are included when no adequate treatment of the subject exists in English.

This being a work of synthesis, I must express my thanks to the countless scholars who have devoted their careers to explicating Qing history and upon whose work I draw. I am especially indebted to my fellow contributors to the three Qing volumes in the monumental *Cambridge History of China*. I cite their scholarship explicitly only when I have leaned on it heavily or borrowed their interpretations and arguments, but the work of them all serves throughout this book as a fount of reference and authority. Misinterpretations and misrepresentations of fact are of course my own. I trust that such errors as remain will quickly be corrected by my fellow practitioners in the field.

I owe special thanks to the three scholars who patiently read my manuscript and offered corrective advice: my Johns Hopkins University colleague Tobie Meyer-Fong, my general editor Tim Brook, and an unidentified reader for Harvard University Press. I am grateful to Kathleen McDermott of the Press for initiating and sponsoring this series on the history of imperial China, and to Susan Wallace Boehmer for editing the manuscript with great sensitivity and skill. Philip Schwartzberg produced Maps 1 and 4 with efficiency and expertise, while Isabelle Lewis did the same for Maps 2 and 3. And finally, I owe deepest thanks to my wife, Jill Friedman, without whose steady encouragement I would never have been so bold as to attempt this book.

INDEX

Academia Sinica, 3
Academy for Critical Examination of the Classics (Jiaoling Shuyuan), 240
Adams, Brooks, 232
Administration: Censorate, 34; as centralized, 7, 10, 38, 39–43, 60, 61–62, 66, 73, 258, 261, 262, 279, 286; circuit intendants, 38; Court of Colonial Affairs/Ministry for Ruling the Outer Provinces, 39–40; governors, 35, 38, 42, 61, 214, 240, 258, 278, 280; governors-general, 35, 37, 38, 42, 61, 75, 80, 205, 207, 208, 210, 214, 221–222, 226, 240, 242, 244, 249, 258, 259, 276; Grand Council, 40–42, 153, 160, 202–203, 248; Grand Secretariat, 33–34, 41; Imperial Household Department, 40, 141, 186; Imperial Maritime Customs, 203, 245–246, 260; inner administration, 33–35; *jingshi/* statecraft, 59–61, 81, 160; Ministry of Commerce, 258–259; Ministry of Education, 258; Ministry of Finance, 258; Ministry of Foreign Affairs, 258, 276; Ministry of Justice, 258; Ministry of Police/Interior, 258; Ministry of Post and Communications, 258, 276; Ministry of Trade, 258; outer administration, 33, 35, 37–39; prefectures, 37, 42, 60, 79, 226, 281; provincial governance, 33–35, 37, 38, 39, 42, 43, 51–52, 61, 160, 204–205, 278–279; smallness of bureaucracy, 33, 48–49, 50, 52, 54–55, 152, 175, 286; Supreme Court, 258; terms of office, 206–207, 257–258; Three Great Administrations, 162; Translation Bureau, 203–204; Zongli Yamen (Office of General Management), 202–203, 220, 222, 223, 242, 245, 258. *See also* Civil service examination system; Grain Tribute Administration; Local governance; Salt monopoly; Six Boards
Agriculture: beans, 123; bondservant labor in, 29; cotton, 55, 123–124, 125, 151, 157, 166, 243; cultural significance of, 73, 100, 134; and ecological deterioration, 95–96, 183; fertilizer, 123; hemp, 124; in highland areas, 93–94, 102, 183; indigo, 102; irrigation, 55; land reclamation for, 93–96, 118, 119, 150, 156, 181; and migration, 91–96; military-agricultural colonies, 32, 69, 75, 92; millet, 124; peanuts, 91; potatoes, 91; production for marketplace, 123, 124–125, 161; productivity of, 32, 55, 65–66, 68, 91, 95, 97, 140, 150–151, 156; rice, 77, 91, 92, 95, 118, 119, 124, 127, 163; slash-and-burn practices, 93; sweet potatoes, 91, 94; tea, 102, 124, 142, 165–166; tobacco, 102, 124; wheat, 91. *See also* Granaries, ever-normal
Aisin Gioro, 14, 132, 201, 210
Alcock Convention, 219, 220
Amherst, Lord, 170
Anderson, Benedict, on imagined communities, 253
Anglo-Chinese War, First. *See* Opium War of 1839–42
Anglo-Chinese War, Second. *See* Opium War of 1856–60
Anhui province, 124, 160, 162, 179, 205; Anhui Army, 196, 197, 205, 229, 259; Anqing, 188; Huizhou prefecture, 99, 112, 130, 199; merchants from, 130, 199; during Taiping rebellion, 196, 197, 205
Annales: économies, sociétés, civilisations, 3–4
Artisans, 109, 127, 212; guilds of, 33, 49, 119